JAN SKANSHOLM

C++
From the Beginning

Addison-Wesley

An imprint of **Pearson Education**

Harlow, England · London · New York · Reading, Massachusetts · San Francisco
Toronto · Don Mills, Ontario · Sydney · Tokyo · Singapore · Hong Kong · Seoul
Taipei · Cape Town · Madrid · Mexico City · Amsterdam · Munich · Paris · Milan

Pearson Education Limited
Edinburgh Gate
Harlow
Essex CM20 2JE
England
and Associated Companies throughout the world

Visit us on the World Wide Web at:
http://www.pearsoneduc.com

The right of Jan Skansholm to be identified as author of this work has been asserted by him in accordance with the Copyright, Designs and Patents Act 1988.

The programs in this book have been included for their instructional value. They have been tested with care but are not guaranteed for any particular purpose. The publisher does not offer any warranties or representations, nor does it accept any liabilities with respect to the programs.

Many of the designations used by manufacturers and sellers to distinguish their products are claimed as trademarks. Addison Wesley Longman Limited has made every attempt to supply trademark information about manufacturers and their products mentioned in this book. A list of the trademark designations and their owners appears on page xiii.

Cover designed by Chris Eley
and printed by The Riverside Printing Co. (Reading) Ltd
Translated and typeset in 10/12 Times by 45
Printed and bound in Great Britain by Biddles Ltd, *www.biddles.co.uk*

First printed 1997

ISBN: 0–201–40377–3

British Library Cataloguing-in-Publication Data
A catalogue record for this book is available from the British Library

Library of Congress Cataloging-in-Publication Data
A catalogue record for this book is available from the Library of Congress

10 9 8 7 6 5 4

04 03 02 01 00

Preface

C++ is without doubt the programming language that has won the greatest popularity during the past few years. It is used in many different applications. For anyone who wants to work professionally writing programs, it is almost a necessity to be familiar with C++. If you want to become a good C++ programmer, your road will be a long one; C++ is a very comprehensive language. This book attempts to make your journey as short as possible, and the recipe is simple: program directly in C++!

C++ is a development of the older, popular programming language C which has been supplemented time and time again. Most of the C++ programmers working today are old C programmers who have taken a step further and learnt C++, so many believe that you should master C before you go on to C++. They argue that C++ is such a difficult language that a detour via C is recommended. This is why most of the books on C++ assume that you already know C and therefore deal with those sections of the language which are found in C++ and not in C. In addition, many comparisons can be made between C and C++.

This book has been planned in a completely different way. There is no onus on the reader to know C, or any other programming language for that matter. Everything is taken in a natural order, from the most simple things such as expressions and assignments, to extremely advanced language constructs such as virtual functions, exceptions and generic classes. Since the goal is to learn C++ and not C, language constructs belonging to C++, and not to C, are used from the very beginning. We will treat C++ as a completely independent language. As a result, there will be no reason to confuse the issue by comparing it with C and discussing the differences between the two languages.

This book is designed both for beginners in elementary programming and those with some programming experience. The aim is to teach C++ as well as the basics of designing 'good' computer programs. For this reason such things as algorithms, objects, classes, modular program development and generic units are discussed. Special emphasis has been placed throughout on developing programs and sections of programs to make them general and reusable.

I have based the tutorial input on many years of teaching programming, both in C++ and in other languages. I have tried to understand which aspects students find difficult and have gone into more detail in these. I have also been well served by my experience of writing other books. This is especially true of my book *Ada 95 from the Beginning*, which, I am pleased to say, has been well received by students. It has been a useful point of departure and has contributed a number of examples.

This book deals with C++ in its entirety, with the exception of some marginal questions. It could, of course, be fun to spend time on these but they are unlikely to be encountered in normal programming. It may be confusing to say 'C++ in its entirety', since the language has been changing continually during the past ten years. At the time of writing no standard has yet been established, although a committee from the American standardization institute ANSI has been given the task of establishing one. This book is based on the draft which the committee has published.

Chapter 1 provides a general background to programming. It gives an overview of how a computer is constructed and how compiling, linking and execution are carried out. In addition, it contains a short account of the most common programming languages. Algorithms and 'software engineering' are also discussed.

The other chapters in the book (except Chapter 6) deal entirely with C++. Chapters 2 to 5 tell you what you need to know to come to grips with the more advanced language constructs. Chapter 2 gives you the basics: variables, expressions, the most common statements and arrays. Chapter 3 describes how you deal with texts. Chapter 4 looks at functions and the guidelines for dividing large programs into files. In Chapter 5, we go through the different types inherent in C++. We also look at pointers and type conversions.

Chapter 6 gives an introduction to object-oriented programming development. Object-oriented analysis, design and programming are discussed in this chapter, together with such important concepts as classes and objects. Various kinds of relations are also discussed.

Chapters 7 to 10 constitute an essential part of the book. Here an account is given of the parts of C++ that deal with classes. Chapters 7 and 8 give basic constructions – member functions, constructors, and so on. Chapter 9 deals with inheritance, virtual functions and dynamic binding. Chapter 10 describes exceptions. I have used the new classes, found in ANSI's draft standard, in order to highlight the kinds of errors which can be found in programs.

Chapter 11 gives an account of streams and files. Up to this point in the book the C++ standard library for reading and writing from the keyboard and screen has been used. This library can also be used to handle different kinds of files and streams and this is demonstrated here. Text files, as well as binary files, are discussed. The way you store 'heterogeneous object collections' (collections where the objects belong to different classes) in files is given particular attention.

Chapter 12 is, in a way, an application of everything which has previously been discussed in the book. The design of dynamic data structures – lists, queues, stacks and trees – with the help of classes, is described here. The concept of iterators is also discussed.

Chapter 13 is of great importance. It shows you how you can design general software with the help of generic program units, or 'templates', as they are called in C++, and in particular how the generic classes and functions, which are a part of the draft standard, are constructed. This is simply to enable the reader to understand and use these standard classes and functions. Chapter 13 also deals with different ways of constructing heterogeneous data collections.

Chapter 14 is a depository for all the material which did not fit into any of the other chapters, such as name spaces, unions and bit operators.

The book contains lots of examples. I have tried, as far as possible, to present 'real-world' examples. The examples should either show fairly complete programs, or demonstrate classes and other parts of programs in a general way and be usable for different purposes. I have seriously tried to avoid fictitious examples of the type, 'a class A which is a subclass of a class B which contains a member function M which happens to write the text: now we are in M'. Every chapter, except Chapter 6, concludes with a set of exercises which the reader can practise with.

Inserted in the text are a good many 'information windows' which contain summaries of rules, language constructs or concepts which have just been dealt with. The purpose of these windows is to give the reader a little revision but they can also serve as a quick reference when a point of language has to be looked up.

All of the program examples in the book have been put to the test, most of them with Borland's C++ compiler on a PC. In spite of this, some errors may exist in the book. All errors discovered will be put onto a World Wide Web page with the address `http://www.cs.chalmers.se/~skanshol/cpp_eng/`. Other information about the book – including solutions to the exercises – can also be found there. If you want to reach me to make comments on the book, the easiest way is by electronic mail, to `skanshol@cs.chalmers.se`.

Finally, I would like to extend warm thanks to everyone who has made this book possible – to my wife and my children who have seen me sitting in front of the computer day after day, hour after hour; to Iréne Andersson at Studentlitteratur Publishing Company who encouraged me and waited patiently for the book to be finished; to Borland in Sweden who provided me with excellent compilers; to all my colleagues at the Department of Computer Science at Chalmers University of Technology for those rewarding discussions on programming languages and the teaching of programming, and last but not least, to all those students, both at Chalmers and outside at various companies, who have given me their constructive points of view on how programming is best learnt. It is these students who have been my foremost source of inspiration for writing this book.

Jan Skansholm
February 1997

Contents

Trademark notice

Borland's C++ is a trademark of Borland International, Inc.

Microsoft's Visual C++, MS-DOS, Windows, Windows NT and Windows 95 are trademarks of Microsoft Corporation

OS/2 is a trademark of International Business Machines Corporation (IBM)

Smalltalk is a trademark of ParcPlace, Inc.

UNIX is a trademark of X/Open Company Ltd

1 Computers and Programming

This book is about programming, or more precisely, about how you write programs in C++. The different chapters will describe different program constructions in C++. This first chapter is an exception, as it is not about C++ but about programming in general and the prerequisites for programming. This chapter gives a short introduction to the way a computer is constructed, its most important components and their functions. We look at a very simple program. Further on we deal with how programs are translated and how the computer is made to carry them out. After this, there is an overview of the most common and important programming languages and their historical development.

Program development is not simply about the act of programming. In a wider perspective, the programming itself is only a part of the total work. Therefore in this chapter there is also a short discussion about *software engineering* and the place of programming in the program development process. The important concepts of *algorithms* and *top-down design* are also introduced.

1.1   A computer's structure and operation

You could say that a computer is a 'machine' which can process and store information. (Computers were of course called *data processing machines* at first.) A very rough illustration of how it looks when you run a program in a computer, is shown in Figure 1.1. We see that the computer can be regarded as a unit into which you put certain data, or *input data*. The computer processes this data and produces *output data*. Indata and outdata can really be anything, text, pictures, or sound. You may think that in principle, a computer communicates with a person via a keyboard, screen and mouse but computers are also used in a variety of different conditions where communication with people is not the main consideration. Computers can, for instance, control industrial manufacturing processes, or they may be components in technical systems (aeroplanes, cars, and so on). Here the indata is often in the form of signals from so-called *monitoring devices* which give the computer information about the current situation in the system concerning, for example, temperatures and speeds. Output data from the computer may then be control signals to relays and motors.

A very important principle, which is clear from the diagram, is that the computer's behaviour is controlled by a program stored inside it. By changing the program, you can make the computer produce different things. It is this which makes the computer so different from an 'ordinary' machine, which, of course, is built to produce certain predetermined things.

Figure 1.2 shows in a little more detail the main components of a computer. The computer's 'brain' consists of the *processor* (the *central processing unit*, or *CPU*). Here you find the *control unit* which controls and coordinates all the computer's activities. The control unit decides which operations the computer will perform and the order in which they will be carried out. It sends out control signals which regulate all the computer's other parts.

There is also an *Arithmetic Logic Unit*, or *ALU*, in the processor which contains electronic circuits to perform various operations on the data to be processed. These might be, for example, addition, subtraction, multiplication and

Figure 1.1

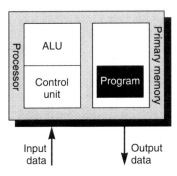

Figure 1.2

division. Advanced processors may contain several ALUs, which means that several operations can be performed in parallel. Modern processors often contain, in addition, a special *mathematics processor*, whose job it is to perform special time-consuming mathematical operations.

Another very important unit in the computer is the *primary memory* (Random Access Memory, or RAM). When a program is performed, or is run, by a computer we say that it is *executed*. For the program to be executed, it must first be placed in the primary memory. In the primary memory, there is also various data and temporary storage space which the executing program needs in order to be able to function.

Execution

When a program is performed (run) in a computer, we say that it is *executed*.

So that the processor can get at the data from the primary memory more quickly, many fast processors often use an extra fast *cache memory* for intermediate storage of data between the processor and the primary memory. The cache memory is often built into the processor.

The primary memory can be thought of as consisting of *memory cells*. (These memory cells are also sometimes called *words*, which do not have anything to do with ordinary words.) Each memory cell has a certain *address* (a number) which gives its position in the memory. The number of memory cells in the primary memory varies, depending on the computer type and model, but it is usually a matter of millions. Each memory cell consists of a certain number of bits (normally

8). Each bit is a *binary digit*, that is, a 'zero' or a 'one'. A group of 8 bits is called a *byte*. You normally express memory size in units of *kilobytes* (Kb), *megabytes* (Mb) and *gigabytes* (Gb), which correspond to 1024, one million and one billion respectively.

A program which is executed and which therefore is to be found in the primary memory, consists of a number of continuous memory cells. A memory cell or a group of memory cells contains an *instruction* in the program. Different instructions can be represented by combining the bits in the memory cells in different ways. Thus a program consists of a sequence of instructions. An instruction tells the computer that it must do a certain particular thing, for instance copy the contents of a memory cell from the primary memory to the central processing unit, or add up two numbers in the Arithmetic Logic Unit.

When a program is being executed, the control unit reads the instructions from the primary memory one by one and sees that the instructions are performed in the order in which they are read.

You could therefore say that an instruction in the program consists of a certain number of ones and zeros. The way these combinations look will depend on the computer. The program must be stored in this form in the primary memory for it to be performed in the computer. You usually say that the program exists in the form of *machine code*. This is a code which is very 'user *unfriendly*', that is, it is difficult for us either to read or to write it. In the infancy of computers, you had to program them directly into machine code. Luckily, things have progressed and normally programmers today don't have to worry about the computer's machine code. As we will see, programs are written in a 'high level language' (for example, C++ or Ada), which is much more user-friendly than the computer's machine code. Nowadays there are special translation programs which translate from high level language to machine code, so that the programs that have been written can be run in the computer.

In Figure 1.3, our computer system has been extended by two very familiar units. In order to communicate with its surroundings, a computer must have one or more *input* and *output* units. The diagram shows the most common input and output

Figure 1.3

units for communication with people, a *screen* (*monitor*), a *mouse* and a *keyboard*. Other common input and output units are printers and loudspeakers.

We saw that a computer's primary memory is used, among other things, to store the program currently being executed but a computer also normally needs to be able to store programs which may not be running. Again, there is a need to store various pieces of information which will be used as input data for different programs. In order to store this type of data, which will be saved more permanently, *secondary memories* are used.

Common types of secondary memory are *disk memory* (hard disks) and *diskettes*. (A hard disk is shown in the diagram.) You can also have secondary memories which are only readable but cannot be written to. The most common example of this is *CD-ROM* (Compact Disk Read Only Memory). These contain completed programs or data.

Disk memories are also used in certain systems to create *virtual memory*. This technique appears to make the primary memory look much larger than it is in reality, which makes things easier for the programmer, who does not have to worry about the primary memory's physical limitations. When you use this virtual memory technique, you only store that data which is currently needed in the actual primary memory. Other data is in fact stored in the disk memory and is retrieved automatically into the primary memory when needed.

Data in secondary memories is usually organized in the form of *files*. A file is a collection of data which belongs together. It may, for example, contain a program or indata for a particular program. You could think of a file as an 'envelope' in which you put data that belongs together. You can create new files, delete files, or make changes in files. Each file is given a special name for easy reference.

It is often important with modern computers to have equipment which makes it possible to communicate with other computers. If the computer is equipped with a *network card*, it can be connected to a local data network, where several computers are connected together, so that they can, for example, access and share each other's disk memories and other input and output devices. If the computer has a *modem*, it can communicate with distant computers. You can be connected to a data network or send electronic mail. It is also often possible to send and receive fax messages.

1.2 How you get the program into the computer

A computer program written in a programming language has the form of normal text. You could write the program on an ordinary piece of paper. In this section, we are going to see what happens when this original *program text*, or *source code*, as it is sometimes called, is translated into the machine's special machine code and

Important components in a computer

- The *processor* (CPU) controls the computer and manipulates the data.
- The *primary memory* is used to store the program to be executed and the data this program needs.
- *Input and output devices* are used to read and print data.
- *Secondary memories* are used to store data permanently.
- *Network cards* make it possible to connect to a local data network.
- With the help of a *modem*, the computer can communicate with distant computers.

loaded in the computer. In order to do this, we will study a very simple program which, when it is run, will only print out the text C++ From the Beginning on the screen:

```
#include <iostream.h>
main()
{
  cout << "C++ From the Beginning" << endl;
  return 0;
}
```

Before we discuss how the program is translated, let's talk about how it looks. (More detailed descriptions of the various program constructions will, of course, come further on in the book.)

·   The language C++ itself contains no special constructions to read and write data but there are a number of complete 'libraries' with resources for reading and writing. One of these is iostream and the first line in the program indicates that the program will make use of this. Actually, 'iostream.h' is the name of an *header file* which contains declarations of the resources to be found in the library. In C, and up to now in C++, it has been a convention that all inclusion files have a name that ends with .h. In the draft of the C++ standard, however, it has been suggested that the suffix .h be abolished. The first line in the program would then look like this:

```
#include <iostream>
```

Since, at the time of writing, the standard has still not been decided and since all existing C++ programs today use the suffix .h in the names of inclusion files, we will also retain this suffix in this book. If you use a compiler that follows the draft standard, you can leave off the suffix.

In a C++ program there can be one or more *functions* which indicate what the program will do. Only one function was shown in the example above. The name of the function is `main`, which is on the second line. A C++ program must contain exactly one function with the name `main` and when the program is run, execution will begin in this function. The empty parentheses after the word `main` indicate that the function lacks parameters. On the third line there is a left brace and on the last line, a right brace. These symbols indicate where the 'guts', or the *body*, of the function begins and ends. (The symbols { and } correspond to the words 'begin' and 'end' which are normally used in many other programming languages.)

On the fourth and fifth lines we find a description of what the function will do. This is expressed in *statements*. A semicolon is normally written after every statement. In this example, there are two statements, one on each line. The first statement indicates that the text `C++ From the Beginning` must be written out. The output operator << from the 'iostream' library is used here. Output takes place with 'cout', which is a pre-defined *output stream*. Whatever is output in this stream will automatically be written in a text window on the screen. The word 'endl' is a *manipulator* which says that the cursor on the screen will be moved forward to a new line (after output).

The fifth line in the program contains a **return** statement. This indicates that execution of the function will come to an end. (The value 0 indicates that execution has finished normally.)

Since the program consists of normal text, it can be entered at the keyboard. There are usually a great many support programs in all computer systems. One such support program which can always be found, is a text editing program, or *text editor*. Figure 1.4 gives an idea of how this program is run. Using the text editor, you can input any text in the computer and store the text in the secondary memory. A file which contains text is usually called a *text file*. With the help of the text editor, you can also easily edit the text, that is, wipe, change, move and add text. You can usually see a part of the text on the screen and so you are able, with the help of the keys or a mouse, to mark parts of the text to be edited. Exactly how the text editor functions and which commands it understands, vary from system to system. A

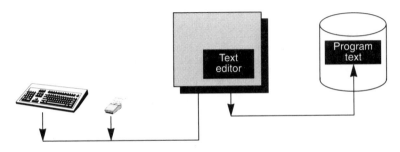

Figure 1.4

simple text editor does not worry about what the text itself contains, but you can also find text editors which 'understand' what kinds of text they are processing. A text editor which knows that it is editing a C++ program can help the programmer by marking different program constructions with different styles or colours.

Let us suppose that we have edited the program text above with the help of a text editor and stored it in the text file with the name `ex1.cpp`. As you can see, the text file has the suffix `.cpp`. In most computer systems, you use suffixes to keep your files in order. Files which contain texts from C++ programs often have the suffix `cpp` but may have other suffixes, such as `c`, or `cc`.

In the next step, the program texts are translated from normal text to machine code. This is done, as shown in Figure 1.5, with the help of a special translating program, a *compiler*. Every compiler is constructed to handle a particular programming language. To be able to translate a C++ program, therefore, you must have access to a C++ compiler. A compiler can either be a separate program, or it can be a part of an integrated program development system. A system like this contains all the resources you need to develop and test run programs, for instance, text editors and compilers. If the compiler is a separate program, it is normally started from a command line.

In a Unix system, the command often has this appearance:

```
CC -c ex1.cpp
```

(Later we will also show examples of an integrated compiler in the Windows environment.)

For every programming language there are special rules for how different programming constructions may look (compare this with the rules for sentence construction in normal languages). We say that every language has a certain *syntax*. The compiler reads the program from the text file created earlier and checks first that the program is following the rules of the language, that is, that the program is following the given syntax. If the compiler finds errors, error outputs will appear on the screen. There may also be warnings for things which may not be clear errors but which the compiler thinks look doubtful. Sometimes, the compiler will try to correct

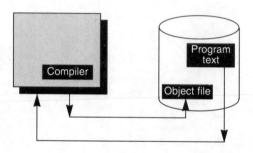

Figure 1.5

the errors if they are not too serious but usually the compiling will break off when errors have been discovered. You then have to go back to the previous step and with the help of the text editor, edit your program text and correct the errors. Once this has been done, you can attempt once more to compile the program. This process normally has to be repeated several times.

If the compiler does not discover any errors, it goes further and translates the program from text to machine code. The compiler usually creates a file with the suffix o or obj, in which it saves the machine code produced. This file is called an *object file*. In our example, the compiler will generate the file ex1.o.

Notice that since different types of computers have different machine codes, object files meant for one computer will not do for another. Different computers must have different compilers. This does not cause the programmer problems, since a C++ compiler always requires a C++ program as indata, whichever computer you are using. Program text developed on one computer system can thus be moved to another system and run there. For this to be done easily, you should not use too many system-dependent details in your program. A program which can be easily moved from one computer system to another is called a *portable* program.

Usually, a program consists of several program parts which have been compiled *separately*. You therefore have several object files. You will have created a number of the object files yourself by compiling your program texts, as with the file ex1.o. There may also exist object files which were created before and which will also be a part of the program. This is true, for instance, with standard functions. In our example the output operator << exists in a prefabricated standard object file. In order to put the various object files together into a program that can be run, you run a special *linking program*, a *linker*. This is shown in Figure 1.6. The linker produces a complete unit, an *executable file*.

Sometimes, a special suffix, for example 'exe', may be used in the file name to indicate that the file contains an executable program. The linker can be a separate program or can be part of a program development system. In a Unix system, the program is linked with the command:

```
CC -o example1 ex1.o
```

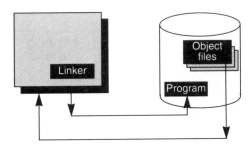

Figure 1.6

We give the names of the object files as arguments. We only have one here, ex1.o. We can see that the linking program automatically finds the standard object files without their having to be indicated. The argument -o is used to indicate what the executable file is to be called. We want it to be called example1.

Linking can either take place *statically* or *dynamically*. With static linking, all the parts of the program are put into the executable file, while with dynamic linking, references to the required object files are placed in the executable file. The object files themselves are not found in the executable file. When a dynamically linked program is run, the different object files will be automatically retrieved and stored in the primary memory when necessary. The advantage with dynamic linking is, of course, that you can save a lot of file space, since different programs often contain common parts, for instance input and output or window handling; these parts do not then need to be copied to all the executable files but can exist in only one copy which all the executable files will refer to.

Now the last step remains, to get the executable program into the primary memory so that it can be run. This leads us to the question: how does the computer know which program it is to run? For the answer, let us look at Figure 1.7.

In earlier diagrams, we have only shown one program at a time in the primary memory, the program being executed. In fact, there are always parts of yet another program permanently stored. This is termed the *operating system*, or OS. Examples of common operating systems are Windows 95, MS-DOS, Unix and OS/2. The operating system is the program which is always run when no 'ordinary' program is being executed. It is automatically started when a normal program has finished being executed, or for some reason, has been broken off. The operating system also begins automatically when the computer is started.

The operating system normally communicates with the user via the screen, keyboard and mouse. The user can write the command on the keyboard, or point and click with the mouse. A common command is for a particular program to be loaded and executed. The operating system then searches for the desired executable file in the secondary memory and copies it into the primary memory, as suggested in the diagram. Control is then transferred to the loaded program which can execute until

Figure 1.7

it has finished or until it is broken off. In order to start our program in a Unix environment, we give the operating system the command

```
example1
```

In a text window on the screen we then get the output

```
C++ From the Beginning
```

We have now seen how a program is written and how it is loaded and run. This process can often be simplified so that you, the programmer, do not need to see all the separate steps and a program can be found which both compiles and links in one step. For instance we would have been able to compile and link our program with the more simple command

```
CC -o example1 ex1.cpp
```

Modern program development systems usually offer the programmer an integrated environment where all the resources necessary to develop programs can be found. Examples of such systems are Borland's C++ and Microsoft's Visual C++. Both of these are for the development of programs under MS-DOS, Windows, or Windows NT.

The different steps

- The program text (the source code) is created with the help of the text editor.
- The compiler translates the program text to an object file.
- The linker puts together several object files to form an executable file.
- The operating system puts the executable file in the primary memory and the program is executed.

A modern program development system not only has the obvious resources of text editor, compiler and linker, it also has support to keep order in the different parts which go to make up a programming project; there is a *debugger* (a program which makes it possible to test run your programs step by step and search for possible errors in them) and there are help texts, documentation and examples. There may also be advanced resources to produce *window-oriented* programs, that is, programs which communicate with the user via menus, windows, click-buttons, and so on.

As an example of a modern program development system, we will show how you write and run our program example in Borland's C++ system. You start the program development system in the usual way, by clicking on its symbol. When the system has started, you get a window like the one in Figure 1.8.

Figure 1.8

For every program that will be developed, there must be a *project*. A project contains a mass of information about the current program. Among other things, it keeps a check on all the files needed to construct the program. In Figure 1.8, you can indicate that you want to start a new project by marking the option 'New' on the File Menu. You then get the window in Figure 1.9.

You have to provide a name for every project (project information is saved in a file which has a name with the suffix .ide.) and you also have to indicate what kind of program it is. For instance, you can indicate that it will be a windows-oriented application, or that it will be a program which uses a simple text window (*EasyWin*). We will choose the second alternative here. The Borland system is able to develop programs for different *platforms*. You can choose Windows with 16 bits, Windows with 32 bits, or MS-DOS.

When the new project has been created, the window in Figure 1.10 can be obtained. Right at the bottom, in the project window, there is a graphics picture of the files that constitute the project.

In our example, we will produce an executable file, ex1.exe, which is constructed from a program text file with the name ex1.cpp. If you click on ex1.cpp in the project window, you will get the text editor window above. You can type in your program text, which is shown in the figure.

The program can be compiled and linked by choosing 'Build All' in the project menu. Then, all the files which constitute the project will be compiled and linked together. If the compiler discovers errors in the program, you will get a message about this and you will be able to see the faulty lines marked in the text editor window. If your program is fault-free, it is linked to a program which can be run. This can be started simply by clicking on the 'run' button, which has a flash of lightning as a symbol. The window in Figure 1.11 will then be shown on the screen. This is a text window in which the program's outputs are shown.

Figure 1.9

Figure 1.10

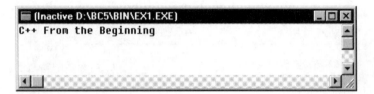

Figure 1.11

Modern applications programs make use of windows, menus, and so on, to communicate with the person running the program, and program development systems such as Borland C++ or Visual C++ make it possible to write such programs. Unfortunately, it is not trivial to construct windows-oriented programs, even if there is adequate support in the program development system, for much depends on the system and the help functions that must be used vary in the different computer systems. This book deals with fundamental programming techniques, so the construction of windows-oriented programs lies outside its framework. We will be dealing with programs that read and write in simple text windows such as that in Figure 1.11.

1.3   Programming languages

The earliest computers had to be programmed, as mentioned earlier, in machine code. A part of a program might then have looked like this:

```
0111000100001111 1001110110110001 1110000100111110
```

Naturally, it was regarded as an enormous advance when *assembler languages* began to be used. The program section above might then be written:

```
LOAD A    ADD B    STORE C
```

In assembler language, every line in the program corresponds to an instruction in the machine code. The program section above thus consists of three instructions. For a program written in assembler language to be run in the computer, a translation program is needed, an *assembler*, which translates into machine code. A translation program like this need not be terribly complicated since the assembler language, in its structure, is very close to machine code.

In spite of the fact that assembler languages were such an improvement, there are still considerable disadvantages to using them. One is that every kind of computer has its own, unique assembler language. An assembler programmer could have to learn many different kinds of assembler languages, which could vary greatly. Another disadvantage is that assembler languages are extremely detailed. Every single instruction must be given to the computer. This means that it is time consuming to use assembler languages and it is very easy to make mistakes.

Programming work was changed radically with the development of high level languages in the mid-1950s. A program written in a high level language is more compatible with the way we express ourselves than with the computer's arranging of instructions. Programs are expressed in a kind of pidgin English and arithmetical calculations are written in a form reminiscent of mathematics.

The program sections above could possibly look like this:

```
C = A + B
```

The programmer can concentrate on the problem to be solved without worrying about the details about of how the computer works. In principle, it is also possible to write programs in one high level language to run on different computers. There is no need to learn a new language for every computer to be used.

The first high level language was *FORTRAN* (FORmula TRANslator), which was introduced in 1954. It was originally intended to simplify writing programs using arithmetical expressions. The great weakness is its poor structure. In addition, the language has poor facilities for input and output. FORTRAN has had a facelift with the new versions FORTRAN 77 and FORTRAN 90.

In 1959 a new programming language, *COBOL*, was introduced, designed for programming in the areas of finance and administration. A few years later the language was standardized and it has become, and remains, one of the most used languages. COBOL programs are very readable in that they resemble ordinary English. The disadvantage of this is that programs in the language are sometimes considered wordy and awkward. What was new about COBOL, compared with FORTRAN, was that it had better ways of describing the data a program had to handle.

A language that came to be very significant for subsequent developments was *ALGOL*, which was presented in 1960. The big advantage of the language is that it has good structure. It is possible to write a program so that the way it works is reflected in its appearance.

Another significant language for later language developments was *SIMULA*, the first version of which appeared in 1967, a direct extension of ALGOL. The language is used primarily, as its names implies, to write simulation programs. SIMULA is significant for being the first programming language that enabled *object-oriented* programs to be written. For instance, *classes* and *inheritance*, two concepts of importance in object-oriented languages today, could already be found in SIMULA.

The *Pascal* language was introduced in 1971. It was to be a simple language, suitable for use in teaching, and it has achieved wide usage in this field. The reason is that it has good program structure, which makes it easy for the beginner to acquire good 'programming style'. Pascal is based directly on

ALGOL and on ideas from SIMULA, although a good many constructs have been deliberately simplified. Even so, variants of Pascal have appeared, for example UCSD Pascal and TURBO Pascal. The greatest weakness of the language is that it lacks constructs for enabling larger programs to be built up in a modular way. Further, it is limited in its handling of text, and in its input and output facilities.

C is a language that has become very popular in spite of its age (it was developed at the start of the 1970s). It is a language which can be said to be a 'high level language at a low level'. It gives the programmer great freedom to control the computer in detail, and has therefore come largely to replace the assembler in the development of system programs. From the beginning C was closely connected to the operating system Unix, but today it is used in most computer environments. Most of today's operating systems and other system programs, such as those handling windows and menus, are written in C. C is relatively small but demands a lot of the programmer, as it is so easy to make mistakes.

Remarkably fast developments in the field of electronics, with more and more powerful components being produced more and more cheaply, led many to believe that it would similarly be possible to construct ever larger and more complex programs. In the event, this assumption was quite wrong. All too many programs either failed to be ready on time, greatly exceeded their budget, contained many errors or did not fulfil the customers' specifications. This phenomenon became known as the *software crisis*. Among the reasons for this crisis was poor project management, and the fact that the programmer often considered the program to be his or her own property. Many individual and curious programming styles developed and it proved difficult to create error-free programs. In order to remedy this, the concept of *structured programming* was introduced, with the aim that a program should be written in such a way that it is both easily understood and free from errors. Structured programming can be said to be a set of rules and recommendations for how 'good' programs should be written. Such programming needs the support of a suitable programming language, and it was this need for well-structured programs that was behind the development of what became known as structured languages, such as Pascal.

During the 1970s, it became clear that even well-structured programs were not enough for mastering the complexity involved in developing a large program system. It was also recognized that it was necessary to support the division of the program into well-defined parts, or *modules*, that could be developed and tested independently of one another, so that several people could work together within one large programming project. One way to divide a program into modules is to use so-called *objects* as building blocks in the program. An object in the program can be thought of as a representation of a real or conceptual thing in the program's environment.

This idea originated from the language SIMULA but was further elaborated in a project at Xerox, where a brand new language, *Smalltalk*, was constructed. The first available version of Smalltalk was presented in 1980 and the concept of *object-oriented* program development was introduced in connection to this project. Many of the special words which are used in the object-oriented programming languages, *messages* and *methods* for instance, come from Smalltalk. In Smalltalk, the concept of object is particularly emphasized. There are no data types in the language and all data in a program are just objects. The syntax of Smalltalk is also somewhat particular; that is, the language looks very different compared with other languages. A Smalltalk system is an integrated interactive environment with a window-oriented user interface. A drawback of Smalltalk that is often mentioned is that the interactive environment demands large computer resources and that the programs produced usually execute slowly. The latter is due to that fact that the program is not compiled, but *interpreted*, at execution.

The US Department of Defense was hard hit by the software crisis. It was an important customer for independent companies producing programming systems. To put this right, the initiative was taken to develop a new programming language capable of meeting the specifications envisaged. Developments continued in the form of an international competition between different research groups and companies. The winning project was given the name *Ada* and was accepted in 1983 as a standard in the USA. Ada also became an international ISO standard. Apart from being a well-structured language, Ada also supports the modular development of programs. The concept of the *package* has been introduced and it is possible to build up libraries of packages which can be put together to make large programs. One thing that distinguishes Ada from most other programming languages is that it can be used to write *parallel programs*, that is, programs which contain several active parts that are to be executed simultaneously and interact with one another. Such programs, called *real time programs*, are encountered in applications for computer control of technical systems.

After a few years of use the decision was made to revise the standard. The new standard is called Ada 95. One important innovation compared with the old standard (Ada 83) is that of object-oriented language constructs. Another important addition is that of child libraries, which further simplify the construction of large programs. Ada is today a fully object-oriented language and an interesting alternative to C++ for anyone who wants to work with object-oriented technology.

C++ is, however, without any doubt the most popular object-oriented programming language at the moment. One of the reasons is that it is an expansion of the popular language C. There are compilers or complete development systems in C++ for all common types of computer.

C++ was constructed by Bjarne Strostrup at AT&T Bell Laboratories. The first commercial version came out in 1985 and is still in the process of development. New versions, with considerable additions, have been introduced gradually. A committee from the American National Standards Institution, ANSI, is working to establish a standard for the language. There is still no official standard but there is a basic document[†] which will be the starting point for the formal standardization of

---

[†] Ellis, Stroustrup, *The Annotated C++ Reference Manual*, Addison-Wesley Publishing Company, 1990.

C++. The standards committee has also published a rough draft[†] to the draft of the standard.

C++ is thus a straight expansion of C. In the basics of the languages there are only marginal differences. You can compile a C program with a C++ compiler but not the other way around; meanwhile the additions made to C are quite comprehensive. It is mainly a question of language constructs for object-oriented programming. The concept of class, central to C++, does not exist at all in C. Again, C++ contains many improvements on C, especially, for instance, the mechanism for the transfer of parameters to functions, which is more reliable. In this book, C++ will be treated as a separate language and we will learn it from the beginning and so we will not be discussing substantial differences between C and C++.

1.4   The process of developing programs

This book is all about programming or, in other words, how one builds or constructs a program. However, developing a program is not only a question of programming. It might be compared with what happens when a house is built – it is not just a case of going ahead and laying the bricks. A good deal of careful preparation is needed. First, you have to decide how the house will be used, then the plans can be drawn, and after that all the calculations have to be made before the actual building can commence. And even when the house is completely built it cannot be left to itself: it needs to be maintained. The work of building a house can thus be divided into a number of *phases* – from the decision about its future usage to its maintenance. This is quite similar to what has to happen if you are going to develop a computer program: the programming, corresponding to the actual carpentry and bricklaying, is only one phase of the whole process.

This is where a useful distinction can be made between *programming in the small* and *programming in the large*. Programming in the small means that you work alone and produce a little program of a temporary nature. Programming in the large means that you work with the development of a larger program and that the work is often the joint effort of a group of programmers. Most programming in education settings is on the small scale, but on occasion it can also be large scale, for example in project-based courses and the sort of applied project work incorporated in many education programmes. In the case of commercial and industrial program development, it is almost always a question of programming in the large.

When you want to develop a program, it is so easy to sit down and start to write it at once – one could call this the direct-programming method. In the case of professional programming, in the large, this practice leads to greater costs and it is

---

[†] Working Paper for Draft Proposed International Standard for Information Systems – Programming Language C++, April 1995. Available on the Internet at `ftp://research.att.com/dist/c++std/wp/`.

questionable whether a functioning and usable program can ever be produced in this way. It is generally admitted that such direct programming brought about the software crisis that was discussed previously. It is less serious to use the direct-programming approach for programming in the small, but even then it is worthwhile to decide in advance what the program should do and how it should do it.

The overall goal when developing a professional program is to produce a high quality program within given constraints of time and cost. A program should match the demands of the user, be reliable, well documented and easy to maintain. To achieve these ends the program has to be developed with a well-structured approach; just as with building a house, this calls for engineer-like work in accordance with a clear plan. The term *software engineering* is often used to refer to such a well-structured approach.

In order to draw up a work plan you need a model for the way in which program development proceeds, and there are several models to choose from. The most widely used is that known as the *waterfall model*, of which there are several variants. The program development process is here divided up into the following phases:

(1)   Requirements analysis and requirements specification

(2)   Design

(3)   Implementation

(4)   Test and installation

(5)   Operation and maintenance.

The reason for calling this the waterfall method is that each phase results in a set of documents that run down to the next phase.

During the first phase, *requirements analysis* and *specification*, the goal is to determine what has to be done. You have to try to understand the environment in which the desired program will have to function. You should specify what the program is required to do, what different functions it should be capable of, and the principles for its communication with the user. Such questions as the sort of computers it should be run on should also be addressed now. This work should result in a written *requirements specification* which clearly states all these demands. The specification is the document which defines the program that is to be constructed and it has to be accepted both by the customer and by the program developer(s). The specification might include a *preliminary user manual* and it can also prescribe *trial procedures*, which state how the final program will be tested.

In the second phase, that of *design*, the question being addressed is *how* should the program meet the demands now specified? You could say that this is producing a blueprint for the program. You decide what different parts should go to make up the program, what each of these should do, how they should interface and how they should communicate with one another. This is done first in outline and then in greater detail. The detailed design really means that you have decided how the program is to be implemented. For example, it is now that decisions are made about suitable algorithms (see the next section) and data structures. The details of the interface with the user are worked out – what it should look like, how commands will be given to the program, what the menus should include, and so on. The documents which are produced during the design phase are firstly a *detailed system description*, laying out the program's design, and secondly a *user manual*, which gives directions for how the program should be used.

It is only in the third phase, *implementation*, that any programming starts to be done, when there is already a detailed system specification and user manual to adhere to. This phase also sees the testing of the parts of the program, one by one, as they are completed. The result of the implementation phase is, naturally, the *program code*, but there might also be *test protocols* resulting from the tests carried out on parts of the program.

In the fourth phase of development, *test and installation*, all the parts of the program are put together for a check that everything works. If the program is to be installed at a particular site, that is also done now. Testing is carried out according to the prescribed test procedures which were defined earlier. This phase results in a *test protocol*, and it is only after this has been found acceptable that the program developer gets paid in full by the customer.

The final phase, *operation and maintenance*, is the longest phase in the life of the product. Now the program is in full use, but errors that were missed in earlier tests have to be put right and the program might have to be adjusted to cope with new demands, for example to work in a more modern hardware environment.

There is a criticism of the waterfall model in that it is too static: if one should happen upon a mistake made in an earlier phase it cannot be corrected. Of course, the waterfall model is not in reality used too strictly: some degree of feedback is allowed. There is, after all, no point in implementing something known to be incorrect or unsuitable. For example, one might discover during the design phase that some of the demands made in the first phase are impossible, or very expensive, to implement, and then it is only natural to relax the demands.

The specifications which are drawn up during the program development process should be as clear as possible, so that there is no possibility of misunderstanding. There are no generally recognized formal methods for writing specifications. The most common method is to use *graphic notation, ordinary text*, or a *program description language*. When using normal text it is usual to make it as formal as possible, by filling in sets of prespecified forms, for example. Program description languages (PDLs) are simplified programming languages which contain certain simple language constructs and which enable one to include explanatory text.

1.5   Algorithms

When designing a program the problem has to be faced of deciding on suitable methods of solving the different partial problems of the whole program. A description of how a particular problem is solved – a computational method – is called an *algorithm*. An algorithm consists of a number of elementary operations and instructions about the order in which these operations should be carried out. Certain demands can be made of an algorithm:

- it should solve the given problem;
- it should be unambiguous (not 'fuzzy' in its formulation);
- if the problem has an end view, such as computing a certain value, then the algorithm should terminate after a finite number of steps.

Note: Not all algorithms have to terminate. For instance, the algorithm that describes the control program for a nuclear power plant should certainly not terminate.

We come across algorithms every day. One example is a recipe. The problem is to prepare a particular dish and the algorithm gives us the solution. Another example is the assembly instructions we get when we buy furniture in kit form; and then there are all the different kinds of instruction manuals. Knitters will recognize that a knitting pattern is nothing other than an algorithm.

Algorithms can be expressed in many different ways. One common way is in natural language. Pictures and symbols can also be used, so can formal languages like mathematical notation. Flow charts have also been popular. Here we are dealing with programming, so what is naturally of interest to us is that algorithms can be expressed in programming languages. The programming language ALGOL, which lies at the root of most of today's conventional programming languages, was designed specifically so that it could be made to express algorithms, hence the name.

Algorithm
Description of how a particular problem is to be solved (a calculation method).

Let us look at an example. We shall describe an algorithm that shows the sum $1 + 2 + 3 \ldots + n$ can be evaluated, if n is a given whole number > 0. One way of describing the algorithm in natural language is:

(1) Set sum equal to 0 and the counter k equal to 1.

(2) Repeat the following steps until k is greater than n:

    (2.1) Calculate the sum of sum and k and save the result in sum.
    (2.2) Increase the value of k by 1.

(3) The result required is now the number in sum.

Expressed as part of a C++ program, the algorithm looks like this:

```
cin >> n;
sum = 0;
for (int k=1; k<=n; k++)
  sum += k;
cout << sum;
```

These lines of program read in the number n from the keyboard and display the calculated sum on the screen.

To describe general algorithms the description method must be able to express the following three constructs:

(1)   A *sequence* is a series of steps that are carried out sequentially in the order in which they are written. An example is the assembly instructions for bookshelves:

> (1)   Put the side pieces in position.
> (2)   Screw the back piece on to the sides.
> (3)   Put the shelves into the frame.

(2)   *Selection.* Selection means that one of two or more alternatives should be chosen. Calculating the absolute value of a number t can be taken as an example:

> if $t > 0$ then the result is t, otherwise the result is $-t$.

(3)   *Iteration.* Part of the algorithm should be capable of repetition either a defined number of times or until a certain condition has been met. We saw an example of repetition a defined number of times in the algorithm above, when the sum $1 + 2 + 3 + \ldots + n$ was calculated. An example of the latter repetition could be:

> Whisk the egg whites vigorously, until they become fluffy.

The most important algorithmic constructs

- Sequence – series of steps
- Selection – choice between alternative paths
- Iteration – repetition

Another kind of construct that is commonly used in algorithms and which can sometimes replace iteration, is *recursion*. This construct seldom occurs in 'everyday' algorithms and may therefore feel a little strange. The principle is to break down the original problem into smaller, but structurally similar, problems. The smaller problems can then be solved by reapplying the same algorithm. The previous example, calculating the sum of the first n positive integers, can be solved with recursion in the following manner:

(1) If n = 0 set the result to 0,

(2) otherwise:

    (2.1) Compute the sum $1 + 2 + 3 + ... (n-1)$ using this algorithm.

    (2.2) The required result is obtained by adding n to the result from step 2.1.

1.6 Top-down design

When a complicated problem has to be solved, it is helpful to split it into smaller subproblems, which are then solved separately. The subproblems can then be split into further subproblems, and so on. This is a very important technique in algorithm and program construction and is known as *top-down design*. Let us look at an 'everyday' algorithm that describes washing your car. A first, rough algorithm may be simply:

(1) Wash car.

This can be quickly refined to:

(1.1) If you are feeling lazy:

    (1.1.1) Wash it at a car wash.

(1.2) otherwise

    (1.2.1) Wash it by hand.

Step (1.1.1) can be refined to:

(1.1.1.1) Drive to the nearest car wash.

(1.1.1.2) Buy a token.

(1.1.1.3) Wait in a queue.

(1.1.1.4) Have the car washed.

Step (1.1.1.4) can be refined further:

(1.1.1.4.1) Check that the doors and windows are closed.

(1.1.1.4.2) Wind down the driver's window.

(1.1.1.4.3) Put the token into the machine.

(1.1.1.4.4) Wind up the window.

(1.1.1.4.5)   Drive into the car wash.

(1.1.1.4.6)   Wait until the car wash is finished.

(1.1.1.4.7)   Drive away.

In this way, different parts of an algorithm can be refined until a level is reached where the solution becomes trivially simple.

Top-down design

- Divide into subproblems.
- Solve the subproblems one by one.
- Divide the subproblems into further subproblems.
- Continue in this way until all the subproblems are easily solvable.

Let us look at another example where iteration is also involved. Imagine the following situation. In your bookcase you have a compact disc holder for ordinary compact discs. You keep your CDs there, neatly arranged alphabetically according to the name of the composer. (For simplicity, assume that you only have classical music.) CD holders are made of small slots each large enough for one CD so that they cannot be moved sideways. We assume that the CDs are kept in the left part of the holder, so that there are no gaps or empty slots on the left, but at least five empty ones on the right.

Now suppose you have bought five new CDs that need to be put in the holder in their correct positions, so that alphabetical order is maintained. Assume also that the bookshelves are so full that there is nowhere to put the CDs, so you have to hold them in your hands while you shift them around. To avoid the risk of dropping any, you cannot have more than one CD in your hand at a time. The five new CDs are on the floor and you pick them up one after the other and position them in the holder.

We can make up a rough algorithm:

(1)   Sort the new CDs into the CD holder.

The first refinement will be:

(1.1)   For each new CD:

(1.1.1)   Lift the CD from the floor with your left hand.

(1.1.2)   Sort it into its correct place.

The way we have written points (1.1.1) and (1.1.2) inset on the line shows that they have to be repeated several times (once per new CD). We have thus introduced iteration into the algorithm. Point (1.1.1) needs no further refinement so we can refine point (1.1.2):

(1.1.2.1) Locate the slot in the CD holder where the new CD is to be placed.

(1.1.2.2) Shift all the CDs to the right of (and including) the located slot one place to the right, so that the located one becomes empty.

(1.1.2.3) Place the new CD in the located slot.

Refining point (1.1.2.1) gives:

(1.1.2.1.1) Put your left index finger on the leftmost slot of the CD holder. (You can do this even though you have the new CD in that hand.)

(1.1.2.1.2) Repeat the following point until the located slot is empty or until the composer's name on the CD in the located slot comes alphabetically after the composer's name on the new CD.

(1.1.2.1.2.1) Move your left index finger one slot to the right.

(1.1.2.1.3) Your left index finger has now located the slot where the new CD is to be inserted.

Point (1.1.2.2) now becomes:

(1.1.2.2.1) Put your right hand on the CD furthest to the right and repeat the following steps until the slot indicated by your left index finger is empty.

(1.1.2.2.1.1) Move the CD held by your right hand one slot to the right.

(1.1.2.2.1.2) Move your right hand to the nearest CD on the left.

If we now put all the refined steps together, we get the following complete algorithm. The numbering of the steps has been removed to make it look neater. Note that the inset lines are repeated a defined number of times.

For each of the newly bought CDs:

Lift the CD from the floor with your left hand.

Put your left index finger on the slot in the CD holder furthest to the left.

Repeat the following steps until the slot pointed to is empty, or until the composer's name on the CD pointed to comes alphabetically after the composer's name on the new CD.

Move your left index finger one slot to the right.

Your left index finger now points to the slot where the new CD is to be inserted.

Put your right hand on the CD which is furthest to the right and repeat the following steps until the slot pointed to by your left index finger is empty.

Move the CD you are holding in your right hand, one slot to the right.

Move your right hand to the nearest CD on the left.

Insert the new CD in the located slot.

We have just seen an example of a *sort algorithm*. This is not the only algorithm that can be used to sort the CDs into position. You could think of several other ways of doing this. Sort algorithms often occur in programming.

There are usually several alternative algorithms for solving a particular problem. In general, it is sensible to design an algorithm that is simple and easy to understand because it will then have the best chance of working as intended.

EXERCISES

1.1   Try to find out the following about the computer system you intend to use:

- What operating system is being used?
- How large is the primary memory?
- How large is the hard disk memory?
- What possibilities are there for communicating with other computers?
- Which C++ compiler or C++ development environment is to be used?
- What other programming languages, apart from C++, are available?

1.2   Write a C++ program to display your name and address at the terminal. Compile, link and test run the program with the help of the compiler or program development environment you intend to use.

1.3   Give an algorithm for calculating the sum

$$\sum_{i=1}^{n} i^2$$

1.4   Find an algorithm for calculating

$$n! = 1 \cdot 2 \cdot 3 \cdot ... \cdot n, \langle n > 0 \rangle$$

1.5   A table contains n different numbers. Design an algorithm which searches the table to find the smallest number. At the end, the algorithm will give the lowest number's position number in the table (an index between 1 and n).

1.6 A table contains *n* different numbers. Design an algorithm which changes the table's contents so that the numbers appear in order of size, the smallest number first and largest last. Use a method which first places the smallest number in the table's first position, the next smallest number in the table's second position, and so on. (*Tip*: The algorithm in the previous exercise may help.)

The Basics

This chapter presents some of the basic concepts behind C++. We shall see how programs that read and write input data are constructed. In this context, we will look at *variables*. A variable is like a container in computer programs; it is used to handle data. There are different kinds of variable and they may contain different sorts of data, or *types*, as they are often called. In this chapter, we will be looking at the most common types so that we can handle different kinds of numbers and we will be going over various forms of arithmetical and logical expressions.

We shall also deal with **if** statements, **while** statements and **for** statements, the most common constructions for performing choice and repetition.

Finally, the various errors that can occur in the programming process are discussed.

2.1   Variables and reading/writing

On page 6 of the first chapter, we saw a simple program to output text. Now we begin to study programs which are more useful, programs that can calculate more important things. We now design, as a first example, a program that calculates how much a car costs to hire. Suppose that you know the number of days you want to hire the car for and how much it costs per day. You give the program this information, and let it calculate the total cost and output it. When the program is running, the output might look like this:

```
Number of days? 3
Rate per day?    42
Total cost:      126
```

The numbers 3 and 42 are called *input data*. They are written by the person running the program. The rest of the output is produced by the program. The number 126 is the result calculated by the program – the *output data*. The program looks like this:

```
#include <iostream.h>
main ()
{
  int day_number;
  int daily_rate;
  cout << "Number of days? ";
  cin  >> day_number;
  cout << "Rate per day?    ";
  cin  >> daily_rate;
  cout << "Total cost:      "
       << day_number * daily_rate << endl;
}
```

The first line says that we want to use the standard library iostream which contains a facility for input and output. (If you have a compiler which follows the draft standard for C++, you can write #include <iostream> instead of #include <iostream.h>.) A variable, as mentioned above, is a kind of container into which data can be put; in this program, the two variables are day_number and daily_rate. A particular variable can only contain information of a certain kind, or *type*. Before you can use a variable in a program, you have to say what you are going to call it and what kind of data it will contain. To do this is to *declare* the variable. In our program, the declarations are made on the two lines which begin with the word **int**. These lines say that the variables will be called day_number and daily_rate and that both of them will contain the values of the type **int**. (We usually say that the variables *are of* the type **int**, or that they *have* the type **int**.) The type **int** is a standard type in C++ and 'int' is an abbreviation of 'integer', which means 'whole number'. The two variables in the program will thus contain whole numbers, that is, numbers without decimal parts.

A function contains, as we have seen, a number of *statements*, which describe what is to be performed. The declarations are often written in front of the statements. In our program, the statements begin on the sixth line.

As we saw in Chapter 1, output from a program can be generated with the help of the output operator <<. The first statement in the program writes out the text Number of days?. The next statement:

```
cin >> day_number;
```

uses the input operator >> to read input data from the input stream cin to the variable day_number. The stream cin is normally connected to the keyboard.

This means that when this statement is carried out, the program will stop for a moment and wait until a number is typed in from the keyboard. When the number has been typed (normally finished by pressing the 'enter' key) the program will continue. The number typed in from the keyboard now lands in the variable day_number. If the user, as in our example, types the number 3, then day_number will get the value 3.

The input data is then read in a similar way for the variable daily_rate, which in our example has the value 42. The output of the result takes the form of the statement:

```
cout << "Total cost: "
     << day_number * daily_rate << endl;
```

First the text Total cost: is written, then the product of day_number and daily_rate. The sign * means multiplication. As we know, many things can be output one after the other in the same output statement. Last of all in the stream is the manipulator endl which generates a new line in the output. There are many different kinds of manipulators and they can be inserted in the outstream to edit the output. We will shortly be looking at a few more common manipulators.

Output on the screen

cout << out1 << out2 << out3... ;

where *outi* can be a constant, a variable, an expression or a manipulator.

In C++ there are a number of *reserved words*, words with particular meanings. There is one in our program called **int**. We often write these reserved words in bold so that they may be seen more clearly and this will be the case in this book.

When you write the program yourself, you don't have to mark reserved words in any particular way. (In modern program development systems reserved words are often marked automatically by special text editors when they are written. See, for example, Figure 1.10.)

The observant reader will notice that we have not put a statement like

```
return 0;
```

as we did in the example on page 6 of Chapter 1. There really ought to be a **return** statement like this at the end of every program but according to the draft of the standard, you can leave out this statement. So we will not include it in our examples from now on. Most of the C++ compilers today will give a warning about this but you can go ahead and compile the program anyway.

Now we shall make some additions to our program so it becomes a little more usable. Suppose you are on holiday in Spain and want to hire a car there. This will mean that the rate per day is given in pesetas. Suppose that you also have to pay an extra, fixed payment of 2000 pesetas in tax. To avoid the mental arithmetic, you want the program to output the total cost both in pesetas and in pounds. For this to be possible, you have to give the current rates of exchange as input data. Here is an example of how the program might look when you run it.

```
Indicate number of days and cost per day: 3 5250
Exchange rate? 0.00479
Total cost: 17750 ptas (£85.0225)
```

The program will then look like this:

```cpp
#include <iostream.h>
main ()
{
  int       day_number, daily_rate, tot_cost;
  const int tax = 2000;
  double    exchange_rate;
  cout << "Indicate number of days and cost per day: ";
  cin  >> day_number >> daily_rate;
  cout << "Exchange rate? ";
  cin  >> exchange_rate;
  tot_cost = tax + day_number * daily_rate;
  cout << "Total cost: " << tot_cost << " ptas"
       << " (£" << tot_cost*exchange_rate << ")"<< endl;
}
```

The three variables `day_number`, `daily_rate` and `tot_cost` are declared on the fourth line. They are all of the type **int**. We can see that we don't have to declare a variable per line but are allowed to enumerate several variables one after another. They must all be of the same type, however.

The constant `tax` is declared on the next line. It has a constant value and may (can) not be changed in the program. The fact that `tax = 2000` is in the program means that the constant `tax` is *initialized* to the value `2000`, and it will have this value during the execution of the entire program.

If a variable is not initialized, its starting value will be undefined. Constant variables must always be initialized, since they cannot be changed later in the program. It is also possible for variables which are not constant to be initialized upon declaration. We might have been able to put it in the following way, where the variables `day_number` and `tot_cost` are initialized to the value `0` and the variable `daily_rate` is left uninitialized.

```
int day_number=0, daily_rate, tot_cost=0;
```

The variable `exchange_rate`, which will contain the exchange rate, is declared on the sixth line of the program. Obviously, the exchange rate cannot be a whole number and so the type **int** will not work. Instead, we have to make use of another standard type, **double**. Variables of this type can contain real numbers, numbers with decimals. (Double actually stands for 'double precision'.)

Variable declarations

type name1, name2 ... ;
⇒ changeable, uninitialized variables

or

type name1=value1, name2=value2 ... ;
⇒ changeable, initialized variables
(each variable is initialized separately)

or

constant *type name1=value1, name2=value2 ... ;*
⇒ constant variables
(each variable is initialized separately)

When you declare a variable, you can decide yourself what to call it. The name of the variable may be as long as you like and can consist of letters, numbers and the underline character. It may not, however, begin with a number. Only the letters 'a' to 'z' may be used in C++. Note that upper case and lower case letters are treated as being *different*. The names `n1` and `N1` thus designate two different variables. Reserved words may not be used as names of variables, so variables such as `while` and `if` may not be declared.

Let us return to our program. In the line

```
cin >> day_number >> daily_rate;
```

the values of the variables `day_number` and `daily_rate` are entered. Several values can be input one after another in the same statement. The user can input freely formatted input data extending to more than one line in the program. The different numbers can either be input one after the other on the same line, or you can press the Enter key after every number. Normally, the operator `>>` automatically skips over all the 'white' characters (spacings, tab stops and end-of-line breaks) in the input stream. Thus input could just as well look like this:

```
Indicate number of days and cost per day: 3
5250
```

Input from the keyboard

> *cin >> variable1;*
> *cin >> variable2;*
> *cin >> variable3;*

or

> *cin >> variable1 >> variable2 >> variable3 ... ;*

Input data is written in free format. Spacings, tab stops and end of lines are normally skipped over.

The variable `tot_cost` is used for storage of the total cost, expressed in pesetas. It gets its value through an *assignment statement*:

```
tot_cost = tax + day_number * daily_rate;
```

The expression on the right of the equation is calculated first. Then, the calculated value is placed in the variable `tot_cost`. A value must have the same type as a variable if it is to be assigned to it. Thus the expression to the right of the equation in an assignment statement must either have the same type as the variable to the left, or the value must be able to be automatically converted into the type of this variable. There is no problem if the types in question are *arithmetic types*, types which contain mathematical numbers, since they can always be automatically converted into one another. When run, the last program statement reads:

```
Total cost: 17750 ptas (£85.0225)
```

When a real number is output, the output operator automatically edits the output to facilitate reading the number as much as possible. (For those familiar with C,

---

Assignment

variable names = expressions;

- The value of the expression to the right of the equation is calculated first.
- This value is then placed in the variable to the left.
- The variable's previous value is destroyed.
- The expression to the right must have the same type as the variable or must be able to be automatically transformed into this type.
- Arithmetic types and possibly others, can be automatically transformed.

---

it should be pointed out that printout is done just as if the function `printf` had been used with a `%g` format.) This means, among other things, that the number of decimals shown will depend on the value of the number. This can be useful, although mostly you might like to control how the number will be output. In our example above, it could well be that you always want two decimals in the output of the sum in pounds sterling. One way of editing the output, is to use manipulators. To do this, you may have to include, the file `iomanip.h` as well in your program. You do this by entering the line

```
#include <iomanip.h>
```

at the beginning of the program. (With a compiler that follows the draft standard, you can instead input `#include    <iomanip>`.) The last statement in our program is then rewritten:

```
cout << "Total cost: " << tot_cost << " ptas"
     << setiosflags(ios::fixed) << setprecision(2)
     << " (£" << tot_cost*exchange_rate << ")"<<endl;
```

Two manipulators have been put into the stream here. The first manipulator, `setiosflags`, is used to give certain characteristics to the current stream. One such characteristic is `fixed`, which indicates that real numbers will be output with a fixed decimal point. (This corresponds in C to the call of the function `printf` with a `%f` format.) The other manipulator, `setprecision`, is used to indicate how many decimals we want to have in the output (in our case, two). The output will be *rounded off* to the number of decimals we indicate. The program will now produce the output

```
Total cost: 17750 ptas (£85.02)
```

Note that the output of the number of pesetas has not been affected. Manipulators only affect the output which comes after them in the stream. A manipulator normally applies not only to the next values which are output but also to the values following these. If, for instance, we were to insert a further series of real numbers into our program, these would also be output with two decimals and a fixed decimal point. In the standard draft, there is a manipulator called `fixed` which is easier to use than `setiosflags`. So an alternative would be:

```
cout << "Total cost: " << tot_cost << " ptas"
     << fixed << setprecision(2)
     << " (£" << tot_cost*exchange_rate << ") " << endl;
```

A commentary should be provided for `precision`. The standard value for `precision` is 6. If the standard format in the output is used, `precision` will indicate the total number of figures in the output; but if you have indicated, as has been done here, that the output form should be `fixed`, `precision` will indicate the number of decimals.

If a return to the default output form is desired, the manipulators `setprecision` and `resetiosflags` can be used:

```
cout << setprecision(6) << resetiosflags(ios::fixed);
```

Let us now look at an example of a program which can be used with the sale of goods. Let us imagine that a customer has bought a certain number of goods of the same kind and that he now wants an invoice. The invoice should say how many articles the customer has bought, what the total cost is (including sales tax) and how much of the cost the sales tax accounts for. When the program is run, it can look like this:

```
Number of articles? 30
Cost per article? 42.50

INVOICE
=======
Number of articles:        30
Cost per article:       42.50
Total cost:           1593.75
Of which sales tax:    318.75
```

Particularly noticeable here is that all the figures in the output of the invoice have been adjusted so that there is a straight right-hand margin. We say that the figures have been *right-justified*. When a number is to be printed, a certain number of positions are used in the output. The number will usually be placed to the right in these positions; the space in front of the number will be filled in with blank characters. If you don't indicate the number of positions to be used, there will automatically be just enough of them for the number. As a result, the number will be left-justified directly after the previous output.

To indicate the number of output positions, the manipulator `setw` is used. The expression `setw(9)` indicates that nine positions will be used in the next output. Note that the manipulator `setw`, unlike `setprecision` and

Some common manipulators in output

The following line must be found at the beginning of the program
```
#include <iomanip.h>
```
- `endl`
    Line feed.
- `setprecision` (*n*)
    Output of numbers of the form `fixed` will occur with *n* decimals. *n*=0 means standard value.
- `fixed` or `setiosflags` (`ios::fixed`)
    Real numbers will be printed out with fixed decimal point and with decimals.
- `resetiosflags` (`ios::fixed`)
    Return to standard kind of output form.
- `setw(n)`
    Next printout will take place with *n* positions.
- `setfill('x')`
    In the next printout, fill-in will occur with the sign 'x' instead of with blanks.

`setiosflags`, only applies to the next output. Note too, that `setw` can be used for all kinds of ouput, not only for outputting real numbers.

The sales tax and the cost with and without sales tax are calculated in three separate variables. The exact percentage for sales tax has been declared as a constant and, since it has been expressed as a percentage, we must divide it by 100. The program then looks like this:

```
#include <iostream.h>
#include <iomanip.h>
main ()
{
  int number;
  double per_art, excl_sales_tax, incl_sales_tax, sales_tax;
  const double sales_tax_percent = 25.0;

  cout << "Number of articles? "; cin >> number;
  cout << "Cost per article? "; cin >> per_art;
  excl_sales_tax = per_art * number;
  sales_tax = excl_sales_tax * sales_tax_percent / 100;
  incl_sales_tax = excl_sales_tax + sales_tax;

  cout << endl <<
  "INVOICE" << endl << "=======" << endl <<
  "Number of articles:" << setw(9) << number << endl <<
  setprecision(2) << setiosflags(ios::fixed) <<
```

```
     "Cost per article:" << setw(11) << per_art << endl <<
     "Total cost:" << setw(17) << incl_sales_tax << endl <<
     "Of which sales tax:" << setw(9) << sales_tax << endl;
}
```

Sometimes you need to indicate the constant values in your programs. In this program, for instance, we have the values 25.0 and 100. Constant values of this kind are called *literals*[†]. Literals need not designate numerical data. You can have literals of another kind, for example literals to designate constant texts, such as "INVOICE". In calculating the sales tax, you could of course have written:

```
sales_tax = excl_sales_tax * 0.25;
```

The constant `sales_tax_percent` would not then have been needed. However, it is a good rule to avoid having numerical literals inserted among statements in a program. If the percentage for sales tax is changed, it could be difficult to find all the places in the program where changes are needed. (The percentage might be used several times in a big program.) If a constant variable is used, as in this example, you only need to make the change in one place.

2.2   Arithmetic expressions

Types used to describe ordinary numbers are called *arithmetic types*. The types `int` and `double` are examples of such types. Often, expressions occur in programs where ordinary numbers are calculated. These expressions are called *arithmetic expressions*. The ordinary arithmetical operations of addition, subtraction, multiplication and division, designated by + − * and / respectively, can be used in these expressions. The most common form of arithmetic expression has two operands which can be variables or literals. Here are some examples of these expressions:

```
i1 + i2      weight + 12.6     1 - i      x - y
x * y        25 * n            i / 10     x / y
```

The two operands may be of different arithmetic types. The result type of the expression will be determined by the types of the operands entered. If both have the same type, the result will also be of this type. If one of the operators is an integer and the other a real number, the result will be a real number. If, for example, the types `int` and `double` are mixed, the result will be of the `double` type.

Division needs to be further explained. It is not unusual for one of the operands to be a real number. Then ordinary division takes place and the result will

---

[†] The term *literal* is used in the draft of the standard for C++ as well as in other programming languages. In the standard for C and in earlier C++ literature, the term *constant* is used.

be a real number, the quotient of the two operands. If, on the other hand, the two operands are of integer type, for instance **int**, *integer division* will be performed. This means that you will see how many times the right-hand operand 'goes into' the left-hand one. If the variables i and j are of type **int** and have the values 14 and 5 respectively, then the expression i/j will give a result of 2, since 5 goes into 14 twice. The result will *not* be 2.8.

To obtain the remainder upon integer division, the *modulus operator* % is used. If as before the variables have the values 14 and 5 respectively, the expression i%j will produce a result of 4. For this operator to give a well-defined result, both operands must be positive.

Unary variants of the operators + and – also occur. These variants only have one operand, which is written to the right of the operator. The unary minus operator is especially useful in the following kinds of constructs:

```
k = -1;    k * (-3)    cout << -k;    k = -k;
```

More complicated expressions can be created by combining several operators. The result will be an expression containing several partial expressions. An example is the expression

```
tax + day_number * daily_rate
```

from the program in the last section. The result of a partial expression will be a value which, in its turn, constitutes the one operand for a new operation. The different priorities of operators in a complicated expression will decide in which order the expression is to be calculated. Operators with a higher priority are calculated before operators with a lower one. Calculation takes place from left to right if two operators have the same priority. In the case of the arithmetic operators discussed, the unary operators + and – have highest priority, then come the operators * / and %, which have the same priority. The ordinary operators + and – have lowest priority. In the above expression, multiplication will therefore take place before addition. Another example is the expression -2+4/2*3 which will have a value of 4. Parentheses can also be used to control the order of calculation. The expression (-2+4)/2*3 will, for instance, have a value of 3. In fact statements like

```
i = i + 1;
k = k - 1;
```

are extremely common in programming.

There are two useful operators in C++, ++ and --, which can be used to increase or decrease a variable's value by 1. With the help of these, the two statements above can be simplified as

```
i++;
k--;
```

These increment and decrement operators occur in two variants. You can put ++

or -- either in front (*prefix* variants) or after (*postfix* variants) the variable's name. The two statements might then have been written

```
++i;   // prefix
--k;   // prefix
```

In the examples above, it does not matter which of the two variants you choose but there is an important difference between them. The expressions i++ and ++i both mean that the variable i is increased by 1 but the *values* of the two expressions are different. The value of the expression i++ is the value i had *before* the increase, and the value of the expression ++i is the value i has *after* the increase. The same holds for the decrement operator. This is best illustrated by a couple of examples.

```
int i, k, m, n;
i = 4; k = 7;
m = i++ * k--; // postfix. m gets the value 4*7, i.e. 28
i = 4; k = 7;
n = ++i * --k; // prefix. n gets the value 5*6, i.e. 30
```

Apart from increasing or decreasing by 1, it often happens that you want to change a variable's value in other ways. You may for instance want to add a value to the variable, subtract a value from it, or multiply it by a certain number. Some examples are

```
i = i + 2;
j = j - k;
k = k * i;
n = n / 3;
```

In these situations it is useful to use the compound forms of the assignment operator. With the help of these, the statements above can be written

```
i += 2;   // same as i = i + 2;
j -= k;   // same as j = j - k;
k *= i;   // same as k = k * i;
n /= 3;   // same as n = n / 3;
```

There are several compounded forms of the assignment operator.

There are often several mathematical functions in the common calculator, and you can usually work out logarithms and trigonometric functions. Are functions of this sort available in C++ and if so, how do you use them? Standard mathematical functions are not built into the programming language itself but they can be found in the standard library. The two most interesting standard libraries are called math and stdlib. (In the draft of the C++ standard they are called cmath and cstdlib, respectively. The letter c at the beginning indicates that these are libraries taken from the programming language C.) The library math contains trigonometric functions, logarithmic functions and square roots. (See the information window on page 41.) The library stdlib contains a number of

Arithmetic operators

+ – *	Addition, subtraction and multiplication.
/	Division (division of integers, if both operands are integral, otherwise ordinary division).
%	Gives the remainder with division of integers.
++	Increases the operand's value by 1. The value k++ is k's old value. The value ++k is k's new value.
– –	Decreases the operand's value by 1. The value k-- is k's old value. The value --k is k's new value.
+= –= *= /= %=	Compound assignment operators. The expression: x •= y; is equivalent to: x = x • (y);

functions of a more general nature but some of them can be used for performing arithmetical calculations.

You should have the following lines at the beginning of your program if you want to have access to the functions in the `math` and `stdlib` libraries:

```
#include <math.h>
#include <stdlib.h>
```

Standard functions in the **math** library

All functions return a real number. The arguments x and y shall also be real numbers. (There are versions of these functions for the types **float, double** and **long double**.)

exp(x)	Gives e^x.
log(x)	Gives the natural logarithm (ln) of x.
log10(x)	Gives the common logarithm (base 10) of x.
sqrt(x)	Gives $\sqrt{x}$.
ceil(x)	Gives the smallest integer which is >=x.
floor(x)	Gives the greatest integer which is <=x.
fabs(x)	Gives the absolute value of x.
pow(x,y)	Gives x^y (If $x<0$, y must be an integer).
fmod(x,y)	Gives the remainder upon division x/y.
sin(x),cos(x),tan(x)	x is given in radians.
asin(x),acos(x),atan(x)	Gives arcsines, etc.
sinh(x),cosh(x),tanh(x)	Hyperbolic functions.

Arithmetic functions in the `stdlib` library

abs (n)	*n* has the type **int**. Gives the absolute value of *n*.
labs (n)	*n* has the type **long** **int**. Gives the absolute value of *n*.

(If you have a compiler which follows the draft standard, you can instead write `#include <cmath>` and `#include <cstdlib>` respectively.)

The call of functions can be a part of arithmetic expressions such as:

```
3.6*sqrt(z)   log(z)/log10(x+y)   fabs(sin(y))
```

As an example, let's look at a program which calculates compound interest. Suppose that your account at the bank is credited with £*b* and that the annual interest rate is *r* %. The capital you will have accumulated over *n* years if you haven't touched the money, is calculated by the formula $b \cdot (1 + r/100)^n$

```
#include <iostream.h>
#include <iomanip.h>
#include <math.h>
main ()
{
    double b, r;
    int n;
    cout << "Amount? "; cin    >> b;
    cout << "Interest? "; cin >> r;
    cout << "Number of years? "; cin >> n;
    cout << setprecision(2) << setiosflags(ios::fixed)
         << "The capital becomes " << b*pow(1+r/100, n);
}
```

2.3 **if statements**

The three most important algorithm constructs, *sequence*, *selection* and *iteration*, were discussed in Chapter 1 on page 22. You can get a sequence in C++ by placing several statements in succession, one after the other. In this section we shall examine the `if` statement, which is one of the most simple and common constructs in C++ for obtaining selection, that is, choice. We begin by giving another variant of the program which calculates sales prices. This time, we will leave out the sales tax. When you run the program, you simply indicate the number of items bought and the cost per item. The program will then calculate the total cost. Let us now suppose that if you spend more than £100, you will get 10% discount on the cost of the goods. If you spend less, you don't get a discount. When you run the program, it can look like this:

```
Number of items? 25
Cost per item? 4.50
The cost becomes: 101.25
```

The program will look as below. Constant variables have been used to indicate how much percentage discount is received and the bound where the discount begins.

```cpp
#include <iostream.h>
#include <iomanip.h>
main ()
{
  int number;
  double per_item, cost, discount;
  const double discount_percent = 10, bound = 100;
  cout << "Number of items? "; cin >> number;
  cout << "Cost per item? "; cin >> per_item;
  cost = per_item * number;
  if (cost > bound)
  {
    discount  = cost * discount_percent / 100;
    cost      = cost - discount;
  }
  cout << "The cost becomes: " <<setprecision(2) <<
  setiosflags(ios::fixed) << cost << endl;
}
```

The interesting part of this program are the four lines preceded by the word `if`. An expression *in parentheses* should come after this word. Here, however, we have the expression cost > bound. If the expression is true, the statements inside the following braces { } will be executed. If the expression is false, these statements will not be executed. It is a good thing to write the left brace immediately above the right brace, so that they can be seen to belong together. We have indented the text so that the conditional statements can be seen more clearly. This indentation facilitates the reading and understanding of your programs.

In an `if` statement, there can be as many statements as you like within the braces. If there is only a single statement, you do not need to put it within braces. For instance, we could write:

Indentation

- A program is made more readable when text on the lines is indented to reflect the program's structure.
- A well-structured program is always indented.
- When writing programs, indentation should always be used.

```
if (cost > bound)
   cost -= cost * discount_percent / 100;
```

An **if** statement can also have an **else** part, a sequence of statements which are executed if the condition is false. You can write, for example

```
if (cost > bound)
{
   discount = cost * discount_percent / 100;
   cost -= discount;
}
else
   cout << "No discount, sorry" << endl;
```

Now *either* the two statements within the braces, *or* the statement after **else**, will be executed.

You can also have several statements in the **else** part but then you must have braces:

```
if (cost > bound)
   cost -= cost * discount_percent / 100;
else
{
   cout << "No discount, sorry" << endl;
   cout << "Buy more next time" << endl;
}
```

Here, we have rewritten the two statements after **if** to make one statement. Note particularly that there must not be a semi-colon in front of **else** when braces include the statements after **if**. When the braces have been left out, however, there must be a semi-colon.

The **if** statement can be used in multiple-choice situations even if it only has two alternatives. Let us suppose that we have two discount levels in our example. If you buy goods totalling more than £500, you will get a 15% discount; if you buy goods totalling less than £500 but more than £100, you get a 10% discount. If anything less than £100 is spent, there is no discount. Let us now then declare two 'boundaries' and two discount percentages:

Different forms of if statements	

if (*expression*)
    statement;
_____
	if (*expression*)
	{
	    one or more statements
	}

if (*expression*)
    statement;
else
    statement;
_____
	if (*expression*)
	    statement;
	else
	{
	    one or more statements
	}

if (*expression*)
{
    one or more statements
}
else
{
    one or more statements
}
	if (*expression*)
	{
	    one or more statements
	}
	else
	    statement;

```
const double  discount_percent1 = 10,  bound1 = 100,
              discount_percent2 = 15,  bound2 = 500;
```

Then we rewrite the **if** statement like this:

```
if (cost > bound2)
  cost -= cost * discount_percent2/100;
else if (cost > bound1)
  cost -= cost * discount_percent1/100;
else
  cout << "No discount, sorry" << endl;
```

Two **if** statements have been put together here with the result that the **else** part of the first **if** statement contains a new **if** statement.

There can be all kinds of statements in an **if** statement, or the **else** part of an **if** statement, even new **if** statements. When one **if** statement is contained within another, we say that the **if** statements are *nested*. This structure will become clearer if the indentation is done slightly differently:

```
if (cost > bound2)
  cost -= cost * discount_percent2/100;
else
  if (cost > bound1)
    cost -= cost * discount_percent1/100;
```

```
else
    cout << "No discount, sorry" << endl;
```

When pure multiple-choice situations occur, as in this example, you usually indent in the way we did first; then the appearance of the program itself becomes a satisfying reflection of its logic.

2.4 Comparison operators and logical operators

The expression within the parentheses after **if**, which will be true or false, can appear in different forms. We usually use *comparison operators*, as in our example. The following comparison operators are used:

```
<   >   <=   >=   ==   !=
```

These mean, 'less than', 'greater than', 'less than or equal to', 'greater than or equal to', 'equal to' and 'not equal to', respectively. Note in particular that the operator 'equal to' is written with two equal signs. (One equal sign of course means 'assignment'). Some examples are given below.

Comparison operators					
==	equal to	<	less than	>	greater than
!=	not equal to	<=	less than or equal to	>=	greater than or equal to

```
if (number == 0)
    cout << "None left";
if (number != 0)
    cout << "Some exist";
if (cost <= 0)
    cout << "Noteworthy pricing" << endl;
```

More complicated *logical expressions* could be constructed using the operators **and**, **or** and **not**, which execute the logical operations *and*, *or* and *not*. The operators **and** and **or** have two operands and the operator **not**, one operand. The expression A **and** B is true if *both* A and B are true but false otherwise. The expression A **or** B is true if *at least one* of A or B is true but false otherwise. The expression **not** A is true if A is false and false if A is true. Some examples:

```
if (temp>20 and temp<30)
  cout << "suitably warm" << endl;
if (i==1 or i==3 or i==5 or i==7 or i==9)
  cout << "Odd number";
if (not(temp>20 and temp<30))
  cout << "Not nice";
```

The operators **and** and **or** have lower priority than the arithmetic operators +, −, * and / and the comparison operators <, >, etc. This means that expressions like

```
i + j > k * l and m == n
```

are interpreted as

```
(i + j) > (k * l) and (m == n)
```

which is quite natural. In the last **if** statement above, the extra parentheses are necessary because the operator **not** has a higher priority than **and** and **or**. Had we not written parentheses, the expression **not** `temp>20` **and** `temp<30` would have been interpreted in the same way as the expression (**not** `temp`)`>20` **and** `temp<30`.

The operators **and**, **or** and **not** have been introduced in the draft standard of C++. The operators &&, || and ! (used in the programming language C and up to now in C++) were used to designate *and*, *or* and *not*, respectively. Using these operators, the last **if** statement, above, would have been written

```
if (!(temp>20 && temp<30))
  cout << "Not nice";
```

It is important to write two & signs or two of the | signs when using these operators, since the two operators, & and |, written singly, also exist. These operators are used when dealing with bits. In C++, you have the choice of using the operators **and**, **or** and **not**, or &&, || and !. We will be using **and**, **or** and **not**

Logical operators		
A **and** *B*	*A* **or** *B*	**not** *A*
A && *B*	*A* || *B*	! *A*
true if *both*	true if *at least one of*	true if *A* is false
A and *B* are true	*A* or *B* is true	

- **and** and **or** have *lower* priority than comparison operators.
- **not** has *higher* priority than arithmetic operators and comparison operators.

throughout in this book because the programs will be easier to read and there will be less risk of confusion with the operators & and |.

Every expression in C++ has a certain type. You need to ask yourself which type the result of an expression with comparison operators, or logical operators, will have. In the draft of the C++ standard, a standard type **bool** has been introduced. The comparison and logical operators give a result which has a value of this type. There are only two values for the type **bool**, **true** and **false**. The **if** statement is constructed in such a way that it expects a value of the type **bool** within the parentheses.

A special type to designate logical values was not found in C++ in the past. Instead, such values were described using the type **int**. As a result the compiler expected the expression within the parentheses in an **if** statement to have the type **int**. When an **if** statement was executed, the value 0 was treated as being 'false' and all other values as 'true'. Comparison and logical operators were also constructed in such a way as to leave integers as a result. If an expression was true, the result was equal to 1 and if an expression was false, the result was equal to 0. Here now are two strange examples:

```
i = 5 > 2; // i is assigned the value 1
if (i)
    cout << "i is not equal to 0";
```

An automatic type conversion, from the type **int** to the type **bool**, has been introduced to ensure old C++ programs can function as they used to when they are compiled with a compiler that follows the latest standard draft. The value 0 is automatically converted into **false** and all other values into **true**. Thus the choice can be made either to use the old style with the type **int** describing logical values, or to use the type **bool**.†

An **if** statement can be used to see if the input has gone as planned. As an example, let us look at the statement

```
cin >> number;
```

where we assume that the variable number has the type **int**. This statement inputs a number from the keyboard and places the input value into the variable number.

---

† If the compiler you use does not as yet support the type **bool**, you can proceed in the following way. Put the program lines below into a text file with the name bool.h.

```
typedef int bool;
#define false 0
#define true  1
#define and   &&
#define or    ||
#define not   !
```

Then let every program start with the extra line

```
#include "bool.h"
```

This will work well, assuming the person running the program actually types in an integer from the keyboard. If incorrect input data is entered (perhaps a letter instead of a number is typed), the input will miscarry and the variable number will remain unchanged, keeping its previous value. The input stream would also get into an error state which would have to be cleared before more data could be entered.

We will now use the fact that the expression cin >> number gives a result value. This value can be automatically converted into the type **bool**. If input has proceeded satisfactorily, the result of the conversion will be **true**; if not, it will be **false**.

```
if (cin >> number)
  cout << "The number was" << number;
else
{
  cout << "Incorrect input";
  cin.clear();
}
```

The statement cin.clear(); clears the error that has arisen in the input stream. This statement must be included if more input data from the stream is to be entered later in the program.

2.5   while statements

Besides sequence and selection, the third important construct is repetition. The easiest way of producing repetition in C++ is by using a **while** statement. Let us begin with a simple example. Suppose that the variable j has the type **int**. The program section

```
j = 0;
while (j < 6)
{
  cout << setw(3) << j;
  j += 2;
}
```

gives the output

```
0 2 4
```

Execution of the **while** statement takes place in the following way. The expression in parentheses after **while** is calculated first. (The same rules hold as for the **if** statement.) If the expression is false, nothing more is done. If, however, the expression is true, the statements within the braces are executed once. When these statements have been executed, the expression in parentheses is calculated once more. If it is false, the **while** statement is terminated; if it is true, the statements within the braces are executed once more, and so on. The **while** statement will be executed three times in the example above. The variable j has the value 0 from the beginning and is increased by 2 at the end of every 'round'. This means that j will have a value of 6 at the end of the third round. The expression j<6 will then be false, and the **while** statement will be terminated.

In a **while** statement, the braces may be left off (exactly as with **if** statements) if only one statement is to be executed at each round.

Different forms of **while** statements	

while (*expression*)
    statement;
	while (*expression*)
	{
	    one or more statements
	}

Our next example will be taken from a somewhat unreal situation. You have been offered a very dangerous job. There is a risk of being seriously injured, or even killed, if you take the job. The settling of wages is also rather unusual. For the first day of work, you are offered 1p, for the second day 2p, for the third 4p, for the fourth 8p, and so on, in other words, the wages are doubled every day. Since you are careful about your health but don't mind taking certain risks to reach your goal and become rich, you want to check out the offer. You ask yourself this question: How many days must I work to become a millionaire? To get an answer to this, we will write the following program:

```cpp
#include <iostream.h>
#include <iomanip.h>
main ()
{
  int number_days = 1 ;
  double daily_wage = 0.01, total_sum = 0.01;
  const double desired = 1000000.0;
  while (total_sum < desired)
  {
    number_days++;
    daily_wage *= 2;
    total_sum += daily_wage;
  }
  cout << "You will be a millionaire after "
      << number_days << " days" << endl;
}
```

The three variables, number_days, daily_wage and total_sum, are used in the program. They are initialized to start values which enable the program to give the situation after one day of work. The constant variable desired has been given a value of one million.

The three statements in the **while** statement will be repeated once per day worked from and including day two. We see that the day counter is increased by 1 for each day, the new daily wage (which is equal to double that of the old) is calculated and added to the total sum. After two days, number_days will have a value of 2, daily_wage a value of 0.02 and total_sum a value of 0.03.

We don't know for how many rounds the **while** statement will be executed. Each round corresponds to a day worked. Remember it was simply the number of days worked which the program was to calculate. Since the value in the variable total_sum increases all the time, the condition after **while** must sooner or later be false. If you run the program you will get the output

```
You will be a millionaire after 27 days
```

We will now look at a more complicated example. We will write a program to calculate the sum of the mathematical series:

$$\frac{1}{1 \times 1} - \frac{1}{2 \times 2} + \frac{1}{3 \times 3} - \frac{1}{4 \times 4} + \frac{1}{5 \times 5} - \cdots$$

The series has an infinite number of terms, so it is impossible to take account of all of them in the program. The signs of the terms alternate between plus and minus and the absolute value[†] of the terms decreases with each new term. The sum of the series therefore approaches a certain limit. (We say that the series is *convergent*.) We will decide to ignore terms that are so small that they won't have any effect on the final result. If the result is to be written to five decimal places, terms with an absolute value of less than 0.000001 can be ignored without any effect on the end result.

To find the solution, we will make use of the technique of top-down design discussed in Section 1.6. First, we produce an algorithm:

(1) Initialize the sum to 0 and the first term to 1.
(2) If the absolute value of the next term >= 0.000001, carry out the following two steps:

  (2.1) Put the next term to the sum.
  (2.2) Calculate a new next term.

(3) Write out the sum.

We can refine step 1:

```
double the_sum = 0, next_term = 1;
```

[†] The absolute value of a number is calculated in the following way: If $x >= 0$, the absolute value is x; if not, it is $-x$.

We have introduced two variables here, `the_sum` and `next_term`. They will both be of real type, since the sum and its terms are real numbers. The second variable is called `next_term`, even if it gives the value of the first term at this stage, because it can then be used in the rest of the program when calculating the values of the remaining terms. (Before beginning, the next term is of course the same as the first term.) We initialize the variables at the same time as we declare them.

In the continuing program construction we will be using *comments* in the program code. Comments serve to help you to construct and clarify your programs. The compiler will not attempt to translate whatever is contained in a comment. In C++ there are two ways of writing comments:

```
// This is a comment
/* This is a comment
   which will continue on several lines */
```

The combination of characters `//` introduces a comment and everything written after these characters on the *same* line will be interpreted as a comment. If the combination of characters `/*` is used instead to introduce a comment, the whole text, including the end mark `*/` will be interpreted as a comment. In the latter case, a comment can extend over several lines.

Step 2 in our algorithm will be a **while** statement. For the time being, we can let the substeps 2.1 and 2.2 be comments. The standard function `fabs` from the `math` library is used to calculate the absolute value of `next_term`.

```
while (fabs(next_term) >= epsilon)
{
   // 2.1 Put next term to the sum
   // 2.2 Calculate a new next term
}
```

We have introduced the constant `epsilon` to avoid having literals in the program. You declare `epsilon` in the following way (`1e-6` means 1×10^{-6}).

```
const double epsilon = 1e-6;
```

Step 2.1 in the algorithm is simply

```
the_sum += next_term;
```

Step 2.2, 'Calculate a new next term' requires a little extra thought. Any particular term in the sum, let us call this term number k, will have the form $1/(k \times k)$. To be able to calculate it, we need a counter k for the number of terms. It is just as well that this counter is an integer which is initialized to 1 and then increased by 1 every time we want to calculate a new term. Thus we get the declaration

```
int k = 1;
```

and the statement

```
k++;
```

which will be executed first in step 2.2.

Having alternate terms that are positive and negative presents a complication. It can be resolved by introducing a variable `sign` which alternately takes the value +1 and -1. If the calculated terms are multiplied by `sign`, they will become alternately positive and negative. For simplicity, we let `sign` be a real variable.

Since term number 1 should be positive, we initialize `sign` to +1. We then get the declaration

```
double sign = 1;
```

By putting in the statement

```
sign = -sign;
```

in step 2.2, we make `sign` alternate between +1 and -1 each time a new term is to be calculated. The actual calculation of the next term is then

```
next_term = sign/(k*k);
```

If we had declared `sign` to be an integer, both the operands of the division operator would have been integers and we would have got integer division, the result of this being an integer. The variable `next_term` should not contain an integer, however, so we let one of the operands of the division operator be a real number and we get an 'ordinary' division. If we put the three statements in 2.2 together, we get

```
k++;
sign = -sign
next_term = sign/(k*k);
```

In step 3, 'Write out the sum', we use a constant variable, `num_dec`, to control the number of decimal places in the output.

```
cout << "The sum is: " << setprecision(num_dec)
     << the_sum << endl;
```

The constant `num_dec` is declared in the following way:

```
const num_dec = 5;
```

This is useful. If on another occasion we want to alter the number of decimal places in the output, all we have to do is change the two constants `num_dec` and epsilon.

Now we can assemble all the steps into a complete program:

```
#include <iostream.h>
#include <iomanip.h>
#include <math.h>
main ()
{
  double the_sum = 0, next_term = 1, sign = 1;
  int    k = 1;
  const  num_dec = 5;
  const double epsilon = 1e-6;
  while  (fabs(next_term) >= epsilon)
  {
    // Put next term to the sum
    the_sum += next_term;
    // Calculate a new next term
    k++;
    sign       = -sign;
    next_term = sign/(k*k);
  }
  cout << "The sum is: " << setprecision(num_dec)
       << the_sum <<endl;
}
```

When the program is run, you get the output:

```
The sum is: 0.82247
```

It is of course possible to have **if** statements inside **else** statements and vice versa. This is shown in the next example. We will look at a program which inputs an arbitrary number of real numbers (>=0) from the keyboard. The program is tailored to write out the largest number and the mean value of all the numbers. The four variables num, max_num, sum and n, are used in the program. One number at a time is input to the variable num. The sum of the numbers is calculated in sum, and n contains the number of numbers entered. The variable max_num is used to calculate the largest number.

```
#include <iostream.h>
main ()
{
  double num, max_num = -1, sum = 0;
  int    n = 0;
  while  (cin >> num)
  {
    sum += num;
    n++;
```

```
    if (num > max_num)
      max_num = num;
  }
  cout << "Largest num: " << max_num << endl
       << "Mean value:  " << sum / n << endl;
}
```

For every number input, a round of the **while** statement is executed. The expression cin>>num in parentheses after **while** may look a little strange. The program tries to read a number from the keyboard using this expression. If input is successful, the expression will be true and the **while** statement will be executed one more time; otherwise, the expression will be false and the **while** statement will be terminated. (Compare with the example on page 49.) This means that the program will be terminated as soon as anything but a number has been input. You can write a letter, for instance, but it is more natural to use a special combination of characters denoting *end of file*. If you are using MS-DOS or Windows, you normally make use of Ctrl-Z to indicate 'end of file'. If you use Unix, the keys will be Ctrl-D.

When a number has just been entered, it is added to the sum and n is increased by 1. The **if** statement is also executed for every new number, since you want to test whether the new number is larger than the largest number (previously found in the variable max_num). If this is the case, the new number will now become the current largest number. Since we have a pre-condition that all input numbers should be greater than, or equal to, zero, max_num will have been initialized to a negative number.

Sometimes it may be necessary to stop a **while** statement in the middle of a repetition. In this case, a **break** statement can be used. A **break** statement can be placed among the statements to be executed in each round. It has the simple form:

```
break;
```

A **break** statement normally lies in an **if** statement and is only executed conditionally.

When a **break** statement is executed, the **while** statement is immediately stopped, and there is a jump in the program to the first statement immediately after the **while** statement. Note that **break** statements can also be used with the two other repetition statements in C++, namely **for** statements, covered in the next section, and **do** statements, described later in the book.

A good opportunity for using **break** statements often presents itself with the use of *interactive* programs. Here, the user is invited to indicate the input. The program then determines the output and presents it to the user at the terminal. Interactive programs are very common. All our examples so far have been examples of interactive programs. We have seen how important it is, in interactive programs, that before each input of data there should be a communication with the user indicating what input should be written. A program stops when it reaches an input

---

break statements

- May be placed among statements executed in every round of a repetition statement.
- They immediately stop the repetition statement.
- There is a jump to the first statement after the repetition statement.
- They are often placed in an **if** statement:

  ```
  if (condition_to_quit)
      break;
  ```

---

statement and does not proceed until the user has entered input data. If there is no message before the input statement, the user will not notice that the program is waiting for input.

A computation of any sort has the following general form:

- Read input data.
- Perform computations.
- Write out the result.

You will often require a program to perform several computations in a row without having to restart it between each computation. The program is thus required to follow this pattern:

- Repeat the following three steps again and again.
  - Read input data.
  - Perform computations.
  - Write out the result.

Repetition should not stop until the person running the program enters special input data to indicate that it is time to stop.

As examples, we will show a couple of variants of a program which calculates the length of the hypotenuse in a right-angled triangle. The input data for the program are the lengths of the two shorter sides. If we designate these to be a and b and the length of the hypotenuse to be c, then c can be easily calculated using the well-known formula: $c = \sqrt{(a^2 + b^2)}$. In our first example, we let the user of the program indicate that it is time to quit by giving a negative value of a or b.

```
#include <iostream.h>
#include <math.h>
```

```
main ()
{
  double a, b, c;
  while (true)
  {
    cout << "Give lengths of shorter sides. " <<
            "Close with a negative number." <<endl;
    cin >> a;
    if (a <= 0)
      break;
    cin >> b;
    if (b <= 0)
      break;
    c = sqrt(a*a+b*b);
    cout << "Hypotenuse has length " << c <<endl;
  }
}
```

The statements occur in the right order inside the **while** statement thanks to the **break** statement. The input comes first in every round and it is preceded by a request to the user to enter input data. When this is read, a check is done to see whether the user has entered the special data indicating that the program should finish. If this is so, the **while** statement is stopped with a **break** statement. Otherwise, the result is computed and output at the end of the round.

Special input data is not always available to indicate that it is time to quit. A little earlier we constructed a program which input an arbitrary number of real numbers and calculated both the largest number and the mean value of all the numbers. In that program, all the real numbers are normal input data and cannot be used as end indicators. Instead we let the user indicate the end of the input by writing the special combination for *end of file*. We can use this technique here too:

```
#include <iostream.h>
#include <math.h>
main ()
{
  double a, b, c;
  while (true)
  {
    cout << "Give lengths of shorter sides. " <<
            "Close with Ctrl-Z. " << endl;
    if(not(cin >> a))
      break;
    if(not(cin >> b))
      break;
    c = sqrt(a*a+b*b);
    cout << "Hypotenuse has length " << c <<endl;
  }
}
```

2.6 **for** statements

We have seen how a **while** statement can be used to produce repetition. In this section we will be looking at **for** statements, which are an alternative to **while** statements. Often, **for** statements are used for repetition where there is a counter to be incremented or decremented for each round in the program. The **for** statement in C++ differs slightly from corresponding statements in other programming languages. After the reserved word **for**, come parentheses which contain three separate parts, an initialization, a condition, and a change part. A semicolon must be placed between the different parts. The **for** statement has the form:

```
for (init; condition; change)
  statement;
```

The statement on the second line can consist of several statements in braces exactly as with **if** statements and **while** statements. Execution is done in the following way: First init is computed and then condition. If condition is true, statement is executed. When this has been done, change is computed; then condition is computed again. If this is still true, another round is executed, which means that first statement, then change are computed again; whereupon condition is computed and tested again. The whole process is repeated until condition is shown to be false.

Note that init is only performed once, before the first round, while the other expressions are computed once per round, condition before each round and change after each round.

Here are some examples of **for** statements. The following statement writes out the multiplication table for 12: 1 times 12, 2 times 12, and so on up to 12 times 12.

```
int i;
for (i=1; i<=12; i++)
  cout << i*12 << endl;
```

If there is a counter, as there is here, it need not be incremented by 1. The counter may be changed at will at the end of each round. For instance, we could easily write

```
int i;
for (i=12; i<=144; i+=12)
  cout << i << endl;
```

The counter can also be declared in the initialization expression; then it will only be recognized inside the **for** statement.

```
for (int i=12; i<=144; i+=12)
  cout << i << endl;
```

The three different parts `init`, `condition` and `change` in the parentheses of the **for** statement can each contain several expressions. Sometimes you may want to initialize several variables at the beginning of repetition, or change more than one counter after each round. Here is an example where x^n is computed. We want x to have the type **double** and n the type **int**. The result will be calculated in a variable r of the type **double**. Both the variable r and a counter i must be initialized before the first round. When one of the parts `init`, `condition` and `change` contains several expressions, then a *comma* should be placed between those expressions. A semi-colon of course serves to demarcate the three parts.

```
for (r=1.0, i=1; i<=n; i++)
   r *= x;
```

Sometimes it happens that the statement to be repeated at every round is an empty statement, when nothing is to be done. In this case you only write a lone semi-colon. The **for** statement above may, for example, be rewritten

```
for (r=1.0, i=1; i <=n; i++, r*=x)
  ;
```

In which case you should, as in this example, write the semi-colon on a separate line so that it will be quite clear that it is an empty statement. Because a semi-colon is counted as an empty statement and will be the statement repeated at every round, you should *never write a semi-colon directly after the end of parentheses*. This also applies to **while** statements.

In a **for** statement, one of the three parts `init`, `condition` and `change` may be left out. If there is no initializing to be done, the initializing part may be omitted. If a part is omitted, this must be indicated by a semi-colon. There should always be two semi-colons in the parentheses of a **for** statement. You can even

---

for statements

for (*init; condition; change*)
    statement;

Is equivalent to the statements:

init;
while (*condition*)
  {
    statement;
    change;
  }

- The parts *init*, *condition* and *change* may be omitted but the semi-colon should remain.
- Each part can consist of several expressions divided by a comma.

omit all the parts. If the `condition` part is omitted, the statement will be regarded as 'true'. An infinite repetition can be produced, for instance, with

```
for (;;)
  cout << "Help, I cannot stop" << endl;
```

2.7 Arrays

A variable of the type **int** or **double** can only contain one value at a time but you will often want to handle aggregates containing different values of the same type. Then you can make use of *arrays*. An array is a kind of table which contains several components, all numbered, of the same kind. Let us begin by declaring an array with 5 components of the type **double**:

```
double f[5];
```

This is a declaration of a variable with the name f. We recognize f as an array and not an ordinary variable from the [5] after the name of the variable. The contents of the square brackets must have a *constant* value indicating the number of elements in the array. The word **double** indicates that the components of the array will be of the same type. Figure 2.1 shows how the variable f looks.

Every component in an array has a unique number, or *index*. Numbering of the components begins with 0, so that the first component has an index of 0. This is *always* the case with arrays. (In C++ it is not possible to indicate, as it is in a number of other programming languages, how the components are to be numbered. The first component always has the index 0.) It follows, therefore, that the last component in an array is always a number which is one less than the number of components in the array. If you want to access a particular component of an array, you make use of the component's index through *indexing*. For example, to give the last component (the one numbered 4) in the array f the value 2.75, we will write the statement:

```
f[4] = 2.75
```

Note the use of square brackets here. The index in square brackets need not be a

Figure 2.1

constant number. It can be an arbitrary integer expression. If the variables i and j are of type **int**, it is possible to write

```
f[i + j] = 2.75;
```

The index expression has to have a value lying inside the bounds of the array. In this example, therefore, the value i+j will lie in the interval from 0 to 4. It is natural to ask what would happen if the index expression's value lay outside the bounds of the array. Would the compiler produce error output? No! In C++, responsibility is completely handed over to the programmer. There is no index check. Even if indexing is incorrect, the program will run; but it will not run as it should and there won't be any warnings or error messages. Suppose, for example, that the value i+j in our example happens to be 5. When the statement above is performed, the value 2.75 is placed in the primary memory in the position where the component number 5 *would* have been *if* such a component had existed. This could of course be disastrous for the program. Any information could be put there, variables which have nothing to do with f, for instance.

Components in an array can be of arbitrary type. We could, for example, declare another array with the name a containing 6 components of type **int**:

```
int a[6];
```

If nothing particular is indicated upon declaration of an array, all its components will be *uninitialized*. An array can be initialized in connection with declaration. We would be able to write

```
int a[6] = {2, 2, 2, 5, 5, 0};
```

The first three components here are initialized to the value 2, the following two to the value 5 and the last to the value 0. The number of components inside the square brackets should conform to the size of the array (but this is not checked by the compiler). When you initialize an array, the compiler itself can compute its size. You can omit the number of components and simply write

```
int b[]= {0, 0, 0, 0, 0, 0};
```

Here the array b consists of six components, all set at zero upon declaration. The initialization expressions inside the braces need not be constants. They can be arbitrary expressions. If the variables i and j have type **int**, we could write

```
int b[]= {i, i-1, i+j};
```

Note that it is only in initializations that you may assign values to all the components all at once. The following statement would not be allowed

```
b = {0, 0, 0, 0, 0, 0}; // Not allowed!
```

If, for example, you want to assign the value 0 to all the components in b, you have to do this for each component one at a time:

```
for (int k=0; k<6; k++)
  b[k] = 0;
```

The following statement is also not allowed

```
a = b; // Not allowed!
```

If you want to assign the whole array b to a, you must instead do it in this way:

```
for (int k=0; k<6; k++)
  a[k] = b[k];
```

Neither can you compare two complete arrays with each other. If we write,

```
if (a == b) // Allowed but not what is intended
 ...
```

it will certainly be allowed but this comparison does not mean that the contents of the two arrays will be compared, only that a check will be made on whether a and b are referring to the same array.

We will now look at a simple program which uses arrays. Ten real numbers, constituting a measurement series, are entered from the keyboard. The program then computes the mean value of the measurements and outputs this data. Finally, the program will output all the measurements which are greater than the computed mean value.

```
#include <iostream.h>
main ()
{
  const int number = 10;
  double meanv, sum = 0;
  double series[number];
  int i;
  cout << "Give measurement values" << endl;
  for (i = 0; i<number; i++)
  {
    cin >> series[i];
    sum += series[i];
  }
  meanv = sum / number;
  cout << "Mean value is " << meanv << endl;

  cout << "Measurements greater than mean value:"<<endl;
```

```
for (i = 0; i<number; i++)
   if (series[i] > meanv)
      cout << "Measurement no. " << (i+1) << " is "
         << series[i] << endl;
}
```

Note in particular that in the program, a constant with the name `number` has been declared. Instead of writing the literal `10`, we have used the constant `number` in the declaration of the array `series`. The constant `number` is also used in other parts of the program itself. By using a constant in this way, the program has become easy to change. If we wanted a measurement series containing 20 numbers, then we would simply have to change the declaration of the constant `number`. Nothing else in the program would have to be changed. It is good practice to use constants in this way.

We will now demonstrate a slightly larger example of the use of arrays. Suppose that a company has a number of sales representatives working on commission. The total number of reps is at most 100 and each rep has a unique identity number (an integer in the interval 1 to 100). Every time a rep has sold something, he or she leaves a record of the sale with the company. A sales record consists of the rep's number and the amount the goods have been sold for. We shall now design a program which inputs a lot of sales records and outputs a compilation of how much the different reps have sold. The program will also show what commission the reps are to receive. This is 10% of total sales if less than, or equal to, £5000. If total sales is greater than £5000, the rep's commission will include 15% of the amount over £5000. If the following data is input into the program

```
78 1000
32 50
2 1200
100 2500
78 6000
2 100
5 6000
```

the program will give the output

```
Number      Amount      Commission
======      ======      ==========
   2          1300          130
   5          6000          650
  32            50            5
  78          7000          800
 100          2500          250
```

No sales records are entered for those reps who have not sold anything. The various sales records can be input in arbitrary order into the program, and if a rep has left more than one sales record with the company, this will be accepted by the program (here, for instance, reps no. 2 and no. 78 each made two sales).

The program looks like this:

```cpp
#include <iostream.h>
#include <iomanip.h>
main ()
{
  const int max_number=100;
  const float bound=5000., pro1=0.1, pro2=0.15;
  float tab[max_number], amount, commission;
  int i, no;
  // reset table
  for (i=0; i<max_number; i++)
    tab[i] = 0;
  // Input sales records
  while (cin >> no and cin >> amount)
  {
    if (no < 1 or no > max_number or amount < 0)
      cout << "Incorrect input data" << endl;
    else
      tab[no-1] += amount;
  }
  // Write compilation
  cout << endl
       << "Number    Amount    Commission" << endl
       << "======    ======    ==========" << endl;
  for (i=0; i<max_number; i++)
  {
    if (tab[i] > 0)
    {
      if (tab[i] <= bound)
        commission = pro1 * tab[i];
      else
        commission = pro1*bound + pro2*(tab[i]-bound);
      cout << setw(4) << (i + 1)
      << setprecision(0) << setiosflags(ios::fixed)
      << setw(12) << tab[i]
      << setw(11) << commission << endl;
    }
  }
}
```

Note that we used constants to indicate the maximum number of sales reps, the bound for getting a higher commission and the two commission percentages. This makes it easy to change the program if these figures should change, for example, if the number of sales reps should increase.

The expression in parentheses in the line

```cpp
while(cin >> no and cin >> amount)
```

will be true if both inputs are successful (compare with the program example, page

54). When the program is run, therefore, you can indicate the end of the input by using Ctrl-Z or Ctrl-D (depending on the operating system).

You will often want to construct computer programs which will search for certain information in tables or lists; then it is natural to use arrays in the programs. There are two operations in particular which you will often perform in arrays: *search* and *sort*. We will first demonstrate a simple way of searching in an array. Suppose that we have an integer array f with n elements and that we want to see whether a certain number is in the array. This is the simplest kind of search, a *linear search*. The array f is searched from the beginning until the element containing the searched number is found, or until the whole array has been searched without producing the number looked for.

```
cout << "What number are you looking for? "; cin >> number;
int k;
for (k=0; k < n and f[k]!=number; k++)
  ;
if (k < n)
  cout << "The number is in place no. " << k << endl;
else
  cout << "The number was not found" <<endl;
```

The first condition in the **if** statement, k<n, tests whether the index k still lies in the array. If so, it will check whether k is the number looked for. If it is not, another round is executed, which means that k is increased by one. The value of k can be examined after the end of the **for** statement. If k had a value inside the bounds of the array, the **for** statement must have been stopped because the partial condition f[k]!=number will have been false. The number looked for will then have been found in position k.

You may often want to have sorted arrays, because they speed up search. There are many ordinary algorithms which describe how an array can be sorted, one of them being the sort algorithm on page 25, when we put compact discs into a CD holder. We will be looking at another sort algorithm here. We will write a program which inputs a maximum of 100 integers, where the input is finished by the user indicating an end to the input by typing Ctrl-Z or Ctrl-D at the terminal. The program puts the integers entered into an array, sorts the array and prints out the numbers in order of size. We use an algorithm called 'search for the least and swap' to carry out the sorting itself. The idea is that the smallest number in the array is found and placed in the array's first position, the second smallest is found and placed in the array's second position, and so on. The algorithm can be described as follows:

(1)   Set k as the index for the first element of the array.

(2)   While k is smaller than, or equal to, the index for the array's last element:

     (2.1)   Search for the smallest element in that part of the array which begins with element k and ends with the last element in the array.

(2.2) Let the smallest element (from step 2.1) and element k swap places.

(2.3) Increase k by 1.

Step 2.1 can be refined to:

(2.1.1) Set m to k.

(2.1.2) Let i run from k+1 to the number of the last element in the array:

(2.1.2.1) If element i is less than element m, set m to i.

(2.1.3) The smallest element is now in the mth position.

Step 2.2 can be refined to:

(2.2.1) Move the kth element to a temporary position.

(2.2.2) Move element m to position k.

(2.2.3) Move the element in the temporary position to the mth position.

Using this, we can now put the program together.

```cpp
#include <iostream.h>
main ()
{
  const int max_number = 100;
  int f[max_number], n = 0; // n is the number of input numbers
  cout << "Write in at most " << max_number << " integers" << endl;
  while (n < max_number and cin >> f[n])
    n++;

  // Sort the array
  for (int k = 0; k < n; k++)
  {
    // Search for the smallest among the numbers no. k to n-1
    int m = k;
    for (int i = k+1; i < n; i++)
      if (f[i] < f[m])
        m =i;

    // Let the numbers no.k and m swap places
    int temp = f[k];
    f[k] = f[m];
    f[m] = temp;
  }

  // print out the sorted array
  for (int j=0; j<n; j++)
    cout << f[j] << ' ';
}
```

2.8   Errors in programs

Writing a computer program is not a trivial task and it is normal to make a number of mistakes. Even an experienced programmer falls into traps of various kinds. It is therefore important when learning to program that we also learn how to find and correct errors in the program. This can be done by designing and writing programs, running tests and correcting any errors found. Three types of error can occur when writing programs:

- *Compiling errors*   These occur when the rules of the language have not been followed. This type of error is discovered during compilation of the program. Usually a listing of different errors is provided. This may include a misspelt variable, a forgotten brace, a lost semi-colon or the wrong key pressed when typing the program.

- *Execution errors*   Such errors do not occur until the program is run. The program may be syntactically correct – the language rules have been obeyed – but it still contains mistakes that prevent it from continuing normally when executed. An example of this is using a pointer to try to change memory space which either does not exist or is input protected. In C++ there is a very poor 'protective net' to catch execution errors. For instance, indexing outside an array does not register as an error. On the other hand, a number of errors can be found through 'exception handling'.

- *Logic errors*   These mistakes are caused by faulty reasoning when designing the program. An incorrect algorithm has been used. This type of error is the hardest to find, since the program can be compiled and run without getting any error messages. A logic error will show when the program is being run, and an incorrect result is obtained. If there is no verified data available for testing the program, it can be hard to be quite certain that the program is free from logic errors. Even if the program works correctly for a particular set of input data, it can be faulty for another set.

We shall demonstrate the different types of error by studying an example. We would like a program to calculate $n!$, that is the product of $1 \times 2 \times 3 \times ... \times n$. We begin by writing in the program:

```
#include <iostream.h>
main ()
{
  int prod = 0, n, i=1;
  cout << "n? ";
  cin >> n;
```

```
while (i<=n)
{
  pro *= i;
  i++;
}
cout << "Result: " << prod << endl;
}
```

We then compile the program. We then get an error message which might be something like

Error line 9: Undefined symbol 'pro' in function main

We are dealing with a compiling error because we happened to write `pro` instead of `prod`. We correct the faulty line:

```
prod *= i;
```

Now the program can be compiled. No error messages appear. We want to test run the program and start it. We try to compute 4 ! which we know should be 24:

```
n? 4
Result: 0
```

To our astonishment, the program returns a result of 0. We test run the program again and this time we input another value for *n*. Whatever the value of *n*, we keep getting the result 0. Something is wrong. There is a logic error in the program. We look at the program to see what the error might be. In the program, we let the counter i run from 1 to n and with every round we multiply `prod` by i, that is, in the first round we multiply by 1, in the second by 2, and so on. This seems to be true but what value does `prod` have from the beginning? The declaration tells us that `prod` has a value of 0 from the beginning. Here is our mistake! If you multiply a number which is 0 by another number, the result will of course always be 0. The variable `prod` should naturally be initialized to 1. We correct this:

```
int prod=1, n, i=1;
```

When the program is run again the result is 24 when we input the number 4 again. The program seems to be correct. We can try other values of n to get larger results. If the number 7 is entered, for instance, the program gives a result of 5040. When we try 8, we get a result of -25216. This is impossible! There has been an error at the execution stage but the program had continued as though nothing had happened. What happened is that the result is so large, it is greater than the largest integer which can be stored in our system by a variable of type **int**. The result is therefore incorrect. If the program is to be able to compute n! for values of n larger than 7, it must be changed. The best solution is to change `prod` to a variable of type **double**. A variable like this is capable of containing much larger numbers than an integer variable. Now the necessary changes are made and the corrected program can be test run after another compilation, as shown now:

```cpp
#include <iostream.h>
main ()
{
  double prod=1;
  int n, i=1;
  cout << "n? ";
  cin >> n;
  while (i<=n)
  {
    prod *= i;
    i++;
  }
  cout << "Result: " << prod << endl;
}
```

Now if we try to compute 8! we will get the correct result, 40320.

Looking for errors in a program and correcting them has come to be known, lightheartedly, as '*debugging*' the program. In some systems there are excellent aids for debugging. For example, it may be possible to test run a program step by step, or stop at particular points in the program, study the values of the various variables and change them. Such debugging aids are very valuable when errors have to be found in more complicated programs. If there is no access to such debugging aids, the values of the variables can still be studied at given points in the program by inserting temporary test printouts, and using them to find possible errors.

EXERCISES

2.1   Write a program to compute and print out how many miles a car has travelled during the last year. When the program is run, it should ask for the daily number of miles and for the number of miles one year ago. The number of miles should be given as whole numbers.

2.2   Modify the program in the previous exercise so that it can compute average litre consumption per mile. In addition to the two readings mentioned earlier, the program should input how many litres of petrol (given as a real number) are used for the year. The printout could look like this:

```
Total mileage:            9290
Total petrol consumption: 1234.5
Consumption per mile:     0.13
```

2.3 When insuring a car, it is common for people to take out comprehensive insurance if the car is new, or not older than five years old. If the car is an older one, then a 'third party' insurance might be sufficient.

   (a) Write a program that gives the type of insurance desired. The program should read the current year, and the year of the car's registration from the keyboard. One of the texts, *Choose comprehensive insurance* or *Choose third party insurance*, should be written out, depending on whether the car is less than, or more than, five years old.

   (b) Some insurance companies have special policies for cars which are at least 25 years old. Modify your program so that it will write out: *Choose a vintage car insurance* if the car is at least 25 years old.

2.4 In the USA, litre consumption is usually given in *miles/gallon*. Write a program which inputs litre consumption given in this way and which translates these figures into the *litres/kilometre* format which is more common in Europe. Use the following conversion factors: *1 mile = 1.609 km* and *1 gallon = 3.785 litres*.

2.5 A running competition consists of two races. The winner is the one with the fastest time for both races together. Write a program to calculate the total time for a runner. The input should be the times for the two races, given in hours, minutes and seconds in the form *hh mm ss*. The results of the program should also be written in this format.

2.6 Write a program to calculate how much change should be received after making a purchase, and in which notes and coins the change should be given. Input to the program should be the price to be paid and the amount given in payment. For the sake of simplicity, assume that no transactions involve coins smaller than 10p or notes greater than £20. For example, if a person bought goods for £62.10 and paid with four £20 notes, the program should print out that the change should be one £10 note, one £5 note, two £1 coins, one 50p coin, and four 10p coins.

2.7 The distance between two points in a coordinate system is given by the formula

$$s = \sqrt{((x_1 - x_2)^2 + (y_1 - y_2)^2)}$$

Write a program to read in the coordinates of the two points and write out the distance between them.

2.8 For radioactive decomposition, the amount of radioactive material, *n*, remaining after a certain time *t*, can be calculated using the formula:

$$n = n_0 e^{-\lambda t}$$

where n_0 is the amount of radioactive material at time $t = 0$ and λ is a constant for the material. This is usually given as a half-life (the time taken for half the radioactive material to decompose). If the half-life is denoted by *T*, it is easy to calculate that:

$$\lambda = \frac{\ln 2}{T}$$

The half-life for the isotope ^{14}C is 5730 years. Write a program to print out what percentage of this isotope is left after S years. S is the input to the program.

2.9 Suppose that a bank gives interest of $p\%$ on invested capital. Suppose further that you want to invest a sum of £k. Write a program which shows how the capital yields interest at compound interest for the first 10 years. The printout should show your capital including interest, after each of the 10 years. The input for the program should be the interest rate and the invested capital.

2.10 The same as for the previous exercise, but this time the program should instead calculate how long your capital should remain in the bank before you have £100 000 at your disposal.

2.11 A local authority has come up with the following forecast for population growth in the next few years: At the beginning of 1997, the borough had 26 000 inhabitants. The number of births and deaths for a year is estimated to be 0.7% and 0.6%, respectively, of the population at the beginning of the year. The number of new residents and people moving out is estimated each year to be 300 and 325, respectively. Write a program to calculate the borough's estimated population at the beginning of a particular year. The year in question should be read in as input data for the program.

2.12 If you don't have access to a library of arithmetical functions, you can use a Maclaurin series to calculate the value of certain common functions. The *sine* function can, for instance, be calculated using the following series:

$$\sin(x) = x - \frac{x^3}{3!} + \frac{x^5}{5!} - \frac{x^7}{7!} + \frac{x^9}{9!} - \dots$$

Write a program which inputs a value of x and which calculates $sin(x)$ using this series. The result should be printed out to four decimal places. Do not therefore include terms in the sum which are smaller than 10^{-5}.

2.13 Write a program which will produce a table for all the integers n in the interval n_1 to n_2. For every integer n, n and n^3 should be printed out. The two integers n_1 and n_2 should be input from the keyboard. Use a **for** statement.

2.14 Design a program to print out a neat table with values for the function
$f(x) = 3x^3 - 5x^2 + 2x - 20$

(a) Let the program print out the value of $f(x)$ for all integer values x in the interval from -10 to $+10$.

(b) Let the program print out the value of $f(x)$ for all values of x in the interval from -2 to $+2$, each time making the step 0.1, i.e. for the values -2.0, -1.9, -1.8 ..... 1.9, 2.0.

2.15 A *prime number* is a positive integer greater than 1 which cannot be exactly divided by any other integer except itself and 1. A number will be a prime number if it cannot be divided exactly by a smaller prime number. Use this fact to design a program to compute the first 50 prime numbers and put them in a table. (If you want to decide whether a certain number k is a prime number or not, check to see whether k can be divided exactly by any of the numbers listed in the table so far.) The program should stop when the table with your 50 prime numbers has been produced.

2.16 On page 65 we demonstrated how a linear search could be performed in an array. Suppose that the array does not contain the number we search for. In that case, the search can be carried out more effectively if the array is sorted. The search is simply stopped before the last element of the array is reached. Adjust the statements on page 65 using this method.

2.17 Write a program to read in a maximum of 100 integers and place them in an array, sorted into ascending numerical order. Your program should be so designed that one number at a time can be read in and put in the array. The numbers read in up to this point should be sorted before each new number is entered.

2.18 There is a very simple but not particularly effective sort algorithm called 'bubble sort'. With this method, you run through the array to be sorted, again and again. As soon as you find two elements in the array lying side by side which are not in the right order, you let them change places. You stop this process when you haven't changed the places of any of the elements. The 'lighter' elements, those having small values, will, during execution, successively 'bubble up' to the front of the array, hence the name of this sorting method. Write a program to read in a number of integers and sort them with this algorithm. The program should stop when the input numbers have been printed out in ascending numerical order.

2.19 Write a program that first reads in an integer k from the terminal. The program should then read in a maximum of 500 integers from the terminal and place them in an array. The numbers in the array should then be rearranged to form two groups in the array. The left-hand group should contain all the numbers $<=k$ and the right-hand group all the numbers $>k$. (The number in each group and the boundary between the two groups will depend on the numbers read into the array and the value of k.)

Example: If k is 20 and the array consists of the numbers:

    23 16 27 3 11 34 25 20 8

then one permissible rearrangement of the array will be:

    8 16 20 3 11 34 25 27 23

Other arrangements would be permissible. Note that it is not necessary to sort the array (even if it is a way of solving the problem).

2.20 Statistics of the rainfall for a certain location have been collected over the past 20 years. Write a program to read in the information for the 20 years and present the results in the form of a histogram. Assume that the annual rainfall lies in the interval from 0–3000 mm. Organize the output as a horizontal histogram, in the format:

```
Year    0           1           2           3         x 1000 mm

 1      ****************
 2      **************************
 3      *************

        etc.
```

Characters and Texts

Most of the data handled by computers is probably not numerical at all, but text, characters and symbols. We will now begin by describing the standard type **char**, which is used to handle individual characters. A character can be a letter, a digit, a special character (such as a question mark, full-stop or colon) or a 'non-printing control character'. Non-printing control characters can be used for communication tasks when the computer needs to make a terminal do certain things, for example, begin a new line, or give a 'chirping' sound.

3.1 Character codes and character literals

To store a character in a computer, a group of eight bits – a *byte* – is most often used. In C, only seven of these bits are used from the beginning. The eighth bit, or *parity bit*, is reserved for purposes of checking. The parity bit is usually the first bit of a byte. The other seven bits can be combined in 128 different ways, which means that there are 128 different character codes. There is a generally accepted standard, called the *ASCII standard*, which determines which characters can be coded with the seven available bits, and for each pattern of seven bits there is one character designated in the standard. For example, '%', '9' and 'A' are represented by, respectively,

```
00100101   00111001   01000001
```

These patterns of bits can be interpreted as binary integers, called *character codes*. The codes start with 0, which means that the character codes lie between 0 and 127; the characters '%', '9' and 'A' thus have character codes 37, 57 and 65, respectively. Even though a C++ compiler does not necessarily have to use the ASCII code, it is nevertheless the norm. This means that a variable of type **char** can contain (at least) the 128 characters in the ASCII standard. It also means that the different characters are represented in the computer in precisely the bit patterns specified by the standard.

The ASCII standard contains the letters a–z (both upper and lower case), the digits 0–9, various special characters ('+', '!' and '.') and a collection of non-printing control characters.

The ASCII standard is an American standard which was developed on the assumption that the language in use is English. The English alphabet has the 26 letters, a–z, derived from the Latin alphabet. Almost all the other living languages use either the Latin alphabet plus other characters, or a non-Latin alphabet or syllabaries. The ASCII standard on the other hand is spread throughout the world. The fact that the ASCII standard only contains the letters a–z has thus been a problem and a constant source of irritation for all those who work in the sphere of programming in countries with languages other than English. The solution to this problem is naturally to allow for more characters in the standard. If we dropped the use of the first bit in each byte as a parity bit, we could have eight bits instead of seven and 256 different characters could be represented instead of 128. We could then use the characters from 128 to 255 to represent new letters and other characters. There is an international standard (ISO 8859) specifying which characters will be designated by the different codes. When you use Windows, or a Unix system (but not MS-DOS or Macintosh) you follow this standard. ISO 8859 corresponds to the ASCII standard for the character codes 0 to 127. Character codes 128 to 255 are used partly for non-printing control characters and partly for a set of printable characters. The set of printable characters contained in the ISO 8859 standard is called *LATIN_1*. Among the characters of LATIN_1 are to be found the letters with diacritics which are used in the languages of Western Europe, for example á, å, è, æ, ö, ü, ñ and ç in both upper and lower case variants. (The only exceptions are the German character ß, indicating a double s and the character ÿ, which are only defined as lower-case letters.) Apart from the letters with diacritical marks, LATIN_1 also contains graphical characters such as §, £ and ¶.

Character literals, that is the constant character values, are written in single apostrophe marks. For instance, if we want to put a plus sign into the variable chtr of type **char**, we can write

```
chtr = '+';
```

In a C++ program you can normally use eight bit codes in texts and comments but not in the names of variables, and so on. The following assignments are allowed, however:

```
chtr = 'ê'; chtr = '¿';
```

An inner order is defined among the different values of type **char**. First come 32 non-printing control characters. Then come the 95 printable characters in the ASCII code and finally the characters with codes from 128–255 (for example, as in LATIN_1). Upper and lower case letters are not treated as the same, and the normal alphabetical order only applies to the letters a–z. The program lines below list two characters and write them out in ascending order. The two variables chtr1 and chtr2 both have type **char** and we see that they can easily be compared in an **if** statement.

```
if (chtr1 < chtr2)
   cout << "chtr1 is smallest" << endl;
else
   cout << "chtr2 is smallest" << endl;
```

Character literals for the printable characters can easily be given as shown above. Exceptions are the characters ′ (single quote), ″ (double quote) and \ (backslash). When choosing these, *escape sequences* must be used. To assign an apostrophe to the variable chtr1, for instance and a backslash to the variable chtr2, you can write:

```
chtr1 = '\''; chtr2 = '\\';
```

Escape sequences are also used to indicate non-printing control characters. Some of the most common control characters have been given special escape sequences. The sequence \n means, for example, the character for a new line and \t means tabulator. If you want to indicate a character that you can't write and which does not have a special escape sequence, you can use an escape sequence where the character's code is given directly. After the character \, an *octal* number, consisting of at most three digits, can be written. Some examples are:

```
'\0'    '\33'    '\177'    '\266'    '\377'
```

Alternatively, the character code can be given in hexadecimal form. An 'x' is then written after the character \. The same examples as the ones above can then be written

```
'\x0'    '\x1b'    '\x7f'    '\xb6'    '\xff'
```

3.2   Single characters, reading and writing

The values of type **char** can be read and written using the common input and output operators << and >>. Let us write a small program to read in and write out a character:

```
#include <iostream.h>
main ()
{
  char chtr;
  cout << "Write a character" << endl;
  cin  >> chtr;
  cout << "The character was " << chtr << endl;
}
```

		Escape sequences
\n	*new line*	Moves the printout position to the start of the next line.
\a	*alert*	Gives a sound signal (e.g. a 'chirp').
\b	*backspace*	Moves the printout position one step to the left.
\r	*return*	Moves the printout position to the start of the line.
\f	*form feed*	Moves the printout position to the start of the next page.
\t	*tab*	Moves the printout position to the next tab stop.
\v	*vertical tab*	Gives vertical tabulating.
nnn		The character with octal character code *nnn*.
xnn		The character with hexadecimal character code *nn*.

In the program we have declared a variable chtr of type **char**. The expression cin >> chtr means that the character the user has written at the terminal will land in the variable chtr. Note that chtr can only contain a single character. If the user were to write several characters at the terminal, only the first one would land in chtr.

The input operator << skips over any white characters. The program will only read and write out the first non-white characters typed in from the keyboard. But there are occasions when you will not want to skip over white characters. An example is when you want to write a program which copies a text exactly as it is written, including all the white characters; then the function cin.get can be used. As an example, here is a small program which reads the input from the keyboard and writes it out at the terminal:

```
#include <iostream.h>
main ()
{
    char c;
    while (cin.get(c))
        cout << c;
}
```

The expression cin.get(c) reads the next character and puts it in the variable c. Like the input operator << , cin.get gives an output value which can be taken to be 'true' if reading in went well and 'false' otherwise. This means that the **while** statement is executed a round for every character the user types in at the keyboard. When the user wants to stop input, 'end of input data' can be indicated by typing Ctrl-Z or Ctrl-D, depending on the operating system being used; then the input of the next character will miscarry, the result of cin.get will be interpreted as being 'false' and the program will be terminated.

It may seem pointless to write a program which reads what is typed at the keyboard and then writes it out at the terminal. Whatever is typed is normally seen on the screen anyway, without needing to run a program like this; but the program can be put to better uses. Certain operating systems, such as MS-DOS and Unix will allow you to redirect the streams cin and cout. Suppose that we have compiled and linked the program above and given the executable program the name, my_copy. When we start the program as usual with the command

```
my_copy
```

the program will function as described above, that is, whatever is typed in will be copied at the terminal. But if instead we start the program with the command

```
my_copy <f1.txt
```

it will display the contents of the text file f1.txt at the terminal. What we have done here is to redirect the stream cin so that it will be connected, not to the keyboard but to the file `f1.txt`. We can also redirect `cout`. We can give the command

```
my_copy >f2.txt
```

in which case the program's output will not appear at the terminal but will instead be stored in the file `f2.txt`. Since both `cin` and `cout` can be redirected, the program can be used to copy the contents of one file to another:

```
my_copy <f1.txt >f2.txt
```

It may be worth mentioning here that there is another variant of the standard function `cin.get` which also reads the next character, whatever it might be, from `cin`. The difference, compared with the first version, is that you get the input character as a result of the function instead of giving the name of a variable as an argument. A call of the other version of `cin.get` can look like this:

```
c = cin.get();
```

There is a standard function called `cin.peek` which functions similarly to the other version of `cin.get`. It 'peeks' at the next character to be read but does not read it. As an example of this we will show a **while** statement which skips the white characters of the input stream. At the beginning of every round, the next character is checked to see whether it is a white character, that is, a blank space, tabulator or an end-of-line character. The **while** statement is stopped as soon as a non-white character is encountered.

```
while (cin.peek()==' ' or cin.peek()=='\t' or
       cin.peek()=='\n')
   cin.ignore();
```

Input and output of simple characters	
`cout << c;`	Outputs the character `c`.
`cout.put(c);`	Outputs the character `c`.
`cin >> c;`	Inputs the next non-white character to `c`.
`cin.get(c)`	Inputs the next character to `c`.
`cin.get()`	Inputs and gives the next character as a result.
`cin.peek()`	Peeks at and gives the next character as a result. The next character remains unread.
`cin.ignore();`	Reads and skips the next character.
`cin.ignore(n,c);`	Reads and skips a maximum of n characters. Ends when the character `c` is encountered.
`cin >> ws;`	Skips the white characters.

We have used yet another standard function in this example, `cin.ignore`. When it is called without arguments, as it is here, it inputs but then skips over the next character. The function `cin.ignore` can also be called with arguments, in which case the first argument will be the maximum number of characters to be skipped and the second argument the character at which you want to stop. We show, as an example, how you can skip all the characters until you come to the character `'X'`. A maximum of 100 characters can be skipped.

```
cin.ignore (100, 'X');
```

Actually there is a much easier way of skipping white characters in the input stream. This may be done with the manipulator `ws` (short for 'white space'):

```
cin >> ws; // Skip white characters
```

We have seen that the first variant of the function `cin.get` gives a result value which can be interpreted as 'false' when *end of file* is entered. The second version of `cin.get`, as well as the function `cin.peek`, both give quite a special value when *end of file* is encountered. This value is called EOF and is defined in the file `iostream`. If you want to test whether there is input data to be read, you can write

```
if (cin.peek()!=EOF)
```

3.3   Character arrays and text strings

In our earlier program example we saw several examples of how to write out text sequences, consisting of several characters. A constant text, a *text string literal*, is indicated by putting it between double quotes, as

```
"This is a text"
```

Note that simple characters of type **char** are put between single quotes, while texts consisting of several characters are put between double quotes. If you want to include non-printable characters in a text, you can use escape sequences. The statement

```
cout << "Line 1\nLine 2\tI \"chirp\" now\a\n";
```

gives the output

```
Line 1
Line 2    I "chirp" now
```

on the screen and some 'chirp' or other sound. After output, the cursor will move to the beginning of the next line.

If you want to write in texts or handle texts in any other way, you must have variables which will contain the texts. Variables of type **char** contain only a single character and cannot, therefore, be used to store whole texts. For this you need to have a *character array*, that is an array where the components are of type **char**. As an example, we will show a program which asks for the name of the user, then writes it.

```
#include <iostream.h>
main ()
{
  char name[10];
  cout << "What is your name?" << endl;
  cin  >> name; // Dangerous input
  cout << "Hello " << name << endl;
}
```

When the program is run, it gives the following printout:

```
What is your name?
Sara
Hello Sara
```

The interesting thing here is the declaration

```
char name[10];
```

which says that the variable name is a character array consisting of 10 characters. As we saw earlier, the numbering of the separate elements in an array always begins with 0, so that the elements in the array name are numbered from 0 to 9. The statement

```
cin >> name;
```

inputs the text typed at the keyboard to the variable name. How this variable looks after input is shown in Figure 3.1. The characters written by the user have landed in the variable name beginning with the element 0. Input finishes with the arrival of a

Figure 3.1

white character (space, tabulator or end-of-line). The input operator >> then automatically puts a special *null character* into the variable name after the input characters. A null character is a byte which contains zeros in all of the eight bits. The null character is usually written with the escape sequence \0 as in Figure 3.1. The elements 5–9 in name will not be influenced by the input in our example. Their contents is therefore undefined.

It is a convention, in C and C++, to use null characters to indicate the end of a text. A sequence of characters terminated by a null character, is usually called a *text string*. We thus differentiate between the concepts of character array and text string. A character array is like a container into which text strings are put. Since each text string terminates with an extra null character, a character array with *n* elements can contain text strings which are at most *n*–1 characters long. When you work with texts in C++, you should always make sure that the texts terminate with a null character, because there are a number of standard functions for handling text strings and they all require the use of null characters. The output operator << in our examples uses, for instance, the null character in the variable name to decide where the text being written out is to finish.

Character arrays and text strings

char a[n];   The variable a is a *character array* with room for n characters.
Numbered from 0 to n−1.

- A *text string* is an arbitrarily long sequence of characters.
- Terminates with a null character, indicated by \0.
- Can be put into a character array. There must then also be room for the null character.

The input statement cin >> name; seems to be easy to use but there are two problems here. The first is that input is broken off when a white character is encountered. This means that if the user writes in both the first and last names of a person, it is only the first name which is read:

```
What is your name?
Peter Pan
Hello Peter
```

Of course you can easily solve this problem by introducing two variables in the program and by writing in the first and last names independently.

The second problem is much more serious. Suppose that the user happens to have a long name:

```
What is your name?
Christopher
```

A pervading characteristic of C++ is that security with the handling of arrays is extremely poor. There are no checks to make sure that texts do not land outside the array. In this example, the text Christopher is 11 characters long but since a null character has also been inserted, 12 characters will be inserted in the variable name in which there is room for only 10. The last two characters will therefore land outside the variable, and the program will be faulty. Anything can happen, and the program can behave in various ways, depending on which compiler you have used. Sometimes the program seems to work as intended, but at other times, vital data in the vicinity of the variable name in the primary memory is destroyed and the program does not work as it should. The worst aspect of this type of error is that it may not be discovered while the program is tested, only later when it is in operation.

We saw in Chapter 2 how the manipulator setw could be used to indicate the number of positions in the output of data; but this manipulator can also be used when data is input. It will indicate how many bytes there are in the array you want to write to. We can change the input line in our program:

```
cin >> setw(10) >> name;
```

Then a maximum of nine characters will be entered. In this case, the input operator will also put a null character last and a position is needed for it. Notice that the manipulator setw will only handle *one* piece of input data; it must be repeated for all new data entered.

The use of setw solves the problem of long names as in our example. The first problem, namely that input stops after the first name, remains. Another alternative is to use the input function getline instead of the operator >>.

```
#include <iostream.h>
main ()
{
  char name[10];
  cout << "What is your name?" << endl;
  cin.getline(name, 10); // safe input
  cout << "Hello " << name << endl;
}
```

The function getline has two arguments. You first indicate which character array you want to write text to and then you indicate how long this array is. Normally, getline writes a whole line from the keyboard but if the input is too long, the function's second argument will determine the number of input characters allowed. If this argument has the value *n*, the function will read at most *n*−1 characters. In both cases, a null character is inserted after the input text. The end-of-line character terminating the input of a whole line is not normally put into the variable. On the other hand, it has been written in (and taken) which means that if you call the function several times in succession, every call will result in the input of a new line.

An input line can contain both spaces and tabulators and these will also land in the variable you are writing data to. We show here two examples of the latter version of the program as it is run.

```
What is your name?
Peter Pan
Hello Peter Pan

What is your name?
Christopher
Hello Christoph
```

Input and output of texts	
`cout << a;`	Types out the text string in character array a.
`cin >> a;`	Reads a text and puts it in a. Puts the null character last in a. Reading stops at the first white character. Dangerous, can put text outside a.
`cin >> setw(n);`	At most n−1 characters may be read in the next input.
`cin.getline(a,n);`	Reads a text and puts it in a. n is the length of a. Puts in the null character itself. Normally reads a whole line, but at most n−1 characters.

Character arrays, like other arrays, can be initialized at declaration. For instance, we can write

```
char name[10] = "Sara";
```

In this case the variable name will look as it does in Figure 3.1, that is the elements 0 to 4 will contain the letters `"Sara"`, element 5 a null character, and the other elements will not be initialized. Note that the null character is also put in automatically here, which means that the character array must be one character longer than the initialized text. Otherwise there will be an error, even though the computer will not necessarily produce an error message from the compiler. When a character array is initialized, its length does not have to be indicated. The array will be exactly as long as is necessary. The variable s in the following declaration will have a length of 4.

```
char s[] = "C++";
```

The syntax for declarations in C++ is somewhat special. Let us look at the following line as an example of this:

```
char a[4], b[4]="xyz", c, d[]="nn";
```

The variables a and b will be character arrays with a length of 4, c will be a simple variable of type **char** (not an array) and d will be a character array of length 3. The variables a and c will not be initialized.

Since character arrays can be *initialized* with text string literals, you would think that it would also be permissible to *assign* them to character arrays. You might want to write, for instance

```
name = "Sara"; // Not allowed !!
```

but this is in fact not allowed in C++. If you want to make assignments to arrays you must use special help functions. We will soon show how this is done.

The next question is whether it is permissible to compare character arrays with each other. If we suppose that the variables a and b have been declared as above and we want to check whether they contain the same text string, we can write

```
if (a == b)   // Allowed but not what is intended
```

As with other arrays, this can be compiled but it doesn't mean, as you might think, that the contents of the variables a and b are being compared. Instead, the expression a==b will determine in this case whether a and b refer to the same variable and of course they do not. The expression will therefore always be false. To compare character arrays, special help functions must be used.

Before we deal with help functions in the context of handling text strings, note that individual elements in a character array can be accessed by the use of *indexing*. To access element number 2 in the array name, for example, you write name[2]. The element you choose to select in a character array will have type **char** and can be handled in the same way as an ordinary, simple variable of this type. Here are some examples of indexing. We suppose that the variable name from the beginning contains the text "Sara", as shown in Figure 3.1.

```
cout << name[2];    // Print an r
if (name[0]=='A')   // See if the first character is an A
name[0] = 'b';      // Change element no.0 to a b
name[3] = '\0';     // Shorten the text to 3 characters
```

It can be seen from this that an individual element can be both read and changed by the use of indexing. After the two assignments in the example, the variable name will contain the text string "bar". The index does not need to be a constant, and an arbitrary integer expression may be written inside the square brackets.

```
cout << name[i];
name[i+j] = 'X';
name[i-1] = name[i];
```

When the index is not a constant but an expression, it is easy to make mistakes when programming so that the index value lands outside the bounds of the array. We have already seen that there are no indexing checks in C++. If you want checks, you have to put them in yourself. Later in the book we will see how classes can be constructed, in which those checks are made.

The use of indexing is illustrated in the next program example. The American style of indicating the date differs from the British style and can sometimes be misleading. For example the date, 15 October 1997, is written in the form 10/15/97, while in Britain the form 15/10/97 is used. The program below can translate a date in the American format into the British format. A date is input using the American format. When the program is run it may look like this:

```
Indicate date in the format mm/dd/yy 10/15/97
The British form of the date is 15/10/97
```

The program appears as:

```
#include <iostream.h>
main ()
{
  char am_date[9], br_date[9] = "  /  /  ";
  cout << "Indicate date in the format mm/dd/yy "
  cin.getline(am_date, 9);
  br_date[0]=am_date[3]; br_date[1]=am_date[4]; // day
  br_date[3]=am_date[0]; br_date[4]=am_date[1]; // month
  br_date[6]=am_date[6]; br_date[7]=am_date[7]; // year
  cout << "The British form of the date is "
       << br_date << endl;
}
```

The variable `br_date` is initialized at declaration. Blank characters have been inserted where the day, month and year numbers should be. These blank numbers are then filled in with day, month and year numbers further down in the program.

3.4   Standard functions for handling text strings

In C and C++ there is a standard library with various help functions for handling text strings. To access this library, you have to include the file `string.h` at the beginning of your program, unless your compiler follows the draft standard in which case `cstring` can be included instead.

We will now give a few examples of the most useful help functions. The function `strlen` computes the length of a text string. If the variable `name` contains the text `"Sara"`, the following statement will give an output of 4:

Assignment and comparison of character arrays

The assignment and comparison of character arrays can *not* be done using ordinary operators. Use the help functions in the standard string library.

```
#include <string.h>
```

The most common help functions:

```
strcpy(s1, s2);
```
copies a string from s2 to s1. No check that there is room.

```
strncpy(s1, s2, n);
```
copies a string from s2 to s1. Max. n characters (including the null character). The null character will be missing in s1 if the length of s2 > n.

```
strcat(s1, s2);
```
puts a copy of s2 last into s1. No check that there is room.

```
strncat(s1, s2, n);
```
puts a copy of s2 last into s1. Max. n characters added. s1 always concluded with a null character.

```
strcmp(s1, s2)          strncmp(s1, s2, n)
```
compares two text strings. strncmp compares at most n characters. Result: <0 if s1<s2, 0 if s1=s2 and >0 if s1>s2.

```
strlen(s)
```
gives the length of the text string in s (excluding the null character).

```
cout << strlen(name) << endl;
```

Note that it is the length of the *text string* in the variable name which is computed, not the length of the variable. The concluding null character is not counted.

The assigning of text strings can be done with strcpy. If we have the declarations

```
char a[4], b[4]="xyz", name[10];
```

we can assign the value of b, that is the text string "xyz", to a

```
strcpy(a,b);        // Does the assignment a=b
cout << a << endl; // Gives the output xyz
```

The whole text string in b, including the null character, is copied to the beginning of array a. A constant text string can also be assigned:

```
strcpy(name, "David"); // name="David"
```

A null character has also been put in at the end of the text here. No check is made to see whether the character array being copied into is big enough to hold the text string:

```
strcpy(a, name); // Dangerous!
```

If you want to make safer assignments, you can instead use the help function `strncpy`. This has an extra argument that indicates the maximum number of characters which may be copied. If we have two character arrays `s1` and `s2`, we can assign from `s2` to `s1`:

```
strncpy(s1, s2, n);
```

Here, a maximum of *n* characters (possibly including the null character) are copied from `s2` to `s1`. This means that if the text string in `s2` (including the terminating null character) is longer than *n* characters, no null character will be copied to `s1`. The text string in `s1` will not then be completed. If we want to make a safe assignment from the variable `name` to the variable `a`, we have to ensure that there is a null character in `a` after the assignment:

```
strncpy(a, name, 3);
a[3]='\0';
cout << a << endl; // Gives the printout Dav
```

The first statement copies the characters 'D', 'a', and 'v' to the elements 0, 1 and 2 in the variable `a`. The second statement puts an end-of-line character last in the variable `a`. You need to have this statement for safety's sake.

When you copy to or from an array, you don't need to start copying at the first element in the array. The statement

```
strcpy(a+2, name+5);
```

copies a string which begins in element number 5 in the variable `name`, to an array `a` which begins at element number 2. (As usual, numbering begins at zero, so that it will be the same thing to write `a+0` as to write `a`.) Using this, we can now write a new version of the date program:

```
#include <iostream.h>
#include <string.h>
main ()
{
  char am_date[9], br_date[9] = " / / ";
  cout << "Indicate date in the format mm/dd/yy "
  cin.getline(am_date, 9);
  strncpy(br_date+0, am_date+3, 2); // day
  strncpy(br_date+3, am_date+0, 2); // month
  strncpy(br_date+6, am_date+6, 2); // year
```

```
      cout << "The British form of the date is "
          << br_date << endl;
}
```

There are two other help functions, `strcat` and `strncat`, which function roughly as `strcpy` and `strncpy`, respectively. The statement

```
strcat(s1, s2);
```

copies the text string in `s2` to the *end* of the text string in `s1`. The earlier null character is thus overwritten. No check is made to see that the result will fit into `s1`. The statement

```
strncat(s1, s2, n);
```

copies the text string in `s2` to the end of the text string in `s1`. A maximum of *n* characters are copied and *then* a null character is put last into `s1`. This always happens (in contrast to `strncpy`). A maximum of *n* characters will thus be put into `s1`, since the old null character is taken away and a new one added. Both `strcat` and `strncat` require `s1` to contain a correct text string from the beginning, otherwise there could be an error, and the assignment could land outside `s1`.

Suppose that we have two variables `name1` and `name2` which contain a first name and a last name, respectively. In addition, we have the variable `name` which, as before, is 10 characters long. We can now combine the first name and the last name:

```
name[0]='\0'; // put an empty string in name
strncat(name, name1, 9-strlen(name));
strncat(name, " ",   9-strlen(name));
strncat(name, name2, 9-strlen(name));
```

The first statement sees that the variable name contains a correct text string (of zero length) from the beginning. Then we add the first name, a blank character and the last name. Note that the blank character should be between double quotes, not single quotes. We don't add a simple character but a *text string* which contains one null character. The total number of 'proper' characters in the variable name should not exceed nine. (There must always be room for the null character.) The text already in name when additions are made consists of a number of 'proper characters' dictated by `strlen(name)`. Thus a maximum number of `9-strlen(name)` new characters can be added each time.

To compare character strings, either of the functions `strcmp` or `strncmp` can be used. Both have two text strings as arguments and these will be compared. The function `strncmp` also has an argument which indicates the maximum number of characters to be compared. If you want to compare the text strings in `s1` and `s2`, you can write the expressions

```
strcmp(s1, s2)        strncmp(s1, s2, n)
```

It is possible to check whether two texts are the same, or whether one is 'bigger' than the other. Ordinary alphabetical order is used. Note, however, that upper and lower case letters are regarded as being different (in the ASCII code, upper case letters are treated as being smaller than lower case letters) while only the letters a–z come in the correct order. If the texts s1 and s2 are the same and they are compared, the functions will give a result of 0. If s1<s2, the functions will give a result less than 0 and if s1>s2, they will give a result greater than 0. As an example, here is a program which inputs and compares two names.

```
#include <iostream.h>
#include <string.h>
main ()
{
  char name1[10], name2[10];
  cout << "Write two names (on separate lines) " << endl;
  cin.getline(name1, 10);
  cin.getline(name2, 10);
  if (strcmp(name1, name2)<0)
    cout << name1 << " comes first" << endl;
  else if (strcmp(name1, name2)>0)
    cout << name2 << " comes first" << endl;
  else
    cout << "The names are the same" << endl;
}
```

A test run gives the following result:

```
Write two names (on separate lines)
Hanna
David
David comes first
```

3.5 The standard type string

As you will have gathered, it can be awkward as well as unsafe to handle texts using character arrays. These language constructs have been inherited from C and they cannot be removed from C++ because they are now too well established. However, there is, in the standard draft, a class called string which can be used instead of ordinary character arrays. There are many operations which have been defined for type string, such as assigning, comparing and the input and output of data. There are also a number of operations for changing the content of a text. Parts of a text may, for instance, be added to, taken away, or replaced. In order to access `string`, you first have to write `#include <string>` in the program. We give here an example which shows some of the operations:

```
#include <iostream.h>
#include <string>
main ()
{
   string s1 = "C", s2, s3, s4;
   s2 = s1;
   s2 += "++";
   s3 = "ANSI-" + s2;
   s4.insert(0, "ISO-");
   s4.insert(4, s3, 5, 3);
   cout << s1 << ' ' << s2 << ' '
        << s3 << ' ' << s4 << endl;
   if (s1<s2)
     cout << s1 << " comes before " << s2 << endl;
   s1 = s2.substr(1, 2);
   s2 = s3.substr(6, 2);
   if (s1 == s2)
     cout << s1 << " is the same as " << s2 << endl;
   s3.remove(4, 2);
   s4 = s3 + s1[1];
   if (s3 != s4)
     cout << s3 << " is not the same as " << s4 << endl;
}
```

When you run the program, you get the output

```
C C++ ANSI-C++ ISO-C++
C comes before C++
++ is the same as ++
ANSI++ is not the same as ANSI+++
```

The normal operator for input `>>` can be used for the input of variables of type `string`. This will first skip white characters, then read on until the next white character. There is also an input function, `getline`, which reads a whole line, including any white characters. The following lines give examples of input.

```
cout << "What is your name? ";
cin  >> s1 >> s2;
cout << "Hello " << s1 << ' ' << s2 << endl;
cout << "Address? ";
cin  >> ws;
getline(cin, s3);
cout << "I see, you live at " << s3 << endl;
```

Some operations for the standard type string	

Suppose that s and s2 have type `string` and that x either has type `string` or is an ordinary character array with type `char[i]`.

`s=x`	Assignment.
`s==x  s!=x  s<x  etc.`	Comparison.
`s+x`	Gives new `string` composed of s and x.
`s[k]`	Indexing without index checks.
`s.at(k)`	Indexing with index checks (gives `s[k]`).
`s.substr(k, n)`	Gives part of s, with beginning in pos. k and length n.
`s.length()`	Gives the length of s.
`s+=x`	Adds x last in s.
`s.remove(k, n)`	Takes away n characters from s with beginning in pos. k.
`s.insert(k, x)`	Puts x into s with beginning in pos. k.
`s.insert(k, s2, k2, n)`	Puts n characters into s with beginning in pos. k copies from pos. k2 in s2.
`s.replace(k, n, x)`	Replaces n characters in s with beginning in pos. k with contents in x.
`s.replace(k,n,s2,k2,n2)`	Replaces n characters in s with beginning in pos. k with n2 characters from s2 with beginning in pos. n2.
`cout<<s`	Prints out s.
`cin>>s`	Inputs to s, stops at a white character.
`getline(cin, s)`	Inputs a whole line to s.

Here is an example of how output may look when these statements have been executed.

```
What is your name? Christopher Long
Hello Christopher Long
Address? London Road, Canterbury
I see, you live at London Road, Canterbury
```

Some of the C++ compilers in use (for example, Gnu's G++) already have a class called `string`. The Borland compiler has in its header file `cstring.h` a class which corresponds to the class `string` in the standard draft.

EXERCISES

3.1   Write a program to read in words from the keyboard to a character array, s1. The program should then copy the text string in s1 to another character array, s2. (In this exercise, you are not allowed to use the help function strcpy.)

3.2   Do the same as in the previous exercise, putting the characters in s2 into the opposite order to which they were in s1.

3.3   A text which can be read forwards or backwards giving the same result is an example of a palindrome (e.g. madam, ada, radar). Write a program which reads in a word and then decides whether the word is a palindrome or not.

3.4   Write a program to enter a text file consisting of several lines and to compute the average number of characters per line in the file. Use redirect cin.

3.5   Write a program to enter a text file and print out the number of letters, digits and other characters in the file. Redirect cin.

4 Functions

When designing programs that are somewhat bigger and more complicated than the ones we have dealt with so far, they have to be divided into several parts, or 'building blocks', which are of a size that can be handled. Essentially, there are only two kinds of building block in C++: functions and classes. In this chapter, we will begin to look at functions. Earlier, we saw how 'ready-made', standard functions could be used. Here, we will be constructing and calling our own functions.

In constructing an algorithm, it is often useful to express certain steps on a 'higher level' than is possible with the fundamental statements in C++. Steps at such a higher level include, for example, 'calculate the logarithm of x', 'sort the table t' or, 'calculate the mean of the measurements'. In C++ functions can be used to join fundamental statements at a higher level. As we have seen, higher-level steps in an algorithm occur naturally when the technique of top-down design is applied to a programming problem.

As we saw in Chapter 1, the program texts of a C++ program can be divided into several program text files, or *source code files*. Every such file can contain one or more functions and the files can be compiled separately. In this chapter, we will be demonstrating the principles for dividing programs in this way.

In several other common programming languages, for example Ada and Pascal, we speak of *subprograms*. There are two types of subprogram, *functions* and *procedures*. The term 'function' is normally used for subprograms which compute a certain value but the term 'procedure' is used for subprograms which 'do something', without this necessarily resulting in a value. In C++ only the concept of *function* is used; this will therefore correspond to both functions and procedures in other languages. There are thus two kinds of functions in C++: those which compute and return a value and those which do not.

4.1 Functions which return a value

We begin by discussing functions which calculate a value. Such a function is like a black box into which one or more values can be placed. A result dependent on these initial values then emerges from the box. As our first example, let us look at the function meanv, which computes the mean value of two real numbers. From the user program's point of view, the function will be like the black box in Figure 4.1.

In C++, the function looks like this:

```
double meanv (double x1, double x2)
{
   return (x1+x2)/2;
}
```

This is called a *function definition*. It consists of two parts – a *function head* and a *function body*. In this example, the function head is on the first line. It will tell the user of the function how the function is to be used. First, the type of the result

Figure 4.1

Function definition

result_type name (type1 param1, type2 param2, etc.)
{
    local declarations
    and statements
}

---

coming out of the function is indicated. In this example, the mean value of two real numbers is to be calculated. The result type is therefore **double**. Then, the name of the function is indicated; here, it is meanv. After the function's name, whatever will be put into the function is indicated by giving a list of the function's *parameters* (also called *formal parameters* or *formal arguments*.) The type and name is given for every parameter. We have indicated here that the function has two parameters, x1 and x2, both of which are of type **double**. You may think that this looks much like a declaration of two variables x1 and x2.In fact, x1 and x2 will come to be regarded as variables inside the function meanv. When the function is called, x1 and x2 will contain the values put into the function.

    The contents of the 'black box' is described by the function body inside the braces but the user of the function need not normally worry about this. A function body looks just like the contents of the function main. First, you normally write declarations (if there are any) and then a number of statements to be executed. There are no declarations in the function meanv, and there is only one statement:

```
return (x1+x2)/2;
```

A **return** statement does two things: it indicates which value is to be given as the function result and it terminates the function. (If another statement were to follow the **return** statement, this statement would not be executed.) There should be an expression after the word **return**. The type of this expression should be the same as the type first indicated in the function head. If this is not the case, there will be an automatic type conversion into this type (if this is possible). A function may

---

return statements

    return *expression*;
- Ends the function and gives the value *expression* as result.
- The expression's type should be the same as the function's result type.

contain several **return** statements but often there is only one, which comes last in the function body.

A function definition is only a description of how a particular computation is done. To actually have a computation done, we have to *call* the function. In other words, we must put something into the 'black box'. In the following example, we have put our function into a complete program which reads in two numbers from the keyboard, computes their mean value and writes it out at the end.

```cpp
#include <iostream.h>
double meanv (double x1, double x2)
{
  return (x1+x2)/2;
}

main ()
{
  double number1, number2, mv;
  cout << "Give two real numbers: ";
  cin >> number1 >> number2;
  mv = meanv(number1, number2);
  cout << "The mean value is " << mv << endl;
}
```

The program consists of two functions, meanv and main. Execution always begins in main. Let us suppose that the user enters the two numbers 2.0 and 2.5. The call of the function meanv takes place in the expression

```cpp
meanv(number1, number2)
```

First there is the name of the function being called and then, in parentheses, there is a list of the *arguments* of the function. (Sometimes the terms *actual parameters* or *actual arguments* are used.) When the call is executed, the values of the arguments are calculated first. (No calculations are necessary in this example, since the values are already in the variables number1 and number2.) The values of the arguments are then put into the function. The arguments' values are *copied* to corresponding parameters. Figure 4.2 illustrates this. When the function is called, the value of the first argument is put into the parameter x1 and the value of the second argument is put into the parameter x2. Note that neither number1 nor number2 are in any way influenced by this or by what will later take place inside the function. This method of transferring the arguments' values to a function is usually termed *call by value* and means that the arguments' values are copied to local copies inside the function. Another way of expressing this is to say that x1 and x2 are *value parameters*. Unless otherwise stated, all parameters in C++ are value parameters.

When the arguments' values are copied to number1 and number2 by a call to meanv, the expression in the **return** statement will be computed. The

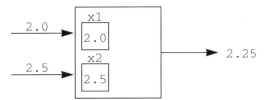

Figure 4.2

function call `meanv(number1, number2)` will thus have the value `2.25`. When the function call is finished, execution will continue as usual in `main` and the value `2.25` will be assigned to the variable `mv`. Note that when the function call has been ended, the two parameters `x1` and `x2` will cease to exist. They are only there while the function is being called. Inside the function they are regarded as ordinary variables, initialized at the start of the function.

The call of a function is regarded as an *expression* and is therefore allowed to be anywhere in the program where expressions may be put. It can, for instance, be a part of a bigger expression

```
mv(number1,number2)/number1*100
```

or be the operand for the output operator. We could have written:

```
cout << "The mean value is " << meanv(number1,number2) << endl;
```

The arguments of a function can also be expressions. They need not be simple variables. You could, for instance, write the expression

```
meanv(number1*number2, number1+10)
```

In this example, the parameter `x1` gets the value `5.0` and the parameter `x2` the value `12.0`. (We suppose that `number1` and `number2` have the same values as before.) The arguments in a function call should have the same type as the corresponding parameters. (Otherwise, automatic type conversion will occur, if this is possible.)

A common misunderstanding where functions are concerned, is that what is put into a function and what comes out of a function should be typed at the keyboard and read at the terminal, respectively; but a function need not have anything whatever to do with input and output. The values going into a function come from the call program and are put in via the arguments (the values will not then be read from the keyboard). Similarly, the function's result value is given to the call program using the **return** statement and will not be displayed on the screen.

In our next example on functions we will look at a function with several **return** statements. The function will compute the larger of two integers.

Function calls

function name(a1, a2, ... an)

- *a1, a2, ... an* are *arguments*. They may be expressions. Their types should agree with those of corresponding parameters.
- A function call is considered to be an *expression*.
- The following occur:
  - (1)   The values of *a1, a2, ... an* are computed.
  - (2)   If nothing particular is indicated, the arguments *a1, a2, ... an* are *copied* to the corresponding parameters. This is called *call by value*.
  - (3)   The statements inside the function are executed.
  - (4)   The function is ended by a **return** statement.
  - (5)   The value of the function call is the value in the **return** statement.
  - (6)   Execution continues after the function call.

```
int max (int x, int y)
{
  if (x > y)
    return x;
  else
    return y;
}
```

The following example shows a program with a max call:

```
main ()
{
  int a, b, c, m;
  cin >> a >> b >> c;
  m = max(a,b);
  m = max(m,c);
  cout << m << " is largest" << endl;
}
```

Three integers are entered in and the largest one of them is computed and output. The function max is called in two places but with different arguments. We can get by without the variable m, if we write instead:

```
cout << max(max(a,b),c) << " is the largest" << endl;
```

The expression `max(max(a,b),c)` means that the function max should be called. The first argument is the expression `max(a,b)`. This expression, which in its turn is a function call, must be computed before the outermost call of `max` can take place. The first thing to happen is therefore that `max` is called with the arguments a and b. The result will be the larger of the values in a and b. This value is then given as the first argument for `max` and the value in the variable c is given as its second argument. The outer call of `max` then takes place, and the result will be the largest of the three values in a, b and c.

A function can have parameters of different types. There can also be an arbitrary number of parameters and their types can be different. Arrays can be parameters. One way of indicating that a parameter is an array, is to write empty square brackets after the name of the parameter, as demonstrated below. Here, the function computes the length of a text string. (Compare with the standard function `strlen`.)

```
int length(char s[]) // gives the length of the text string in s
{
    int n = 0;
    while (s[n] != '\0')
        n++;
    return n;
}
```

In the function, there is a *local variable*, n, which gets the value 0 from the beginning. You then run through the array from the beginning, increasing n by 1 for every character until you find a null character. The function can be called with character arrays of different lengths. If we have the declarations

```
char a[100]="Hanna", b[10]="X";
```

then the statements give

```
cout << length(a);
cout << length(b);
```

the outputs 5 and 1, respectively. Note that it is the lengths of the text strings that is computed and not the lengths of the character arrays.

Here is another example of a function which has an array as a parameter. This function will have an array where the elements have type **int**. The function should calculate the sum of all the elements in the array and give this sum as the result. The function will appear as:

```
int sum(int a[], int n) // sums up the elements in a
{
  int s = 0;
  for (int i=0; i<n; i++)
    s += a[i];
  return s;
}
```

That the parameter a is an array, can be seen by the empty square brackets. An extra parameter n, indicating the length of the array, is needed to establish the number of elements in the array within the function. Here is an example of a program section which uses the function sum to calculate the sum of a number of integers entered. The counter k indicates the number of the elements in the array used. The value of k will be given as the second argument of the function sum.

```
int tab[1000], k=0;
while (cin >> tab[k])
  k++;
cout << sum(tab, k);
```

We will give yet another example of functions which have arrays as parameters. Here, a method of making a more effective search than the linear one discussed on page 65 will be demonstrated. We will write a function which searches for a given number in an integer array, a prerequisite being that the array to be searched will have been *sorted*. We will use the following idea:

Look first at the element lying in the middle of the array. Suppose that this element contains the value *m*. If the number searched for is less than *m*, we will know that it must lie, assuming that it exists, in the array's left-hand side, since the array has been sorted. If the number searched for is bigger than *m*, it must lie in the right-hand side of the array (again, assuming that it exists). A third possibility is that the number is equal to *m*, in which case the solution is trivial, since we happen to have found the number straight away. Thus, having looked at the number in the middle of the array, we will either have found the desired number, or we will know which half of the array we should continue to search.

If we continue our search, we can consider the half to be searched as a new array, smaller than the original one. We can then use the same idea again, that is looking at the element lying in the middle of the new, smaller array. If the desired number is not the one having the value of this element, we can decide whether we want to search in the array's left- or right-hand side. We now apply the same method yet again to the new, still smaller, partial array to be searched. The whole procedure is repeated again and again with ever-decreasing partial arrays, until either we have isolated the number we are looking for, or until the partial array we are left with is so small that it cannot contain any elements. In the latter case, the desired number will not be in the array.

The method just given is a search method usually called a *binary search* (so called because it halves, at every step, the array to be searched).

We now show what the function looks like. It has three parameters, the first being the number we are searching for. The second parameter is the array, and the third is an integer which gives the number of elements in the array. The function gives as result an index for the position in the array occupied by the desired number. If the number does not happen to be in the array, a value of -1 is returned. We use the variables first and last so that we will know the first and last index in the partial array we are searching in. These variables are initialized so that they will describe the whole array from the beginning.

```
// Binary search
int bin_sch(int searched, int f[], int n)
{
  int first = 0, last = n-1;
  while (first <= last)
  {
    int middle = (first + last)/2;
    if (searched < f[middle])
      last = middle-1;
    else if(searched > f[middle])
      first = middle+1;
    else // equal
      return middle;
  }
  return -1; // not found
}
```

This search method is much more effective than a simple linear search. For instance, if you have an array with 100 elements, the binary search algorithm will need to investigate seven elements in the array, if it should come to that, to see whether a particular number is there or not. With a linear search, this 'worst case' would have meant investigating 100 elements. The bigger the array, the greater the efficiency of the method. In an array of 1000 elements, a binary search would have needed to investigate a maximum of only 13 elements at any one time while with a linear search, this figure would have been 1000.

Functions can be constructed which do not have parameters. As an example, let us write a function get which enters an integer from the keyboard. The function should give as result the number entered. To make the function usable, we will design it so that it will ensure input from the programmer. In other words, if the person running the program happens to make an inputting mistake resulting in a number not being an integer, the function will give an error message warning the user to make a fresh attempt at typing an integer. The function will continue in this way until the user has typed a correct integer and only then will it return the number entered. We will use the result value from the input operator << to decide whether a correct integer was entered or not. (Compare with the discussion on page 48.)

```
int get()
{
  int i;
  while (not(cin>>i) or cin.peek()!='\n')
  {
    cout << "Incorrect integer. Try again: ";
    cin.clear(); // clear error state
    cin.ignore(1000, '\n'); // jump to next line
  }
  return i;
}
```

Note that there must be empty parentheses after the function name on the first line. It would also have been permissible to have used the reserved word **void** and then to have written

```
int get(void)
```

The expression `cin>>i` on the fourth line in the function gives the value 'true' if input to the variable number has gone well and the value 'false' otherwise. The expression **not**`(cin>>i)` will then be 'true' if input to number has miscarried. The expression `cin.peek()!='\n'` is computed if input to the variable number has gone well. The function `peek` peeks at the next character waiting to be input. This character should be an end-of-line character, since the user is expected to press the Enter key after the integer has been typed. If the next character is not an end-of-line character, incorrect data have been input after the integer.

A round of the **while** statement is executed every time the user inputs incorrect data. First, an error message is given, then `clear` is called to discontinue the error condition in the input stream. The standard function `cin.ignore` is used to skip the whole of the incorrect line the user has written. Of course the user would welcome the opportunity of writing a new number from the beginning. The argument `1000` of `ignore` means that at most 1000 characters may be skipped in the input stream and the argument `'\n'` denotes that characters should be skipped until an end-of-line character has been encountered. The end-of-line character will then be the last one to be skipped. The statements

```
cout << "Write an integer: ";
n = get();
cout << n;
```

can give the following output at the terminal when the program is run:

```
Write an integer: xy23
Incorrect integer. Try again: 12.6
Incorrect integer. Try again: 45
45
```

When you call a function which does not have parameters, you still need the parentheses in the call. Thus, we wrote `get()`. If the parentheses are forgotten, an error message will appear saying that the types are incorrect. Sometimes the outcome can be even worse: the program may be compiled but the function will not be called. Instead you will get a pointer to the function as a result. (Pointers will be dealt with later in the book.)

4.2   Functions which do not return a value

Up to now, we have shown functions of a particular category – those which compute and return a value. Now we shall give some examples of functions of another category – functions which do not return a value but only perform something. As our first example, we will show a simple function which ensures that printout begins on a new line at the terminal. We call this function, `new_line`.

```
void new_line() //Gives new printout line
{
    cout << endl;
}
```

The reserved word **void** which comes first, indicates that the function will not return a value. A function which does not give a result does not need a **return** statement. Execution in the function stops when you come to the last right-hand brace. You can have **return** statements in functions which do not return a value but then there should not be an expression after the word **return**. When you call a function which does not leave a value, there will not, of course, be a value to deal with. The function call becomes a statement as, for example

```
new_line();
```

In the function `get`, on page 104, we called the standard function `cin.ignore` to skip all the input characters up to the beginning of the next line. We made the call `cin.ignore(1000,'\n');` This does not look very nice; besides, an upper bound must be given for the number of characters to be skipped. We will therefore write our own function `skip_line` which will accomplish the same thing but which does not have any parameters. It also does not have an upper bound for the number of skipped characters. The function is called by writing

```
skip_line();
```

After the call, the first character comes on the next input line waiting to be read. The function is very simple. It reads one character at a time until either an end-of-file mark is encountered, or until an end-of-line character has been read in.

```
void skip_line() // Jumps to the next line to be read
{
   while (cin.peek() != EOF and cin.get() != '\n')
      ;
}
```

The functions `new_line` and `skip_line` did not have parameters. In the next example, we will look at the function `change_to`, which will not return a value but which has parameters. The purpose of the function is to change text strings. It changes a character to another character every time it occurs in a text string. How it is intended to function is best shown by the example below. The lines of the program

```
char a[100] = "C\tfor\tyourself";
cout << a << endl;
change_to(a, '\t', ' ');
cout << a << endl;
```

change all the tabulator characters in the text string in a to spaces. The output will be

```
C       for     yourself
C for yourself
```

Here is the function:

```
void change_to(char s[], char c, char cnew)
{
   int n = 0;
   while (s[n] != '\0')
   {
      if (s[n] == c)
         s[n] = cnew;
      n++;
   }
}
```

It is remarkable, if you think about it, that the argument a in the call should be changed. We stated earlier that values of arguments were *copied* to a function's parameters and that the function then worked with these copies; in which case it should not be possible for a to be changed. That this in fact happens, stems from the fact that a is an array. The rules for arrays are rather special. When a function is called, the values in an array are not copied to a corresponding parameter. The parameter will instead contain a pointer to the array. The parameter s in our example thus points to the array a, and this is why a is changed. We will be studying linkage between pointers and arrays in much more detail later in the book.

We saw in the previous chapter that when you read in text strings, you had to combine the input operator << with the manipulator setw so as not to run the risk of data landing outside the character array being read to. An alternative was to use the standard function cin.getline but this always reads an *entire* line. We shall now write our own function which accomplishes the same thing as the operator << in combination with setw, that is it skips white characters and then reads up to the next white character. This function is called get:

```
void get(char s[], int n)
{
  int i = 0;
  cin >> ws; // skip over white characters
  while (i < n-1 and
          cin.peek() != ' ' and cin.peek() != '\t' and
          cin.peek() != '\n' and cin.peek() != EOF)
  {
    cin >> s[i]; // read a non-white character
    i++;
  }
  s[i] = '\0';
}
```

The function has two parameters; the first, s is the character array we want to read in to and the other, n, is an integer which indicates the size of the array. The function reads at most n-1 characters from cin. Before it ends, it always puts a null character last in the text string in s. We first use the manipulator ws within the function to skip all initial white characters. Then comes a **while** statement which reads all the non-white characters. The **while** statement is ended when a new white character is encountered, or when the input data has finished.

The variable i is a counter which notes where the next character is to be inserted in the character array s. If we call the function get when there is no longer any input data to be read, no rounds of the **while** statement will be executed. This means that the variable i has the value 0 in the function's last statement and that the null character is placed first in s. The character array s will thus contain a text string of length 0.

As we saw in Chapter 2, it can be rather difficult to edit outputs in C++. This is especially true of real numbers when the correction to a certain number of decimal places and right-hand justifying is required. Then the manipulators setprecision, setiosflags and setw must be used. We shall now construct a function which we will call put and which is much easier to use. We let the function have three parameters. The first one is the number which will be written out, the second gives how many positions the function will write out in front of the decimal point and the third gives how many decimals are to be written out. Let us suppose, for example, that we want to write out the values in the variables y and z with 3 positions in front of the decimal point and to 2 decimal places. We can then call our new function put:

```
put(y,3,2);
new_line();
put(z,3,2);
```

(Here we have also called the new function new_line, which we defined on page 105). If y contains the value 23.907 and z the value 318.2, the function will write out

```
 23.91
318.20
```

The function looks as given below. The different manipulators for writing out and editing the parameter x are used on the first two lines inside the function. The last line restores the output stream to its standard values, so that any output coming after will not be affected by this output.

```
void put(double x, int before, int aft)
{
   cout << setprecision(aft)   << setiosflags(ios::fixed)
        << setw(before+aft+1) << x
        << setprecision(6)    << resetiosflags(ios::fixed);
}
```

Let us now discuss for a moment the function main. Why does it look so different? We normally write

```
main()
{ ...
}
```

Shouldn't **void** be written in front of the function name to indicate that main will not leave a result? No, it would certainly be possible to do this but it would not be quite correct, since main actually leaves a value of type **int** as a result to the operating system. For historical reasons (an inheritance from C), it is assumed that the function will return a value of type **int** if a return type from a function has not been indicated. It would therefore be more correct to write

```
int main()
{ ...
    return 0;
}
```

The first way of writing this is more pleasing. But the draft of the standard permits you to omit having a **return** statement at this point in the function `main`.

4.3   Declaration scope and visibility

In programs you use entities, for example, variables or functions, which you yourself have declared. Entities can be declared at many different places in a C++ program. Common functions are always defined at the outermost level in a program. It is in fact permitted to define variables there. Variables may also be declared in *blocks*. A block is an area of the program included in braces. All the variables seen so far have been declared within blocks. A third place where declarations may be made is in the function head, where function parameters are declared. Apart from these, declarations may also be made in classes and name spaces but these will be discussed later in the book. Here are some examples of declarations:

```
int x;
int f1(char c)
{
    double y;
    while (y>0)
    {
        char x;
        ...
    }
    int w;
    ...
}
void f2()
{
    int y, z;
    ...
}
```

The integer variable x and the functions `f1` and `f2` are declared at the outermost level. The variables y, w and z, together with the **char** variable x, are declared in blocks. The variable w is an example to show that in C++ declarations can be put anywhere in a block. Thus they do not have to come before the statements.

An important concept is the *declaration scope* of an entity. The declaration scope of a program is that area of the program for which the declaration is valid. For all entities (except for members of classes), the declaration scope begins at that point of the program where the entity is declared. How far the declaration scope extends, will then depend on the position of the declaration. If the declaration occurs at the outermost level in a program, the declaration scope will extend right to the end of the program text file. If a declaration occurs in a block, the declaration scope will extend to the end of the block (to the right-hand brace), and if the declaration concerns a function parameter, the declaration scope will extend to the end of the function body (to the last right-hand brace).

Special rules apply to **if** statements, **while** statements, **for** statements and **switch** statements. (We will discuss **switch** statements later.) If an entity is declared inside the parentheses following **if**, **while**, **for** or **switch**, the declaration scope will include both the area inside the parentheses and one or more statements controlled by the statement. Here are some examples:

```
if (int k = n)
{ // declaration scope for k
  ...
}
else
{ // k is also declared here
  ...
}
// Here k is NOT declared

for (int j=1; j<=n; j++)
{ // declaration scope for j
  ...
}
// Here j is NOT declared
```

For an entity to be used in a program, it must be *visible* (for example, the use of a variable or the call of a function). An entity is visible in the whole of its declaration scope as long as it is not *hidden* (see below) by another entity of the same name. In the example on page 109, the parameter c and the **double** variable y are only visible in the function body of f1 (also inside the inner block after **while**); the variable x of type **char** is only visible in the inner block of f1; the variable w is only visible in the last part of f1; the variable z is only visible inside f2.

Normally, you may not declare several entities with the same name in a particular declaration scope. On the other hand, it is permissible to have the same name in different declaration scopes. In the previous example, for instance, we were allowed to have two variables called x and two called y since they did not lie in the same block. If an entity *e1* is declared in an inner block and if in the surrounding block there is another entity *e2* with the same name, the *e1* entity will hide the *e2* entity in the innermost block. (In the outer block, *e1* is not visible and *e2* is not hidden there.) In our example, the integer variable x is hidden in the inner block of f1. If x is written there, it would denote the **char** variable x.

If you want to access a hidden entity, the operator : : can be used. For instance, we can write, in the innermost block of f1:

```
cout << x;    // the char variable is written out
cout << ::x; // the integer variable is written out
```

Where functions are concerned, there is in C++ an important exception to the rule that several entities may not have the same name in a declaration scope. It is permissible to have several different functions with the same name. In the previous section, on page 108, we constructed a function with the name put, which wrote out and edited real numbers. We can produce two other functions with the name put. One will write out and edit integers and the other one will write out text strings:

```
void put(int i, int width)
{
   cout << setw(width) << i;
}
```

```
void put(char s[])
{
   cout << s;
}
```

Now suppose that we have the following program lines:

```
double y = 43.138;
int k = 8;
put(y, 3, 2);
put(" and\n");
put(k, 3);
```

We then get written out

```
43.14 and
  8
```

When two or more functions have the same name, we say that the functions are *overloaded*. It is permissible to have overloaded functions on the condition that they have different parameters. The number of parameters and/or parameter types must be different. This is a condition because the compiler has to be able to compare the actual arguments with the parameters and 'understand' which function is to be

---

Overloaded functions

Several functions may have the same name, or be overloaded, if they have a different number of parameters or parameter types.

called. Only one of the overloaded functions may pass; if this were not so, the program would be ambiguous.

4.4 Function declarations

The first complete program example in this chapter had the structure

```
#include <iostream.h>
double meanv (double x1, double x2)
{
  return (x1+x2)/2;
}
main ()
{
  ...
  mv = meanv(number1, number2);
  ...
}
```

We see that the definition of the function `meanv` has been put before the definition of the function `main`. This is because a function in C++ must be visible before it can be called. If `main` had been put before `meanv`, `meanv` would have been unknown to the compiler when the call came up in `main`. The option still exists of putting `main` before the definition of `meanv`, however. In this case, a separate *function declaration* (also called a *prototype*) of the function `meanv` must be inserted before `main`.

In C++, the difference between the concepts `declaration` and `definition` is pointedly emphasized. When an entity is *declared*, it is given a name and its characteristics are listed. A *definition* gives an entity a name as well, but a definition also sees to it that memory space is reserved for the thing defined. A definition can be said to be that place in a program where the thing defined really 'exists', while a declaration is only an indication of something that exists somewhere else. You may often only have a definition, for example, when you declare a variable in a function. Then this also serves as a declaration.

A function *declaration* contains only the function head itself. When you have a separate function declaration, the complete *definition* of the function must exist in some other place; for instance, later in the program text. Our program could have the following structure:

```
#include <iostream.h>
double meanv (double x1, double x2); // declaration
main ()
```

```
{
  mv = meanv(number1, number2);
  ...
}
double meanv (double x1, double x2) // definition
{
  return (x1+x2)/2;
}
```

In a function declaration, it is permissible to omit the names of the parameters; only the types have to be indicated. Thus the declaration of the function meanv could have looked like this:

```
double meanv (double, double);
```

For someone who only wants to call a function, it may of course be of little interest what the names of the parameters are inside the function. The important thing is to know what types they have; but sometimes it can be be useful to remember the parameter names, since they shed light on the order in which they are to come; this can be hard to remember if you have several parameters of the same type.

Function declarations

Before a function can be called, it must be *declared*.
This can either be done in a function *definition* or in a function *declaration*. A function declaration contains only the function head (it is also called a *prototype*):

result_type names (type1 param1, type2 param2, etc.);
The parameter names may be omitted.

4.5   Division of programs

We shall now discuss how you can divide a program into several program text files, or source text files, so that the different files can be compiled separately. As an example, we will write a program which reads in a text, word for word, and computes the number of words in the text, as well as the average length of a word. We can use several of the functions we constructed earlier in this chapter. We will construct the following program and put it into a text file with the name main.cpp.

```
main()
{
char a[30];
double    sum' = 0;
int n = 0;
get (a,30);
while(strlen(a) > 0)
{
  n++;
  sum += strlen(a);
  get(a,30);
}
put("Number of words:");
put(n, 13);
new_line();
put("Average length:");
put(sum/n, 3, 1); new_line();
}
```

If we try to compile this file as it is here, the compiler will complain that it does not recognize the functions get, strlen, put and new_line. We begin by discussing the function strlen.

This is a standard function. We know from experience that the following line must first be inserted in the program:

```
#include <string.h>
```

But why is it in order to call strlen when this line is included? The file string.h is a quite normal text file which contains program text. It is an example of a *header file*. Other header files we have met before are iostream.h and iomanip.h. There is a header file for each library of standard functions. It is an old tradition (an inheritance from C) that header files have names which end with .h , where the 'h' stands for 'header'. (This does apply to the standard library in the draft of the C++ standard.) Suppose now that you have a program text file with the name file1, and that you insert a line with the directive #include <file2> at a certain position in this file, then the compiler, when it is about to compile file1, will read and compile all the text which is in file2, exactly as if this text had been in the position indicated in file1. So what kind of text is there in a header file? Most header files contain a number of function *declarations*, that is declarations of function heads. Header files do *not*, however, contain function definitions, the complete functions. There is in the file string.h, for example, a line which roughly looks like this:

```
int strlen (char s[]);
```

After the file string.h has been included in our program, the function strlen will have been declared and can be called.

We have written the other functions which are called in the program, that is
`get`, `put` and `new_line`, ourselves. They are useful in reading and writing and
could be useful in other programs, too. We therefore choose to put their *definitions*
into a separate file with the name `simpleio.cpp`. The functions must be *declared*
in `main` so that they can be called there. One way is to put the following function
declarations in the file `main.cpp` before the definition of `main`:

```
void get(char s[], int n);
void put(double x, int before, int aft);
void put(int i, int width);
void put(char s[]);
void new_line();
```

This is not a good solution, however. The first problem is that all the function heads
in the file `main.cpp` must be written again. This is troublesome, and there is a
great risk of making mistakes when typing; as a result the contents of the function
definitions may not be exactly the same as in the file `simpleio.cpp`. The other
problem is that lines at the beginning of every new program have to be entered to
call the functions in `simpleio.cpp`.

A much better solution is to use a header file, just as you do for standard
functions, since header files can also be created for functions you write yourself. If
you include the file `myfile.h` which you yourself have created, you should give
the directive

```
#include "myfile.h"
```

The file name is put between double quotes instead of the signs < >, which are only
used for standard files. When double quotes are used, the compiler will know that
it is a personally created file and it should search for this file in the programmer's
current directory in the file system. When you include standard files, the compiler
will look in another section of the file system.

We will now make a text file with the name `simpleio.h` and in it
put declarations of the functions `get`, `put` and `new_line`. We will also include
the function `skip_line` in the file, although it will not be called in this example.
The file `simpleio.h` will afterwards be included in the main program. Our
program will now consist of three files, `main.cpp`, `simpleio.h` and
`simpleio.cpp`:

```
// The file main.cpp
#include <string.h>
#include "simpleio.h"
main()
{
   ... // as before
}
```

```
// The file simpleio.h
void get(char s[], int n);
void skip_line(); // Jumps to the next input line
void put(double x, int before, int aft);
void put(int i, int width);
void put(char s[]);
void new_line(); // Gives new output line
```

```
// The file simpleio.cpp
#include <iostream.h>
#include <iomanip.h>
#include "simpleio.h"

void get(char s[], int n)
{
  int i = 0;
  cin >> ws;   // Skip white characters
  while (i < n-1 and
         cin.peek() != ' '  and cin.peek() != '\t' and
         cin.peek() != '\n' and cin.peek() != EOF)
  {
    cin >> s[i]; // Read a non-white character
    i++;
  }
  s[i] = '\0';
}

void skip_line() // Jumps forward to next input line
{
  while (cin.peek() != EOF and cin.get() != '\n')
    ;
}

void put(double x, int before, int aft)
{
  cout << setprecision(aft)  << setiosflags(ios::fixed)
       << setw(before+aft+1) << x
       << setprecision(6)     << resetiosflags(ios::fixed);
}

void put(int i, int width)
{
  cout << setw(width) << i;
}

void put(char s[])
{
  cout << s;
}

void new_line() // Gives new output line
{
  cout << endl;
}
```

> ### Division of programs into several files
>
> - A program can consist of several separate parts. Each part contains a pair consisting of a *definition file* and a *header file*.
> - A definition file contains function definitions.
> - A header file contains function declarations.
> - The header file is included in its corresponding definition file and in other files where the functions in use will be called.

This is a general model which illustrates the division of programs. Files are always constructed *in pairs*. For every file which contains function definitions or *definition file*, a corresponding header file is written.

All the functions in the definition file capable of being called from other parts of the program, should be declared in the header file. Note particularly, that the header file is to be included in the definition file. In our example, the file simpleio.h has been included in the file simpleio.cpp (on the fourth line). This may seem strange. Do you need to declare the functions again in the definition file? No, this is not actually necessary, although it's a very good habit to cultivate, for then the compiler, when the definition file is compiled, will check that the declarations in the header file really accord with the definitions in the definition file. You can then be sure that the header file is correct.

In order to run our example program, it must of course be compiled. Two separate compilings are needed, one for the file main.cpp and another for the file simpleio.cpp. Then the whole program will be linked together. In a Unix system, for instance, the following commands may be needed:

```
CC -c main.cpp
CC -c simpleio.cpp
CC -o wordprog main.o simpleio.o
```

The first two lines compile the files main.cpp and simpleio.cpp. The result of these compilings will be two object files, main.o and simpleio.o, respectively. The last command links together the two object files into a program that can be run. The argument '-o wordprog' indicates that the program to be run will be called wordprog. Note that the header file simpleio.h does not need to be compiled separately. It will be compiled as soon as it is included in the other files.

This model can be generalized to programs which are made up of any number of separately compiled files. All the files (except the file with the main program) will be in pairs, every pair consisting of a definition file and a header file.

4.6 Reference parameters

On page 104, we wrote a function, `get`, which reads in an integer from the keyboard. If incorrect input data is entered, the function will output an error message asking the person running the program to enter the number again. The function can be called by writing

```
n = get();
```

This is a useful function, so we will want to put it into our `simpleio` package from the previous section. We would also like to have a corresponding function there with the name `get`, which reads in a real number instead of an integer. This could be called in the following way (y has type **double**):

```
y = get();
```

We should then have two functions with the declarations

```
int get();
double get(); // Incorrect overload
```

But it does not work! The overload mechanism in C++ is only valid for parameters and not for result types. For two functions to have the same name, they must have different parameters. If we redesign our `get` functions so that they do not give the number entered as a result but instead have a parameter, then overloading will work. They can then be called in the following way:

```
get(n);
get(y);
```

We begin by trying to rewrite the function `get` which reads integers:

```
void get(int i) // Incorrect function
{
  while (not(cin >> i) or cin.peek() != '\n')
  {
    cout << "Incorrect integer. Try again: ";
    cin.clear();
    skip_line();
  }
}
```

(Here, the function `skip_line` from page 105 has been used.) Now we call the function `get` with the following lines:

```
int n=0;
cout << "Write an integer: ";
get(n);
cout << "The number is: " << n;
```

A test run will give the output

```
Write an integer: 45
The number is: 0
```

Now something is wrong here! In Section 4.1, we discussed how function calls were implemented and we saw that when a function was called, *value calls* were normally used; this meant that the values of the arguments were *copied* to corresponding parameters where the parameters could be considered as *local* variables inside the function. What happens here when get is called, therefore, is that a value of 0 is copied to the parameter i. The parameter i is a local variable inside the function, and in the expression cin>>i an integer is read to this local variable. The variable n is not at all affected by this! It will still have a value of 0. But it is of course the variable n we want to read an integer to. How is get to be formulated so that this happens? To write cin>>n inside get is, of course, a silly idea because we cannot always be sure that the name of the argument will be n and the variable n is not visible in get. The solution is to use a *reference parameter.*

```
void get(int& i)
{
  while (not(cin >> i) or cin.peek() != '\n')
  {
    cout << "Incorrect integer. Try again: ";
    cin.clear();
    skip_line();
  }
}
```

The only change made is that the parameter type i has been changed from **int** to **int**&. The character & is the important thing here. It indicates that i is not an ordinary value parameter but a *reference parameter*. The parameter i is a *reference* to a variable of type **int** and it will refer to the variable given as an argument when the function is called. This means that i can no longer be considered to be a local variable inside the function get. Instead, it can be thought of as an alternative name for the argument given in the call. If, as before, the call

```
get(n);
```

is made, then i is a reference to n and can be considered as an alternative name to n. This means that if the variable i in get is changed, the variable n will in fact be

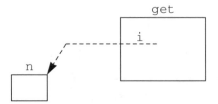

Figure 4.3

changed. An integer will thus be read into n. This is of course exactly what we wanted. Figure 4.3 shows how it looks. When reference parameters are used, we say that we use *call by reference* instead of 'value call', which is the usual mechanism in C++.

We can now write the second get function, the one which reads a real number:

```
void get(double& x)
{
  while (not(cin >> x) or cin.peek() != '\n')
  {
    cout << "Incorrect real number. Try again: ";
    cin.clear();
    skip_line();
  }
}
```

The overload mechanism will now work. If the variable n has type **int** and the variable y type **double**, we can carry out the following call, and the compiler will be able to decide which get is to be called.

```
get(n);
get(y);
```

We can now supplement our simpleio package with the two get functions. The definitions are put into the file simpleio.cpp and the declarations into the file simpleio.h which will look like this:

```
// The file simpleio.h
void get(char s[], int n);
void skip_line();
void get(int& i);
void get(double& x);
void put(double x, int before, int aft);
```

```
void put(int i, int width);
void put(char s[]);
void new_line();
```

Thus there are now three overloaded functions with the name get here. We discussed the first of these on page 107. It reads a text into a character array. Note that you never have reference parameters when the parameter is an array because the name of an array is already a kind of reference to the array. You could say that arrays are always called by reference.

When a function with reference parameters is called, the current argument must be able to be changed. Normally, a variable name is given to it. For example, the following call of get is not allowed:

```
get(n+k); // Incorrect reference call
```

A reference parameter must be used if an argument is to be changed in a function call. This may be necessary if you construct a function which gives more than one result. (Of course, only *one* result can be given with a **return** statement.) As an example of this, we will construct a function rooter to calculate the two real roots of a second-order equation of the form $x^2 + px + q = 0$, the roots of which are given by the formula

$$x = \frac{-p}{2} \pm \sqrt{\left(\frac{p^2}{4} - q\right)}$$

We let the function we want to write have two reference parameters, root1 and root2, in which the calculated roots are given as a result. The expression within the square root sign, the discriminant, must be greater or equal to zero if the equation has real roots. The function can therefore only calculate the roots if that is the case. For the function to be able to tell the caller whether or not the roots were calculated, it is given a third reference parameter ok which we set to 'true' if the real roots were calculated and to 'false', otherwise. The parameter ok may have type **bool**. (If a compiler which does not recognize type **bool** is used, let the parameter ok instead have type **int** and give a value of 0 or 1 as result.)

Here is a program where the function rooter is called. We will make use of the input and output functions in simpleio in this example, to demonstrate how you can use your own packages with help functions.

```
#include <math.h>
#include "simpleio.h"
void rooter(double p, double q,
            double& root1, double& root2, bool& ok)
```

```
{
  double d = p*p/4-q;
  if (d < 0)
    ok = false;
  else
  {
    ok = true;
    root1 = -p/2+sqrt(d);
    root2 = -p/2-sqrt(d);
  }
}
```

```
main ()
{
  double a, b, r1, r2;
  bool went_well;
  put("p? "); get(a);
  put("q? "); get(b);
  rooter(a, b, r1, r2, went_well);
  if (went_well)
  {
    put("The roots are "); put(r1,1,2);
    put(" and "); put(r2,1,2);
  }
  else put("No real roots");
}
```

We have now discussed the two kinds of parameters you can have in functions – value parameters and reference parameters. When you want to write a function, you must choose the parameters you need. A particular function can have parameters of both kinds. 'Value parameter' and 'reference parameter' are terms which reflect the technical aspect of how to transfer parameter values. Another way of looking at it is not to worry about the technical aspect at all but, instead, to think of which values will go *in* and which values will come *out* of a function; then the terms *inparameter* and *outparameter* are often used. Inparameters are used to carry data into a function from the calling program and outparameters are used to carry data in the opposite direction. In the function rooter above, for example, p and q are inparameters, while root1, root2 and ok are outparameters. Sometimes there is also a third category of parameters, *in/outparameters*. These are used to both carry data into and out of a function. If we write a function with a parameter p which is a character array and the function's task is to change all the lower case letters to upper case in the text string in p, then p can be considered to be an in/outparameter. The text string's old values must, of course, be carried into the function for it to know which characters are to be transformed, and the altered text string must be carried out of the function.

What then is the relationship between in- and outparameters and value and reference parameters? You could say that if a choice must be made between an in-

---

Reference parameters

Function name(*type*& p);   // declaration

Function name(a);   // call

- The parameter p is a reference to argument a.
- Can be thought of as another name for a.
- The argument a must be changeable, e.g. to a variable.
- Are not used for arrays. An array is already a kind of reference.

---

or outparameter (or possibly an in/outparameter), then it is a question of choosing the one which gives the correct technical solution; you can choose either value parameters, or reference parameters. For arrays, there is no choice – you must always have some kind of reference parameter, since a parameter which is an array is, in fact, a reference to the array given as argument when the function is called. If it is not a question of an array, you have to choose. Outparameters and in/outparameters are the simplest to use. Here you must always have reference parameters.

In terms of inparameters, we have used, in all our examples so far, value parameters. Since an inparameter should only be used to carry data into a function, corresponding arguments in the call should remain constant and, technically speaking, this is the case with value parameters. Now you might not see why you should not use reference parameters as inparameters, since the function could get at the argument's value directly. The problem here is that it would be possible to change the argument's value inside the function, but this is not meant to be possible for inparameters. There are occasions when it is more effective to use reference parameters as inparameters. This is when you have large parameters which need a great many bytes of memory space. It is impractical here to use value parameters, since the entire argument value must be copied when a call is made. A reference, on the other hand, always consists of a small number of bytes and is therefore always easy to transfer. To eliminate the risk of an argument's value somehow changing inside the function, you can declare the parameter as a reference to a *constant* value.

Before we give an example, let us simply discuss which parameters can be considered to be large. The built-in types as, for example, **int** and **double**, are not large. They can be transferred as quickly as a reference. When you have inparameters of one of the built-in types, it is therefore easiest to use ordinary value parameters. It is the types which are not built-in which can be large. In C++ you normally use classes to define your own types which are not built-in. This will be described in more detail later in the book but we have in fact already come upon a type which was defined with the help of a class. This was the standard type string discussed in Section 3.5 on page 91. A variable of type string can be very large. (Note that the type string is not an array. A variable of type string contains more information than simply the text string itself.)

As an example, we will now construct a function with the name word, which will check whether a variable of type string contains a word. As result, the function will leave the value **true** or **false**. When we speak of a 'word', we mean a text which only consists of letters. The variable to be checked is given as argument for the function. It is clear that here we should use an inparameter. The variable's value must, of course, be carried into the function in order to be checked but it may not be changed. It would be inappropriate to let the parameter be a value parameter in this example, since it could be large and then copying would be unproductive. Instead, we will let the parameter be a reference to a constant string. In this example, there is also a main program which reads the groups of characters typed in at the keyboard and indicates whether they can be considered to be words.

```cpp
#include <iostream.h>
#include <string>
bool word (const string& s)
{
  int i = 0;
  while (i<s.length())
  {
    char c = s[i];
    if ((c >= 'a' and c <= 'z') or
        (c >= 'A' and c <= 'Z'))
      i++;
    else
      return false;
  }
  return true;
}
main ()
{
  string w;
  while (cin >> w)
    if (word(w))
      cout << "A word"  << endl;
    else
      cout << "No word" << endl;
}
```

4.7   Parameters with default values

If a function has a certain number of parameters, then normally the same number of arguments must be indicated when the function is called. In C++, however, it is possible to leave out certain arguments when making the call. A condition for this is that the corresponding parameters should have default values. An example will best show how this works. We will construct a function, write_several, which has two parameters. The first one indicates a character to be written and the second indicates how many times the character should be written.

```
void write_several (char c, int num=1)
{
  for (int i=1; i<= num; i++)
    cout << c;
}
```

We have given the parameter num a default value of 1 here. This value will automatically be used if the corresponding argument is omitted in a call. If the argument is not omitted, then its value will be used as usual. Examples of calls which are allowed are:

```
write_several('x', 4); // Four 'x's are written out
write_several('y');    // One 'y' is written out
```

A default value may not be redefined, not even to the same value. This means that if you have a separate function declaration (prototype), you ought to indicate the default value in it and not in the complete function definition. This is shown here for the function write_several:

```
void write_several (char c, int sum=1); // declaration
void write_several (char c, int sum)    // definition
{
  ...
}
```

If a parameter has a default value, all the parameters *following* it must have default values. For instance, we could extend our function with yet another parameter which indicates whether or not each character should be written on its own line.

```
void write_several (char c, int num=1, bool separate_lines=false)
{
  for (int i=1; i <= num; i++)
  {
    cout << c;
    if (separate_lines)
      cout << endl;
  }
}
```

Here are a few examples of calls:

```
write_several('+');          // One + is written
write_several('?', 7);       // Seven ?s on the same line
write_several('%', 5, true); // Five %s on separate lines
```

4.8   Recursive functions

We have seen that a function can call another function. Furthermore, a function can call itself and such a function is called a *recursive function*. Recursive functions are used to solve certain types of problem. The problems for which recursion is most useful are those which are defined from the start in a recursive way: this occurs often in mathematical calculations. The most common example of a recursive function – an example that occurs in almost all books about programming – is a function to calculate the factorial of a number n. We studied this problem earlier (in Section 2.8, page 67). We then used iteration to solve the problem but now we shall see how recursion can be used instead.

The factorial of a number n, written $n!$, can be defined by:

$$n! = \begin{cases} 1 & \text{if } n = 0 \\ 1 \times 2 \times 3 \times ... \times n & \text{if } n > 0 \end{cases}$$

Another way of writing the definition is:

$$n! = \begin{cases} 1 & \text{if } n = 0 \\ n(n - 1)! & \text{if } n > 0 \end{cases}$$

There is one case where the value is given (that is $0! = 1$) and one case where induction is used to express the solution in terms of values already defined. This second definition leads naturally to the following C++ function:

```
int nfac(int n) // calculate n!
{
   if (n <= 0)
     return 1;
   else
     return n * nfac(n-1);
}
```

It is the last line but one which is the most interesting. There the function `nfac` calls itself. (The parameter n should never be less than zero but we have written the condition n<=0 in the **if** statement to avoid problems if the function should be incorrectly called with a negative value in the parameter.)

Those who have not worked with recursion before usually think that it is a little strange. But remember a fundamental rule: recursive function calls work in *exactly the same way* as other function calls. There are no special rules for recursion. This means that when a function is called (itself, or another one), the current parameters are calculated first. Memory space is then generated for the called function's formal parameters and the current parameters are copied into this space. More memory space is generated for the formal parameters at *every* new call. If a particular function is called several times, this will mean that *each* instance of the function will have its *own instance* of the formal parameters. The statements are then executed in the function called. When these statements are completed, you return to the point where the function was called. Thus if a function calls itself, you return to a point inside the function in question.

Let us take a concrete case and discuss exactly what happens. We will suppose that in a program there is the following statement

```
m = nfac(3);
```

The function `nfac` is called. Space is generated for the formal parameter n, which will have a value of 3. Since n is greater than 0, the statement after **else** will be performed. Now there is a new call of the function `nfac`. The value of the current parameter n-1 will be 2. New space is generated for the formal parameter n, and this space has the value 2. At this moment, then, there will be two different formal parameters, both with the name n. The first one, with a value of 3, belongs to the first instance of `nfac` and the second one, with a value of 2, belongs to the second instance of `nfac`.

In the second instance of `nfac`, n is greater than zero as well, so the statement after **else** is performed. Now `nfac` is called for the third time, and another formal parameter n, which has a value of 1, is generated. The statement after **else** in the third instance of `nfac` will also be executed, since 1 is greater than 0. The function `nfac` is called for the fourth time and this time another formal parameter with the name n is created. This will have a value of 0. No less than four different formal parameters with the name n will be existing at the same time.

In the fourth instance of `nfac`, the condition after **if** will be true. The statement

```
return 1;
```

will therefore be executed. As usual, this means that the function is interrupted, a result value of 1 is returned, and there is a jump to the point where the call took place. Since the fourth call of `nfac` took place from the statement

```
return n * nfac(n-1);
```

the function will jump back to this point. That the result value is 1 means that the expression n*1 should be calculated. But what value does n have? In the fourth instance of nfac, n had a value of 0, but the fourth instance has now been terminated. We have returned to the third instance and there n had a value of 1. Thus the expression 1*1 is calculated. Now execution of the **return** statement can be completed, which means that the third instance of nfac will now be terminated. A result value of 1 is returned, and the function jumps back to the point where the call took place. We return again to the statement

```
return n * nfac(n-1);
```

Since we now return to the second instance of nfac, n will this time have a value of 2. Therefore the expression 2*1 is calculated. Instance number two is now terminated with a result value of 2, and the function jumps back again to the point of the call, that is to the statement

```
return n * nfac(n-1);
```

We have now returned to instance number one of nfac, where n had a value of 3. Since the result value of the expression nfac(n-1) was 2, the expression 3*2 will now be calculated. Thus the result of instance number one of nfac will be a value of 6. Now instance number one will be terminated, and there will be a return to the point of call. The first call of nfac took place from the statement

```
m = nfac(3);
```

so the return will be to this point, and the variable m will be assigned a value of 6.

Recursive functions

- A function that directly or indirectly calls itself.
- During execution there are as many instances of the function as the number of non-terminated calls made.
- Each instance of the function has its own values for formal parameters and local variables.

Recursive solutions always follow the same pattern. Given a problem, first identify one (or more) special case(s) where the solution is trivial (n=0 in nfac). Then try to reformulate the problem so that it somehow becomes simpler (($n-1$)! is simpler than n!). You may then have the idea that the function you are trying to write already exists, and this will solve the simpler problem.

As an example of this, we will construct a recursive function which reads text from the terminal and writes it out backwards. To solve this problem, we use the following recursive idea:

(1)   Try to read the first character in the text and store it.
If it could be read, do the following:

(1.1)   Read in the rest of the text and write it out backwards.
(1.2)   Write out the first character of the text.

The trivial special case is that the text has no characters, in which case we do not do anything. In step 1.1, we assume that there already exists a function which can read the text and write it out backwards. We make use of this function to solve the simpler problem which arises when the text is one character shorter than it was at the beginning. If we now translate this algorithm to a C++ function, we will get:

```
void backwards() // reads a text and writes it out backwards
{
  char c;
  if (cin.get(c))
  {
    backwards();
    cout << c;
  }
}
```

We suppose that the user will terminate the text by marking the end of the file (with Ctrl-Z or Ctrl-D). The function will occur in as many instances (plus one) as the number of characters in the text. The first instance will read the first character. This instance will not be terminated until all of the others have been terminated. The last thing to happen will therefore be that the first character will be written out. Note that each instance of the function has its own unique instance of the local variable c. Thus there are in principle as many variables c as there are characters in the text.

In the examples we have looked at, recursion has always occurred because a function called itself. This is called *direct recursion*. It is also possible to have *indirect recursion*. A function f can call another function g which, in turn, calls f. Then f and g are said to be *mutually recursive*. It is even possible for recursion to occur through several stages (f calls g which calls h which calls f).

We will see several examples of recursion later in the book. We will find recursion especially useful when we deal with such dynamic data structures as lists and trees.

EXERCISES

4.1   Write a function to evaluate the sign of an integer in the following way. The function should return as its result the value 1 if the integer is greater than 0, the value 0 if the integer is equal to 0 and the value −1 if the integer is less than 0.

4.2 A number can be shown to be a prime number if it is exactly divisible only by itself and by 1. Write a function which checks whether or not a given number is a prime number.

4.3 A 'perfect number' is a number where the sum of its factors, including 1 but not the number itself, is equal to the number. A couple of examples are the numbers 6 and 28. Write a function which decides whether or not a given positive number is perfect.

4.4 The binomial coefficients can be defined for non-negative integers n and k in the following way:

$$\binom{n}{k} = \frac{n!}{k! \cdot (n-k)!}$$

Write a function, with the help of the function `nfac` on page 126, which evaluates the binomial coefficients for two numbers.

4.5 Write a function that uses the following Maclaurin series to calculate the value of e^x. Exclude terms that are less than 10^{-7} from the sum.

$$e^x = 1 + \frac{x}{1!} + \frac{x^2}{2!} + \frac{x^3}{3!} + \frac{x^4}{4!} + \dots$$

4.6 Construct a function `raise`, which evaluates x^y where both x and y are real numbers. Using common mathematical formulas for the calculation of logarithms, we find that

$$x^y = e^{y \cdot \ln(x)}$$

4.7 *Euclid's algorithm* for evaluating the greatest common divisor of two positive integers m and n can be described as follows:

- Divide m by n and denote the remainder by r.
- If $r=0$, the evaluation is finished and the result is in n.
- Otherwise, set the value of m to that of n and the value of n to that of r and return to step 1.

Use this algorithm to write a function `gcd` that evaluates the greatest common divisor of two positive integers. Then write a program that reads in an arbitrary number of pairs of positive integers and writes out the greatest common divisor for each pair.

4.8 To calculate the square root of a number x we can use Newton's Method as follows:

Start by guessing a number $g \geq 0$. When we guess g, we know that there must be a number h such that $g \cdot h = x$. (The number h can thus be written as $h = x/g$.) If we are very lucky and made a good guess, g and h are approximately equal and we have found the solution. In general, however, guesses are not that good. A new better guess is the mean of g and h:

$$g_{new} = \frac{g + \dfrac{x}{g}}{2}$$

Now we can replace g by the new guess and calculate a new value of h. By taking the mean of the new values of g and h we can get a still better guess and so on. Use this method to write a function that evaluates $\sqrt{x}$. Use $x/2$ for the first guess and let the guesses continue until the difference between two consecutive guesses is less than 10^{-6}.

4.9 All the previous exercises 4.1 to 4.8 require the construction of functions of a mathematical character. These functions can be useful in a number of different contexts. Show how, with the help of a header file and a definition file, a 'package' with these functions can be created. Then in a separate file, write a main program which uses at least two of the functions.

4.10 Write a function which determines whether a given text string contains a variable name allowed in the C++ sense (see Chapter 2 page 33). The function will return as result the value **true** or the value **false**. Use this function to write a program which reads in a line with a number of words from the terminal and which writes out how many of the words are permissible variable names. The different words on the line are separated by one or more blank characters.

4.11 Write a function which determines how many lower and upper case letters (in the interval a–z) there are in a given text string. The result should be given in two outparameters.

4.12 Write a function that takes two text strings, t1 and t2, as parameters. The function should determine whether t1 is a substring of t2. If this is true, the function should return as a result the index of the start of the substring in t2. (An index is normally calculated from 0.) If t1 is not a substring of t2, the function should return as result a value of –1. If, for example, t1 has the value "declaration" and t2 the value "General declaration office", the function should give as the result a value of 8.

4.13 Do the same thing as in the previous example but use the standard type string instead of ordinary text strings. Use reference parameters which refer to constants.

4.14 In the Romany language, all the consonants are doubled and an 'o' is placed between the doubled consonants. Vowels and other characters remain unchanged. Write a function put_romany which has a text string written in the Romany language as parameter. The function should write out the text in plain English. If, for example, the parameter contains the text "hoheyoy alollol yoyou roromomanoniesos", the function should write out "hey all you romanies". Use the function to write a program which reads a text file containing a secret message in Romany. The program should write out the secret message in plain English at the terminal. Redirect `cin`.

4.15 Write a function which decides whether two integer arrays are equal. (Two arrays are equal if they contain the same number of components and the corresponding components are equal.) The function should have as parameters the two arrays and two integers which indicate the length of the arrays. The function should give a result of type **bool**.

4.16 In an array of integers, 'rotation to the right' can be defined as an operation that moves each element one place to the right and the last element into the first position. Write a function that rotates an array an arbitrary number of places to the right. The function should have three parameters, the array to be rotated, the length of the array and an integer that gives the number of places to be rotated.

4.17 In this chapter we constructed the 'package' `simpleio`, which contains two output functions with the name `put`. These write out integers and real numbers and edit them. Both functions have parameters which indicate how editing is to proceed. Complete the declarations of the functions so that their edit parameters take on appropriate default values. In which file should the changes be made, the header file, or the definition file?

4.18 A trade union makes the following offer for a long-term wage agreement:

- The first year (year number 1) each employee will receive a monthly wage of £790.
- In the following years (years number 2, 3, 4, and so on) there will be an increase of 4% over the previous year's wage and an additional general rise of £30 per month.

Write a recursive function that will calculate the monthly wage for a particular year according to the scheme presented here. The only input parameter is to be the year number.

4.19 Write a recursive function `gcd` that evaluates the greatest common divisor of two positive integers m and n based on the following definition.

$$gcd(m, n) = \begin{cases} m & \text{if } m = n \\ gcd(m-n, n) & \text{if } m > n \\ gcd(m, n-m) & \text{otherwise} \end{cases}$$

4.20 By making use of the output operator $<<$, integers can be written out in decimal, octal or hexadecimal form but the operator will not write out in binary form. Write a recursive function which will produce a positive integer in binary form.

5 Types

When we talk about phenomena in the real world, we nearly always use a technique known as *abstraction*. Abstraction means creating a concept of something so that it can be talked about and described. The word 'truck', for example, is an abstraction for a vehicle that can be used for transporting things. We can talk about a truck and say that it has certain properties, such as capacity, length, running cost, and so on.

The abstraction can be made at different levels. For a maintenance mechanic it is natural to think of a truck as consisting of many components, such as a gear box, brake system, and so on. To go down another level, it can be said that the gear box is made up of many parts, axles, gear wheels, and so on. This level is appropriate for the design or repair of a gear box. The level of abstraction chosen, therefore, depends on the context in which the phenomenon is to be studied. The advantage of deliberately choosing an abstraction is that it allows nonessential details to be ignored in favour of those properties important for the study in hand. The driver of a truck is not interested in how the different gear wheels inside the gear box are moving. He or she only needs to know how to use the gear lever.

The concept of a *type* is used in a computer program to indicate characteristics for data objects. When a variable is said to have a certain type, this explains *both* which values the variable can have *and* which operations are allowed to be performed on the variable. In earlier chapters use has been made of the predefined data types `int` and `double`. These are examples of *arithmetic types* (or *numeric types*), useful when numbers in mathematics are dealt with. The type `int` is an *integer type* and can be used to describe things which can only have integer values, such as counters and numbers of different kinds. The type `double`, which is a *real type* (or *floating point type*), can be used to deal with other kinds of numeric values, physical characteristics such as temperature and length, for instance.

A question could be raised on the need for two number types: surely the standard type `double` would be sufficient to handle all numeric figures? In principle, the answer is a guarded yes. We still keep the type `int` as well because most computers handle integers more quickly than real numbers. Again, integers can be stored in a very exact way in the computer while real numbers are stored more approximately.

We will go through all the arithmetic types in C++ in this chapter and give a short account of how they are represented in the computer. We will also be looking at *enumeration types* which in C++ are treated as a kind of integer type. When programming in C++, often so-called *pointers* have to be used. Ordinary texts, such as those discussed in Chapter 3, are in fact represented with the help of pointers. In this chapter we will be describing how pointers work.

In order to make models of more complicated objects than mere numbers, we must be able to declare our *own* types where we can say how an object of the type is to be constructed (and which values it is to have) and which operations it will be possible to perform on the object. The important language construct *class* is used in C++ to declare our own types. We will be looking at classes in more detail later in the book.

We also discuss *type conversions* in this chapter. When working with different types, it is sometimes necessary to convert data from one type to another. We will be discussing when this can happen and what then takes place.

5.1   Integer types

5.1.1   Storing integers in a computer

In order to understand the characteristics of integer types, we give here a brief description of the principles for the storage of integers in a computer. The details here are not essential for the programmer to know and may be skipped on a first reading.

As we stated in Chapter 1, the memory of a computer consists of a number of memory cells. Each memory cell is made up of a certain number of bits, and every bit can hold a binary digit, (a zero or a one). This means that numbers are naturally stored in binary form in a computer's memory. Let us therefore begin by considering the *binary number system*.

In our culture the decimal system dominates (presumably because we have ten fingers). So if we write a number, such as 158.32, we assume automatically that it is expressed in the decimal system where the base is ten. We interpret 158.32 as:

$$1 \times 10^2 + 5 \times 10^1 + 8 \times 10^0 + 3 \times 10^{-1} + 2 \times 10^{-2}$$

Expressing this more generally, we can say that a decimal number:

$$a_n a_{n-1}...a_1 a_0 . d_1 d_2 ... d_m$$

(where the as denote the integral part and the ds the decimal part) really means:

$$a_n \times 10^n + a_{n-1} \times 10^{n-1} + ... + a_1 \times 10^1 + a_0 \times 10^0 + d_1 \times 10^{-1} + d_2 \times 10^{-2} + ... + d_m \times 10^{-m}$$

Using base 2 instead of base 10, the binary number:

$$b_n b_{n-1} ... b_1 b_0 . c_1 c_2 ... c_m$$

is interpreted as:

$$b_n \times 2^n + b_{n-1} \times 2^{n-1} + ... + b_1 \times 2^1 + b_0 \times 2^0 + c_1 \times 2^{-1} + c_2 \times 2^{-2} + ... + c_m \times 2^{-m}$$

Here, the bs denote the integral part and the cs denote what is sometimes called the *bicimal* part. For example, the binary number 10111.101 can be interpreted as:

$$1 \times 2^4 + 0 \times 2^3 + 1 \times 2^2 + 1 \times 2^1 + 1 \times 2^0 + 1 \times 2^{-1} + 0 \times 2^{-2} + 1 \times 2^{-3}$$

or:

$$16 + 0 + 4 + 2 + 1 + 0.5 + 0 + 0.125 = 23.625$$

When an integer is stored in a computer, a certain number of the bits are used. The actual number of bits used varies from computer to computer but it is commonly either 16 or 32. If, for example, the integer 23 has to be stored in 16 bits, we get the binary pattern:

```
0000000000010111
```

If every bit is allowed to represent a binary digit, an *unsigned* storing form is obtained. The greatest number which can be stored in unsigned form with N bits is then $2^N - 1$. If there are 16 bits, the greatest number which can be stored then becomes $2^{16} - 1 = 65535$. The unsigned form for storing integers cannot be used to store negative numbers. So the smallest number that can be stored using an unsigned form is always 0.

Generally, it is desirable to be able to use both positive and negative integers. To make this possible, a form of storing numbers called *two's complement* is used. With this form, the bit on the extreme left gives the number's sign; zero and one indicating a positive and negative number, respectively. The greatest positive number that can be stored in 16 bits is therefore:

```
0111111111111111
```

This is actually $2^{15} - 1 = 32767$. Using the two's complement form, the number -1 is stored in 16 bits as:

```
1111111111111111
```

The number -2 is obtained by subtracting 1 from this, thus getting:

```
1111111111111110
```

The number -3 is:

```
1111111111111101
```

By continuing to subtract one at a time we see that the least number (that is, the most negative number) that can be stored in 16 bits is:

```
1000000000000000
```

This has the value $-2^{15} = -32768$. In general, it can be stated that if integers are stored in N bits, the least number that can be stored is -2^{N-1}, and the greatest is $2^{N-1} - 1$.

Values of the standard type `int` are normally stored in this form and can, therefore, be both positive and negative. As we shall see, there are also standard types where integers are stored in unsigned form. The programmer does not need to know exactly how the storage works because the compiler takes care of it.

There is a certain risk attached to using a standard type such as `int`. Because the size of the numbers that can be stored depends on the design of the particular computer being used, the type `int` will not have the same properties in all implementations of C++. Suppose we develop a program in a computer that uses 32 bits for storing integers of the type `int`. Now suppose a variable of type `int` at some point in the program takes the value 100 000. This is fine because there is room in 32 bits to store 100 000. But if we want to transfer our program to another computer that uses 16 bits to store integers we would have a problem. The program would not run as it should.

5.1.2   Predefined integer types

There are eight different predefined integer types in C++. These are divided into two groups – signed types, that is, types which allow both positive and negative numbers, and unsigned types, which will only allow storage of positive numbers. The signed integer types are **signed char**, **short int**, **int** and **long int**. For every one of these four, there is a corresponding unsigned type. The unsigned integer types are **unsigned char**, **unsigned short int**, **unsigned int** and **unsigned long int**. Signed integer types and the corresponding unsigned types (for example, **int** and **unsigned int**) are always stored in the same number of bits in the computer. When variables of different integer types are declared it is sometimes permissible to omit key words. For example, the word **int** is understood if it is omitted. So if we write

```
unsigned m;
```

it will mean the same as

```
unsigned int m;
```

Furthermore, the word **signed** is understood except for type **char**. The line

```
long n;
```

is equivalent to

```
signed long int n;
```

For the type **char**, unfortunately, the notation can be ambiguous (for historical reasons). If you write

```
char c;
```

it will not be clear whether the variable c is **signed** or **unsigned**. How it is interpreted depends on which version of C++ is implemented. If the variable c is to be used to store 8-bit character codes, it can be useful to declare c as an **unsigned char**. (The character codes, of course, have values from 0 to 255.)

      The draft of the standard does not state exactly how many bits are used to store the different types. This obviously depends on implementation. It can be stated, however, that the type **char** is usually stored in eight bits, the type **short int** in 16 bits, the type **int** in 16 or 32 bits and the type **long int** in 32 bits.

      With unsigned types, arithmetic overflow can never occur. We say that computations are carried out 'modulo 2^N', where N is the number of bits for the type in question. Suppose, for example, that the type **int** is stored in 16 bits and that we have declared a variable u of type **unsigned int**. The greatest number which can be contained in u is then 65535, and we can make the following assignment

```
u = 65535;
```

The statement

```
u = u + 1;
```

now does not result in overflow and the result is 0. If instead we had made the statement

```
u = u + 2;
```

the result would have been 1, and so on.

Integer types	
Signed types *Can have both positive and* *negative values*	*Unsigned types* *Can only have positive* *values*

`signed char`
`short int`
`int`
`long int`
	`unsigned char`
	`unsigned short int`
	`unsigned int`
	`unsigned long int`

Which integer type should be chosen when a variable is declared? If the variable is to be used for counting, the normal choice would be type `int`. When dealing with large integers, which cannot be stored in `int`, the type `long int` must be used. If there are many small integers to be stored, possibly in large arrays, then a great deal of memory space can be saved by using the types `short int` or `signed char`. Unsigned types are used to calculate modulo 2^N, and may also be used to store bit patterns. Naturally, the type `char` is used primarily to store texts.

The arithmetic operation symbols +, -, * and so on, are defined for all the integer types and may therefore be used for these operations in variables of type `char`. If c has type `char`, we can write

```
c = c * 3 - 5;
```

This may seem surprising at first. The type `char` is mainly used to store printable (or non-printable) characters, so we would not expect arithmetic operations of this kind to be performed with `char`. Upon reflection, however, we can see that what is stored in a variable of type `char` is the *code* for the character we want to store, and the code is, of course, an integer. In certain situations it might be natural to use arithmetic operations to handle character codes. If, for example, we want to write out all the lower-case letters from 'a' to 'z', we might have the statement

```
for (char c = 'a'; c <= 'z'; c++)
  cout << c;
```

The expression c++ increases the character code in c by one which means that c
will store the next letter.

That the type **char** should be counted as one of the integer types indicates
something even more surprising, namely, that character literals are in fact a kind of
integer literal. If we write

```
c = 'a';
```

this will mean that the variable c should be assigned the character code for the letter
a. Since this character code has the number 97, we could just as well have written

```
c = 97;
```

This is quite correct but may not be easy to recognize. The use of character literals
is, therefore, an alternative way of writing integers. A character literal has type
char and so is an integer. The character literals '+', '5', 'ñ', '\33' and '\\', for
example, are equivalent to the integer literals 43, 53, 241, 27 and 92, respectively.

To demonstrate that the type **char** is an integer type, we will first look at a
function where the values of this type are used for indexing. The function
determines whether two texts are each other's anagram. (Anagrams are created by
jumbling the letters in a word or phrase so that another word or phrase is formed.)
The function will have as parameters, called s1 and s2, the two texts to be
examined, and the function will return a result value of type **bool**. Two integer
arrays, f1 and f2, used internally in the function, serve to count the number of
different letters in the two texts. The character codes for the different characters in
the texts are used as an index in f1 and f2. Because there are 256 different
character codes, the arrays f1 and f2 must each have 256 components. As an
example, let us take the letters 'a' and 'é'. The character code for 'a' is 97 and for
'é' it is 233. The components f1[97] and f1[233] will then contain the
number of lower case *a*s and lower case *é*s, respectively, in the text s1. When the
two arrays f1 and f2 have been filled, we can decide whether s1 and s2 are each
other's anagram simply by comparing f1 and f2. If they are the same, s1 and s2
are each other's anagram. The function looks like this:

```
bool anagram(char s1[], char s2[])
{
  int f1[256], f2[256], i;
  // Put f1 and f2 to zero
  for (i=0; i<256; i++)
    f1[i] = f2[i] = 0;
```

```
// Count the number of different characters in s1
for (i=0; s1[i]; i++)
  f1[(unsigned char)s1[i]]++;
// Count the number of different characters in s2
for (i=0; s2[i]; i++)
  f2[(unsigned char)s2[i]]++;
// Compare f1 and f2
for (i=0; i<256; i++)
  if (f1[i] != f2[i])
  return false;
return true;
}
```

Let us comment on some of the details in this function. The statement f1[i]=f2[i]=0; means that both f1[i] and f2[i] are set to 0. (Assignment of values goes from right to left.) The statement

```
f1[(unsigned char)s1[i]]++;
```

also needs explaining. The expression s1[i] has type **char** and is component number i in the text s1. This component is, as we now know, a character code – an integer. Because it is not clear whether type **char** is unsigned or not, we do not know whether the value of s1[i] lies in the interval from −128 to 127 or the interval from 0 to 255. If we want to use the value of s1[i] as index in the array f1, we must ensure that s1[i] is understood to be a number in the interval from 0 to 255. This we can do by writing (**unsigned char**) in front of s1[i]. (We are actually making a *type conversion* from type **char** to **unsigned char**. We will be discussing type conversions in greater detail later.) The expression (**unsigned char**)s1[i] is therefore a number in the interval from 0 to 255, and we use this number as index in the array f1. The component we then get is increased by one.

There is a standardized header file limits.h which contains information about the different standard types for integers, including type **int**. (If you use a compiler which follows the draft standard, this file is called climits.) The two constants INT_MIN and INT_MAX indicate the least and greatest number, respectively, which can be stored by the type **int**. (There are corresponding constants for the other integer types.) A test program to determine which numbers can be stored in a computer can look like this

```
# include <limits.h>
# include <iostream.h>
main()
{
  cout << "The smallest int is: " << INT_MIN << endl;
  cout << "The largest int is: " << INT_MAX << endl;
}
```

5.2 Floating point types

5.2.1 Storing real numbers in a computer

In science and engineering, to avoid using too many zeros in a number, standard notation is often used for writing very large and very small numbers. In standard notation the numbers 350 000 000 and 0.000 000 73, for example, are written as:

0.35×10^9 0.73×10^{-6}, respectively

The same technique is employed for storing real numbers in a computer but the base 2 is used instead of 10. The decimal number 10.5 can be translated into binary form, giving the binary number 1010.1, and this can be written as

0.10101×2^{100}

The first part, 0.10101, is usually called the *mantissa* and the second part, 100, the *exponent*. Both the mantissa and exponent are written as binary numbers (the exponent 100 meaning 4 in base 10).

When a real number is stored in a computer, its mantissa and exponent can each use a certain number of bits, the numbers varying from computer to computer. In addition, one bit is used to store the sign of the number.

The principle of storing real numbers is demonstrated in the following example, where we assume that the decimal number 10.5 is stored in a computer that uses 32 bits to store real numbers; the first of the 32 bits holds the sign (0 for plus, 1 for minus), the next eight bits are used for the exponent, and the remaining 23 bits are used to store the mantissa. The integral part of the mantissa does not need to be stored because it is always zero. (Sometimes, the first digit in the mantissa is not stored either because it is always possible to adjust the number so that this digit is 1.)

```
t exponent      mantissa
0 00000100      10101000000000000000000
```

It should be noted that the details of storing real numbers vary considerably from one computer to another. This example merely shows the general principles.

Note that the exponent can also be negative when a small number is stored. For example, the number 0.06125 (= 1/16) would be stored as follows, using the same format as the previous example:

```
0 11111101 10000000000000000000000
```

Here, the value of the exponent (−3) is expressed in the two's complement form.

This method of storing real numbers means that some numbers, such as the example of 10.5 above, can be stored exactly, whereas others, such as 0.6, cannot.

If the number −0.6 is to be stored in a computer using the form outlined above, the pattern of bits would look like this:

```
1  00000000  10011001100110011001100
```

The bit pattern in the mantissa should be repeated infinitely many times, but only 23 bits are available.

The number of significant decimal figures obtained depends on the number of bits used to store the mantissa. (It takes, on average, 3.32 bits per decimal figure.) The number of bits used for the exponent determines the largest and smallest numbers (excluding zero) that can be stored. The number zero is usually handled specially and stored exactly, using a particular pattern of bits.

The type **double** uses the above technique to store real numbers. This means that the number of significant figures is the same over the whole range of possible numbers and that the position of the decimal point 'floats'. It is said the numbers are stored as floating point numbers and that **double** is a floating point type.

Storing real numbers is therefore complicated but it is reassuring to know that the programmer need not worry about the details of what is happening. However, he or she should be aware of the accuracy the decimal numbers retain. Furthermore, the programmer should remember that real numbers are not always stored in their exact form, that is, care must be taken when determining whether two real numbers are equal. Even if they are equal in principle, they can still differ by one bit in their mantissas, and the computer will then see them as unequal.

5.2.2   Predefined floating point types

There are three floating point types in C++: **float**, **double** and **long double**. They are all stored according to the principles described in the previous section. Exactly how many bits are required is not specified in the draft standard, and will depend on the installation used. The type **float** is often stored in 32 bits and the type double in 64 bits. The floating point type most often used is that of **double** because in many compilers **float** only offers accuracy to six or seven significant figures.

The header file float.h (or cfloat if your compiler follows the draft standard) contains miscellaneous information about the different standard types for real numbers. If we want to find out the number of significant figures and the largest

Floating point types
•   `float`
•   `double`
•   `long double`

and least number which can be stored for type **double**, the constants DBL_DIG, DBL_MAX and DBL_MIN, respectively, can be used. (For the type **float**, the corresponding constants are FLT_DIG, FLT_MAX and FLT_MIN; for the type **long double** the constants are LDBL_DIG, LDBL_MAX and LDBL_MIN.) This is demonstrated in the following test program.

```
# include <float.h>
# include <iostream.h>
main()
{
  cout << "Characteristics for type double" << endl;
  cout << "Sig.Figs: " << DBL_DIG << endl;
  cout << "Largest number: " << DBL_MAX << endl;
  cout << "Least number: " << DBL_MIN << endl;
}
```

5.3 The `sizeof` operator

If we want to find out how many bytes an expression or type consists of, we can use the operator **sizeof**. We write either

```
sizeof expression
```

or

```
sizeof (typename)
```

If we suppose that type **int** consists of four bytes and type **double** of eight bytes, then the following expressions will give the values 1, 4 and 8, respectively.

```
sizeof (char)
sizeof (unsigned int)
sizeof (double)
```

The **sizeof** operator can also be appplied to expressions. We can write

```
cout<<"The variable k is " << sizeof k <<" bytes";
cout<<"The expression a+b is " << sizeof (a+b) <<" bytes";
```

If the **sizeof** operator is used in an array, it will give the number of bytes for the whole array. If, for example, an array f has 10 elements of type **double** and type **double** is stored in eight bytes, the following expression will give a result of 80.

```
sizeof f
```

A common trick to find out the number of elements in an array is to write

```
sizeof f / sizeof f[0]
```

where the length of the whole array is quite simply divided by the length of one element.

5.4   Pointers

5.4.1   Primary memory addresses

When a program is run, the program variables will be in the computer's primary memory. We saw from Chapter 1 that the primary memory consists of a number of memory cells, each cell being made up of eight bits or one byte. These memory cells are numbered, with each cell having a unique number called a *primary memory address* or, quite simply, an *address*. A variable can consist of one or more memory cells (bytes). How many bytes a variable may have will depend on the type of the variable. The type **char**, for instance, normally takes up one byte and the type **int**, two or four bytes. As a variable lies in the primary memory it can be said to have a primary memory address. This address is the same as the address of that variable memory cell which has the lowest address.

As we know, the size of the primary memory depends on the computer. Its physical construction may also be different. But from the programmer's point of view, the primary memory consists logically of a memory, which, in principle, is infinitely large and where each byte has a unique address.

Numbering of the cells begins at zero and continues upwards. The operating system and the computer's hardware takes care of the generating process from the logical memory the programmer sees, to the computer's physical primary memory. The size of memory addresses which can be indicated depends on the computer's construction and the characteristics of the operating system. Modern operating systems (Windows 95, Windows NT and Unix, for example) permit 32-bit addressing, which means that the largest memory address that can be indicated is equal to $2^{32} - 1 = 4294967295$. Older computers and operating systems may be more limited. MS-DOS, for example, uses 20-bit addresses which are put together by combining two 16-bit words. Primary memory addresses are usually indicated as octal or hexadecimal numbers. For example, the largest memory address which can be indicated with 32 bits can be written, in hexadecimal form as ffffffff, or in octal form as 37777777777.

In a C++ program we can work with a special kind of variable which contains primary memory addresses. These are called *pointers*. Suppose, for example, that we have a variable k of type **int** and that this variable happens to have the primary address 00000561234 (octal form). If we now have another variable, with the name p and this variable contains the number 00000561234, then we say that p *points to* k.

Modern programs are normally designed to be loaded anywhere in the memory when they are to be executed. Programs do not have to be found at a special, predetermined place in the memory in order to function. We say that programs like this are *relocatable*, and we also use this term for the variables in the program. A variable can therefore land in different places in the primary memory and have different addresses every time the program is run. Only in special cases is it meaningful to give an absolute primary memory address of `00000561234` in a program. (The only occasion when this might be necessary is in the writing of system software, such as drive routines.) When values are to be given to pointer variables, therefore, only what the pointer variables point to should be indicated and not exact addresses. We say that we work with *relative addresses*. As a program is loaded to be run, the loader will automatically convert the relative addresses to absolute addresses valid for that particular run.

5.4.2   Pointer variables

Let us now look at our first example of the use of pointers. The syntax used for declaring pointer variables is rather unusual. To declare a pointer variable `pi`, which is allowed to point to an **int**, we write

```
int *pi;
```

The asterisk shows that the operation involves a pointer. C++ distinguishes between pointers for different types. A pointer variable declared as a pointer for the type **int** may not, for example, point to a value of type **double** or **char**. Two further pointer variables, one for type **double** and another for type **char**, are declared here:

```
double *pd;
char    *pc;
```

The & operator is used to find the address for a particular variable. For example, we can declare a variable k of type **int** and let the pointer `pi` point to k:

```
int k = 15;
pi = &k;
```

The operator & can be read as 'address for'. Figure 5.1 illustrates this.

Figure 5.1

Several pointers may point to the same variable. We can write

```
int *pi2;
pi2 = pi;
```

The value in the variable pi is a pointer for k, that is, the primary memory address for k. This value has here been assigned to the variable pi2. We then have the situation shown in Figure 5.2 (we would naturally have arrived at the same situation if we had instead written pi2=&k;).

The * operator should be used to get at whatever a pointer points to. For example, the following statement can be given to write out the variable that pi points to.

```
cout << *pi; // writes out 15
```

The * operator can also be used to the left of the equality sign when making an assignment. We can write the following statement which assigns a value of 20 to the variable k:

```
*pi = 20;
```

Note the difference between changing a pointer and changing what the pointer points to. If we have the following lines, where pi points to k and pi2 to n

```
int k = 15, n;
int *pi, *pi2;
pi   = &k;
pi2  = &n;
*pi2 = *pi;
```

the last line will assign a value of 15 to the variable n. If the last line had instead been

```
pi2 = pi;
```

the pointer pi2 itself would have been changed and the situation in Figure 5.2 would have been the result.

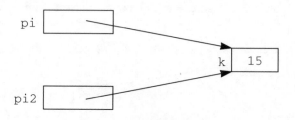

Figure 5.2

Several pointer variables can be declared on the same line. We wrote

```
int *pi, *pi2;
```

Note that the asterisk must be repeated. If an asterisk had not been written in front of pi2, the variable name, pi2, would have been understood as a common **int**. Declarations of common variables and pointer variables can also be combined on the same line. Of course, the different variables can also be initialized in a declaration. The first four lines of the above example could have been written in a single declaration with initializations:

```
int k=15, n, *pi=&k, *pi2=&n;
```

Note also that an asterisk can be used in two different ways; these should not be confused! When a pointer variable is declared, the asterisk is used to indicate that the variable should be a pointer but an asterisk can also be used as an operator to get at the value a pointer points to.

Sometimes a pointer variable may not be pointing at anything for the time being, in which case a value of zero is put inside the pointer. (Integers may not really be assigned to pointers without a type conversion but the constant 0 is an exception.)

```
pi = 0;
```

A pointer which contains a value of zero is called a *null* pointer. When variables are declared in C++, they are uninitialized as long as an explicit initialization is not made at the same time; this also applies to pointer variables. Thus, pointer variables are not automatically null when they are declared.

There may also be pointers which point to constants. Suppose that we make the following declarations:

```
int k;            // changeable int
const int c=100;  // constant int
const int *pc;    // pointer for constant int
int *pi;          // pointer for changeable int
```

Then the following is allowed:

```
pc = &c;
pc = &k;
```

but this is not allowed:

```
pi = &c;  // Error! pi may not point to a constant
*pc = 0;  // Error! pc points to a constant
```

Finally, note the difference in the declaration below, where a constant pointer, cp, is declared.

```
int *const cp = &k;
```

The pointer cp may not itself be changed as it always points to the variable k; but k may be changed via the pointer.

Pointers	
type *p;	p has the type 'pointer to *type*'
p = &v;	p is assigned the address for v
*p	means 'what p points to'
p1 = p2	p1 will point to the same thing as p2
*p1 = *p2	what p1 points to will be changed

5.4.3 Pointers and arrays

We discussed arrays in Section 2.7. Arrays and pointers are closely connected to each other in C++. Every time we work with arrays we make use of pointers. In this section we will attempt to describe how they are connected. We begin by declaring an array where the elements are of type **float**:

```
float f[4];
```

The variable f has the type 'array with 4 elements of type **float**'. Suppose now that we wish to declare a pointer which can point to the array f; the problem is then to indicate the right type for the pointer. A pointer for an array can be considered to be a pointer for the first element of the array, so the pointer's type can be given as a pointer for the element's type. A pointer with the type 'pointer to **float**' can therefore point to the array f. We will now declare this pointer:

```
float *pd;
```

Then pd can be made to point to the first element in f (element number 0):

```
pd = &f[0];
```

We first choose element number 0, using indexing, and then we apply the address operator &. There is, however, a much easier way of obtaining the address of the array's first element. We simply write:

```
pd = f;
```

At first glance, this may seem strange. What is on the left of the equality sign is a pointer and what is to the right of it is an array. Surely you can't assign a whole array to a pointer! The secret lies in the fact that array names are treated rather specially in C++. As soon as an array name occurs in an expression, there is an automatic type conversion to a pointer, and the pointer will point to the first element in the array. If the array has the type 'array with an *n* number of T', the automatic conversion will result in the type 'pointer to T'. In the assignment above there is, therefore, an automatic type conversion to the type 'pointer to **float**', the same type as the variable pd has. The assignment above is then correct, since the type is the same on both sides of the equality sign. In Figure 5.3 we see how this looks after the assignment has occurred.

We can now get at the first element in the array via the pointer pd. We can write out, for example:

```
cout << *pd;   // Write out element number 0 in f
```

If we want to get at another element in the array via the pointer pd, we must take care to point to the desired element. We may write, for example:

```
cout << *(pd+3);   // Write out element number 3 in f
```

It may seem strange that the expression pd+3 points to element number 3 in the array. The variable pd, of course, contains the primary memory address of the array f. If we suppose that the type **float** is stored with four bytes in the computer, then pd+3 should point somewhere to the middle of the first element of f. That this is not the case is due to the fact that C++ makes use of what is normally called *pointer arithmetic*. If there is an expression of the form p+n, n+p or p-n, where p is a pointer and n an integer, then n is interpreted as the number of *steps* and n is automatically multiplied by the length of the step. The length of a step depends on what the pointer p is pointing to. If the pointer points to a **char**, the step is equal to 1; if the pointer points to something that is two bytes long, the step will be equal to 2, and so on. If we suppose that type **float** is stored with four bytes, the expression pd+3 will mean 'the address which is in pd plus 12'. If pd points to the array's first element, therefore, pd+3 will be the address of the element number 3 (the fourth element) in the array. The expression *(pd+3) also means 'that which is where the address pd+3 points', that is, element number 3 in the array.

The difference between two pointers can also be calculated. Suppose that there are two pointers p1 and p2 which both point to the same type. Then we can

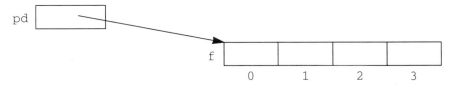

Figure 5.3

calculate the expression p1-p2, the result of which is an integer which indicates the number of steps between what the pointers point to. When working with pointer arithmetic, we never need to know how many bytes a step represents. The compiler will automatically take care of this.

Let us now look at another strange thing. If an expression is written in the form x[n], the compiler will interpret this as if *(x+n) had been written. Therefore, we could also have written out element number 3 in the array f by giving the statement

```
cout << pd[3];    // Write out element number 3 in f
```

When an expression of the form x[n] is written, where x is an array, an automatic type conversion to a pointer is performed. If x has the type 'an array with an *n* number of T', then a conversion to the type 'pointer to T' will occur, as before. This means that the four expressions f[3], *(f+3), 3[f] and *(3+f), are identical. All of them will give element number 3 in the array f.

When programming in C++, we often use pointers for indexing when we want to run through an array. If, for example, we want to set all the elements in the array f to zero, we can of course do this with the statements:

```
for (int i=0; i<4; i++)
   f[i] = 0;
```

But this can be done just as easily with pointers:

```
for (float *p=f; p < f+4; p++)
   *p = 0;
```

The pointer p is initialized to point to the first element in f. Figure 5.4 shows how this looks just after p is initialized and before the first round has been run through. At the end of each round, p is increased by one step (pointer arithmetic comes in here). Thus in the first round, p will point to f[0], in the second round to f[1], and so on. The condition for continuing another round is that p is *less* than f+4. But since the array only consists of four elements, the last one will have the number 3, and there will not be an element number 4. As a result the last round to be run through is the one where p points to f[3].

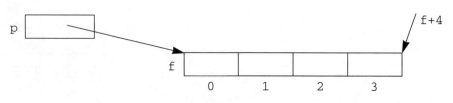

Figure 5.4

We have seen that when the name of an array occurs in an expression there is an automatic type conversion to a pointer, and this also applies to function calls. We demonstrated, in Chapter 4, page 102, how a function with the name sum calculated the sum of elements in an array of integers. The function sum has two parameters, an array and an integer which indicates the number of elements. If we have an array with the declaration

```
int b[] = {1,2,3,4,1,2,3,4,1,2};
```

we can calculate and write out the sum of the elements with the statement

```
cout << "The sum is " << sum(b,10) << endl;
```

When the function is called, the first argument b will be automatically converted to a pointer for type **int** and this pointer will point to the first element in the array b. The function sum will therefore get as first parameter, not a copy of the whole array b but a *pointer* to it. This accords with what was discussed in Chapter 4, namely, that arrays are always transferred as a kind of reference parameter. Here is an alternative version of the function sum:

```
int sum(int *a, int n)    // Sums the elements in a
{
   int s = 0;
   for (int *ip=a; ip < a+n; ip++)
     s += *ip;
   return s;
}
```

In the list of parameters, **int** a[] could have been written (as was done earlier in the book) instead of **int** *a. Both ways of writing mean exactly the same where function parameters are concerned, namely, that the parameter is a pointer to an element of type **int**.

The constant 10 in the call of sum indicates that the array has ten elements. When writing programs, it is often desirable to make them easy to change. To insert constants in this way can, therefore, be dangerous. It would be easy to forget to change the constant 10 if later the array b had to be changed to a different length. The operator **sizeof** (see Section 5.3) is therefore used instead to calculate the number of elements in b. We then write:

```
cout << "The sum is "
        << sum(b,sizeof b/sizeof b[0]) << endl;
```

The observant reader will realize that no conversion of b to pointers occurs in the expression **sizeof** b; instead, the number of bytes in the whole array is calculated.

Pointers and arrays

```
type a[...];
```

- The array name a is automatically converted to the type *type* *
  in expressions, and the value becomes a pointer to the array's
  first element.
- Applicable to assignments and function calls, for example.
- Arrays as parameters can either be declared as *type* a[] or as
  type *a
- *Pointer arithmetic*: p+n means the pointer value p plus n *steps*
- *(p+n) is the same thing as p[n]
- *(a+n) is the same thing as a[n]

In certain cases, it can be practical to have recursive functions which in turn have pointers to arrays as parameters. To demonstrate this, we will write an alternative version of the function sum. As before, the first parameter, a, is a pointer to the array in question and the other parameter, n, indicates how many elements there are in the array.

```
int sum(int *a, int n)   // sums the elements in a
{
  if (n <= 0)
    return 0;
  else
    return *a + sum(a+1, n-1);
}
```

The recursive idea is simple. The trivial case is that the array has no elements, in which case the sum will be equal to zero. If there are elements in the array, the sum of these can be calculated by adding the value of the first element, that which a points to, to the sum of all the other elements in the array. The expression a+1 is a pointer to the second element in the array. The function sum thus calls itself recursively in order to calculate the sum of the elements in an array which is one element shorter than the original one.

We shall demonstrate another example in which recursion is used in connection with arrays. A function which carried out a binary search in a sorted array was shown on page 103. A new, recursive variant of this function will now be constructed. The new version will have three parameters: the first will be the number desired; the second parameter, a pointer to the array's first element; and the third, a pointer to the array's last element. As a result, we allow the function to give a pointer to that element in the array where the desired number is. If this is not in the array, we will let the function return a value of 0. If, for example, we have an array b with 100 elements, we can get a pointer to the element which contains the value 317 by making the call:

```
int *p = bin_search (317, b, b+99);
```

The function will look like this:

```
int *bin_search (int searched, int *first, int *last)
{
  if (first > last)   // The array has no elements
    return 0;
  int *middle = first + (last-first)/2;
  if (searched < *middle)
    return bin_search (searched, first, middle-1);
  else if (searched > *middle)
    return bin_search (searched, middle+1, last);
  else   // Equal, the desired number lies in the middle
    return middle;
}
```

If the pointer to the array's first element points to the right of the pointer to the array's last element, the array will not have elements and the desired number cannot therefore be found. If the array contains elements, we let the pointer middle point to the element lying in the middle of the array. We then decide whether the desired number lies in the array's left-hand half, its right-hand half, or whether it is the same as the middle element. If the last case is true, we have found the number we were looking for and can return a pointer to it. In the recursive calls of bin_search, middle-1 means a pointer to the element lying to the left of the middle element and middle+1, a pointer to the element lying to the right of the middle element.

5.4.4 **Pointers and text strings**

Text strings were discussed in Section 3.3. We stated there that text strings were stored in character arrays with the type 'arrays with *n* number of **char**'. We can, for example, make the declarations

```
char txt[5];
char name[] = "Sara";
```

The variable name will automatically get a length of 5 and be initialized with the text "Sara", which is terminated with a null character. An automatic type conversion to a pointer is performed when the name of a character array occurs in an expression, exactly as for other arrays. For character arrays, this pointer gets the type 'pointer to **char**', that is **char** *. We can therefore write

```
char *p;
p = name;
cout << p << endl;      // Sara is written out
cout << p+2 << endl;    // ra is written out
cout << *(p+2) << endl; // r is written out
```

Figure 5.5 illustrates this. Note that when the output operator << has an operand of the type 'pointer to **char**' as on lines three and four above, it writes out all of the text string the operand points to. If separate characters are to be written out, the * operator may be used, as on the last line.

There can also be pointers to constant text strings:

```
const char *q = "Hanna";
```

A text string literal, such as "Hanna", has the type 'array with *n* number of **char**' but when it occurs in an expression as it does here, it is automatically converted into the type 'pointer to **char**'. This means that the pointer q will point to the text string "Hanna". The pointer q is one of several variables in our program but the text "Hanna" is itself at another position in the primary memory.

Since the pointer q has the type 'pointer to a *constant* **char**', what q points to cannot be changed. But what would happen if we used the pointer p instead, which has the type 'pointer to **char**'?

```
char *p = "Hanna";
*(p+1) = 'i';         // Doubtful!!
```

It is not clear what happens here. In the draft standard it is stated that the result of an attempt to change the contents of a text literal remains undefined. Different C++ compilers may function differently. The operation may work but it may also result in an execution fault.

Pointers are often used instead of indexing when working with text strings. As the first example of this we will write our own version of the function strlen, which calculates the length of a text string. If the variable p, as above, points to the

Figure 5.5

text string `"Sara"`, the call `strlen(p)`, for example, should give a value of 4 as result, and the call `strlen("C++")` a value of 3. The function looks like this:

```
int strlen (const char *s)      // Gives the length of s
{
  for (const char *p=s; *p++;)
    ;
  return p-1-s;
}
```

The parameter s has the type 'pointer to a constant **char**'. This means that the function cannot change the text, the length of which is to be calculated. But the function can be called with pointers to constant and non-constant texts. In the **for** statement a help pointer, p, initialized to s, is used; that is, it points from the beginning to the same text string as the parameter s. If, for example, we suppose that the function is called with a pointer to the text `"Sara"` as parameter, p will point to this text. This was illustrated in Figure 5.5.

In the **for** statement, the third part inside the parentheses is empty and so is the statement performed at every round. This means that the only step to be performed in the **for** statement occurs in conjunction with the calculation of the test expression `*p++`. Expressions in this form are very common in connection with the handling of text. In the case of unary operators (operators with only one operand), those *after* the operand have a higher priority than those *before* the operand. In the expression `*p++`, therefore, `++` has a higher priority than `*`. So the partial expression p++ is calculated first. This expression increases the pointer p by one so that p will point to the next character in the text string, that is, to the character 'a'. Note, however, that the resulting value of the partial expression p++ is the old value for p, that is, a pointer to the character 'S'. The operator `*` is then applied to this old value and the result is the character 'S'. Since the character code for 'S' is not equal to zero, the result of the test expression `*p++` is understood as 'true', and the **for** statement will be performed for another round.

This process is repeated time after time. At the beginning of every round, the pointer p is increased by 1, so that it points to the next character. The character that p pointed to in the previous round is then tested. If it is 'false', that is, equal to zero, the **for** statement is terminated. Since the text string is terminated by a null character, the **for** statement will stop in the position where p has just been changed so that it points to the character after the null character. Then p-1 must point to the null character. The length of the text string can then be calculated by calculating the difference between p-1 and the pointer s, which will still point to the beginning of the text string.

Here is another example of a function for the handling of text strings where pointers are used instead of indexing. We will write our own version of the function `strcpy` which copies one text string to another. This function has two parameters. The first, s1, is a pointer to the character array to which the text string will be copied and the second, s2, is a pointer to the text string which is to be copied. Since it should not be possible for the function strcpy to change the text to be copied, s2 can be declared as a pointer to a *constant* **char**. The function looks like this:

```
void strcpy (char *s1, const char *s2)
{
  while (*s1++ = *s2++)
    ;
}
```

An empty statement is also performed with this function at every round of the repetition statement. Let us suppose that strcpy(txt, "ab") has been called. The copying of all characters occurs in conjunction with the calculation of the test expression in parentheses. This test expression is an assignment. First, the expression to the left of the equality sign is calculated. This expression first increases the pointer s1 by 1 but the result of the expression is the character s1 was pointing to before the increase, that is, txt[0]. The expression to the right of the equality sign is similarly calculated. The pointer s2 is increased by 1 but the result of the expression is the character s2 was pointing to, that is, the character 'a'. As a result, at the beginning of the first round, the character 'a' will be copied to txt[0]. The resulting value of the assignment is the assigned value, the character 'a', which is understood as 'true'. One round of the **while** statement is therefore performed. Similarly, the character 'b' will be assigned to txt[1] at the beginning of the second round. When the function tests whether a third round should be performed, the third character in the text string "ab", that is, the null character, will be copied to txt[2]. The **while** statement will now be terminated since this character is understood as 'false'. As a result, a third round will not be performed.

Here are examples of calls to the function strcpy.

```
strcpy(txt, q);        // "Hanna" is copied to txt
strcpy(txt, name);     // "Sara" is copied to txt
strcpy(txt+4, " Maria");
cout << txt << endl;   // "Sara Maria" is written out
```

The elements of an array may have any type whatever. It is permissible to have arrays where the separate elements are pointers. This is useful when constructing tables with different texts, as in the following example.

```
const char *mess[4] =
            {"Put on your safety belt", "Start the motor",
             "Release the handbrake", "Close the door"};
```

The variable mess is an array consisting of four elements where each element has the type 'pointer to constant **char**'. Figure 5.6 illustrates this. We note, for

Figure 5.6

example, that the element mess[0] contains a pointer to the text string "Put on your safety belt" and that mess[1] contains a pointer to the text string "Start the motor". Note that the four text strings pointed out automatically have a null character last, as usual. If we want to write out a particular message, we can simply index in the array mess:

```
cout << mess[i] << endl;
```

If necessary, this can be written out with the help of a function

```
void write(const char *pp[], int i)
{
  cout << pp[i] << endl;
}
```

Message number 2 can, for example, be written out with the call write(mess,2);. The type of the parameter has been indicated here as '**const char** *pp[]' but we know that a type conversion automatically occurs when the name of an array is indicated in the call of a function, sending a pointer to the array as a parameter for the function. A pointer of this kind has, as we have seen, the type 'pointer to the array's element type'. Because the element type in the array mess is '**const char** *', the function write will get a pointer of the type 'pointer to **const char** *' as parameter. The parameter pp is therefore *a pointer to a pointer* and can be declared, alternatively:

```
void write(const char **pp, int i)
  as earlier
```

These two ways of indicating the type of the parameter pp are equivalent.

5.4.5   Memory allocation

In order to work with a variable, there must be a space reserved for the variable in the computer's primary memory. When we reserve memory space for a variable, we usually say that we *allocate* memory space; when memory space is no longer needed for a variable, we say that we *deallocate* this memory space. We normally speak of a variable's *life*, this being the time that memory space is allocated for the variable. When a variable has been declared in the usual way, memory space will be allocated and deallocated *automatically*. But the programmer need not worry about this. For variables declared within a function (or local variables) and function parameters, memory space is automatically allocated each time the function is called, and automatically deallocated each time a return from the function occurs. A function parameter or a local variable will, therefore, only have a life for the duration of a particular call. Each time a function is called, memory space is once again allocated for the parameters and local variables. On the other hand, a variable declared at the outermost level in a program, outside all functions, will have a life as long as the program is being executed.

For the great majority of cases, the programmer will know how many variables are needed. The variables can then be declared in the usual way and the problem of memory allocation can be ignored, since it will happen automatically. For some applications, however, it will not be known in advance how many variables will be necessary, nor of what size they need to be. One example is when we need an array but do not know the exact size when writing the program. Another example is when we work with *dynamic data structures* that increase or decrease during execution. Examples of such dynamic data structures are lists, stacks and trees. (Dynamic data structures will be dealt with in Chapter 12).

In our examples up to now, we have seen that pointers point to other variables. The variables pointed to have been variables which we declared in the usual way. Pointers are very useful to us, but not simply because they can point to ordinary variables. Why make a detour with a pointer when it is much simpler to use the variable's name? Pointers prove particularly useful when memory space is allocated dynamically, for they are used to point to the memory space which has been allocated.

To allocate memory space, a **new** expression is used. This consists of the reserved word **new** followed by a type name. To allocate memory for a variable of type **double**, for example, **new double** is written. The result of a **new** expression is a pointer to the allocated memory space. The type of pointer will correspond to the type of the memory space. If memory is allocated for a variable of type **double**, the **new** expression will return a result of the type 'pointer to **double**'. This result can be placed into a suitable pointer variable. We can write, for example

```
double *pd;
pd = new double;
```

The variable for which memory space is allocated does not have a name. The only way of getting to the memory space, therefore, is via a pointer. To assign a value to the allocated memory space, we can write

```
*pd = 2.5; // Initialize the allocated space
```

If memory space is to be allocated for an array, the number of elements desired can be indicated in the **new** expression. In the following lines an array consisting of n integers is allocated. The number n is read as input data.

```
int n;
cin >> n;
int *pi = new int[n];
```

The allocated memory space will be uninitialized (as long as objects with constructors are not allocated; a discussion of which occurs later in the book). If we wish to set all the n elements in the array to zero, we can write

```
for (int i=0; i<n; i++)
  pi[i] = 0;
```

Variables that have been allocated dynamically will have a life until their memory space has been expressly deallocated, and this can be done with a **delete** expression. To deallocate the memory the pointer pd points to, we can write

```
delete pd;
```

If we wish to deallocate a memory space that has been allocated for an array, we should use the alternative form

```
delete[] pi;
```

(Note that the square brackets may be left out but, generally speaking, it is important for them to be used when the allocated array contains objects with their own destructors. Otherwise the destructors will not be called for all the objects that are deallocated. Destructors will be dealt with later in the book.) In this case, all of the array pointed to by pi and consisting of n **int**, is deallocated. The pointer in a **delete** expression will have got its value earlier from a **new** expression. The number of bytes deallocated automatically will be exactly the same as the number allocated earlier. (This is possible since the system automatically registers the number of bytes of memory space allocated and the pointer value which points to the allocated memory space.) It is also permissible to have a pointer with a value of 0 in a **delete** expression; in this case nothing happens.

As an example of the allocation of arrays, we will look at a function read_line which can be used to read one line at a time from the keyboard. We saw earlier that input could either be effected with the input operator >>, or with the

Memory allocation	
`p = `**`new`**` type;`	Allocates space for a variable of the type `type`. p points to the allocated space.
`p = `**`new`**` type[n];`	Allocates space for an array with n elements of the type `type`. p points to the array.
`delete`` p;`	Deallocates what p points to (not arrays).
`delete``[] p;`	Deallocates the array p points to.

help of the standard function `cin.getline`. We could, for example, write `cin >> a`, where a must be an array sufficiently large to accommodate the text read in. The new function `read_line`, which we will now write, does not require an array to have been declared in advance. Instead, the function reads a line and then itself allocates a memory space exactly large enough to accommodate the line read in. The characters that are read in are put in the allocated memory space, and, as a result, the function `read_line` gives a pointer to the allocated memory space. Here is an example of a call of this function.

```
char *s;
cout << "What is your name? ";
s = read_line();
cout << "Hello " << s << endl;
```

The function `read_line` looks like this

```
char *read_line()   // Reads a line
{
  char temp[1000];
  cin.getline(temp, 1000);
  char *res = new char[strlen(temp)+1];
  strcpy(res, temp);
  return res;
}
```

The standard function `cin.getline` is called first to read in a whole line from the keyboard. The input line is then placed in the local variable `temp`, an array big enough to hold lines of up to 1000 characters. An array as big as the text to be read is now allocated. The length of the text is calculated with the function `strlen`. This length must be increased by 1 in order to accommodate the null character, which comes last. Finally, the text that has been read is copied from the local array `temp` to the allocated memory space.

5.4.6 Common errors

To program using pointers is not always a simple matter. It places big demands on the programmer, and mistakes are easily made. Such mistakes may be discovered during compiling; it is possible, for example, to confuse a pointer value with the value the pointer points to, resulting in a type error. However, a number of mistakes may not be discovered during compiling, and may then cause problems later when the program is being executed. The following are common errors:

- using a pointer which is uninitialized or contains a value of 0;
- using a *lingering pointer*, which points to a memory space, allocated earlier but now deallocated;
- allocating new memory space repeatedly, without deallocating memory space no longer needed.

Here is an example of the first kind of error, often made by inexperienced programmers. Since the name of an array is automatically converted to a pointer in an expression, it may be assumed that it doesn't matter whether a variable is declared as an array or as a pointer. Look at the following program lines:

```
char a[10];
char *p;
*a = 'X';  // OK! a[0] = 'X'
*p = 'X';  // Execution error!
```

Since initializing of the pointer p does not occur when it is declared, it will contain an undefined, worthless value. When an attempt is made on the last line to copy the character 'X' to the place where p points, there is of course an error, since p may be pointing anywhere.

As an example of the problem with lingering pointers we will look at the following, incorrect version of the function read_line from the previous section.

```
char *read_line()    // Incorrect function!!!
{
  char temp[1000];
  cin.getline(temp, 1000);
  return temp;       // Return of lingering pointer
}
```

Here, too, a line is read in with the use of the standard function cin.getline, and the characters read in are placed in the array temp. The function read_line should as a result give a pointer to the characters read in. Since these are now in the array temp, we try to get a result by quite simply giving a pointer to this array. This can be compiled and, possibly, also test run. But the problem is that the array temp has a life that stops as soon as the function call is terminated. This means that the pointer given as a result points to a memory space no longer reserved for the array temp but which later, in the program can be used to store other variables and input data. If we were to try to change something in the line read in using the pointer obtained as a result from read_line, we could really make a mess of things, and the program might well behave in the most unexpected ways.

The third kind of common error can be illustrated by the following program lines, where the function read_line (the correct version) is called again and again.

```
while(true)
{
  cout << "Write input data";
  s = read_line();
  // Make calculations
  ...
}
```

A program containing these lines may certainly function excellently. However, problems may arise if it is designed to be in continuous operation. With every new round, memory is allocated for the line read in but the allocated memory is not returned anywhere. If the program is in operation for a long time, the accessible memory space must end sooner or later. The result will be an execution fault.

5.4.7 Pointers and references – a comparison

In C++ there is a language construct called a *reference*. References are closely related to pointers, and the inexperienced programmer may easily confuse them. So let us try to clarify the two terms.

A reference can either be declared as an ordinary variable, or as a function parameter; this was discussed in Section 4.6, page 118. Let us look at the following declarations:

```
int n;
int &ri = n;
```

A reference with the name ri is declared on the second line. The character & indicates that we are dealing with a reference. Do not confuse the character & used here with the address operator used in connection with pointers. A reference can be understood as a *constant* pointer to a particular variable. A reference is said to be a constant because it always refers to the same variable and cannot itself be changed. Since references are not changeable, they must always be initialized, which is what happens on the second line above. The reference ri is initialized so that it refers to the variable n. A reference could also be understood as an alternative name for another variable. We could write, for example,

```
ri = 15;       // same as n = 15
cout << ri;    // same as cout << n;
```

Note that, although `ri` is a reference, a `*` operator should not be included – as it is with pointers – to get to what `ri` refers to; because `ri` is constant, we mean 'what `ri` refers to' when we write `ri`.

There are two exceptions to the rule that references must always be initialized. One of these has to do with reference parameters. As we saw in Section 4.6, a reference parameter is automatically initialized with every function call so that it refers to a corresponding actual parameter. The other exception applies when a reference is a data member of a class, in which case it must be initialized through a special initialization function called a constructor. This will be discussed in Chapter 7.

To shed some light on the difference between references and pointers, we show here two versions of a function which changes the values of two variables of type `int`. The first version of the function uses references:

```
void change1 (int& a, int& b)
{
  int c = a;
  a = b; b = c;
}
```

To change the values of two variables `i` and `j`, the following may be written:

```
int i = 5, j = 10;
change1(i, j);   // i gets a value of 10 and j a value of 5
```

Since the parameter `a`, for the whole of the call, refers to the variable `i` and the reference `b` to the variable `j`, the variables `i` and `j` will change values after the call of `change1`.

Alternatively, the same result can be achieved with pointers, instead of references. Let us look at the second version of the function:

```
void change2 (int *pa, int *pb)
{
  int c = *pa;
  *pa = *pb; *pb = c;
}
```

Here the parameters are of the type 'pointers to `int`', so we must change the `*` operator within the function to get at what they point to. When the function `change2` is called, the *addresses* to the variables that are to change values must be given as actual parameters. This can look as follows:

```
int i =5, j =10;
change2(&i, &j);   // i gets a value of 10 and j a value of 5
```

Note that the use of references makes everything a little simpler for the programmer both within the function and when the function is to be called. When we need to use changeable function parameters in this book, therefore, we will use reference parameters instead of pointers. This does not apply to arrays, of course, since array parameters, as we have seen, are always transferred via pointers.

5.4.8 Pointers to functions

A pointer may point to a function and functions may be called via pointers. We begin by declaring a pointer pf which may point to functions. The syntax is not particularly easy to read. (The rules for interpreting complicated declarations are discussed in Section 5.5.)

```
float (*pf)(int);
```

This should be understood as, 'pf is a pointer to a function which has an **int** as parameter and which returns a **float**'. We can see that this is a function because the word **int** is in parentheses after the variable name. The first parentheses, around *pf, are necessary. If they had not been put there, the declaration would have indicated instead that pf was a function with an **int** as parameter, which returned a pointer to a **float**.

Now suppose that we have the function g with the declaration

```
float g(int);
```

Then the pointer pf can be made to point to this function by making the assignment:

```
pf = g;
```

An automatic type conversion occurs here so that the part on the right is converted to a pointer to a function. (Compare this with automatic type conversions where names of arrays are indicated.) Now the function that pf points to can be called:

```
x = pf(n);
```

Here, the function g is called but if pf had pointed to some other function, this one would have been called instead.

Note that the pointer pf may only point to functions which have an **int** as parameter and which return a **float**. If a pointer to another kind of function is required, another pointer must be used. The following line, for example, declares a pointer pf2 which may point to functions with three parameters – a **double**, a pointer to a **char** and an **int** – and which does not give a result (returns **void**).

```
void (*pf2)(double, char *, int);
```

Pointers to functions can be handled like other pointers. Arrays can be formed, for example, by pointers such as these.

```
float (*apf[10])(int);
```

Here `apf` is an array where the elements are pointers to functions with an **int** as parameter, which return the type **float**. We can, for example, calculate the function number `i` with the parameter `n`:

```
x = apf[i](n);
```

Pointers to functions are very useful. They are often used in connection with numeric calculations. Many numeric functions are formed so that they have a pointer to a mathematical function as one of their parameters. A function which performs mathematical integration has, for example, a parameter which indicates the mathematical function to be integrated. As an example, we will construct a function `zeropos` which calculates a zero position for mathematical functions. The function `zeropos` will have the declaration:

```
double zeropos(double (*f)(double),
               double a, double b, double eps=1e-10);
```

The first parameter `f` is a pointer to the mathematical function for which a zero position is to be searched. The two parameters `a` and `b` indicate in which interval the search for the zero position is to occur. We are thus looking for a value `x` in the interval $(a, \ b)$ such that $f(x)=0$. We suppose that the function `f` points to, is monotonous and that it has exactly one zero position in the given interval. The parameter `eps` indicates the greatest error that may be found in the result. We have given this parameter a default value of 10^{-10}. We will use the notion of 'surrounding' the zero position by moving the end points `a` and `b` ever nearer to each other. The definition of the function will be:

```
double zeropos(double (*f)(double),
               double a, double b, double eps=1e-10)
{
  if (f(a) > 0 and f(b) < 0)
  { // Change a and b
    double temp = a;
    a=b; b=temp;
  }
  if (not (f(a) < 0 and f(b) > 0))
  {
    cout << " No zero position " << endl;
    abort();
  }
  // Now holds f(a) < 0 < f(b)
```

```
    while (fabs(a-b) > eps)
    {
      double xm=(a+b)/2, fm=f(xm);
      if (fm < 0)
        a=xm;
      else if (fm > 0)
        b=xm;
      else
        return xm; // We happened to find the zero position
    }
    return (a+b)/2;
}
```

In the first part of the function we ensure that the condition f(a)<0<f(b) is true. If it turns out that f(b)<0<f(a), we quite simply exchange a with b: If f(a) and f(b) are both greater than zero or less than zero, a zero position can be absent from the interval. In that case, an error printout is given, and the program is terminated. This is done with the standard function abort, which is declared in the header file stdlib.h.

We then calculate the mid-point xm in the interval (a, b) and the function's value at this point. This is done in the call f(xm). Here the function which f points to, is called. If the function value is less than zero, the zero position must lie to the right of xm. Then we make a change inside the interval so that a is set to xm. If the function value is greater than zero, the zero position must similarly lie to the left of xm, and b is changed to xm. This process is repeated until the interval (a, b) is shorter than eps or until we happen to find the zero position.

The function zeropos can now be used to calculate the zero position for different functions. For example, if we have the two functions,

```
double f1(double x)
{
  return x-1;
}
double f2(double x)
{
  return 2*x*x*x - 3*x*x - 18*x - 8;
}
```

their zero positions can be calculated and written out with the statement:

```
cout << zeropos(f1, -10, 10)  << endl
        << zeropos(f2, -1, 1)   << endl;
```

Another very important area of use for pointers to functions should be mentioned here. Most modern programs today use a graphic user interface; in other words different windows and menus are shown on the screen, and the user communicates with the program through the medium of a mouse. To work in this way a program has to have a special structure. The program is started by calling prepared help functions in the windows system and specifying which windows, menus, etc., are to be found. Then a special wait function in the windows system, which allows the user to wait until an event occurs, is called. An event can be the moving of the mouse, or the pressing of a key or a mouse button.

Before the wait function is called, it is necessary to indicate what should be done when different events occur. This is effected by calling the help functions which should have as parameters, pointers to *callback functions*. These are functions that we write ourselves and that are to be called for various events. For example, a callback function can be written specifically to be called when the user clicks with the mouse on a certain button on the screen. Thus we need to know how to make pointers to functions.

5.5   Complicated declarations – `typedef`

Declarations in C++ are not always very easy to read, particularly when we begin to handle more complicated types such as arrays of pointers. First of all here are some fundamental examples:

```
float f(int);   // f is a function
float a[10];    // a is an array
float *p;       // p is a pointer
```

Variable names, type names, ordinary parentheses, braces and the character * are some examples of what might occur in declarations. (References can also be declared but these are not often complicated.) Ordinary parentheses coming after a name which is declared signify a function; square brackets coming after the name signify an array; and when the character * precedes a name, it is a question of a pointer. This is relatively simple as long as not too many of these characters – ( ), [ ] and * – appear in the same declaration.

Here are some more complicated examples:

```
float *fp(int);   // fp is a function which returns
                  // a pointer to float
float *ap[10];    // ap is an array where the elements are
                  // of the type pointer to float
float **pp;       // pp is a pointer to a pointer
                  // to a float
```

The following rules may be used to interpret these declarations correctly:

(1)   Begin by finding the name of what is to be declared (example: 'fp is').

(2) If there is a (. .) or a [. .] directly after what is being declared, this will have highest priority. In this case, read 'a function', 'an array', respectively. Repeat this point until there are no more (. .) or [. .] following to the right.

(3) If there is a * in front of what is to be declared, read 'pointer to'. Repeat this point until no more * are left.

(4) Last of all, read the type name that comes first.

Simplifying matters we can say that (. .) and [. .] have higher priority than * in a declaration but if this order of priority is not satisfactory, it can be changed by including extra parentheses. We could, for example, write:

```
float (*pf) (int);      // pf is a pointer to a function
                        // which returns a float
float (*pa) [10];       // pa is a pointer to an array
                        // where the elements are of type float
float (*apf[10])(int); // apf is an array where the elements
                        // are pointers to functions
```

Unfortunately, declarations can be even more complicated than those illustrated in these examples. In order to simplify the treatment of declarations and to understand them more easily, a language construct called **typedef** can be used. If we have a complicated type, we can use **typedef** to give it a name and subsequently use this name instead of the complicated type formulation. Suppose, for example, that we wish to work with variables of the type **unsigned long int**. This may be awkward to write in some places, so we can make the following declaration:

```
typedef unsigned long int ulong;
```

A **typedef** declaration has exactly the same form as an ordinary variable declaration. The only difference is that the word **typedef** comes first. In a **typedef** declaration, we declare a type name, not a variable name. Thus, we declared the name ulong here. This name can then be used as a simple type name wherever a type can be indicated. We can, for example, declare a variable with the name u1:

```
ulong u1;
```

The variable u1 will get the type **unsigned long int** just as if we had written it in the declaration. The use of **typedef**, therefore, does not lead to the creation of a new type; we have simply found an easier way of indicating the type **unsigned long int**. Let us show a few examples:

```
typedef char *text;
typedef float array[10];
typedef float (*funct_point)(int);
```

The type names `text`, `array` and `funct_point` have been entered here. Now pointers to text strings can be declared more simply:

```
text t = "Hello";
```

The type names can be used to give simplified declarations of the variables `a`, `pf`, and `apf` that were used above:

```
array a;
funct_point pf;
funct_point apf[10];
```

5.6   The type void

There is a standard type called **void**. This is no common type. There are, for instance, no values of type **void** and variables of this type may not be declared. The most important use of the type **void** is at the declaration of functions, when it is used to indicate that a function will not return a result:

```
void f(int);
```

We can also write **void** to show that a function has no parameters. The following two lines have the same meaning:

```
int g();
int g(void);
```

Variables of type **void** may not be declared; neither is it permissible to have references to type **void** but it is permissible to declare variables and parameters with the type 'pointer to **void**':

```
void *p;
int f(void *q);
```

Because there are no values of type **void**, it is not permissible to try to find out what a pointer of this kind is pointing to; neither is it allowed to perform pointer arithmetic on the **void** pointer:

```
cout << *p;     // Not allowed!!
p++;            // Not allowed!!
```

Pointers to **void** can be used as intermediate results when we wish to make conversions between different pointer types. (See Section 5.7 below.)

5.7   Type conversions

Every expression computed in a C++ program has a certain type, and the compiler will keep a careful account of the types that different expressions have. However, the value of an expression can be converted in certain cases from one type to another. Either this happens *automatically*, without anything particular being written by the programmer, or *explicitly*, when the programmer writes a *type conversion expression*.

5.7.1   Automatic type conversions

Let us begin by listing the occasions when the compiler tries to produce an automatic type conversion.

- When an expression of the form x•y is written, where • is an operator, the compiler tries to convert the operands x and y so that the operation can be carried out. If, for example, we have the expression a + k, where a has type **double** and k type **int**, then the value of k is automatically converted to type **double**. (Naturally, the variable k itself is not changed by this. What is converted is a copy of the value of k.)

- With assignments and initializing, for example, x = y. Then an attempt is made to convert the part on the right so that it gets the same type as the value in the left-hand part. (Assignment is actually a special case of the point above.)

- When a function is called, the compiler tries to convert the arguments' values (the actual parameters) so that they correspond to the types of the formal parameters. The same applies to a **return** statement. Then the value after the word **return** is refashioned to the type the function should return.

- In an **if** statement, the value in parentheses should be of type **bool**. If it is not, the compiler will try to carry out an automatic type conversion.

- In a **switch** statement (which we have not yet dealt with), the expression after **switch** should be of integer type. An automatic type conversion can also occur here.

What kind of type conversions are possible with automatic type conversion? For example, can a pointer be automatically converted to an **int**? We list here some of the possible kinds of automatic type conversion:

- *Arithmetic type conversions.* A value of arithmetic type can be converted to a value of another arithmetic type. A value of an enumeration type (see Section 5.8) can also be converted to an integer. In many cases, the value is not changed as a result of this conversion, but sometimes it is. An example of this occurs when a conversion is made from a long integer type to a short integer type. Then the bits furthest to the left which will not fit in, are cut off. Another example is a conversion from a floating point type to an integer type, when the decimals will disappear.

- *Conversion to and from the type* **bool**. An arithmetic value, an enumeration value (see Section 5.8) or a pointer value can be automatically converted to the type **bool**. A value of 0 is then interpreted as **false** and all other values as **true**. A value of the type **bool** can alternatively be automatically converted to the type **int**. A value of **false** will then be converted to 0, and a value of **true**, to 1.

- *Arrays and functions*. The name of an array or a function can be automatically converted to a pointer to the array's first element or, in the case of a function, to a pointer to the function.

- *Null pointers*. The integer literal 0 can be automatically converted to a pointer type and will then mean 'null pointer'.

- *Pointers to* **void**. A pointer of the type 'pointer to T' can be automatically converted to the type 'pointer to **void**'. Note that type conversions in the other direction cannot take place automatically.

- *Classes*. A number of automatic type conversions can also occur when we work with classes. We will be describing these later in the book. For the sake of completeness, we will simply name here which automatic type conversions can occur:
  - If there are user-defined type conversions (type conversion constructors or type conversion operators) to be carried out, these can be carried out automatically.
  - If D is a class with a base class B, a value of type D can be converted to type B. In the same way, a pointer of the type 'pointer to D' will automatically be converted to the type 'pointer to B'. Special rules also apply to pointers to class members.

5.7.2   Explicit type conversions

If, in a particular situation, a type conversion has to be made and this does not occur automatically as described above, an *explicit type conversion* can be effected. It is permissible to carry out several different types of type conversion. For example, conversions may be made between pointers and integers and between different kinds of pointer types. It should be noted that the normal safety mechanisms in the compiler will no longer function when explicit type conversions are made. A program that contains explicit type conversions can, therefore, behave strangely if no extra care is taken. In C++, there are two alternatives for indicating an explicit type conversion. Either a type conversion expression of the form

```
(typename) expression
```

can be used, or the form

typename (expression)

C++ has inherited the first form, called a *cast*, from C. We write in parentheses which type we want the expression to be converted to. Here are some examples:

```
char *p = (char *) 07650;   // integer → pointer
long int i = (long int) p;  // pointer → integer
double *q = (double *) p;   // pointer → another pointer
void *v;
q = (double *) v;           // void pointer → another pointer
```

The other, newer form of explicit type conversion is reminiscent of a function call. A couple of examples are:

```
cout << int(p);      // pointer → integer
typedef char *text;
cout << text (v);    // void pointer → another pointer
```

To be able to use the second form, we have to be able to express the type we want to make the conversion to, with a simple type name. In order to achieve this, we can, as in the second example, give the type a simpler name using **typedef**.

It should be pointed out here, that the four type conversion operators **dynamic_cast**, **static_cast**, **reinterpret_cast** and **const_cast**, have been introduced in the draft standard, the intention being that these should be used instead of the ones shown above. Using an explicit type conversion is always risky. If errors arise in a program when it is test run the explicit type conversions should always be checked to make sure they are correct. But it can be difficult to find all the places where explicit type conversions have been made. If the four operators suggested in the draft standard are used, the problem disappears, since it would be an easy matter to search for the word 'cast' in the program text.

5.8 Enumeration types

We have seen that much use is made of integer types when designing programs, but there are many phenomena in the real world that are described in words rather than numbers, for example, the days of the week. The second day of the week is usually called Tuesday rather than day number 2. In the same way, the suits in a pack of cards are not numbered but have names: clubs, diamonds, hearts and spades. To describe the state of something, we commonly use different terms rather than numbers, such as the state of an elevator being 'going up', 'going down', or 'stationary'. If phenomena like these are to be represented in a program, numeric types will not suffice. Instead, there is the opportunity to use *enumeration types*.

When an enumeration type is declared, the possible values are simply enumerated or listed.

Let us look at three examples already mentioned: the days of the week, the suits in a pack of cards and the states of an elevator. We can make the following declarations:

```
enum day_of_the_week {Monday, Tuesday, Wednesday, Thursday,
                      Friday, Saturday, Sunday};
enum suit {clubs, diamonds, hearts, spades};
enum elevator_status {going_up, going_down, stationary};
```

The words day_of_the_week, suit and elevator_status will now designate three new types. These types can be used in the same way as the built-in types. We can, for example, declare the variables:

```
day_of_the_week today, tomorrow;
suit current_trump, suit_played;
elevator_status condition_1 = stationary;
```

The variables today and tomorrow will be of the type day_of_the_week, current_trump and suit_played of the type suit and condition_1 of the type elevator_status. A variable of enumeration type may only accept one of the enumerated values for the type. The variable suit_played may, for example, only accept one of the four values clubs, diamonds, hearts and spades. Although we are perhaps accustomed to values being numeric, we must also become accustomed to the notion that diamonds is a value of type suit just as 257 is a value of type **int**.

Here are some examples of statements that are allowed:

```
suit_played = diamonds;
current_trump = suit_played;
if (condition_1 == stationary)
   cout << "The elevator is stationary" << endl;
```

It is not permissible to mix types. The following are incorrect:

```
int i = 4;
today = i;          // Error!
today = diamonds;   // Error!
```

In fact, enumeration values are stored as integers but it is not permissible to assign an integer to an enumeration value. On the other hand, we may assign an enumeration value to an integer, so it would have been correct to write:

```
int i = today;      // OK!
```

If nothing else has been indicated, the first enumeration value will be represented by the integer 0, the second by the integer 1, and so on. The value Friday is represented, for example, by the integer 4. The programmer may choose which integer is to be used to represent the different enumeration values. Look at the following declaration, for example:

```
enum etype {a, b = 100, c = -10, d};
```

Here a will be represented by the value 0, b by the value 100, c by the value −10 and d by the value −9 (the previous value +1). Enumerations can be used as an alternative way to give integer constants. We will find this useful when we work with classes later. We could define two constants, k and number, for example:

```
enum {k = 100, number = 200};
```

Note that it is not necessary to indicate a name for the enumeration type. The enumeration values can then be used as constant integers. An example is:

```
double array[number];
```

We must have a way of reading and writing enumeration values simply for it to feel natural to use enumeration types. Unfortunately, there are no input and output operators for enumeration types in C++. If we were to carry out the following statements:

```
today = Saturday;
cout << "Today it is " << today << endl;
```

we would get written out

```
Today it is 5
```

The enumeration value is thus converted automatically to an **int** and is written out as an integer. One way to get the printout in fully written out text is to declare a table:

```
const char *day_tab[] =
            {"Monday", "Tuesday", "Wednesday", "Thursday",
             "Friday", "Saturday", "Sunday", 0};
```

The variable day_tab is an array where each element is of the type **const char** *, that is, a pointer to a constant text. The table contains an entry for each enumeration value, and we have added an extra null pointer in an extra element at the end of the array. This null pointer will be useful later when we come to use the table for input. It is quite complicated to write the type of the table; therefore it will be convenient to introduce a name for it, using **typedef**:

```
typedef const char *enum_txt[];
```

The type `enum_txt` is called and the table `day_tab` can now be declared more easily:

```
enum_txt day_tab =
          {"Monday", "Tuesday", "Wednesday", "Thursday",
           "Friday", "Saturday", "Sunday", 0};
```

The value of an enumeration variable can then be written out by indexing in the table:

```
cout << "Today it is " << day_tab[today] << endl;
```

If the variable `today` has the value `Saturday`, as before, the sixth element in the table (the one with number 5) will be written out. We then get the printout:

```
Today it is Saturday
```

We also want it to be possible for the user of the program to write input data in fully written out text. The following lines might be wanted in a program:

```
cout << "What day of the week is it today?";
cin >> today;    // ERROR!!
```

and it might be desirable to have the user be able to reply, for example,

```
Sunday
```

This is simply not possible, unfortunately. For the input therefore, we must construct a help function with the declaration

```
int get_enum(enum_txt tab);
```

The function will get as argument a table containing a text for each enumeration value. As result, the function will return an integer that is equal to the number in the integer value. If the call of the function looks as follows, for example:

```
cout << "What day is it today? ";
today = day_of_the_week(get_enum(day_tab));
```

and the user writes the value `Sunday`, the function will return a value of 6. (Numbering takes place, as usual, from 0.) Since the return value is of type **int**, we must make an explicit type conversion to the correct enumeration type, here the type `day_of_the_week`, before we can assign the next read value to an enumeration variable. Here is the definition of the function `get_enum`:

```
int get_enum(enum_txt tab) {
  char s[100];
```

```
if (cin>>s) {
  for (int k=0; tab[k]; k++)
    if (strcmp(s, tab[k])==0)
      return k;
    cout << "Error in input data" << endl;
}
return -1;
}
```

The function begins by reading the next word from the keyboard. The expression cin>>s will be true if reading went successfully. The text will then be in the text array s. The function then compares the text with each one of the texts described by the parameter tab. These comparisons occur with the standard function strcmp which returns a value of zero if the two texts compared are the same. If the text read is the same as a particular text in tab, the number k, equal to the text's number in the table, is returned. The expression tab[k] is used in the **for** statement as the condition to continue for one more round. The elements in tab are pointers to texts. All the pointers, except for the last one, which was intentionally set to 0, contain non-null pointers and can therefore be understood as true. If the text in s is not the same as one of the texts described by tab, the **for** statement will be interrupted when we reach the last (false) element in tab. An incorrect word must then have been written by the user, with the result that the function gives an error printout. A result of -1 is then returned. This value is returned even if the input cin>>s has miscarried, for example if the user typed Ctrl-Z (or Ctrl-D).

It should be pointed out that output and input of enumeration values using a text table will not function if we indicate our own integers for the enumeration values.

We shall conclude this section on enumeration types by illustrating a program that mixes colours. The colours are described by enumeration types. The program asks the user to indicate two of the colours red, yellow and blue. The program then writes out which colour is obtained by mixing them. Here is an example of how this can look when the program is run:

```
Indicate two of the colours red, yellow, blue.
yellow blue
The colour mixing will be green
Indicate two of the colours red, yellow, blue
yellow yellow
The colour mixing will be yellow
Indicate two of the colours red, yellow, blue.
The user writes here Ctrl-Z (or Ctrl-D)
```

The program looks like this:

```
# include <iostream.h>
# include <string.h>
```

```
typedef char *enum_txt[];

int get_enum(enum_txt tab) {
  as above
}

main() {
  enum colour {red, yellow, blue, mauve, green, orange};
  enum_txt tab1 = {"red", "yellow", "blue", 0}
  enum_txt tab2 = {"red", "yellow", "blue",
                   "mauve", "green", "orange", 0};
  colour colour1, colour2, mixing;
  while (true) {
    cout << "Indicate two of the colours red, yellow, blue."
         << endl;
    if ((colour1=colour(get_enum(tab1)))<0 or
        (colour2=colour(get_enum(tab1)))<0)
      break;
    if (colour1==red     and colour2==yellow or
        colour1==yellow and colour2==red)
      mixing = orange;
    else if (colour1==yellow and colour2==blue or
             colour1==blue   and colour2==yellow)
      mixing = green;
    else if (colour1==red   and colour2==blue or
             colour1==blue  and colour2==red)
      mixing = mauve;
    else
      mixing = colour1; // same colour
    cout << "Colour mixing will be "
         << tab2[mixing] << endl;
  }
}
```

5.9   Multidimensional arrays

In the array types studied so far there has been an index that could be used to select particular components from an array. This type of array is excellent for describing collections with several data objects, where these could be imagined lying in a long line. Texts are an example of this. Sometimes, however, we are confronted with tables, and these do not lend themselves to being described in this way. An example is Table 5.1, which gives the daily air temperature and water temperature in the Algarve in Southern Portugal. In C++, arrays with several indexes, or *multi-dimensional arrays*, can be used to describe this type of table. If we wish, for example, to have a table consisting of 3 rows and 4 columns, where the elements in the table are integers, we can do this with the help of the following variable declaration:

```
int m[3][4];
```

Table 5.1 Daily air temperature and water temperature in the Algarve.

	January	February	March	April	May	June	July	August	September	October	November	December
Minimum	11.5	12.0	12.9	13.5	17.0	20.5	22.2	22.5	21.5	16.0	13.5	9.9
Maximum	19.0	20.5	21.0	23.0	27.0	29.0	33.0	35.0	31.5	27.0	22.0	20.0
Mean	15.0	15.5	17.0	19.0	20.1	24.0	27.0	27.4	26.5	22.7	17.5	14.5
Water	17.0	17.5	20.5	21.0	21.5	23.0	25.0	26.0	26.0	22.7	21.0	17.5

A two-dimensional arrangement with numbers is usually called a *matrix*. We can therefore say that the variable m is a matrix with 3 rows and 4 columns. In a declaration, we are allowed to have as many indexes as we would like. In practice, however, it would be unusual to have more than two, so we will only describe this case.

The variable m is actually a common one-dimensional array with 3 elements, where every element is in turn an array consisting of 4 elements of type **int**. We say that m is an *array of arrays*. An illustration of the variable m is shown in Figure 5.7.

Multidimensional arrays can be initialized in connection with the declaration. Table 5.1 can be described with the variable temp, which is declared in the following way:

```
float temp [4] [12] =
  {{11.5, 12.0, 12.9, 13.5, 17.0, 20.5,
    22.2, 22.5, 21.5, 16.0, 13.5,  9.9},
   {19.0, 20.5, 21.0, 23.0, 27.0, 29.0,
    33.0, 35.0, 31.5, 27.0, 22.0, 20.0},
   {15.0, 15.5, 17.0, 19.0, 20.1, 24.0,
    27.0, 27.4, 26.5, 22.7, 17.5, 14.5},
   {17.0, 17.5, 20.5, 21.0, 21.5, 23.0,
    25.0, 26.0, 26.0, 22.7, 21.0, 17.5}};
```

We see that in the initialization expression every line in the table is included in braces. It would have been permissible to omit the first index in the declaration, in

m

0   1   2

Figure 5.7

which case the compiler itself would have computed the number of lines with the help of the initialization expression.

The easiest way of getting at a particular element in a multidimensional array is to use indexing. We can write, for example:

```
m[1][2] = 14;
cout << temp[2][4];
```

On the second line, it would have been appropriate to use enumeration types to make it more readable. If we make the declarations

```
enum month { January,   February, March,    April,
              May,       June,     July,     August,
              September, October,  November, December};
enum temp_type {min, max, mean, water};
```

we can instead write:

```
cout << temp[mean][May] << endl;
```

To run through multidimensional arrays, we normally use repetition statements nested inside each other. For example, if we want to set all the elements in the variable m to zero, we write:

```
for (int i=0; i < 3; i++)
  for (int j=0; j < 4; j++)
    m[i][j] = 0;
```

Where one-dimensional arrays were concerned, we saw that the array name was automatically converted to a pointer when it occurred in an expression. The pointer's type was then 'pointer to the element type'. What is the case with multidimensional arrays? Let us declare a pointer variable

```
int *p;
```

We are allowed to write

```
p = &m[0][0];   // OK
```

since the first element is of type **int**. By contrast, the following is not correct:

```
p = m;    // Error!!
```

The reason for this is that the array name m is converted to the type 'pointer to an array with 4 **int**s', since m is really a one-dimensional array, the elements of which are in turn arrays. If we wish to be able to assign the variable name to a pointer, the pointer must have this type:

```
int (*q)[4];    // Pointer to an array with 4 ints
q = m;          // OK
```

We saw that for ordinary arrays, pointers were often used instead of index-ing. This can be done for multidimensional arrays but it becomes more complicated:

```
p = &m[0][0];
cout << *(p+6);       // Writes out m[1][2]
q = m;
cout << *(*(q+1)+2);  // Writes out m[1][2]
```

It is permissible to have multidimensional arrays as parameters of functions. The following function will write out the contents of a matrix where the number of columns is 4:

```
void write (int a[][4], int row_num)
{
  for (int i=0; i < row_num; i++)
  {
    for (int j=0; j < 4; j++)
      cout << a[i][j] << ' ';
    cout << endl;
  }
}
```

The parameter row_num indicates how many rows there are in the matrix but in the declaration of the parameter a, it is not necessary to indicate this. It can vary from call to call. Note, however, that the number of columns there are in each row must be indicated. This number is fixed and cannot be changed. To write out the matrix m, we can make the call

```
write (m, 3);
```

We conclude by showing a function which adds two matrixes a and b, element by element, and places the result in a third matrix c:

```
void add (int a[][4], int b[][4], int c[][4], int n)
{
  for (int i=0; i < n; i++)
    for (int j=0; j < 4; j++)
      c[i][j] = a[i][j]+b[i][j];
}
```

As the number of columns must always be fixed when the parameters are two-dimensional arrays, we cannot make the functions as general as we would like them to be. One solution to this is to consider a two-dimensional array as a one-dimensional array and to give as parameters both the number of columns and the number of rows. Another solution would be to declare, using a class construct, an entirely new matrix type; this type would also be more flexible. (This is done in Chapter 13.)

EXERCISES

5.1   Find out how many bits are used to represent the predefined numeric types in the C++ compiler you use.

5.2   Find out (try) what happens if you write a program that tries to retrieve the value a null pointer points to.

5.3   Write a function which puts the characters in a text string in reverse order. The function should use two pointers. The only parameter of the function should be a pointer to the string.

5.4   Write a program to read in a number of integers (1000, at most) from the terminal and print them out in the same order with any given integer only being printed once. If the integer has been printed already, it should not be printed again. For example, if the following numbers are read from the terminal:

```
45 77 -22 3 45 0 21 -1 3
```

the program should output the following:

```
45 77 -22 3 0 21 -1
```

Use pointers to deal with the array in which you have stored the numbers.

5.5   The amplitude of a vector $(v_1, v_2, \ldots v_n)$ can be calculated using the formula:

$$l = \sqrt{(v_1^2 + v_2^2 + \ldots + v_n^2)}$$

Write a function to calculate the amplitude of a vector whose components are real numbers. Formulate the function so that it can calculate the amplitude of vectors with an arbitrary number of components.

5.6   Two vectors $(u_1, u_2, \ldots u_n)$ and $(v_1, v_2, \ldots v_n)$ are said to be *orthogonal* if the sum

$$\sum_{k=1}^{n} u_k v_k$$

is equal to zero. Write a function that determines whether two integer vectors are orthogonal. The function may assume that the vectors have the same number of components but the actual number should be different from one call of the function to another.

5.7 Write a function that copies one text string to another. As well as pointers to both character arrays, the function will get a parameter which indicates the size of the array into which the text should be copied.

5.8 As we know, the function `strcat` copies a text string to the end of another text string. Using pointers, write the function `strcat`.

5.9 The value of an integral

$$I = \int_a^b f(x)dx$$

can be approximated, using the *trapezoid rule*, by the formula

$$I = h\left(\frac{f(a)}{2} + f(a + h) + f(a + 2h) + \ldots + f(a + (n-1)h) + \frac{f(b)}{2}\right)$$

We have split the interval a to b into n subintervals of length h, that is

$$h = \frac{b - a}{n}$$

Write a function `integral` that calculates the integral of an arbitrary function whose argument and result value have the type **double**. As parameters, `integral` should have a pointer to the function to be integrated and the values a and b which indicate the integration interval. Perform, in the function `integral`, repeated calculations of the integral until the difference between two calculations is sufficiently small. With every new calculation the number of intervals, n, is doubled.

Use the function `integral` to calculate the value of the integral

$$\int_1^5 x^2\, dx$$

5.10 Write a program that records temperatures taken at one o'clock in the afternoon, for one week. The program should compute the highest recorded temperature and the mean of the recorded temperatures. The program variable that indicates the current day should be of the type `day_of_the_week` (see page 173).

5.11 Assume that the enumeration type `day_of_the_week` is declared as on page 173. Declare a table `tomorrow` that can be used to find out which day comes after a particular given day. The expression `tomorrow[Tuesday]` should, for example, have the value `Wednesday`, and `tomorrow[Sunday]` should have the value `Monday`.

5.12 Roman numerals are indicated by the letters I, V, X, L, C, D and M, standing for 1, 5, 10, 50, 100, 500 and 1000, respectively. First declare a table that can be used for translating a Roman numeral into an ordinary numeral (for example, L to 50). Use an enumeration type to describe the Roman numerals. Then write a program to read in a Roman number and translate it into an integer. The Roman number is to be read as input to the program. Terminate input by using the character combination for *end of file*. For simplicity, it can be assumed that when a Roman number is input at least one space is left between the numerals. The user can write, for instance, M X M V I I at the terminal. The program should then print out 1997. *Tip*: Use the function `get_enum` on page 175.

Remember that in a Roman number, if the Roman numeral P stands immediately to the left of another Roman numeral Q and if P denotes a number smaller than Q, then the value of P is subtracted from the total number (for example, LIX means 59), otherwise P is added to the total number (for example, LXI means 61).

5.13 Write a function to determine whether an $n \times n$ matrix is symmetric. In a symmetric matrix A, $a_{ij} = a_{ji}$ for all i and j.

5.14 A magic square is an arrangement of numbers with n rows and n columns. The sums of the values in each row, column and diagonal are the same. The following square is a magic square, for example:

```
16    9    2    7
 6    3   12   13
11   14    5    4
 1    8   15   10
```

Write a function that determines whether such an arrangement is a magic square. The number of rows and columns is arbitrary.

Another condition for an arrangement of numbers with n rows and n columns to be a true magic square is that it contains all the integers 1, 2, ... n^2. Amend the function so that it also checks for this condition.

5.15 The simplest form of noughts and crosses is played on a board with 3×3 squares. One player plays crosses and the other noughts, and éach takes it in turn to put his or her character in a square. During the game, therefore, a given square can be empty, contain a cross, or contain a nought. The first player to get three characters in a row, column, or diagonal, has won. Write a function which gets the board as parameter and as result indicates whether a player has won.

5.16 Tables can be constructed showing how different countries border each other. An example is shown in Table 5.2. Write a function `number_neighbours` that will

Table 5.2 Countries that border each other.

	Belgium	France	Italy	Holland
Belgium	–	yes	no	yes
France	no	–	yes	no
Italy	no	yes	–	no
Holland	yes	no	no	–

result in a table like this one and a country as parameters. As a result, the function should give the number of countries the given country borders. The call number_neighbours (tab, France) should, for example, give a value of 2. (We only consider countries with land boundaries.)

5.17 The Morse code for the alphabet is shown in the following table, where dots and dashes are used to represent short and long signals, respectively.

```
A .-      B -...    C -.-.    D -..     E .       F ..-.
G --.     H ....    I ..      J .---    K -.-     L .-..
M --      N -.      O ---     P .--.    Q --.--   R .-.
S ...     T -       U ..-     V ...-    W .--     X -..-
Y -.--    Z --..
```

Write a program that reads in a message and codes it into Morse code.

Then write another program that reads in a message in Morse code, decodes it and writes out the decoded message. In the Morse message letters are separated by one space, and words are separated by two spaces.

5.18 An efficient way of sorting the elements of an array goes under the name of *quicksort*. The method can be described by the following recursive algorithm:

(1) If the array has no elements or only one element, then it is sorted. Otherwise, perform the following steps:

(2) Choose an arbitrary element in the array and call it *k*.

(3) Move the elements around in the array so that two groups are formed. The element *k* should be placed between the two groups. All the elements that are less than, or equal to, *k* should be placed in the group to the left of *k* and all the rest in the group to the right.

(4) Sort the part of the array to the left of *k* using this algorithm.

(5) Sort the part of the array to the right of *k* using this algorithm.

Write a function that sorts an array with elements of type **double**. Use the quicksort algorithm. The function should be able to sort arrays of different lengths.

Object-oriented Program Development

6.1 Basic concepts
6.2 Object-oriented analysis

6.3 Object-oriented design
6.4 Object-oriented programming

'Object-oriented' is one of the latest in-words in the computer world. You hear of object-oriented design, object-oriented programming, object-oriented analysis, and so on. What does 'object-oriented' mean? There is no absolute definition. One way of trying to describe object-orientation is to say that it is a new approach to program development, in which a program system is built up according to the objects it involves rather than according to the functions it should perform. Another way of looking at object-orientation is from a more technical perspective and trying to describe the idea of 'object-oriented programming'. In object-oriented programming, a program is built up of a number of well-delimited units called objects.

In this chapter we shall give an introduction to object-orientation. We will discuss the basics of object-oriented programming and what the different words mean. In particular, we will be discussing the concepts of *class* and *object*. When a large program is to be developed using object-orientation, we say that we carry out *object-oriented program development*. Object-oriented program development is normally divided into the three different phases of object-oriented analysis, object-oriented design and object-oriented programming, and we will be discussing these three phases.

6.1   Basic concepts

In Chapter 1, we gave the traditional picture of a data program. This was a 'box' into which input data was placed and out of which came output data. The program's function was to transform a flow of data. This way of understanding is usually called the *function-oriented* view. The *object-oriented* view is rather different. In this, a computer program is understood to be a kind of *model* of the reality alongside which the program has to work. The different variables in a program, the *objects*, are then models of real or devised things in the program's environment and the computer program is designed to manipulate these objects. Let us begin by discussing the concept of 'object' in more detail.

Every object has a unique identity. In a program, we access objects via names or pointers. For example, we can construct an object called `the_lift`, which represents a real lift; or an object `date` can describe a day. Each object has a set of *attributes* which define its properties. There are two categories of attribute. The first is the *data attribute*. (Different object-oriented languages use different terms for a data attribute. In C++ it is called a 'data member'; in Ada a 'component'; and in Smalltalk it is an 'instance variable'.) Each object has its own, unique set of data attributes. Normally, they are hidden within the object so that they are not accessible from outside and can only be changed by the object itself. This is called *information hiding*. Data attributes are used to keep track of the object's status, since each object has a definite status which can be changed during execution. As an example, we can study the object `the_lift` whose status can be described with two data attributes, `direction` and `floor`. The attribute `direction` can have one of the values `stationary`, `up`, or `down`, while the attribute `floor` can contain an integer stating which floor the lift is currently at.

The second category of attributes for an object are the *operations* that can be performed on it. (In C++ such an operation is called a 'member function'; in Ada the term 'primitive operation' is used; and in Smalltalk it is called a 'method'.) For the object `the_lift`, for instance, there might be the operations `go_to`, `stop` and `which_floor`. The operation `go_to` is used to get the lift to a particular floor, `stop` is used to stop the lift, and `which_floor` is used to find out which floor the lift is currently at.

An object is thus a model of a real or devised thing. How then is an object described in a program? This is where the concept of *class* comes in. A class is a kind of template, or pattern, which defines the appearance of a collection of objects

---

Objects

- Model of a real or devised thing.
- A kind of variable.
- Have two kinds of attribute: data attributes and operations. In C++, these are called *data members* and *member functions*, respectively.

with a common construction and set of properties. A class is thus a *description*, and different classes can describe different sets of objects. Figure 6.1 illustrates the class `Lift`. The data attributes have been placed above and the operations below.

An object which belongs to a particular class is said to be an *instance* of the class. There can be several of these. Figure 6.2 shows two instances of the class `Lift`. One lift is on the way up and is currently on the second floor and another one has stopped on the fifth floor. For every object, the class it belongs to is given at the top, and then the values of the data attributes are shown underneath.

Many programmers involved in object-oriented programming understand a class as a type (as it is in certain languages, such as C++). Declaring a class is then the same thing as declaring a type and, using the same analogy, objects are a sort of variable. An instance of a class C is simply a variable which has type C. This analogy between classes and types, however, is not entirely satisfactory in all languages (in Smalltalk, for instance, there are no types, and a class, strangely, is itself an object) but to think in this way makes the different concepts more readily understandable.

In C++, there is a special and important language construct called **class**, and we shall be making a great deal of use of this construct from now on.

```
The_lift
─────────
direction
floor
─────────
go_to
stop
which_floor
```

Figure 6.1

Figure 6.2

6.2   Object-oriented analysis

Object-oriented program development, described above, can be said to be a kind of model building. The first question you ask yourself, is 'What shall I build a model

Classes
● Description of a group of objects with the same properties. A kind of type.

of?' In the section called 'The process of developing programs', in Chapter 1, an account was given of the different phases involved in the design of a program. During the first phase, requirements analysis and requirements specification, we had to try to understand and establish what the program had to do. In object-oriented program development, this phase is termed *object-oriented analysis,* and in a similar way we have to 'get into' the problem, understand the conditions involved and make a first, fairly rough model of our program. To put this in more concrete terms, we must:

● find the objects which will be part of the model;
● define the different attributes of objects;
● establish the relations between the different objects.

It may be necessary to go through these steps repeatedly, since we have to make sure that all the required operations are carried out by an object. The result of the object-oriented analysis is documented in various forms by diagrams that describe how the model looks, and these diagrams can be complemented with tables and other written information.

The first step, to find the objects, may seem complicated. How do we find the 'right' objects? If the program is considered as a model of reality, there is a natural way to let every real 'thing' in the environment be represented as an object where objects constructed earlier should be used again, if possible. Examples of these are different types of data holders, such as tables or lines.

Another strategy that has been suggested is to write down, in words, an informal description of what the system should do. Here we underline all the nouns and let them be candidates for an object. All the verbs will be candidates for the operations carried out on the objects. This may seem too easy, but some will say that the problem with this strategy is that there will be too many objects. However, every noun need not designate a prospective object; a noun could also indicate a property, or a condition of an object.

We could also study how the system works as a whole and select a number of *use cases*, or scenarios. If we think of an object as something that provides services, we can check that all these services in the use cases are available. If, for example, a program is to be designed to check a bank's cashpoint, we could look at the use cases, 'a customer wants to withdraw money', 'a customer wants to check the balance of an account', and so on.

Of course, no one collection of objects will be the right one. One collection can result in a program design which is just as good as another but quite clearly, the quality of a program will finally depend on the experience, knowledge and intuition of its creator.

To be able to carry out an object-oriented analysis in a large program development project, we must have the support of a *system development process*. This is a sort of work schedule which indicates how we will accomplish the process of finding objects, attributes and relations. This process can also suggest the different forms of the diagrams to be produced, and it will usually provide software support, that is, programs which help with the selection of diagrams and other necessary information. Examples of some common object-oriented system development processes are OMT (see Rumbaugh *et al.*, 1991); Objectory (see Jacobson *et al.*, 1992); and Coad/Yourdon's OOA-OOD (see Coad and Yourdon, 1991a; 1991b). (The notation used in the illustrations in this section is taken from OMT.)

An object-oriented analysis should thus establish the relations between the various objects. Three different kinds of relation can be said to exist:

(1) *has*

(2) *knows*

(3) *is.*

The simplest of these is the *has* relation, which states that an object is constructed with the help of another object, that it has this object as one of its parts. For example, a car has a motor and a book has a number of different chapters. Figure 6.3 gives a graphic illustration of how a car has a motor. (The 'diamond' on the line can be read as 'has'.)

An object can also have several objects as its constituents. Figure 6.4 illustrates how a motor can be described as having several cylinders. (The black 'ball' means 'none or more').

Of course, an object can consist of several different sub-objects. In Figure 6.5 we illustrate that a car is composed of a motor, wheels, body and interior.

To say that an object A is constructed with the help of another object B, is really the same thing as saying that the object A has B as a component. In other words, B can be seen as one of the attributes of A, and it is not necessary to use a *has* relation; instead, B can be described directly as being an attribute of A. As we

Figure 6.3

Figure 6.4

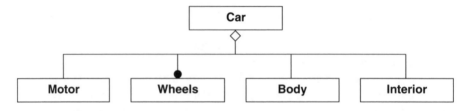

Figure 6.5

shall see later, when program codes are written to define classes, the *has* relations are simply given as data attributes. The use of *has* relations in the analysis phase is kept to differentiate those data attributes which are fully-fledged objects with their own operations from the less advanced data attributes. We only describe simple object properties that can be defined with ordinary built-in types – for example, numeric values and texts – by simple data attributes.

The next relation we will describe is the *knows* relation, which is also known as *association*. This relation is used to denote that an object knows and communicates with another object, without necessarily stating that it is constructed with the help of the other object. A person can, for instance, know his or her own, as well as another person's, address; and a car can, for instance, have a person as its owner. This is demonstrated in Figure 6.6.

This is a bidirectional association: 'a car has an owner' and 'a person owns no, or several, cars'. (As before, the black ball means 'none or more'.) The words on the line are called role-names. Associations may also exist between objects of the same class. A person may be married, for example, and therefore have an association with his wife or her husband. This is demonstrated in Figure 6.7. (The circle means 'none or one'.)

It is easy to confuse the *knows* relation with the *has* relation. Do not be fooled by the word 'has'. That a car has an owner does not mean that an owner is a component in the construction of the car. The *knows* relation is represented in programs by a pointer or by a reference. To describe, for example, that a car has an owner, we let the class `car` contain an attribute which is a pointer to an object belonging to the class `person`. We will return to this later in the book.

The third important relation in object-oriented program development is the *is* relation. This denotes that a class has certain general properties that can be common to other classes: 'a squirrel is a mammal', 'a dog is a mammal'. These common properties are then described in a separate main class (in our example, in

Figure 6.6

Figure 6.7

the class `Mammals`). We can have *is* relations in several stages: 'a mammal is an animal', 'an animal is a living thing'. Figure 6.8 illustrates *is* relations for different kinds of vehicle. (The 'triangle' means 'is a'.)

In object orientation, we make use of the concept of *inheritance* to describe *is* relations. When we have to describe a class, we can begin with a class that already exists and add or subtract attributes. The new class is said to *inherit* the properties of the old class which is said to be a *superclass* of the new class. The new class is then a *subclass* of the old class. Suppose, for example, that we have a class `person` which defines persons. Some of the data attributes in this class will be `name` and `address`. Suppose further that we wish to define students at a university. We can then create a new class `student` which is a subclass of the class `person`. This means that the new class will automatically get all the attributes in the class `person`. Therefore, we do not have to redefine the attributes `name` and `address`. The only thing that we need to do is to declare the new attributes and relations we want to have in the subclass `student`. We could conceive of relations that indicated which courses a student had taken, as well as an operation that could give a printout of the grades the student had got. Figure 6.9 uses both *inheritance* and *knows* relations to illustrate the classes `person`, `student`, `teacher` and `course`. Both students and teachers are persons. A student takes a number of courses. A teacher teaches a certain number of courses. A course has a teacher. A course has several students.

Figure 6.8

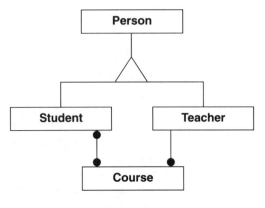

Figure 6.9

A class which is a subclass of another class can in turn be a superclass with its own subclasses. A class can also have several subclasses. This means that a class hierarchy can be built, with a tree-like structure. One of the ideas behind inheritance is that the programmer can make use of 'ready-made' classes kept in a *class library*. In doing so, he or she will not need to continually write new program code. In addition, the 'ready-made' classes should be better tested and therefore contain fewer errors than classes constructed in other ways. (Some critics have stated that this method of programming leads to a situation where a great number of program parts have to be used, many of them superfluous to the needs of the programmer. This makes a program larger and more incomprehensible than it would be if only modules containing what was really needed were used, and not inheritance.)

6.3 Object-oriented design

Up to now, we have mainly discussed object-oriented analysis – the first phase in object-oriented program development. After this phase comes the *object-oriented design* phase, where plans are drawn up and drawings made for the object-oriented program.

The boundary between the analysis and design phases is a little vague. It could be said that in the analysis phase an idealized model is made, while in the design phase this model is made more concrete. Another way to express this is to say that during the analysis phase we think about *what* is to be done, while in the design phase, we consider *how* these things are to be done.

The design phase can be divided into two parts: *system design* and *object design*. System design has to do with making global decisions for the system. At this point, we ask questions such as how the new system is to be split into subsystems and how it will communicate with its environment. The operating system to be used is also something that needs considering. Part of the environment for our new system might well be a windows handling system (such as Windows or X Windows), database handlers and communications programs.

During the object design phase, we start with the objects that have been selected in the analysis phase and add a number of details until each object has the form we want it to have. This may involve the application of appropriate algorithms, decisions on how the different operations are to be performed and what parameters they are to have, and so on. We also make decisions on the objects' internal construction during this phase and decide whether we can use previously constructed objects again.

A decision on which programming language will be used to write the program must be made before the design phase is over, for the program language will affect aspects of different objects as well as the system's ability to communicate with its environment.

It should be pointed out again here that object-oriented analysis and design often merge; it is not unusual for the analysis phase to encroach on the design phase. It is also an *iterative* process, where a return to the analysis phase may be necessary if something in the design phase has to be changed. The programmer can be flexible in developing object-oriented programs and does not have to work as rigidly as in the classical waterfall model discussed earlier.

6.4 Object-oriented programming

Our goal in the programming phase is to implement the system, that is, to realize it in the form of a computer program that can be run. Naturally, we try to write as 'good' a program as possible. A program is 'good' if it satisfies the following requirements:

- it is correct,
- it is effective,
- it is reusable,
- it is adaptable.

The first requirement is that the program should be *correct*. It should be able to perform the operations defined in earlier phases of the program development without error. Naturally, this is a very important requirement. If a program contains errors, good properties will not redeem it.

The next requirement is that a program should be *effective*, that is, it should use the resources of the computer system well. Under certain conditions, this may be a deciding factor in whether the program can be used or not, but it may not always be of such importance.

Is a correct and effective program always a good program? It depends on what we mean by 'good'. To shed some light on the question, we can look at the costs of producing software. These can be divided into two parts: development costs and maintenance costs. Program development would be simplified if there were more opportunities to use ready-made program components in the same way that we have with mechanical and electronic systems. In other words, software should be required to be reusable. If stocks of computer software consisted of complete, reusable and well-tested components, we would soon be in a position where:

- program development costs were lower,
- program development went more quickly,
- software quality improved.

Many programmers spend a great deal of time creating variants of satisfactorily developed programs. Why is this so?

One of the reasons may be that programmers are not used to reusing programs. They may think that it must take at least as long to find a program component and find out how it works as to write it themselves. Also, it is not as easy for a programmer to find an appropriate program component as it is, say, for an electronics design engineer to find a VLSI circuit. If software components are to be reusable, they must conform to certain conditions in terms of the operating system or the ability to handle certain kinds of data. The number of variants can be endless. A reusable program component should be applicable under different conditions. In other words, it should be 'general'.

It is basically a matter of 'packaging'. How should a program component be packaged to make it 'general', so that its functions are easily understood and clearly defined?

Before continuing with our discussion of reusable programs, something needs to be said about the other side of program development costs: *maintenance costs*. A program does not deteriorate, so software maintenance costs cannot be compared with those for a car, for instance. The two main aspects of maintenance costs are correcting errors in the software that should already have been discovered during its design, and adapting software to new circumstances and requirements. That the latter should be necessary is probably caused by incorrect program specifications, or the problem of forecasting future applications.

Maintenance costs can be low if a program has been kept free of errors from the beginning (by the use of well-tested components, for example) and if the program is intrinsically adaptable.

We can adapt a program more easily if it is constructed from several independent modules, each one being employed for a special, well-defined task. Then changes in the program will simply entail a procedure where a component is exchanged or removed (as with, for example, the repair of a TV set). As far as possible, we want to avoid interfering with the structure of programs. If changes have to be made, they should be thought out well.

Our ability to take in a complex situation is limited. It is extremely important to keep the number of contact situations between modules, as well as the number of each module's 'boundaries' in a system to a minimum. All the information in a module that is local, that is only necessary to be known for the module itself, should be hidden. When the module is used, the user should not need to think about its internal construction. This is where the concept of *information hiding*, which was touched on earlier, comes in. Again, packaging can have a favourable effect on both development and maintenance costs.

In object-oriented programming, we should try to write programs that are correct, effective, reusable and adaptable, by allowing individual modules in a program to be constructed from objects which facilitate information hiding. Such objects will be found in the design phase.

For the result to be satisfactory, an *object-oriented programming language*, a language with relevant constructs, should be used. Above all, there are two constructs that are usually required of an object-oriented programming language:

- *Information hiding*   It should be possible to put everything that defines an object's properties into one place in a program. This includes both data and information. The details of a particular object should be hidden so that other objects can neither 'see' them nor 'get to' them.

- *Inheritance*   When defining an object, we should begin with the properties of other objects, adding the new properties as required. In other words, we should try to use previously constructed objects and, making use of the inheritance mechanism, modify and adapt them to our own requirements.

There is a third programming language construct which has proven to be at least as useful as inheritance for writing reusable programs:

- *Generic program units*   A generic program unit is a kind of template that can be adapted to create new program code. Generic program units are specially useful when different kinds of *container* are created. A container is an object that can contain several other objects, an example of this being a list.

C++ and Ada are examples of programming languages that have the three important constructions – information hiding, inheritance and generic program units. C++ has a special language construct called **class**. Objects can be defined easily using this construct. It also facilitates the use of information hiding and inheritance. To construct generic program units in C++, we use something called a *template*.

Classes, inheritance and generic program units will be dealt with at some length later in the book.

References

Coad, P. and Yourdon, E. (1991a). *Object-oriented Analysis*, 2nd ed. Englewood Cliffs NJ: Prentice Hall.

Coad, P. and Yourdon, E. (1991b). *Object-oriented Design*. Englewood Cliffs NJ: Prentice Hall.

Jacobson, I. *et al.* (1992). *Object-oriented Software Engineering*. Wokingham: Addison-Wesley.

Rumbaugh, J. *et al.* (1991). *Object-oriented Modeling and Design*. Englewood Cliffs NJ: Prentice Hall.

7 Classes

In the previous chapter we discussed object-oriented program development and established that the concept of *class* was central to the subject. In this chapter, therefore, we will look at how classes are constructed in C++. We will see how the different attributes a class can have are defined and implemented, as well as how information hiding and the two relations 'has' and 'knows' are realized. (The relation 'is' is saved until Chapter 9.)

In C++, a class is the same thing as a type. This chapter may therefore also seem to follow on from Chapter 5, where the built-in types in C++ were discussed. Classes are more advanced types than the basic, 'ordinary' types, such as integer types and array types. For the ordinary types, there is a collection of predefined operations available to the programmer. For example, integers can be added, and indexing can be carried out in arrays. In the case of ordinary types, data is also stored in a predefined way. An array, for example, consists of a series of similar elements lying one after the other in a row; indexing here always takes place from 0, and the length of the array is not stored. Where classes are concerned, it is left entirely to the programmer to decide what operations are to be used and how data is to be stored. We can declare our own array types, we can keep track of the array's length, and we can let indexing start at a value different from 0, from 1 or 100, for example. Types that contain components of different kinds can also be defined with the aid of classes. If we want to define persons, for instance, we can define a class `Person` containing both a name (a text string) and a length (an integer).

In computer science, a type constructed entirely by the programmer, who also defines exactly which operations to use and how to store data, is called an *abstract data type*. In C++, abstract data types can, therefore, be said to be constructed with classes.

7.1   Class definitions

As a first example, let us look at the following lines, which describe a clock.

```
class Clock {
public:
    void set (int hour, int min, int sec);
    int read_hour ();
    int read_min ();
    int read_sec ();
    void write(bool write_sec=true);
    void tick();
private:
    int h, m, s;
};
```

The above lines constitute a *class definition*. A definition of this kind is always introduced with the word **class**, which is a reserved word in C++. After the word **class**, the name of the class is indicated, in this case, `Clock`. Note that the name starts with a capital C. We will continue to let all class names begin with a capital. It will then be easier to keep track of which identifiers denote variables and which denote classes. Since a class is the same thing as a type, `Clock` can be said to be the name of a *type*, just as **int** and **double** are the names of types. From now on, all types defined with the aid of classes will be called *class types* (when we need to differentiate them from different kinds of types, such as integer types and pointer types).

Objects belonging to the class `Clock` have nine attributes – the six operations `set`, `read_hour`, `read_min`, `read_sec`, `write` and `tick` as well as the three data attributes h, m and s. We will use the conventional terminology in C++ and call the operations, therefore, *member functions* and the data attributes

> ### Definition of class
>
> **class** *name* {
> **public**:
>   *declarations of visible*
>   *member functions and data members*
> **private**:
>   *declarations of hidden*
>   *member functions and data members*
> };

data members. The data members h, m and s are used to keep track of hours, minutes and seconds. The member function set can be called when the clock is to be set. The member functions read_hour, read_min and read_sec return values of h, m and s, respectively. The member function write gives a printout in the form hh:mm:ss or hh:mm, depending on whether the parameter write_sec is **true** or **false**. (The parameter write_sec has the default value **true**.) The member function tick is called every time a second has passed.

A declaration of a member function looks just like that of an ordinary function declaration, the only difference being that it is placed *inside* the class definition. In the same way, a declaration of a data member looks just like an ordinary variable declaration, the difference being that a member variable is declared inside the class definition. The reserved words **public** and **private** are used to obtain information hiding. The word **public** indicates that the attributes that are declared in the subsequent part of the class definition should be *visible*, that is, accessible everywhere, while the word **private** indicates that the subsequent attributes should be *private*, that is, only accessible inside the class. If neither of the words **public** or **private** are indicated, all the members of a class will be considered to be private.

In C++, declarations of members can be placed in any order, and this applies to the reserved words **public** and **private**. We have chosen here to put the **public** sections with the member functions first and the **private** sections with the data members last. Most authors usually put members in this order but the **private** sections are sometimes put first. In this book we will be putting the **public** sections first because the **public** section of a class definition is the most interesting for the user of the class. This section should therefore come first so that it can be seen more easily. Since the user of a class does not have access to whatever is declared in the **private** section, this part will be irrelevant to all the program sections except those where the class is implemented. For these reasons the **private** sections have been put last.

Let us look at a small program which uses the class Clock:

```
main()
{
  Clock k;
  int hh, mm, ss;
  cout << "Set the clock!" << endl
       << "Indicate hour, min and sec" << endl;
  cin >> hh >> mm >> ss;
  k.set(hh, mm, ss);
  cout << "How many seconds should tick? "; cin >> ss;
  for (int i=1; i<=ss; i++)
    k.tick();
  cout << "The time is now "; k.write();
}
```

A test run of the program could look like this:

```
Set the clock!
Indicate hour, min and sec
17 58 0
How many seconds should tick? 130
The time is now 18:00:10
```

To get an object which belongs to the class Clock, we have to create an *instance* of the class. This can be done in C++ with an ordinary variable declaration. On the third line of the program, the variable k, which has type Clock, is declared.

```
Clock k;
```

The type Clock is handled exactly as an ordinary type. For instance, we can declare how many variables we want of this type, or declare pointers or references to variables of type Clock.

A member function can be called with the aid of the *dot operator*. We write the name of the object we want to perform the function for, followed by a dot, and then the function call itself with its arguments. The line

```
k.set(hh, mm, ss);
```

is, for example, a call of the member function set for the object k. As usual, hh, mm and ss indicate the actual parameters (arguments). In more 'object-oriented' terminology it can be said that 'the message set is sent with the arguments hh, mm and ss to the object k'.

Note that each object of a class, that is, each variable of a type, has its own data members which are *independent* of other objects. For instance, if we declare yet another clock

```
Clock k2;
```

this one will have its own data members hh, mm and ss. The lines

```
k.set (10, 30, 45);
k2.set(15, 20, 00);
cout << k.read_hour() << ' ' << k2.read_hour();
```

give the printout

```
10  15
```

We can have pointers to other objects which belong to classes, exactly as for other types. We can write, for example

```
Clock *p;
```

The variable p is then a pointer to a Clock. To get p to point to a certain clock, the address operator & can be used as usual, or memory space can be allocated dynamically with the help of the operator **new**:

```
p = &k;          // p points to the variable k
p = new Clock;   // p points to a nameless new Clock
```

When a member function for an object is called via a pointer, we should use not the dot operator but the *arrow operator* -> as in the following example

```
p->set(21, 56, 30);
p->tick();
```

The dot operator can also be used with pointers but then the * operator must first be employed to access the object the pointer points to. The second line above could then be written in the following way. Parentheses are necessary since the dot operator has higher priority than the * operator.

```
(*p).tick();
```

So far, we have seen how the class Clock is defined and how it can be used in a program. In the class definition for each member function we have only written its *declaration*, that is, the line which says what the function is called, what parameters it has and what result type it returns. For a class to be used, the *definitions* of the member functions, containing the complete implementations of the functions, must of course exist somewhere. In C++, there are two alternatives here for the definitions of member functions. Either they can be placed directly in the class definition, or they can be placed separately, outside the definition. To demonstrate the first alternative, we will create another variant of the definition of the class Clock. We now place the definitions of the three simplest member functions read_hour, read_min and read_sec directly into the class definition:

```
class Clock {
public:
  void set (int hour, int min, int sec);
  int read_hour () {return h;}
  int read_min () {return m;}
  int read_sec () {return s;}
  void write(bool write_sec=true);
  void tick();
private:
  int h, m, s;
};
```

Note that the data members are directly accessible inside the member function although they were not declared in the function or given as function parameters. But this only applies to member functions. If we had had another function, not a member function in the class Clock, we would not have been able to access h, m and s in the function. When we indicate the name of a data member inside a member function, that data member is meant that belongs to the object for which the member function is called at that moment. If, for example, we make the call

```
k.read_hour()
```

then by h inside the definition of read_hour is meant the h belonging to the variable k. If we had instead made the call

```
k2.read_hour()
```

h in the definition of read_hour would have meant the h belonging to the variable k2.

The three remaining member functions, set, write and tick are defined separately, outside the class definition:

Members' accessibility

- *Outside* the class only *visible* members can be accessed, those which have been declared in the **public** section of the class definition. Then the dot operator or arrow operator is used:
  object_name . member_name
  pointer_to_object –> member_name

- *Inside* a member function, all the members can be accessed without dot notation.

```
void Clock::set(int hour, int min, int sec)
{
   h=hour; m=min; s=sec;
}
void Clock::write(bool write_sec)
{
   cout << setw(2) << setfill('0') << h
   <<':'<< setw(2) << setfill('0') << m;
   if (write_sec)
     cout << ':'<< setw(2) << setfill('0') << s;
}
void Clock::tick()
{
   s = (s+1) % 60;
   if (s==0)
   {
     m = (m+1) % 60;
     if (m==0)
       h = (h+1) % 24;
   }
}
```

Member functions are no ordinary functions. They have special properties which ordinary functions do not have. A member function has, for example, direct access to the data members of a class. When a member function is defined separately, outside the class definition, it is not enough to write the name of the member function. We must also indicate which class the function is a member of. This is done by writing the class name in front of the name of the member function with a double colon between them. In our example, therefore, we wrote the function names Clock::set, Clock::write and Clock::tick.

It can be handy to define the member functions directly in the class definition since there would be less to write but there is good reason to be careful here. This is because the program's readability will suffer. The user of a class studies the class definition. If this is full of codes, lacking in interest, it could be difficult to distinguish what is important. The user is only interested in how the member functions should be called and not what they look like inside.

Something else should be known about the placement of the definitions of the member functions, and this has to do with how the C++ compiler translates the member functions into machine code. When a function call is made (this applies both to ordinary functions and member functions), the compiler usually generates machine code; this means that the program *jumps* to another place in the code where there is code for the function called. When the machine code for the function has been executed, there is a *jump back* in the program to the position where the call was made. The machine code for the function itself is, therefore, only found in one position, and all calls will result in a jump to that position. There must be a certain number of instructions at every call to enable these jumps back and forth and to transfer the function's parameters. If a function is very simple and only consists of one or two statements, it is very likely that the machine instructions for a call will be more complicated and will demand greater primary memory space than the machine instructions for the function itself. When this is the case it would be much better not to perform a jump to the function but instead to execute the function's machine instructions directly where the call is made. Then a function is said to be *inline* and so it is called an *inline function*. The code for an inline function is, therefore, duplicated at all the places in the program where the function is called.

Member functions are often very short as, for example, the functions read_hour, read_min and read_sec, so it could be useful to call these *inline* sometimes. If the *definition* of a member function (that is, the member function's code) is placed in the class definition, the compiler will automatically try to convert these functions into inline functions. Since long functions are not supposed to be inline functions, it is not appropriate to define functions longer than a couple of statements in a class definition. These functions should be defined separately.

There is much to be said for keeping class definitions free of function definitions, even if it means writing a little more. They look better and are easier to read. So all functions should really be defined separately, outside the class definition, even very short ones. If we want the functions we have defined separately to be inline functions, we can always add the reserved word **inline** in the function definition. For instance, we can indicate that we want the member function set to be an inline function by letting the separate definition look like this

```
inline void Clock::set(int hour, int min, int sec)
{
  h=hour; m=min; s=sec;
}
```

Definition of member functions

- Should be placed separately, outside the class definition:
  result_type class_name::function_name(parameters)
  { local declarations and statements }

- Very short member functions can be defined directly in the class definition (not recommended). Then they are *inline* functions.

- Separately placed functions can also be defined as *inline*:
  inline *result_type class_name::function_name(parameters)*
  { local declarations and statements }

7.2 **Placement of classes**

We have now seen how classes are defined and how they can be used in a program. The question now is how to divide a program into program text files and place class definitions, definitions of member functions and user programs in the best way. When writing a very small program, it is possible in principle to put everything in the same file but this is not adequate when the program is bigger. In Section 4.5 we discussed how programs could be conveniently divided up. We were dealing with functions then, and we decided that we should construct program files *in pairs*. For every definition file that contained function *definitions*, or complete functions, we were to have a corresponding header file in which we placed corresponding function *declarations*, that is, declarations of the function heads. The header files were to have names that ended in '.h', and the definition files were to have names ending in '.cpp' (or a similar suffix). We should use similar principles when working with classes; we should create pairs of files, a header file and a definition file. A class definition is placed in the header file, and in the corresponding definition file are placed definitions of member functions. If we have a group of classes that are close to each other, we can put several class definitions in the same header file. In this case, the corresponding definition file should contain the definitions of member functions in all the classes.

The term class *declaration* and not class *definition* would seem to be in keeping with the terminology we have used up to now since function declarations, and not function definitions, are put into header files. But the term 'class declaration' is used for constructs of the form

```
class MyClass;   // class declaration
```

where we only indicate that the name MyClass denotes a class and that the complete definition will come later. We will see that such constructs are needed when classes have to cross-refer to each other.

As an example, let us look at a new class Flight, which will describe regular flights. A header file is constructed with the name flight.h which contains the definition of the class Flight. The file looks like this

```
// The file flight.h
#ifndef FLIGHT_H
#define FLIGHT_H
#include "clock.h"
class Flight {
public:
  void init(char flight_no[],
            int dep_h, int dep_m,
            int arr_h, int arr_m);
  void info();
  void delay(int min);
```

```
private:
  char no[7];
  Clock dep, arr;
};
#endif
```

The second, third and last lines require some commentary. In C++ it is not allowed to define a class more than once in a compilation. For instance, if we wanted to have the definition of class Flight twice in our program, we would get a compilation error because the compiler would understand that we are trying to define two classes with the same name, which is not allowed. The risk of writing the same class definition twice in the same program text file may not be very great, but when we use header files, this may very well happen. Suppose, for example, that in the file f1.cpp both the file f2.h and the file flight.h are included. Further suppose that we need, in file f2.h, the class Flight and have, therefore, also included file flight.h there. This means that when file f1.cpp is compiled, file flight.h will be read twice by the compiler.

The second, third and last lines of file flight.h are there to prevent file flight.h being included more than once in a compilation. FLIGHT_H is the name of a *macro*, a kind of constant which we define ourselves. On the second line, there is a check as to whether a macro with this name has been defined (#ifndef means 'if not defined'). If it has not, the compiler will read the whole text until the line #endif. The first time the compiler comes upon file flight.h, the macro FLIGHT_H has not been defined. The compiler will, therefore, read the text. A definition of the macro FLIGHT_H (the macro is not given a value but it is not needed; getting the definition is enough) occurs on the third line, which begins with #define. If the compiler should come upon file flight.h a number of times, it would jump over the text up to and including the line with #endif. The class Flight can, therefore, never be defined twice. We recommend this procedure for all header files containing class definitions. It is advisable to let the macro have the same name as that of the file but with capital letters.

Let us now look at the class Flight itself. It has three data members, a character array no, which contains the flight number, for example, BA2078, and two clocks with the names dep and arr to indicate the departure time and arrival time, respectively. Here we have an example of the *has* relation which we discussed in Chapter 6. An object of class Flight 'has' two clocks. We suppose that the definition of class Clock is in a header file with the name clock.h. To access class Clock, we must therefore include this file. This happens on the fourth line.

The class Flight has three member functions. The first one, init, is used to initialize a flight. The flight number, together with departure and arrival times, must then be indicated as parameters. The member function info writes out information about a flight, and delay is called when the flight is delayed, the length of the delay being a parameter. The function delay will then update the departure and arrival times for the flight in question.

Where functions are concerned, header files should not contain definitions with function bodies, only the function declarations. This principle also applies when we deal with classes. So we put the definitions of the member functions into a corresponding definition file with the name `flight.cpp`:

```
// The file flight.cpp
#include "flight.h"
#include <iostream.h>
#include <iomanip.h>
#include <string.h>
void Flight::init(char flight_no[]
                  int dep_h, int dep_m,
                  int arr_h, int arr_m)
{
  strcpy(no, flight_no);
  dep.set(dep_h, dep_m, 0);
  arr.set(arr_h, arr_m, 0);
}
void Flight::info()
{
  cout << "Flight no " << no;
  cout << ", Dep "; dep.write(false);
  cout << ", Arr "; arr.write(false);
  cout << endl;
}
void Flight::delay(int min)
{
  for (int i=1; i <= min*60; i++)
    dep.tick();
  for (int j=1; j <= min*60; j++)
    arr.tick();
}
```

Note especially that file `flight.h` must be included to make the definition of class `Flight` accessible. (File `clock.h`, on the other hand, does not need to be included, since it is already included in file `flight.h`.)

The data members `dep` and `arr` are objects of class `Clock`, and the member functions for class `Clock` are called to handle these objects. The data members in `dep` and `arr` cannot be accessed directly since they lie in the private section of class `Clock`.

A program using class `Flight` must include the file `flight.h`. As an example, we show below the following simple main program, which we will place in a file with the name `demo.cpp`.

```
// The file demo.cpp
#include "flight.h"
```

```
main()
{
  Flight f;
  f.init("SK1853", 8, 10, 10, 55);
  f.delay(15);
  f.info();
}
```

The printout from this program will be

```
Flight no SK1853, Dep 08:25, Arr 11:10
```

For the program to be run, it must be compiled and linked. If we suppose that the definitions of the member functions for class Clock are in a file with the name clock.cpp, then three compilations will be needed. Files demo.cpp, flight.cpp and clock.cpp must be compiled. If a compiler which is started from the command line is used, the following commands will be necessary. (This example is from a Unix system.)

```
CC -c demo.cpp
CC -c flight.cpp
CC -c clock.cpp
CC -o demo demo.o flight.o clock.o
```

The last line contains the command to link the program. Alternatively, everything can be done with one command:

```
CC -o demo demo.cpp flight.cpp clock.cpp
```

If an integrated program development system, such as Borland's C++ compiler, is used, the compilation commands will not be written in this way. Instead, what is called a *project* is defined, where files demo.cpp, flight.cpp and clock.cpp are indicated as being parts of the project. A command is then chosen from one of the menus which compiles and links all of the files in the project.

A header file should not contain separate definitions of member functions, but an important exception is the inline functions, which have to be defined in the header file. This applies to inline functions defined in the class definition as well as to those defined separately. The file clock.h, for example, can have the following appearance:

```
// File clock.h
class Clock {
public:
  void set (int hour, int min, int sec);
  int read_hour () {return h;}
  int read_min () {return m;}
```

```
    int read_sec () {return s;}
    void write(bool write_sec = true);
    void tick();
private:
    int h, m, s;
};
inline void Clock::set(int hour, int min, int sec)
{
    h=hour; m=min; s=sec;
}
```

Division of classes into files

- For every class, or group of associated classes, two files are created: a *header file* and a *definition file*.

- The *header file* contains the class definition and definitions of possible member functions which are inline functions.

- Use #ifndef and #endif to avoid duplicating definitions.

- The *definition file* contains definitions of all member functions which are not inline functions.

Here we have chosen to let the functions read_hour, read_min, read_sec and set, be inline functions. Note that if the function set had not been defined inline, it would have been put instead into file clock.cpp.

From here on in the book, we will be assuming that class definitions and definitions of member functions have been placed in program files in the way described in this section. We will not be discussing file division, therefore, when we give different examples of classes.

7.3   Constructors

When ordinary variables are declared, we may wish to initialize them. This is not permissible for the data members of a class:

```
class C {
    int i = 0;        // ERROR! initialization forbidden
    const int k = 0;  // ERROR! initialization forbidden
};
```

When an object of a class is declared, all the object's data members will be uninitialized unless the object is initialized in some other way. The easiest way to initialize objects automatically is to use something called a *constructor*. A constructor is a special kind of initialization function which is *automatically* called every time a variable of a certain class is declared, or when an object of the class is created in some other way – with **new**, for example.

7.3.1 Declarations of constructors

Let us return to the class Clock and take it as an example. We will make a new variant of the class definition:

```
class Clock {
public:
  Clock ();
  Clock (int hour, int min, int sec);
  void set(int hour, int min, int sec);
  int read_hour(){return h;}
  int read_min(){return m;}
  int read_sec(){return s;}
  void write(bool write_sec = true);
  void tick();
private:
  int h, m, s;
};
```

What is interesting here are the two new lines

```
Clock ();
Clock (int hour, int min, int sec);
```

A constructor is a kind of member function which has the *same name* as the class it is a member of. We have, therefore, declared two constructors here, both with the name Clock. In C++, as we know, it is possible to have overloaded functions, functions with the same name but different parameters. This also applies to member functions as well as to constructors. The two constructors Clock have different parameters, so they are overloaded. The first constructor has no parameters and the second one has three parameters of type **int**.

A constructor that can be called without arguments is called a *default constructor*. That a default constructor can be called without arguments means either that it has no parameters, or that it only has parameters with default values. If a constructor for a class is not defined, a default constructor will automatically be defined for it. (This cannot happen, however, and the program will be faulty if the class contains data members that are constants or references or that are of a class type without default constructors. In addition, the class is not allowed to have a base class without default constructors. See Chapter 9.) An automatically defined default constructor does not do anything when it is called, and if we declare a constructor,

---

Declaration of constructors

class_name(*list of parameters*);

- Initializes an object. Is called automatically when an object is created.

- Has same name as the class.

- Several can be overloaded with different parameters.

- A constructor which can be called without arguments is called a *default constructor*.

- A default constructor is automatically defined if no constructors have been declared by the programmer. (Compilation error if the class contains data members that are constants, references or objects lacking default constructors, or if the class has a base class without default constructors.) An automatically defined default constructor does not do anything.

---

of any kind, no default constructor will be automatically defined. In this case, therefore, if we want to have a default constructor, we have to define it ourselves.

Note that no return type has been indicated for the constructors. This is because constructors differ from ordinary functions in that they cannot leave a result. It is not even permissible to indicate the type **void**.

7.3.2 Definitions of constructors

Constructors are defined in the same way as other member functions, either directly in the class definition, or separately. If we want to define the first constructor directly in the class definition, we can write

```
Clock () {h=m=s=0;}
```

Here we see that this constructor simply sets the three data members, h, m and s to 0. If we prefer not to have the definition of the constructor in the class definition, we can instead give a separate function definition:

```
Clock::Clock ()
{h=m=s=0;}
```

Note the rather clumsy way of indicating the function name. The first word Clock indicates that a member function of the class Clock is involved, while the second Clock indicates that the member function is called Clock (which implies that it is a constructor, its name being the same as the class name).

We can define the second constructor separately in a similar way:

```
Clock::Clock(int hour, int min, int sec)
{h=hour; m=min; s=sec;}
```

Here we see that the member variables have been assigned values from the parameters.

Instead of carrying out assignment in the function body, we can have an *initialization list* in constructors, where we indicate what initialization value each data member is to have. We can then write the definition of the second constructor as

```
Clock::Clock(int hour, int min, int sec)
: h(hour), m(min), s(sec) {}
```

The initialization list is written immediately after the parameter list and is introduced by a colon. Here we see that the data member h should be initialized to the value hour, m to min and s to sec. A function definition must always have a function body, so after the end of the initialization list there must be a function body even if, as in this case, it is empty.

It is also possible to mix the initialization of data members. Some can be initialized with the initialization list and some using ordinary initialization:

```
Clock::Clock(int hour, int min, int sec)
: h(hour), m(min) {s=sec;}
```

In this constructor it does not matter if we use an initialization list or carry out ordinary assignments; but sometimes it is necessary to use an initialization list, for instance if we have to initialize data members that are constants or references, since we are not allowed to assign to these. Moreover, initialization lists can give more effective code when we initialize data members that are objects. It is therefore advisable to use initialization lists if possible and we will be making use of them from now on.

Definition of constructors

class_name::class_name(parameter list) initialization list
{function body}

- An initialization list can be omitted. Initialization lists have the form:
  :*d1*(*expression*), *d2*(*expression*) ...
  where *d1, d2* ... are names of data members.
- References and constants must be initialized with the initialization list.

7.3.3 Calling constructors

Constructors are not called in the same way as ordinary functions. Let us, as an example, look at some program lines that create objects of the class `Clock`:

```
Clock k1;
Clock k2(8,25,30);
Clock k3 = Clock(22,15,10);
Clock *p1, *p2;
p1 = new Clock;
p2 = new Clock(14,5,40);
```

In the first line, the default constructor for class `Clock` will be automatically called, which means that the data members for `k1` are set to 0. The second and third lines show an alternative way of initializing an object when it is declared. In both of these cases, the second constructor, the one with three arguments, will be called. The style of the second line is recommended, for if that of the third line is adopted, the compiler may create a temporary object of class `Clock`, which would be later copied to `k3`. On the penultimate line, an object is created dynamically using **new**. Since no arguments are indicated, a default constructor will be called for the object created. The last line illustrates that arguments can be given when an object is created dynamically. Here the constructor with three parameters is automatically called. The following statements can be added:

```
k1.write();   cout << endl;
k2.write();   cout << endl;
k3.write();   cout << endl;
p1->write();  cout << endl;
p2->write();  cout << endl;
```

which result in the printout

```
00:00:00
08:25:30
22:15:10
00:00:00
14:05:40
```

An expression of the form C (*parameter list*), where C is the name of a class, is an explicit call of a constructor for class C. What happens, is that a temporary object of class C is created and initialized with the constructor. For example we can write,

```
k1 = Clock(19, 05, 45);
f(Clock(23, 40, 00));
```

In the first line, a temporary object is created, which is then assigned to `k1`. In the second line, a function `f` is called with a temporary object as argument. If we suppose that the function `f` has a formal parameter p of type `Clock`, the temporary object will then be copied to the parameter p. In certain cases, the compiler is allowed to jump over a stage to form a temporary object. When the function f is called, it is possible, for instance, for the parameter p to be directly initialized with the help of the constructor without the creation of a temporary object.

We will now see what happens when we create arrays where the elements are objects. We make the declaration

```
Clock cf[3];    // The default constructor is called
```

The variable cf is an array with three clocks. When this declaration is carried out, the default constructor (the one without parameters) will be automatically called for each of the three elements in the array. For this to happen, there must be a default constructor for the actual class. If this is not so, we will get a compilation error. The default constructor is also called automatically when arrays are allocated dynamically. In the following statement, for example, the default constructor will be called five times.

```
p1 = new Clock[5]; // The default constructor is called
```

An array can be initialized using a constructor other than the default constructor. If we write

```
Clock aa[] = {Clock(9,35,20), Clock(14,55,50)};
```

we get an array with two clocks both of which are initialized with the constructor that has three parameters. (Temporary objects may be formed and these will then be copied to the elements in the array aa.) We can see what some of the clocks contain:

```
aa[0].write();   // write 09:35:20
aa[1].write();   // write 14:55:50
cf[2].write();   // write 00:00:00
p1[4].write();   // write 00:00:00
```

If a class contains data members which are objects of another class, these data members can also be initialized with constructors. In order to demonstrate this, we will return to class Flight to add two constructors, a default constructor and one with parameters:

```
class Flight {
public:
  Flight();
  Flight(char flight_no[],
         int dep_h, int dep_m,
         int arr_h, int arr_m);
as earlier
```

```
private:
  char no[7];
  Clock dep, arr;
};
```

The definition of the default constructor looks like this:

```
Flight::Flight()
{ strcpy(no,""); }
```

We will now define a variable of type `Flight`:

```
Flight f1;
```

No parameters are given, so the default constructor will be called. We see in the definition that the only step to be performed explicitly is the copying of a text string of length 0 to the data member no. The other two data members, dep and arr, are objects of class Clock. What also happens is that the default constructor for class Clock is automatically called, both for dep and arr. These data members will then be automatically initialized to the time 00:00:00.

If we want an object of type Flight to get a proper flight number, and the departure and arrival times to be initialized to the correct values at declaration, we should ensure that the second constructor, the one with the parameters, is called. We therefore proceed as follows:

```
Flight::Flight(char flight_no[],
               int dep_h, int dep_m,
               int arr_h, int arr_m)
: dep(Clock(dep_h, dep_m, 0)),
  arr(Clock(arr_h, arr_m, 0))
{ strcpy(no, flight_no); }
```

We use an initialization list here to initialize the data members dep and arr. Both of them are initialized with explicit calls of a constructor for the class Clock. If we declare a variable

```
Flight f2("TP0255", 11, 25, 13, 05);
```

the departure and arrival times for this flight will get the values 11:25:00 and 13:05:00, respectively.

7.3.4 The copy constructor

When an object is declared, it can be initialized so that it becomes a copy of another object of the same type. We can then write, for example:

```
Clock ca(7, 35, 30);
Clock cb = ca;
```

In the second line, object `ca` will be copied to object `cb`. What actually happens is that a special constructor, the *copy constructor*, for class `Clock` is called and it is this constructor which copies the data members, one at a time, from `ca` to `cb`. We can, as we shall soon see, ourselves define a copy constructor for a class, but if we do not do this, one will be defined automatically.

An object can contain several *subobjects* which are either data members or so-called *base class subobjects* (see Chapter 9). The automatically defined copy constructor copies each subobject individually in the following way. Subobjects of a simple kind (scalars and pointers) are copied bit by bit, exactly as with ordinary assignments. If a subobject is of class type, the copy constructor for this class is called to do the copying. If, finally, a subobject is an array, each element in the array is individually copied according to the rules above. We can, for instance, declare an object, `f2`, of type `Flight` and initialize it with another object:

```
Flight f1;
Flight f2 = f1;
```

When `f2` is initialized, the automatically defined copy constructor for type `Flight` is called. This copies the data member `no` from `f1` to `f2` but since `no` is an array, each element in the array is considered as a subobject to be copied individually. The elements in `no` are scalars (of type **char**) and are, therefore, copied by a simple assignment. The data members `dep` and `arr` are subobjects of class type, so the copy constructor for class `Clock` is called for each one of them.

The copy constructor is not only called when variables are initialized. It is also called when parameters are transferred to functions, or when values are returned from functions. We also count as 'initialization' the initializing of data members using an initialization list. For example, we can declare another constructor for class `Flight`:

```
Flight(char flight_no[],
       Clock dep_h, Clock arr_h);
```

Apart from the flight number, this constructor has two parameters which are objects of class `Clock`. The definition of the constructor looks like this:

```
Flight::Flight(char flight_no[],
               Clock dep_h, Clock arr_h)
: dep(dep_h), arr(arr_h)
{ strcpy(no, flight_no); }
```

If this constructor is called, which happens, for instance, if we make the declaration

```
Flight f3("AA7089", ca, cb);
```

the copy constructor for class `Clock` will be called twice, once at the initialization of `dep` and once at the initialization of `arr`.

Note that the copy constructor can only be called with initializations and not with ordinary assignments. If we write, for example

```
Flight f4 = f3;   // The copy constructor is called
f4 = f3;          // The assignment operator is called
```

the copy constructor will be called in the first line but *not* in the second. Instead, the assignment operator will be called in the second line. We will return to this later in the book.

In most cases, there is no point in defining a copy constructor since the automatically defined copy constructor does exactly what we want. But when we are working with classes that allocate memory space dynamically, we often have to define our own copy constructor so that everything goes according to plan. To demonstrate this, we will construct a class with the name `Vector`. This class will describe arrays of arbitrary length with element types which are **int**. Unlike ordinary arrays, the class `Vector` will also contain the length of an array. Another difference is that indexing will not always need to start from 0. Instead, we will be able to choose which number the array's first element should have. Indexing will also be safe, so that it will not be possible to make the mistake of indicating an index lying outside the array.

We will use the standard function `assert` to carry out checks in the program code. An expression should be written as argument for `assert`, for example:

```
assert(n>0);
```

The function will check that the expression is true. If the expression were false, we would get an error printout of the form

```
Assertion failed: n>0, file vector.cpp, line 25
```

and the program will then be terminated. In order to use the function `assert`, the file `assert.h` (or the file `cassert` if your compiler follows the draft standard) must be included.

```
#include <assert.h>
```

The function `assert` is a good one to use during the program's development, when we are checking that everything is working as it should. When the test run is finished and we are absolutely sure that everything is correct, we can do away with checks to increase the effectiveness of the program. This is most easily done by adding the line

```
#define NDEBUG
```

just before the line which includes the file `assert.h`.

Now to class `Vector`. It has the definition

```
class Vector {
public:
  Vector(int first_index=1, int number=0);
  Vector(const Vector& v);
  int first() {return i1;}
  int last() {return i1+num-1;}
  int length() {return num;}
  int read(int index);
  void change(int index, int value);
private:
  int *p;
  const int i1;
  int num;
};
```

There are two different constructors. The first gets two integers as parameters and these indicate the lowest index allowed and the number of elements. If, for instance, we want to create a vector that is indexed from 101 and has 50 elements, we write

```
Vector va(101, 50);
```

Both parameters have default values. If the second parameter is omitted, we get a vector which (for the time being) has no elements. The second constructor is the interesting one here, since it is our own copy constructor, which replaces the one generated automatically. We can tell that it is a copy constructor from the parameter's type because a copy constructor for a class X always has a parameter of type **const** X& (or only X&), that is, the parameter is a *reference* to another object of type X. This constructor is called automatically if we have declarations like:

```
Vector vb(va);
Vector vc = va;
```

There are three data members in the class `Vector`. The constant integer `i1` indicates the first allowable index and `num` indicates the number of elements. The pointer `p` is a pointer to an array with `num` elements. The space for the array must be allocated dynamically in the constructor every time a new vector is created.

The three member functions `first`, `last` and `length` can be called if we want to keep track of a vector's first or last index, or its length. Since these functions are trivial, they have been defined directly in the class definition. The two member

---

The copy constructor

class_name(**const** *class_name&*);

- Has a parameter that is a reference to another object of the same class.
- Is called automatically if there are declarations of the form
    ```
    X  x1=x2;
    X  x1(x2);
    ```
  where X is a class and x2 belongs to class X.
- Is called only with declarations, *not* with ordinary assignment.

---

functions `read` and `change` are called to read and change, respectively, a particular element in a vector. (We shall later replace these two member functions by an indexing operator.) The integer parameter `index` indicates which element is concerned.

Let us look at how the different member functions have been defined. We begin with the constructors. The first constructor has the definition

---

```
Vector::Vector(int first_index, int number)
: i1(first_index), num(number)
{
   assert(num>=0);
   p = new int[num];
}
```

The data member `i1` is a constant and must therefore be initialized in the initialization list. The standard function `assert` is then used here to check that the number of elements is not negative. (But a zero number of elements is allowed.) If the number is correct, space is allocated for the array, and the pointer to the array is kept in `p`.

Our own copy constructor has the definition

```
Vector::Vector(const Vector& v)
: i1(v.i1), num(v.num)
{
   p = new int[num];
   for (int i=0; i<num; i++)
     p[i] = v.p[i];
}
```

The new vector that is initialized with this constructor should be a copy of the vector v given as parameter. The new vector should have the same index boundaries and length as the vector v, so first the values of i1 and num are copied from the vector v to the new vector. The next step is to allocate an array that has as many elements as the corresponding array in vector v. Finally, we run through all the elements in vector v and copy them to the array in the new vector.

Why do we have to define our own copy constructor? Isn't the one that is automatically defined sufficient? Unfortunately, this one will not work here. If we used it, every data member in the vector v would be copied independently to the new vector, and if we copied the pointer v.p, we would get a pointer that pointed to the *same* array as v did. This would mean that the new vector and vector v would *share* the array, and each change that was made in one of the vector elements in the one vector would change the corresponding vector element in the other vector, which would be absurd of course. We have to copy the *whole* array, not a pointer to the array. This procedure is called carrying out a *deep copy*, in contrast to using an automatically defined constructor which results in a *shallow copy*. Generally speaking, we can state that when memory space is to be created dynamically for data members in a class, we need to have our own copy constructor.

Now all that remains is to give the definitions of the member functions that are left:

```cpp
int Vector::read(int index)
{
   assert(index >= i1 and index <= last());
   return p[index-i1];
}
void Vector::change(int index, int value)
{
   assert(index >= i1 and index <= last());
   p[index-i1] = value;
}
```

These functions check both with the help of assert and see that the index indicated lies within the permitted boundaries.

To conclude this section, we will include an example of a program which uses the class Vector. The program reads a number of test values, then computes and writes out both their sum and the sum of the squares of the values. Two help functions are defined in the program: sum and square. The function sum calculates the sum of the elements in a vector, and the function square changes the contents of the vector so that each element is squared. Note that the two help functions are not member functions of the class Vector. They are, therefore, called in the usual way, and they can only use whatever is declared in the **public** section of the class Vector. Two vectors are declared in the program: v1 and v2. The program begins by reading how long the vector v1 is to be and then declares v1. Vector v2 is initialized to be a copy of v1, and we use our own copy constructor.

```
#include "vector.h"
#include <iostream.h>
int sum(Vector& v)
{
  int s = 0;
  for (int i=v.first(); i<=v.last(); i++)
    s += v.read(i);
  return s;
}
void square(Vector& v)
{
  for (int i=v.first(); i<=v.last(); i++)
  {
    int x = v.read(i);
    v.change(i, x*x);
  }
}
main()
{
  int n, x;
  cout << "Number of test values? "; cin >> n;
  Vector v1(1,n);
  cout << "Indicate test values" << endl;
  for (int i = 1; i<=n; i++)
  {
    cin >> x;
    v1.change(i,x);
  }
  Vector v2 = v1;
  square(v2);
  cout << "The sum: " << sum(v1) << endl;
  cout << "The sum of the squares: " << sum(v2) << endl;
}
```

7.3.5   Type conversion constructors

In Section 5.7.2 we discussed explicit type conversions and we saw that an expression of the form

typename(expression)

was a type conversion from the expression's type to the type indicated in the type name. A constructor that can be called with only one argument has exactly this form and is therefore called a *type conversion constructor*. (That a constructor can be called with one argument means that it must have at least one parameter. If it has more than one, all of these except the first one will have default values.) Let us take a simple example. We define the following class RatNum, which describes the rational numbers.

```
class RatNum {
public:
  RatNum() : numer(0), denom(1) {}
  RatNum(int i) : numer(i), denom(1) {}
  declarations of several member functions
private:
  int numer, denom;
};
```

Rational numbers are numbers that can be written exactly as a quotient of integers, usually called the numerator and the denominator. (For example, the numbers 2/3, 19/5 and 23/1 are rational numbers.) We therefore let class RatNum have two data members which only contain the numerator and denominator. We have defined two constructors. The first has no parameters and is therefore a default constructor. The second constructor has a parameter, so it is a type conversion constructor. If we write

```
RatNum r1, r2(5);
```

then r1 will be initialized to 0/1 with the default constructor, and r2 will be initialized to 5/1 with the second constructor.

The interesting thing about type conversion constructors is that the compiler tries to use them to make *automatic* type conversions. If we now write, for example

```
r1 = 9;
```

then there are different types to the left and right of the assignment operator. On the left we have the type RatNum and on the right, the type **int**. For the assignment to be made, therefore, the value to the right must be converted to type RatNum. The compiler discovers that there is a type conversion operator converting from type **int** to type RatNum and so turns out code, which means that this constructor is called automatically. The result is then the same as if we had made an explicit type conversion:

```
r1 = RatNum(9);
```

Type conversion constructors can be called on all the occasions where the compiler tries to produce automatic type conversion.

A constructor can be both a default constructor and a type conversion constructor at the same time. For example, in class RatNum, we can manage with a single constructor:

```
RatNum(int i=0) : numer(i), denom(1) {}
```

By giving the parameter a default value, this constructor can be called with either zero, or an argument.

Let us look at yet another example. As we have seen, it is not easy to handle texts in C++. It is therefore natural to define a class that simplifies text handling. (The class `string` in the draft standard is an example of a class like this.) Here we shall define a class `Text` which describes objects that contain text. We can describe a text with two member variables, an integer that indicates the length of the text and a pointer that points to a memory space allocated dynamically when an object is created.

```
class Text {
public:
  Text(int n=0);
  Text(char *s);
  declarations of several member functions
private:
  char *p;
  int length;
};
```

We have declared two constructors here. The first initializes an object so that it will contain a text consisting of n blank spaces. The second constructor initializes an object so that it contains a copy of the text the parameter s points to. We make the definitions of the constructors separately:

```
Text::Text(int n) {
  assert(n>=0);
  length = n,
  p = new char[length+1];
  for (int i=0; i<length; i++)
    p[i] = ' ';
  p[length] = '\0';
}
Text::Text(char *s) {
  length = strlen(s);
  p = new char[length+1];
  strcpy(p, s);
}
```

We can now make the declarations

```
Text t1(5), t2("Beware of the dog");
```

The object `t1` will contain a text consisting of five blank characters and `t2` will contain the text `"Beware of the dog"`. Since both constructors can be called with one parameter, they are type conversion operators; so that we can get automatic type conversion in expressions such as

```
t1 = "C++";
t2 = 3;
```

We sense that the first of these assignments is a natural one. We change t1 so that it will contain the text "C++". The other automatic type conversion does not occur as intuitively. If we tried to assign an integer to a text, this would generally be understood as a programming error. In fact, it is possible here. What happens is that t2 will contain a text consisting of three blank characters. If the compiler turns out a great deal of non-intuitive automatic type conversions, it can be very difficult to understand what is happening in a program. It can, therefore, be desirable to prevent some of these automatic type conversions from occurring in the first place. In the draft standard, there is a construct which makes it possible to prevent certain type conversion constructors being used with automatic type conversion. The reserved word **explicit** is written in the declaration of the constructor:

```
explicit Text(int n=0);
```

And now the second of the above assignments will be incorrect. If we really want to create a text object containing a text with three blank characters, we have to make an explicit type conversion. This is still allowed:

```
t2 = Text (3);
```

7.4 Destructors

We recall from Section 5.4.6 that it is a common error, when working with dynamically allocated memory space, not to release memory space that is no longer needed. In class Vector, which we constructed earlier in this chapter, we allocate memory space, for example, every time a new object of class Vector is created, and this happens in one of the two constructors. As we know, a constructor is called automatically every time an object is declared or created with **new**. There is a corresponding language construct that is automatically called every time an object ceases to exist. This is called a *destructor*. A destructor is a member function without parameters, and it is exactly like a constructor in that it is not allowed to have a result type. The name of a destructor is the same as the class name, except that it has a ~ (tilde) in front. A destructor is declared, like other member functions, in the class definition. We can add a destructor to the class Vector:

```
class Vector {
public:
```

```
~Vector();   // Declaration of a destructor
  as earlier
};
```

The destructor ~Vector is automatically called when objects of type Vector cease to exist. If an object has been declared in the usual way, a destructor vector will be automatically called when we leave the block in which the object has been declared. Again, if an object has been allocated with **new**, this will happen when we want to deallocate the object with **delete**:

```
{
  Vector v1;        // A constructor for v1 is called
  Vector *pv;
  pv = new Vector;  // A constructor for *pv is called
  ...
  delete pv;        // The destructor for *pv is called
}                   // The destructor for v1 is called
```

If a class C1 has a data member belonging to another class C2, the destructors for both class C1 and class C2 will be called when an object of type C1 ceases to exist. For example, if we have a class VV:

```
class VV {
  Vector y, z;
  ...
};
```

then the destructor for y and z will be called if an object of class VV ceases to exist:

```
{
  VV w;    // Constructors for y, z and w are called
  ...
}          // Destructors for w, z and y are called.
```

A destructor has the task of 'cleaning' and returning any memory space we ourselves have allocated. This means that for class Vector, the destructor should release the array the member variable p points to. Of course, the destructor can be defined directly in the class definition. Then we write

```
~Vector () { delete[] p;}
```

But we can also define the destructor separately:

```
Vector::~Vector()
{ delete[] p;}
```

By constructing our own vector for class `Vector`, we can be sure that all the memory space we have allocated will be returned.

Destructors

~class_name();

- Used to 'clean' an object.
- Automatically called when an object ceases to exist.
- Has the same name as the class with the character ~ in front.
- Is always without parameters. Cannot be overloaded.

7.5   An object-oriented example

It is now time to show a longer example constructed according to object-oriented principles, which will also illustrate how some of the material we have covered in this chapter can be used. We'll write a program that allows the user to play the card game 'Twenty-one' with the computer. The game is played in the following way: the user receives one card at a time and after each card makes a decision whether or not to have another card. The user has to try to make the sum of a 'hand' as near to 21 as possible, without overstepping this number. An ace is counted as either 1 or 14. If the number 21 is overstepped, the user loses and the computer wins. But if the user stops at a number under 21, the computer has to draw one card at a time, after each card deciding whether to continue or not. If the computer has more than 21 points or a score lower than the user's, the user wins; otherwise the computer wins. The computer is, therefore, the winner if both have the same number of points.

We begin by defining a class `Card`, which defines the cards. We can create new cards, read a card's suit or value, or write information about a card. The parameters for the constructor have default values allowing it to function as a default constructor.

```
enum suit {clubs, diamonds, hearts, spades};
class Card {
public:
  Card(suit = clubs, int = 1);
```

```
  suit su() { return f; }
  int value() { return v; }
  void write_out();
private:
  suit f;
  int v;
};
```

The definition looks like this:

```
Card::Card(suit ff, int vv)
{
  assert(vv >=1 and vv <= 13);
  f=ff;
  v=vv;
}
void Card::write_out()
{
  const char *tab1[] = {"Clubs", "Diamonds", "Hearts", "Spades" };
  const char *tab2[] = {"Jack", "Queen", "King" };
  cout << tab1[f] << ' ';
  if (v == 1)
    cout << "Ace";
  else if (v <= 10)
    cout << v;
  else
    cout << tab2[v-11];
}
```

To define a collection of cards, we define the class `Cardstack`. An object of class `Cardstack` can either define a card in a player's hand or the whole pack of cards.

```
class Cardstack {
public:
  Cardstack() : number(0) {};
  void throw_cards() { number = 0; }
  int number_cards() { return number; }
  Card look_at (int no);
  Card deal_top();
  void lay_top(Card k);
  void new_pack();
  void shuffle();
private:
  Card stack[52];
  int number;
};
```

A cardstack consists of ('has') a maximum of 52 cards, and we put these into the array `stack`, which is a private data member. We can thus keep track of how many cards are currently in the stack. For this purpose we use the data member `number`.

The constructor creates an empty stack of cards. To lay new cards at the top of the stack, we use the member function `lay_top`. If we want to change a cardstack so that it contains a new pack with all 52 cards, we can call the function `new_pack`. Cards are taken from a stack with the function `deal_top`. There is also a function `throw_cards`, which removes all the cards from a stack. The cards may be looked at without removing them from the stack, with the function `look_at`, and this will have a card number as parameter. Number 1 represents the top card in the stack, while the number of the card at the bottom can be found by calling the function `number_card`, which gives the current number of cards in the stack. Finally, the function `shuffle` will shuffle the cards in a stack. This is especially necessary if the stack contains a new pack that is to be shuffled before the game begins.

The definitions of the member functions in class `Cardstack` are given here:

```
Card Cardstack::look_at(int no)
{
   assert(no >= 1 and no <= number);
   return stack[number-no];
}

Card Cardstack::deal_top()
{
   assert(number > 0);
   return stack[--number];
}

void Cardstack::lay_top(Card k)
{
   assert(number < 52 );
   stack[number++] = k;
}

void Cardstack::new_pack()
{ int n = 0;
   for (suit f=clubs; f<=spades; f=suit(f+1))
     for (int v=1; v<=13; v++)
       stack[n++] = Card(f, v);
   number = 52;
}

void Cardstack::shuffle()
{
   srand(time(0));
   for (int i=1; i<1000; i++)
   {
     int n1 = rand() % number;
     int n2 = rand() % number;
     Card temp = stack[n1];
```

```
    stack[n1] = stack[n2];
    stack[n2] = temp;
  }
}
```

In the array stack, the bottom card lies at place number 0 and the top card at the place with the number number-1. In the parameter no of the function look_at, 1 means the top card, 2 the next one down, and so on. To take the right card, therefore, we must pick the card with the index number-no from the stack. In the function deal_top, it is extremely important that we write --number and not number-- because the decrease of number must occur *before* we do the indexing. Similarly, it is important that in the function lay_top, we write number++ and not ++number, since it is the *old* value of number we shall be indexing with.

We run through all the combinations of suits and values in the function new_pack. The constructor for class Card is called once for each combination.

The most difficult member function is shuffle, which will run for 1000 rounds. At every round, it randomly chooses two integers n1 and n2, in the interval 0 to number-1. It then changes the places of the cards for places n1 and n2 in the pack. The standard function rand is called to elicit random numbers. When it is called, this function returns a random integer >= 0 as result. In order to get a number in the interval 0 to number-1, we divide this result by number and see what the remainder is. This remainder must, of course, lie in the required interval.

The function rand calculates a random number using the formula:

$$s_n = K \cdot s_{n-1} + L$$

where s_n is the new random number, s_{n-1} is the previous random number that was calculated and K and L, two appropriately chosen constants. Repeated calls of rand will therefore generate a sequence of integers. We should note especially that if we generate several sequences of numbers, each time starting with the same value, s_0, then the same sequences of numbers will be generated every time. In our case, this would mean that the cards would be shuffled in exactly the same way every time we ran the program and there would not be anything particularly random about the procedure. To find a remedy for this, we have to make sure that the start value s_0 is different each time the cards are shuffled. To indicate a start value for the function rand, we call another standard function srand. This will have an integer s_0 as parameter. To give a random value to s_0, we call a third function, time, which will return a large integer (equal to the number of seconds which have passed since a certain date). Every time we run our program, time will return different values as result. Different random sequences will be generated. We have to include the file stdlib.h to be able to use the standard functions rand and srand, and to be able to use the standard function time, we have to include the file time.h.

Note that both `Card` and `Cardstack` are completely independent of the game that will be played. They are quite general in character and could just as easily be used to write a program for a game of patience.

Our next class is the class `Player`, which describes a participant in the game Twenty-one. This class is, of course, intended only for this game.

```
class Player {
public:
  Player(Cardstack& cardpack, bool is_computer)
  : pack(cardpack), computer(is_computer) {};
  int play();
private:
  Cardstack hand;
  Cardstack& pack;
  const bool computer;
  int points();
};
```

A player has three data members: `hand` is a cardstack that describes the cards in the hand of the player, `pack` is a *reference* to the pack used in the game and `computer` indicates whether the player is a computer or a person. The data member `computer` has been declared as a constant, since a player's properties will not change during the course of the game. The data member `pack` is an excellent example of the relation 'knows'. A player must know the pack of cards used in the game to be able to draw cards from it. It is important for both players to use the same pack, so the relation 'has' will not work here. If we had written

```
Cardstack pack;   // ERROR!
```

each player would then have his or her *own* pack of cards to play with, and this would be completely independent of the pack the other player played with. Clearly, it is important to have a reference to a stack of cards in order to describe the whole pack. We could also have used pointers, in which case we would have written

```
Cardstack *pack;   // Would have been all right
```

The relation 'knows' can, thus be described either with references or with pointers. Since a reference is a constant that cannot be changed once it has been initialized, it is appropriate to use references to describe constant 'knows' relations. In this example, a player will know the same pack of cards for the duration of the game. If we want to describe relations which can be changed during execution of the program, we should use pointers.

The data members in objects of class `Player` are initialized in the constructor. This has two parameters, a reference to the pack of cards used and a value of type **bool** which states whether the current player is a computer or not. An initialization list must be used here to initialize the data members `pack` and `computer`, since both are constants and can not be initialized in an assignment. The third data member, `stack`, is not named explicitly but will be automatically initialized with the default constructor for class `Card`.

The member function `play` is called when it is the turn of the current player to play. This function returns as result the number of points the player scored. Coming last, in the private section of the class definition, is a declaration of a member function with the name `points`. This is a help function that is used internally at the definition of the function `play`. It is not meant to be called from outside, so it has been declared in the private section of the class definition.

Before we see how the member functions in the different classes are defined, let us look at the main program:

```cpp
#include "player.h"
#include "cardstack.h"
#include <iostream.h>
main ()
{
  Cardstack pack;
  Player you (pack, false);
  Player I (pack, true);
  char answer[10];
  cout << "Welcome to twenty-one" << endl;
  while (true)
  {
    cout << "New game? "; cin >> answer;
    if (answer [0] != 'y') break;
    pack.new_pack();
    pack.shuffle();
    int p1 = you.play();
    if (p1 > 21)
      cout << "You lost!" << endl;
    else if (p1 == 21)
      cout << "You won!" << endl;
    else
    { // The computer must play
      int p2 = I.play();
      if (p2 <= 21 and p2 >= p1)
        cout << "You lost!" << endl;
      else
        cout << "You won!" << endl;
    }
  }
}
```

Now it only remains to write the definitions of the member functions in class `Player`. First comes the internal help function `points`, which calculates how many points the player's hand is worth:

```
int Player::points()
{
  int p = 0, number_aces = 0;
  for (int i=1; i <= hand.number_cards(); i++)
  {
    int v = hand.look_at(i).value();
    if (v == 1) {
      p += 14;
      number_aces++;
    }
    else
      p += v;
  }
  for (int j=1; j <= number_aces and p > 21; j++)
    p -= 13;   // counts an ace as 1
  return p;
}
```

The function play, which is called every time it is a player's turn, looks as below. The variable continue indicates whether the player would like another card or not. When this applies to the computer, we use the strategy of 'sticking on' 16 points or more.

```
int Player::play()
{
  bool continue = true;
  int p;
  while (continue)
  {
    Card k = pack.deal_top();
    hand.lay_top(k);
    p = points();
    if (computer) {
      cout << "The computer got "; k.write_out();
      cout << endl;
      if (p >= 16)
      {
        cout << "The computer has " <<p<< " points" << endl;
        continue = false;
      }
    }
    else
    { // Person
      cout << "You got "; k.write_out();
      cout << " and have " << p << " points" << endl;
      if (p < 21)
      {
        char answer[10];
        cout << "One more card? "; cin >> answer;
```

```
        continue = answer[0] == 'y';
      }
    else
      continue = false;
    }
  }
  hand.throw_cards();
  return p;
}
```

Finally, here is an example of how the program can look when it is run:

```
Welcome to twenty-one
New game? y
You got Clubs 5 and have 5 points
One more card? y
You got Clubs 7 and have 12 points
One more card? y
You got Hearts 4 and have 16 points
One more card? n
The computer got Diamonds 4
The computer got Spades 4
The computer got Hearts 6
The computer got Hearts Jack
The computer has 25 points
You won!
New game? y
You got Clubs 8 and have 8 points
One more card? y
You got Diamonds 6 and have 14 points
One more card? y
You got Diamonds Jack and have 25 points
You lost!
New game? n
```

EXERCISES

7.1   Construct a class `Counter` that counts integers which can only take on values in a certain interval. When a counter is initialized, the start value should be indicated, as well as the least and greatest values the counter can take on. (If no boundary values are indicated, the counter should take on all the values of type **int**.) There should be member functions with which we can count up and down a counter with the number 1. If a counter should then get a value which is not allowed, an error printout should result. We should also be able to read a counter's value.

Then use the class `Counter` in a program to read in a text and calculate how many blank characters occur in the text. Divide the text into appropriate files.

7.2   Complete the class `Text` on page 223 so that there are operations with which a particular character in a text can be changed and read. There should also be an operation enabling us to find out how long a text is. Construct an appropriate destructor for the class.

7.3   Construct a class `Person`. A person should have a name, an address and an age. Make use of the class `Text`. Formulate a constructor and some appropriate member functions for class `Person`.

7.4   For class `Clock` on page 198 there is a member function that advances a clock by one second. It is not practical to call this function again and again if we want to advance the clock by a larger time interval. Write a member function for class `Clock` which can advance a clock by an arbitrary number of seconds at one time.

7.5   To define a point in a two-dimensional coordinate system, it is most common to use the form (x, y), called *rectangular coordinates*. Construct a class `Point` which describes points in this way. Write appropriate constructors and a member function which calculates the distance between a given point and another. The distance between two points (x_1, y_1) and (x_2, y_2) is given by the formula

$$d = \sqrt{((x_1 - y_1)^2 + (x_2 - y_2)^2)}$$

7.6   In the previous exercise, points were described using rectangular coordinates. An alternative way of defining points is by using polar coordinates (r, θ), where r is the distance of the point from the origin. If we imagine a straight line drawn through the origin and the point, this line will form an angle with the x-axis, and this is θ. Conversion from polar coordinates to ordinary rectangular coordinates can be effected with the formula

$$x = r \cdot \cos \theta$$
$$y = r \cdot \sin \theta$$

First define a class `Rpoint`, where the points are defined using polar coordinates, then write a type conversion constructor for class `Point` in the previous exercise, which converts from an `Rpoint` to a `Point`.

7.7   Complete the class `RatNum` on page 222 with a constructor that gets both a numerator and a denominator as parameters. When the new rational number is initialized, you should make sure that the denominator is never negative and that the nominator and denominator do not have common factors. (*Tip*: Use the function `gcd` from Exercise 4.7.)

Now write a member function `add_to` that gets another rational number `r` as parameter. The function should add `r` to the actual number. You should make sure that here, too, numerator and denominator do not have common factors.

7.8   Construct a class `Passenger` that will define a passenger on a flight. Each passenger can have a maximum of ten departures during a flight (use class `Flight` on page 205).

A passenger must therefore know (contain pointers to) this. There should be a constructor that initializes a passenger with appropriate flight departures. Here you should check that times and flights correspond, so that a person will not take a flight that leaves before the previous flight has arrived. There should also be a member function with which you can replace one flight by another. Check here, too, that times and flights correspond. If a flight is delayed, a passenger may need to change the flight that follows. Write a member function that checks whether this is necessary for a particular passenger. To solve this exercise you must add two member functions which make it possible to examine the departure and arrival times of a flight.

7.9   Complete the class Cardstack in Section 7.5 by an operation which combines two cardstacks in one. Then use the classes Card and Cardstack to construct a program which plays the card game *Starve the Fox*. This game is played by two players. First, all the cards are dealt out with each player getting a stack of 26 cards. One of the players plays his top card, after which the two players take it in turns to play a card. The player who first plays a higher card of the same suit as the card first played may then take all the cards on the table and put them under his stack. If the card that is played first happens to be an ace, it is counted as 1; aces are worth 14 points otherwise. The player who loses all his cards also loses the game.

7.10   A company has a warehouse that contains several different types of article, and there may be several different examples of each article in stock. The following information will be interesting to know for each article: the *article identification* (a code of four characters), the *article description* (a text with at most 30 characters) the *number of articles* of a particular kind in stock and the *sales price*. Write a class Article, which defines the articles.

You need a program that keeps track of all the articles in stock. Write a program that first reads in this information about the articles and places the information into an array with elements of type Article. (Assume that there are no more than 1000 kinds of article in the warehouse.) Input can terminate when, for example, the article definition '0000' is given. The program will then repeatedly read commands from the terminal and perform the tasks required. The different commands are as follows, where xxxx stands for an article definition code:

info xxxx	Write out all current information about article xxxx.
sell xxxx n	Register that *n* items of article xxxx have been sold.
buy xxxx n	Register that *n* items of article xxxx have been put into the store.

8 More about Classes

We have now learnt how to construct our own types with the aid of classes. In this chapter we will be going further and learning more about what we can do with classes. The emphasis will be on how to create our own operators to work with objects in the same way as if they were built-in standard types. This we must do if the classes we construct are to be functional and maintain their 'general' character.

In order to be able to make the operators as general as we would like, we will have to waive some of our principles regarding information hiding, for we will be describing what are known as friends – functions or other classes – which give an insight to the private sections of classes.

In this chapter we will also be discussing constant objects and functions as well as static data members, class variables only found in an instance which is shared by all the objects in a class.

8.1   Constant objects

We know that an object is a variable whose type is a class, and we have seen that constant variables and function parameters can be declared. This also applies to objects. For example, we can write

```
const Clock ck;
```

If we now try to call a member function which changes a constant object

```
ck.tick();      // ERROR!
```

or call a function that has a pointer or reference to a changeable `Clock` as parameter

```
void f1(Clock *cp);
void f2(Clock& cr);
f1(&ck);        // ERROR!
f2(ck);         // ERROR!
```

the compiler will discover this and give a compilation error.

Some member functions do not change the data members of the actual object. These are called *constant functions*. The function `read_hour` is an example of a constant function. Ordinary member functions cannot be called for constant objects but it ought to be possible to call constant member functions. The problem is that we will get a compilation error if the compiler does not know that the member function is constant. For instance, we would get a compilation error if we wrote

```
int hour = ck.read_hour();
```

But we can still indicate explicitly which member functions are constant in a class definition. We do this by writing the reserved word **const** after the parameter list in a function definition. We now adjust the definition of class `Clock` and indicate that the functions `read_hour`, `read_min`, `read_sec` and `write` are constant:

```
class Clock {
public:
  Clock ();
  Clock (int hour, int min, int sec);
  void set(int hour, int min, int sec);
  int read_hour() const {return h;}
  int read_min() const {return m;}
  int read_sec() const {return s;}
  void write(bool write_sec = true) const;
  void tick();
```

```
private:
  int h, m, s;
};
```

We are now allowed to call the functions for constant objects:

```
ck.write();              // OK
int min = ck.read_min(); // OK
```

The compiler checks that we keep our word. For instance, if in the definition of the member function `write` we try to change the actual object all the same, we would get a compilation error:

```
Clock::write() const
{
  h = 0;    // ERROR!
  tick();   // ERROR!
  ...
}
```

It is a good habit to indicate which functions are constant in the class definition, since we do not then limit the functions' usefulness unnecessarily. We will be developing this habit from now on.

Constant member functions

- Member functions that do not make changes in the actual object.
- Are indicated by the word **const** in the function definition
  result_type function_name(parameter list) **const**;

8.2   The pointer `this`

When a member function is called, it is always for a particular object. If we make the call

```
k1.tick();
k2.tick();
```

the member function `tick` will be called for the object `k1` in the first line and for the object `k2` in the second. No object name is indicated inside the member function `tick`. Only something like this can stand there

```
s++;
```

How can the member function tick know that in the first call it should change the data member s in the object k1 and in the second, that it should change the s that is in k2? The answer is that all *member* functions get an extra hidden parameter that is not seen, either in the parameter list or at the call of the function. This hidden parameter is always called **this**. Its type is 'pointer to C', where C is the name of the class in question. All member functions in class Clock, for example, have a hidden parameter **this** of type Clock *.

The pointer **this** is initialized automatically so that it points to the actual object whenever it is called. Thus, at the call k1.tick(), **this** will point to k1 and with the call k2.tick(), to k2. When the name of a member m is written inside a member function, the compiler will interpret this as if (**this**->m) had been written. If we write s++ in the function tick, it will mean (**this**->s)++. Since **this** points to k1 in the first call and to k2 in the second, the correct object will be changed.

Generally speaking, we do not have to think about the pointer **this**, because the compiler automatically deals with it. But there are two occasions where we must explicitly make use of **this** in a member function. The first is when we need to call, from inside a member function, another function that will have an object of the actual class as parameter. Suppose, for example, that there is a function with the declaration

```
void plan(Flight& f);
```

which gets a reference to a flight and places this in a list of aircraft. Further suppose that we want to be able to call this function from a member function mf in the class Flight. We can then write the following:

```
void Flight::mf()
{
  ...
  plan(*this);   // give this object as argument
}
```

Another fairly common occasion when **this** must be used is when we want to return the actual object – or a reference or pointer to it – as result from a member function. This is necessary if we want to write member functions capable of being called in a single sequence. (Compare with the write-out operator <<.) If we want to write

```
k.set(10, 25, 30).tick().tick().write();
```

the member functions set and tick must be changed. The result from a call of these must be the actual object, so that we can directly apply the dot operator. We make the declarations

```
Clock& set(int hour, int min, int sec);
Clock& tick();
```

Here we let the member functions return a *reference* to the actual object and not to a copy of the object. The definitions of the two member functions must also be changed:

```
Clock& Clock::set(int hour, int min, int sec)
{
  h=hour; m=min; s=sec;
  return *this;
}
Clock& Clock::tick()
  { as earlier
  return *this;
}
```

Interesting here is the last line, with the expression `*this`. This expression means 'what `this` points to', that is, the actual object. It is a reference to this object, which will be returned. There could be a question why **return this** is not used instead, since a reference really is a kind of pointer but this would be an error, because the compiler automatically ensures that there is a reference to the object. On the other hand, if the return type from the function had been a pointer to a `Clock`, that is, `Clock *`, it would have been correct to write **return this**.

8.3 Friends

We have stated that information hiding is a very important ingredient in object-oriented programming style, and this is corroborated by the way we construct classes in C++. Whatever is declared in the private section of a class definition, is not visible outside the class. The rules of the language guarantee that only the member functions of a class have access to what has been declared there. But as we know, there cannot be rules if there are no exceptions, and so it is here. There has had to be a compromise on information hiding in C++. This is because the member functions in certain situations serve to limit the various possibilities. Now, we may indicate in a class definition that a class has certain *friends*. A friend can either be an ordinary function, which is not a member function, or another class. A friend is allowed to view a class in its entirety.

Let us take a couple of examples. On page 221, we showed a program which used the class `Vector`, and in this program there is a function `square`, which squares the elements in a vector. Now we can indicate in the definition of class `Vector` that this function will have a friend:

```
class Vector {
public:
```

```
friend void square(Vector& v);
    ...
private:
  int *p;
  const int i1;
  int num;
};
```

With this, the function `square` will have knowledge of the data members p, i1 and num in the private section. We can now write a more effective variant of the function `square` where, instead of calling the member functions `read` and `change`, we can directly make changes in the array the data member p points to.

```
void square(Vector& v)
{
  for (int i = 0; i <= v.num; i++)
    v.p[i] *= v.p[i];
}
```

Note that `square` is not a member function. It does not belong to the class `Vector`. We use a normal function call to call it, without indicating an object in front of the function name. We can write, for example:

```
Vector vv;
square(vv);
```

It is controversial to use friend functions in this way, since it is contrary to our ideas on information hiding. It is important that we use friends with some discretion and common sense. If we define our friend functions with the member functions, in the same file, they could be understood to be operations which are part of the class concerned, in spite of the fact that they are not member functions. Then the function `square` might as well have been formulated as a member function, which might have been a good idea. But there are occasions when it seems natural to use friend functions, or when we simply cannot use member functions. This latter case will be discussed later in connection with operators. One instance where it is better to use friend functions is when we are dealing with *symmetrical* operations with two or more objects of the same kind as arguments. Then it does not make sense to take one of the arguments and put it in front of the function name, while the other arguments are given in the usual way. Suppose that we want to construct a function `earliest`, which gets two strikes of a clock as arguments and as result gives the earliest of the two. If the strikes of the clock, k1 and k2, are to be compared and the earliest of them is to be placed in the variable k3, then writing

```
k3 = earliest(k1, k2);
```

will be more satisfactory than writing

```
k3 = k1.earliest(k2);
```

We can produce the first example if we formulate the function `earliest` as a friend function rather than as a member function:

```
class Clock {
public:
  friend const Clock& earliest(Clock& ca,  Clock& cb);
  declarations of other member functions
private:
  int h, m, s;
};
```

We put the definition in the file `Clock.cpp` and it looks like this

```
const Clock& earliest(Clock& ca,  Clock& cb)
{
  if (ca.h<cb.h or (ca.h==cb.h and (ca.m<cb.m
            or (ca.m==cb.m and ca.s<cb.s))))
    return ca;
  else
    return cb;
}
```

Not only functions can be friends. Another class can be declared as a friend, in which case all of the member functions in one class can access the private members of another. This is how the class `Clock` indicates that the class `Flight` is its friend:

```
class Clock {
public:
  friend class Flight;
  ...
};
```

This makes it possible to construct a much more effective variant of the function `delay` than the one shown earlier (see page 207).

```
void Flight::delay(int min)
{
  dep.h = (dep.h + (dep.m+min)/60) % 24;
  dep.m = (dep.m+min) % 60;
  arr.h = (arr.h + (arr.m+min)/60) % 24;
  arr.m = (arr.m+min) % 60;
}
```

Here we do not have to make the clock tick forward one second at a time. We can simply add the necessary minutes.

We should exercise extreme caution before we make an entire class into the friend of another. A class C1 should only make another class C2 its friend when C1 is simply a 'help class' of C2, that is, used to implement C2. We will be showing examples of this in Chapter 12 when discussing linked data constructs.

Note, finally, that friendship is one-way in C++. A certain class itself chooses who is to be its friend and share its secrets. A class or function cannot ask to be friends with another class or function.

Friends

- In a class definition a particular function or class can be made to be a friend.

  ```
  class C {
      friend type f(parameters);
      friend class C2;
      ...
  };
  ```

- The function f and the class C2 then have access to the private members of C.

8.4   Operators

In C++ there are a number of predefined operators that can be applied to the built-in standard types. For instance, we can add two variables of type **int** using the operator +, and we can compare two values of type **double** using the operator <=. These predefined operators are actually overloaded, as each one of them can be used for several standard types. For instance, one + operator is used for type **int** and another for type **double**. Where classes are concerned, there are almost no predefined operators. (The most important ones are the assignment operator =, the dot operator, the arrow operator and the address operator.) When, using classes, we declare our own types, we often wish that there were operators for these. For instance, it would seem entirely natural if for type RatNum, which was discussed on page 222, there were an operator + enabling us to write expressions of the form r1+r2, where r1 and r2 are of type RatNum. What we can do, is define our *own* operators for our classes, and these will be superimposed on the predefined operators. For instance, if we define our own operator + for type RatNum and write the expression r1+r2, the compiler will automatically discover that it is a personally defined plus operator that must be called.

We shall now look at how we define our own operators for our classes, how we *overload* operators. When we declare our own operator, we write a function with the name **operator**X, where X is an operator symbol. If, for instance, we were to write our own addition operator, the function we declared would have the name **operator**+. The word **operator** is reserved in C++. We will be giving several examples, but first some general comments are needed.

Almost all the predefined operators for the standard types can be overloaded. This applies to the following operators:

new	delete	new[]	delete[]					.
+	–	*	/	%	^	&	|	~
!	=	<	>	+=	-=	*=	/=	%=
^=	&=	|=	<<	>>	>>=	<<=	==	!=
<=	>=	&&	||	++	--	,	->*	->
()	[]							

Among these are, for instance, numeric and logical operators. Of special interest are the assignment and comparison operators, which, as we note, can be overloaded. The two operators () and [] on the last line represent a function call and indexing, respectively.

When we define our own operators we must, therefore, use one of the operator symbols from the above table. We are not allowed to use a combination of our own, for instance, <>, which does not appear in the table. We must also remember that there should be an equal number of operands for an operator as for the corresponding predefined operator. For instance, if we define our own comparison operator ==, this must have two operands and if we define our own operator !, it must have one operand. Some of the predefined operators exist in two variants, with one operand (unary) or with two (binary). The – operator is an example of this. We may write our own versions of these operators in both the unary and the binary variants.

When we write our own operator, it will have the same priority as the corresponding predefined operator. If for class RatNum we have defined both our own plus operator + and our own multiplication operator *, the multiplication operator will have higher priority and so will be called first in the expression r1+r2*r3.

In order to preserve clarity in the way a program functions, we should try to formulate our own operators so that they logically correspond to predefined operators. For example, it would be appropriate if we defined our own + operator

---

Operators

- Functions with the name **operator**X, where X is the operator symbol.
- Most of the predefined operators may be overloaded for class types.
- Can have one operand (unary) or two operands (binary).
- The number of operands and the priority are the same for a corresponding predefined operator.
- Can be constructed as a member function or friend function.

---

for type RatNum so that it really added two rational numbers and did not carry out some other operation on them, subtraction, for instance.

We have two ways of constructing our own operators, either by formulating them as member functions or as friend functions. While it is customary to use member functions, sometimes we have to use friend functions; we will be describing both ways here. We begin by dealing with how we use member functions to construct our own operators. In the following sections we use class Vector, defined on page 218, as an example. (The only difference is that we now declare first, last and length as *constant* member functions.)

8.4.1   Binary operators

In our first example, we will define our own operator == for class Vector. This operator makes it possible to compare two vectors v1 and v2 as in, for example

```
Vector v1, v2;
if (v1 == v2)
```

We formulate the operator as a member function. As with other member functions, the declaration of the operator should lie in the class definition:

```
class Vector {
public:
  bool operator== (const Vector& v) const;
  declarations of the other member functions
private:
  int *p;
  const int i1;
  int num;
};
```

Note that the function **operator**== only has *one* parameter and we previously stated that a comparison operator had to have *two* parameters. This is because the first parameter is understood and will automatically become the actual object. If, for example, we write the expression

```
v1 == v2
```

the compiler will understand it as if we had written

```
v1.operator==(v2)
```

that is, the function **operator**== is called for the object v1, and v2 is given as argument. Thus, the function's formal parameter v will correspond in this call to v2, and the pointer **this** will point to v1. It *is* permissible to call our own operators in this way, even if it is more normal to write an expression such as v1==v2. As a general rule, binary operators always have *one* parameter and unary operators have *no* parameters, where operators are declared as member functions.

Note that in the declaration we indicated that the function **operator**== should be a constant function. Of course, the actual object should not be changed when it is compared with another object. Note, too, that we did not indicate that the parameter v should be of type Vector but a *reference* to a constant Vector. By using a reference, we avoid copying a whole vector in every call, and by saying that it is a reference to a constant, we guarantee that the right-hand operand is not changed when a call of the operator == is made.

We write the definition of the function **operator**== separately. Two vectors are equal if they contain the same number of elements, each element being equal to the corresponding element in the other vector. But the first index value of the vectors need not be the same.

```
bool Vector::operator== (const Vector& v) const
{
  if (num != v.num)
    return false;
  for (int i=0; i<num; i++)
    if (p[i] != v.p[i])
      return false;
  return true;
}
```

If the function here is called with the expression v1==v2, num will mean the num that is in v1, and v.num will mean the num that is in v2.

If the operator == has been declared, there should also be a != operator. This is not automatically declared when the equality operator is declared. Instead, we have do this ourselves. We therefore add the following declaration in the definition of class Vector:

```
bool operator!= (const Vector& v) const;
```

We can use the operator == we have just constructed, in the definition:

```
bool Vector::operator!= (const Vector& v) const
{
  return not((*this)==v);
}
```

If we suppose that the function is called from an expression v1!=v2, the pointer **this** will point to v1. The expression *this then means v1. Since v refers to v2, what we will be doing is comparing v1 and v2 to find out if they are equal. We then return the inverted value from this test.

In the next example, we construct an operator that adds two vectors, element by element. For this to be possible, the two vectors must contain the same number of elements. First we must explain what we mean when we say that the operator will add two vectors. By way of explanation, let us look at type **int**. If we have two integers m and n and write the expression m+n, this will mean that a new, temporary integer has been formed and that this contains the sum of the two integers. Neither m nor n will be changed because we write m+n. If we want to change one operand, we should instead use the operator += and write, for example, m+=n. Then the number in n is added to the number in m, and m will be changed. We would like to apply the same principles to our own type Vector, and so we construct two different addition operators, += and +. First we deal with the operator +=. We can write the declaration

```
const Vector& operator+= (const Vector& v);
```

The definition looks like this

```
const Vector& Vector::operator+= (const Vector& v)
{
  assert(num==v.num);
  for (int i=0; i<num; i++)
    p[i] += v.p[i];
  return *this;
}
```

It is also understood here that the left-hand operand is the actual object. The parameter v refers to the right-hand operand. Since this should not be changed we will have a reference to a constant. When this function is called, it is done, for the most part, in statements such as

```
v1 += v2;
```

but the operator could also be a part of more complicated expressions such as

```
if (v3 == (v1 += v2))
```

Thus the operator += should leave a result which we can continue to work with. This should be a copy of the left-hand operand's new value, in our example, a copy of the new value of v1. In the declaration we have indicated that the result type should be a reference to a constant Vector, and on the penultimate line we write that the value *`this` should be returned. What will be returned is quite simply a reference to the actual object, or v1, in our example. We could also have stated that the result type should be Vector but the function would then have copied the actual object and left the copy as result. By using a reference, we avoid ineffective copying. It is important that the result type be indicated as a reference to a *constant*. Naturally, it would not be possible to change the actual object via the result value that has been left. For instance, the following would not be allowed,

```
(v1 += v2) = v3;   // ERROR!
```

Let us turn now to the second addition operator. The declaration is:

```
Vector operator+ (const Vector& v) const;
```

We have declared the function as constant since the actual object should not be changed by this operator. Here is the definition:

```
Vector Vector::operator+ (const Vector& v) const
{
   assert(num==v.num);
   Vector temp(*this);   // Create a copy of this vector
   temp += v;
   return temp;
}
```

In this function we cannot leave a reference to the actual object as result, since this object is not to be changed. Instead, we declare a local, temporary variable of type Vector inside the function. As initializion value for this temporary vector we give the argument *`this`, that is, the actual vector. The vector temp will then be initialized with the aid of the copy constructor and will contain a copy of the actual vector. If, for example, we call the function with the expression v1+v2, temp will be a copy of v1. We then apply the operator += on temp, causing it to be changed. It will then contain the sum of the actual vector and the right-hand operand, that is, the sum of v1 and v2 in our example. We give as result a copy of temp.

It may seem strange that we have not specified that the result type of this function should be a reference, as we did for the operator +=. If we had, the function would

Binary operators
• Should have *one* parameter if it is a member function.
• Actual object == the left-hand operand.
• The parameter == the right-hand operand.
• Be careful to differentiate between operators whether or not an actual object is changed.

have given a reference to the variable `temp` as result. This would not have been correct, as `temp` only exists inside the function **operator**+. Once the function has finished being executed, `temp` will no longer exist. As we know, a reference is a kind of pointer to a variable. If we had returned a reference as result type, therefore, we would in fact have returned a lingering pointer. (See our discussion of common errors when using pointers on page 161.)

We will now construct two more addition operators for type `Vector`, and these will also be called += and +. The new operators both have an integer as the right-hand operand. We should be able to write `v1+=5` to add the number 5 to each element in `v1` and `v1+10` in order to compute a vector which gives a copy of `v1` but with the number 10 added to all the elements. The declarations are:

```
const Vector& operator+= (int d);
Vector operator+ (int d) const;
```

The definitions are made in the same way as before:

```
const Vector& Vector::operator+= (int d)
{
for (int i=0; i<num; i++)
  p[i] += d;
return *this;
}
Vector Vector::operator+ (int d) const
{
  Vector temp(*this);
  temp += d;
  return temp;
}
```

We shall now construct a slightly more complicated operator, a concatenation operator which we will call &=. With this, we will be able to extend a vector and add another vector onto the end of it. If, for example, the vector `v1` contains the three elements [1, 5, 7] and the vector `v2` the two elements [0, 3], we will

be able to write v1&=v2. After this operation, v1 will contain the five elements
[1, 5, 7, 0, 3]. The declaration is simple:

```
const Vector& operator&= (const Vector& v);
```

We also return a reference to the changed object here in order to continue working
with the result. For instance, it will be possible to write v3=(v1&=v2). The
definition is:

```
const Vector& Vector::operator&= (const Vector& v)
{
  int *q = new int[num+v.num];  // Create new space
  for (int i=0; i<num; i++)
    q[i] = p[i];                // Copy this vector
  for (int j=0; j<v.num; j++)
    q[j+num] = v.p[i];          // Copy v
  delete[] p;                   // Release old memory
  p=q;                          // Point to the new space
  num += v.num;                 // Increase length
  return *this;
}
```

The actual object should be changed to ensure it contains a longer vector than
previously; in order to bring this about, we have to allocate new memory space that
will be big enough. It will have to accommodate num+v.num elements. We let the
provisional pointer q point to this new memory space. We then copy to it the
original elements of the actual vector followed by the elements in the right-hand
operand. The memory space allocated earlier for the actual vector must then be
released so that we do not consume memory that will never be released. When
this has been done, we let the member variable p point to the newly allocated
memory space.

We can also make a variant of the concatenation operator, one which does
not change the actual object but only gives a unified vector as result. We will call
this operator &. If v1 as before contains the three elements [1, 5, 7] and vector
v2 the two elements [0, 3], we will be able to write v3=v1&v2. Then v3 after
this operation will contain the five elements [1, 5, 7, 0, 3]. Vectors v1 and
v2 will be unchanged. We now write the definition:

```
Vector operator& (const Vector& v) const;
```

The definition can be written quite simply using the operator &=

```
Vector Vector::operator& (const Vector& v) const
{
```

```
Vector temp(*this);  // Create a copy of this vector
temp &= v;
return temp;
}
```

As with the operator +, we create here a local copy of the actual vector. We then apply the operator &= to this copy.

Using these operators as models, we can construct several binary operators for class Vector. We could, for instance, write operators for subtraction, multiplication and division.

8.4.2 Unary operators

As an example of a unary operator, we will construct a unary minus operator. If we have a vector v1, we should be able to write -v1. We would then get a copy of v1 where all the elements are replaced by corresponding negative values. The declaration of the binary operator is very simple:

```
Vector operator- () const;
```

Note that when a unary operator is formulated as a member function, the function should *not have parameters*. The operator will only have one operand where it is understood that this operand is the actual object. When we write:

```
-v1
```

it is the same thing as if we had made the function call:

```
v1.operator-()
```

It is permissible to write it in this way as well. The definition can now be written separately:

```
Vector Vector::operator- () const
{
  Vector temp(*this);  // Create a copy of this vector
  for (int i=0; i<num; i++)
    temp.p[i] = -temp.p[i];  // Negate each element
  return temp;
}
```

There are a couple of unary operators that present special problems. These are the increment and decrement operators ++ and --. We will remember from Chapter 2 that these two operators exist in two variants, a prefix variant, where ++

Unary operator
● Should not have parameters if it is a member function.
● The actual object == the operand.

---

or `--` is placed in front of the variable name, and a postfix variant where `++` or `--` is placed after the variable name. (See page 40.) Both variants increase or decrease their operand but the difference between them is that the prefix variant gives the operand's new value as result, while the postfix variant gives as result the operand's old value.

We look at the increment operator here, constructing our own operator `++` for type `Vector`. (The decrement operator can be treated analogously.) We therefore make the declaration:

```
const Vector& operator++ ();   // prefix ++v
```

Since the operator `++` is a unary operator, we have declared it as a function without parameters. The problem is that both the prefix and postfix variants of the operator `++` are unary. Therefore, they should both have exactly the same declaration, and it should not be possible to tell them apart. In C++, a special style of writing the declarations has made it possible to declare both the prefix and postfix variants of the increment and decrement operators. (This did not exist in earlier versions of C++, when only the prefix variant could be declared.) If we write as above, we mean the declaration of the prefix variant. If we want to declare the postfix variant, we have to declare an operator with the name `++` that has a parameter of type **int**. The declaration would then look like this:

```
Vector operator++ (int);   // postfix v++
```

We can pretend that the operator `++` is binary! The integer parameter has only been added, however, to mark that we are dealing with the postfix variant. The parameter does not get a value when the function is called, and it is not used in the function definition. It has not even been given a name.

It is now time to look at the definitions of the two variants of the operator `++`. We begin with the prefix variant, which increases all elements in the actual vector by 1 and then returns the new value:

```
const Vector& Vector::operator++ ()   // prefix ++v
{
  return (*this) += 1;   // Return the new value
}
```

> ### The operators ++ and --
>
> - For class X:
>   ```
>   const X& operator++();   // prefix ++x
>   X operator++(int);       // postfix x++
>   ```
> - The integer parameter is not used. Only marks the postfix variant.

Here we have been able to make things very easy by making use of the operator +=, which has an integer as a right-hand operand and which we constructed in the previous section. As usual, we return a reference to the actual object instead of copying unnecessarily.

The postfix variant of ++ can be made almost as simple. The only difference is that instead of returning the actual vector's new value, we return a copy of the vector's old value. (We cannot return a reference because we would have problems with lingering pointers.)

```
Vector Vector::operator++ (int)    // postfix v++
{
  Vector temp(*this); // Create a copy of this vector
  (*this) += 1;       // Increase this vector
  return temp;        // Return the old value
}
```

8.4.3 The assignment operator

In Section 7.3.4 we dealt with the copy constructor, which is called when initializing an object. Then, we had various problems when making initializations, and we will experience similar problems with making assignments. When we make an assignment, as for example:

```
v1 = v2;
```

the *assignment operator* is called for the class. In most cases, the compiler itself automatically defines an assignment operator. (But this will not happen if a class has a data member which is a constant or a reference.) The automatically defined assignment operator works well for most classes. The way in which it makes assignments corresponds to the way in which the automatically defined copy constructor makes initializations: a subobject of simple type (scalars and pointers) is copied bit by bit, just as with ordinary assignments. If a subobject is of class type, the assignment operator for this class will be called to do the copying. If, finally, a subobject is an array, each element in the array will be copied according to the foregoing rules.

In Section 7.3.4, we stated that the automatically defined copy constructor did not work for classes which themselves allocate memory space. In order to carry out deep copying, we had to define our own copy constructor. On page 219 we gave a copy constructor for class `Vector`. We needed to carry out deep copying when making initializations, and the same is true when we make assignments. We also need to construct our own assignment operator. A copy operator for a class X will have the name **operator**= and have a single parameter that will be of type X, X& or **const**X&. We can declare our own assignment operator for class `Vector`:

```
const Vector& operator= (const Vector& v);
```

This will now replace the automatically defined assignment operator and will be called every time we assign one vector to another. (With initializations, however, the copy constructor will be called.) We write the definition:

```
const Vector& Vector::operator= (const Vector& v)
{
  if (this != &v)        // Copying to itself?
  {                      // No
    delete p;            // Release old memory
    num = v.num;
    p = new int[num];    // Allocate new space
    for (int i=0; i<num; i++)
      p[i] = v.p[i];     // Copy the elements
  }
  return *this;
}
```

First there is a check that an assignment has not been made to itself. If so, nothing needs to be done. But it is important to include this test, as otherwise the memory space for the vector would be wrongly released.

Assignment operator

operator=

- Has a parameter that is an object of the same class or a reference to an object of the same class.
- Is automatically called with assignments
    ```
    x1=x2;
    ```
- If we need to write our own copy constructor, we normally also need our own assignment operator.

If there is no assignment to the same object, the assignment operator will do the same thing as the copy constructor, that is, it will allocate memory space for an array that will contain the new value and copy the elements one by one to the new array. In addition, the memory space containing the old value must be released.

8.4.4 The indexing operator

In the previous chapter, we used the two functions `read` and `change`, to read and change different elements in an object of type `Vector`. This was rather clumsy. It would have been much simpler to use indexing, exactly as for ordinary arrays. This is possible if we construct our own indexing operator. It will have the name **operator**`[]` and one parameter. We can make the declaration:

```
int& operator[] (int i);
```

If we now wrote an indexing expression such as `v[j+n]`, for example, it would be interpreted as though we had written:

```
v.operator[](j+n)
```

that is, the vector we are indexing in becomes the actual vector, and the index value is given as argument. An indexing expression should be able to stand both on the right and on the left in an assignment. For instance, it should be possible to write:

```
v[j+1] = v[j];
```

To make this possible, the function **operator**`[]` must return a *reference* to an element so that this element can be changed via the reference. If the function had only returned an **int**, the result would have been a *copy* of the chosen element, and it would not have been possible to change this. Let us look at the definition. We use the function `assert` to check that the index lies within the allowed limits.

```
int& Vector::operator[] (int i)
{
  assert(i >= i1 and i <= last());
  return p[i-i1];   // Return a reference
}
```

There is a little problem with this operator. Suppose that we write:

```
const Vector cv;
cout << cv[1];
```

When we try to compile, we can get the error printout:

Indexing operator

```
element type& operator[](int index);
element type& operator[](int index) const;
```

- The object we index in becomes the actual object.
- Index given as the only parameter.
- Appropriate to define two overloaded variants.
- Called automatically upon indexing
    x[i]

---

non-const function called for const object

Although the indexing operator does not change in the actual object, it makes it possible for the caller to change a particular element. So it should not be declared as a constant function (with the word **const**). This means that it cannot be used on occasions such as the one above, where we want to read a particular element in a constant object without changing anything. The solution is to overload the index operator. We are allowed to overload two member functions with the same parameters, where one function is constant and the other is not. We declare here a constant variant of the indexing operator:

```
int operator[] (int i) const;
```

We return a copy of element number i, instead of a reference. The definition looks almost exactly the same as for the non-constant variant:

```
int Vector::operator[] (int i) const
{
    assert(i >= i1 and i <= last());
    return p[i-i1];   // Return a copy
}
```

8.4.5   The function call operator

The next operator we shall look at is rather special. It is the *function call operator*, indicated by the parentheses (). We call this operator by making what looks rather like a function call. We can decide how many parameters we want the operator to have. For instance, if we decide it is to have no parameters, we can call it by writing:

```
x();
```

where x is an object. If we had decided that the function operator should have three parameters, a call would then have the form:

```
x(p1, p2, p3);
```

¯As an example of the way we use this operator, let us construct an operator which will help us to cut *slices* out of a vector. For example, if we have a vector v1, consisting of 5 elements numbered from 1 to 5, then the elements 3, 4 and 5 constitute a slice consisting of 3 elements. An appropriate way of representing this slice is to write v1(3,5). We can use this style if we formulate the function call operator in the right way. For instance, we can write:

```
Vector v1(1,5), v2, v3;
for (int i=1; i<=5; i++)
  v1[i] = i;
v2 = v1(2,4);              // v2 == [2, 3, 4]
v3 = v1(3,5) & v2(1,2);    // v3 == [3, 4, 5, 2, 3]
```

A declaration of the function call operator should look like this:

```
Vector operator() (int from, int to);
```

It evidently has two parameters that indicate the first and last index for the slice that will be cut out. As result it gives a copy of the required slice. The definition is:

```
Vector Vector::operator() (int from, int to)
{
  assert(from<=to and from>=i1 and to<=last());
  Vector temp(from, to-from+1);  // Create a slice
  for (int i=0; i<temp.num; i++)
    temp.p[i] = p[from-i1+i];    // Copy the elements
  return temp;
}
```

Function call operator
return type **operator**() (*parameters*);
● Can have an arbitrary number of parameters.
● Automatically called with expressions of the form   x(p1, p2, p3 ...) where x is an object of the actual class.

Note that the function call operator returns a copy of the slice. This means that the operator cannot be used in expressions such as `v1(1,3)=v2` and `v1(1,3)++`, where the intention is to change inside a particular slice. For this to be possible, both the slice and the whole vector must refer to the *same* physical integer array (their data members `p` should point to the same array). But then we will have problems with constructors and destructors. Clearly, we do not do things in this way, otherwise we shall just get into a muddle.

8.4.6 Friend functions as operators

In the introduction to this chapter, we stated that operators could either be formulated as member functions or as friend functions. Why is the alternative necessary? Is it not possible to simply use member functions as we have seen in so many examples? The problem is that there is one occasion when member functions cannot be used. All operators used as member functions require the type of the left-hand operand (or the only operand) of an operator to be of the actual class. When, for example, we use the type `Vector` and write such expressions as `v1+v2`, the member functions only work if `v1` has type `Vector`. Earlier we constructed an operator that had a vector as left-hand operand and an integer as right-hand operand. This made it possible to write expressions such as `v1+5`. For reasons of symmetry, we would like to write `5+v1`, when the result should be the same. But we cannot do this with member functions, so we have to use a friend function. We therefore place the following declaration in the definition of class `Vector`:

```
friend Vector operator+ (int d, const Vector& v);
```

A friend function is not a member function and so there is no 'understood' parameter. Instead, all the parameters must be indicated in the parameter list. If a binary operator is involved here, it should have two parameters. The first parameter will indicate the left-hand operand and the second, the right-hand operand. This function can be said to belong to class `Vector`, in spite of the fact that it is not a member function. We therefore put it with the definitions of member functions in the file `Vector.cpp`.

```
Vector operator+ (int d, const Vector& v)
{
    return v+d;
}
```

This is extremely simple. By changing the order of the operands, we can call the member function + which is already there. (Actually, the function does not have to be a friend function, since it does not make use of anything declared in the private section of class `Vector`.)

We shall give another example of a useful friend function for class `Vector`. We shall write our own output operator. To obtain output at the terminal or in files, we usually use the output operator `<<` in C++. This operator is declared as a member function in the standard class `ostream`, which is defined in the file `iostream.h`. Class `ostream` defines what is called an *output stream*. (The variable `cout`, which we have used extensively, is, for instance, a predefined object of class `ostream`.) Since the operator `<<` is a member function of the class `ostream`, the left-hand operand of the operator should always be of this class. The right-hand operand will be the value that is output. The output operator `<<` is overloaded. There is a variant for every one of the built-in standard types. The following two member functions enable output to be made from the standard types **int** and **double**, for example:

```
ostream& operator<< (int);
ostream& operator<< (double);
```

These operators are called when we want to write, for instance

```
cout << i;   // i has type int
cout << d;   // d has type double
```

It is important to note that the operator `<<` always gives as result a reference to the actual output stream. This makes it possible to construct chains by calling the operator. For instance, we can write:

```
cout << i << d;
```

Here, the partial expression `cout<<i` gives as result a reference to `cout`, which means that the right-hand operator `<<` gets an output stream as left-hand operand.

We will now write our own operator `<<` to function for type `Vector`. Since the operator will function in the same way as the standard variants of `<<`, it must as left-hand operand have a reference to an output stream of type `ostream`, and as right-hand operand have a value of type `Vector` The result type should be a reference to the actual output stream. We must formulate our output operator as a friend function of class `Vector`, so we place the following definition in the class definition:

```
friend ostream& operator<< (ostream& o, const Vector& v);
```

We place the definition of our operator separately in the file `Vector.cpp`:

```
ostream& operator<< (ostream& o, const Vector& v)
{
  o << '[';
```

```
if (v.num>0)
  o << v.p[0];
for (int i=1; i<v.num; i++)
  o << ", " << v.p[i];
o << ']';
return o;
}
```

The function writes the individual elements in a vector in square brackets. The standard variant of the operator $<<$ is used to write output inside the function. The actual output stream is indicated by the parameter o, and a reference to this is also given as result. We can now write, for instance:

```
Vector v1(1,5);
for (int i=1; i<=5; i++)
  v1[i] = i;
cout << v1;
```

On the last line our new output operator is called. The parameter o will refer to the output stream cout. This output is then written as:

```
[1, 2, 3, 4, 5]
```

We can also let our output operator be part of the call chains, as in:

```
cout << "v1 contains " << v1 << endl;
```

We usually construct our own output operators for our classes, and the input operators are constructed in a similar way. The left-hand operand is a reference to an object of the standard class istream, and the result type is a reference to istream. If we constructed an input operator for class Vector, it would have the following appearance:

```
friend istream& operator>> (istream& in,Vector& v);
```

Friend functions as operators

       friend *return_type* **operator**X (*parameters*);

- Should have the same number of parameters as operands.
- Must be used when the left-hand operand does not belong to the actual class.

8.4.7   Type conversion operators

In the last chapter we learnt that a constructor which could be called with only one parameter carried out a type conversion to the actual class. The class RatNum was declared, for instance:

```
class RatNum {
public:
  RatNum (int i=0) : numer(i), denom(1) {}
  declarations of several member functions
private:
  int numer, denom;
};
```

The constructor functions here as a type conversion from type **int** to type RatNum. It can therefore be called automatically, without this being revealed in the code. If a variable r has type RatNum, the constructor will be called automatically if we write, for instance:

```
r=5;
```

Constructors can only function as type conversions if the type we are converting *to* is a class. If we want to define a type conversion to a type which is not a class, we have to do it in a different way. We can then define a type conversion operator. Let us take the class RatNum as an example. A rational number can be represented exactly as a quotient of two integers. Sometimes, however, we may want an approximate value of this quotient. It will then be a real number which can be defined by the standard type **double**. Thus we construct a type conversion operator that converts from type RatNum to type **double**. The following declaration will be placed in the definition of class RatNum:

```
operator double() const;
```

There are some special rules for type conversion operators: their names should be the same as the names they are converting to; they should not have parameters; and no result type can be specified. Of course, the result type should always be identical to that of the type they are converting to. We write the definition separately:

```
RatNum::operator double() const
{
  return double(numer)/denom;
}
```

Type conversion operator

operator *type*() **const**;

- Member function.
- No parameters or result type can be specified.
- Converts from the actual class to type *type*.
- Is called automatically when type conversion is needed.

Here we simply give as result the quotient of the numerator and denominator. For it to be a real number division and not an integer division, we have to make an explicit type conversion of one of the operands to type **double**.

This type conversion operator can now be called automatically when a type conversion from type RatNum to **double** is needed. This happens, for example, in the statement d=r. (Suppose that the variable d has type **double** and r type RatNum.)

8.5 **Static members**

Sometimes there are components common to all objects which belong to a class. In an object-oriented context, these are usually called *class variables*. In C++ they are called *static members*, so we will be using this term here. Interestingly, a static data member only exists in a single instance but this instance is shared by all objects belonging to the actual class. A good example of a static data member is that of a variable which keeps track of how many objects of a certain type there are at a given moment. Take a bank account, for example. For every bank account, there is a particular balance and a particular account holder. These items of data must, of course, be available in one instance for each account, and so they are ordinary data members. The interest rate, on the other hand, is a static data member. We will use this example of a bank account to write the class definition:

```
class Account {
public:
Account() : customer_no(0), bal(0), int_earned(0) {}
  void open_account(long int customer) {customer_no=customer;}
  double balance() const {return bal;}
  void transaction(double amount);
  void daily_interest();
  void add_interest();
  static double current_interest() {return interest_rate;}
  static void change_interest(double new_interest);
```

```
private:
  long int customer_no.;
  double bal, int_earned;
  static double interest_rate;   // declaration
};
```

For every account there are three ordinary, non-static data members: a customer number and `bal`, which contains the current balance and `int_earned`, which contains the interest earned during the year. Interest earned is calculated on a daily basis but is not added to the balance until the end of the year.

First, we will define the member functions that have nothing to do with static data members. The constructor initializes a new account so that the three non-static data members are set to zero. The member function `open_account` is used to open a new account. A unique customer number is indicated as parameter. The function `balance` is called when the balance in a particular account is required. The function `transaction` is called each time a deposit or withdrawal is made on the account. Deposits are given by a positive amount and withdrawals by a negative amount. The function `daily_interest` will be called once every day and calculates how much interest is earned during this day. The interest earned is added to the data member `int_earned`. The function `add_interest` is called at the end of the year (or when the account is closed). This function adds the total interest earned during the year to the balance after which the data member `int_earned` is set to zero.

There is a static data member, `interest_rate`. This is indicated by the reserved word **static**. There are also two member functions, `current_interest` and `change_interest`, which are used to read and change the interest rate. These functions are special in that they do not deal with individual accounts and do not use non-static variables. Member functions with this property are called *static member functions* and are marked by the word **static**.

A static data member exists only in a single instance, and there is not one for every object. We *declare* a static data member in the class definition, as was done here with `interest_rate`, but the *definition* of a static data member (the place where the variable 'is') must lie outside the class definition. We usually place it in the same file as the definitions of separate member functions. Here we put the definition of `interest_rate` into a file with the name `account.cpp`. The definition looks like this:

```
double Account::interest_rate = 0.0;   // definition
```

Note that the word **static** will *not* be put here. A static member variable can be initialized in the definition. Here it has been initialized to a value of 0. Constructors are not used to initialize static member variables, and they cannot be destroyed by a destructor.

Static data members that have been declared in the private section of a class are, like other members, only accessible inside the class, in the member functions

---

Static data members

> **static** *type_name;* // declaration
> - The definition is placed outside the class definition:
>   *type class_name::name = initialization_value;*
> - Only exists in a single instance. Shared by objects in the class.

---

of the class (and in the friend functions or friend classes of the class.) A static data member declared in the **public** section of a class definition is visible and accessible from outside. We then write *class name::member name*. If interest_rate had been declared in the **public** section, we would have been able to write, for instance:

```
Account::interest_rate = 5.0;   // Not for private members
```

Static member functions can be defined, like other member functions, either in the class definition, or separately. We defined the function current_interest directly in the class definition but defined the second static member function separately. The word **static** cannot be put here, either.

```
void Account::change_interest(double new_interest)
{
  assert(new_interest >= 0);
  interest_rate = new_interest;
}
```

A static member function is not called for any object in particular, in fact it can be called even when there are no objects of the actual class. To change and read the interest, we can make the call:

```
Account::change_interest(10.0);
cout << Account::current_interest();
```

We indicate that the functions are member functions for class Account by indicating their full names Account::change_interest and Account::current_interest. Like other functions, static member functions can be called by writing the name of an object in front of the function name. For instance, we are allowed to write:

```
k.change_interest(10.0);
```

Static member functions

```
class C {
  static return type name(parameters);
};
```

- Are defined like other member functions.
- Can only use static data members.
- Are not called for any special object.

```
C::name(parameters)   // call
```

if k is a variable of type Account. But this is quite meaningless since the function change_interest does not, in any way, read or change in k.

Ordinary, non-static member functions have access to static data members and can read and change these. For example, the interest rate is needed in the function daily_interest to calculate the interest for the day:

```
void Account::daily_interest()
{
  int_earned += bal*interest_rate/100/365;
}
```

If we change a static data member in a member function, the change will have an effect on all the objects of the actual class, since all of them share the static member variable. Now to complete our example, here are the remaining member functions for class Account:

```
void Account::transaction(double amount)
{
  if (amount<0 and bal+amount < 0)
    cout << "Withdrawal not possible!" << endl;
  else
    bal+=amount;
}
void Account::add_interest()
{
  bal += int_earned;
  int_earned = 0;
}
```

EXERCISES

8.1   Complete the class RatNum so that it contains operators for the addition, subtraction, multiplication and division of rational numbers. You should also be able to perform these operations when one of the operands (any one) is an integer. Make sure that the denominator in a result is never negative and that the numerator and denominator do not have common factors (see Exercise 7.7).

8.2   Add operators for subtraction, multiplication and division for the class Vector.

8.3   Overload the operators &= and & for type Vector so that a vector can be extended by one single integer. You should be able to write expressions such as v&=5, v&19 and 27&v.

8.4   Add an input operator for class Vector.

8.5   The *scalar product* of two vectors of equal length $(u_1, u_2, ... u_n)$ and $(v_1, v_2, ... v_n)$ can be defined as the sum

$$\sum_{k=1}^{n} u_k v_k$$

Complete class Vector with an operator to calculate the scalar product of two vectors. The operator should check that the two vectors have the same number of components but numbering need not be the same. Since C++ does not allow the overloading of functions whose difference is only discernible in the return type, you cannot use the operator symbol * (it has already been used in Exercise 8.2). The symbol ^ can be used instead.

8.6   A *complex* number k can be written in the form $k = a + b \cdot i$, where a and b are ordinary real numbers and i is an *imaginary* number such that $i \cdot i = -1$. The number a is normally called the *real* part and the number b, the *imaginary* part of the number k. Construct a class Complex which makes it possible to work with complex numbers. Choose appropriate constructors and operators. (You need not write a division operator.)

8.7   Write a class Dictionary to define a very simple dictionary. A dictionary should consist of a number of entries (an array). Each entry consists of two parts, a reference word and an explanatory text. Use an extra help class Entry to define this. For class Dictionary there should be a member function with which new entries can be added. (The array does not have to be sorted.) There should be an indexing operator [] that gets a *text* as parameter. This text should be a reference word. The operator should look up the reference word in the dictionary and as result give a pointer to a corresponding explanatory text (or 0 if the reference word is not present).

8.8   Write a class that contains a static variable which automatically keeps track of how many objects of the class there are at any given moment. In addition, the class should contain a static member function that returns the value of the static variable.

8.9   A polynomial such as:

$$f(x) = 7.4x^5 + 3.1x^2 - 10.2x + 14.9$$

can be represented by an array in which every element defines a term in the polynomial. In each element is stored the term's coefficient and degree. Construct a class `Polynomial` that defines polynomials in this way. There should be operations to add, subtract and multiply polynomials, and the results should be new polynomials. There should also be a member function that calculates the polynomial's value for any value of x. This value of x should be given as a parameter of the function. In addition, write an operator that gives the derivative of a polynomial. The derivative of a polynomial

$$P(x) = a_n x^n + a_{n-1} x^{n-1} + \ldots + a_1 x + a_0$$

can be written as

$$P'(x) = n a_n x^{n-1} + (n-1) a_{n-1} x^{n-2} + \ldots + a_1$$

9 Inheritance

The special thing about object-oriented programming is that it uses *inheritance*. Using inheritance, you can create new types on the basis of existing types which you extend with further attributes. In the two previous chapters, we saw how *has* and *knows* relations were created. The third important relation, the *is* relation, is created by the use of inheritance. For instance, we can express relations such as 'an athlete is a person' or, 'a book is a document'. In C++ inheritance is introduced by creating subclasses of existing classes. In this chapter we will be looking at how this is done.

Using inheritance, we can create objects that are only partly equal to other objects. Such objects are defined by what are called *polymorphic*[†] *classes*. When objects belong to polymorphic classes, we can have operations with the same name carrying out the same operation on the different objects, even though the operations may carry out different things, depending on the kind of object involved. Suppose, for example, that we have two different kinds of bank account, one where the interest is

---

† of many forms

calculated on a daily basis and another where a certain sum has had to be in the account for a certain time before it can accrue interest. The operation 'calculate interest' will carry out, logically speaking, the same thing for the two different kinds of account but the actual calculation will proceed differently in each case. In an object-oriented language, there is a mechanism called *dynamic binding*. This enables us to handle such objects uniformly. We do not actually need to see what kind of object is involved. Instead, the language mechanism ensures that the correct operation is performed automatically when the program is executed. We will see how we can make use of dynamic binding in this chapter.

9.1   Derived classes

First, let us look at an example. We begin with a class `Person`:

```
class Person {
public:
  Person();
  const char *is_called() const;
  void change_name( const char *n);
  void write_info() const;
private:
  char name[30];
};
```

A person has a name. There are operations to read and change the name. We can get a printout of the name, and there is a default constructor. We will put the definitions of the member functions separately, in the interests of clarity:

```
Person::Person()
{ name[0] = '\0'; }
const char *Person::is_called() const
{ return name; }
void Person::change_name( const char *n)
{ strcpy(name, n); }
void Person::write_info() const
{ cout << "Name: " << name << endl; }
```

If we want to described persons in employment, we can define a new class:

```
class Employee : public Person {
public:
  Employee() : salary(0) {};
  long int earns() const;
  void change_salary(long int new_salary);
  void write_info() const;
private:
  long int salary;
};
```

By writing `Person` after the colon in the first line, we indicate that the new class `Employee` is a *subclass* of class `Person`. (We will not explain just now why **public** is in the first line.) We say that class `Employee` is *derived* from class `Person` and that class `Person` is a *direct base class* (or *superclass*) of `Employee`.

The definitions of the member functions `earns` and `change_salary` are very simple. (We will not give the definition for `write_info` yet.)

```
long int Employee::earns() const
{ return salary;}
void Employee::change_salary(long int new_salary)
{ salary=new_salary; }
```

A derived class inherits all the data members from the base class. We say that it contains all of the base class as a *base class subobject*. This means that an object of class `Employee` will have the data members `name` and `salary`. This is illustrated in Figure 9.1, where we initially declared two variables p and e, such that p belongs to class `Person` and e to class `Employee`.

```
Person   p;
Employee e;
```

Figure 9.1

We see that the variable p only has a name, while the variable e has both a name and a salary.

Member functions can also be inherited. As a result, an object of class Employee will have the member functions is_called, change_name, write_info, earns and change_salary. We can also write the statements

```
p.change_name("David");
p.write_info();
e.change_name("Neil");
e.change_salary(20000);
long int s = e.earns();
e.write_info();
```

But we could not write p.change_salary() or, p.earns(), since these member functions do not exist for class Person.

We are allowed to indicate the same name of a member in a subclass as in a base class; as a result, we get a new member that *hides* the member of the base class. For instance, if we had also declared a data member called name in class Employee, an object of class Employee would have had two data members called name, but the first one would have been hidden by the second.

A new member function with the name write_info is declared in class Employee. This will hide the member function write_info which was declared in class Person. If we write e.write_info(), where e is an object of type Employee, the write_info that was declared in class Employee will be called. But if we write p.write_info(), the write_info that was declared in class Person will be called, since the variable p is a member of that class. The definition of write_info for class Employee looks like this:

```
void Employee::write_info() const
{
  Person::write_info();
  cout << "Salary: " << salary << endl;
}
```

The third line is interesting. It shows how we can access a hidden member. To access a hidden member with the name m that has been declared in a base class B, we write B::m. Here we have written Person::write_info(), which means that the write_info declared in base class Person will be called. The printout from the statements above will be:

```
Name: David
Name: Neil
Salary: 20000
```

The first line is written out by the call p.write_info() and the two other lines by the call e.write_info().

We must avoid function overloading between inheritance hierarchies. If a function is declared in a subclass, all the functions with the same name will be hidden in the base class, irrespective of what parameters they might have.

```
class C1 {
public:
  void f(int);   // C1::f
}
class C2 : public C1 {
public:
  void f();      // C2::f, hides C1::f
}
main()
{
  C1 a;
  C2 b;
  a.f(5);        // OK!     C1::f is called
  b.f();         // OK!     C2::f is called
  b.f(5);        // ERROR!  C1::f is hidden
}
```

There are a number of functions that cannot be inherited. These are constructors, destructors, friend functions and the assignment operator =. Constructors and destructors will be dealt with in detail in Section 9.2. The assignment operator cannot be inherited since one is always defined automatically for each class (see page 254). It hides the assignment operator of a base class.

A derived class can also have subclasses. We can, for instance, declare a class Programmer that is a subclass of class Employee:

```
class Programmer : public Employee {
public:
  Programmer();
  const char *read_favourite() const;
  void change_favourite(const char *f);
private:
  char fav[10];
};
```

The data member fav indicates a programmer's favourite programming language. The member functions are defined separately:

```
Programmer::Programmer()
{ fav[0] = '\0'; }
```

```
const char *Programmer::read_favourite() const
{return fav;}
void Programmer::change_favourite(const char *f)
{strcpy(fav,f);}
```

The classes `Person` and `Employee` are *base classes* of class `Programmer`. The class `Employee` is a *direct base class*, since it is indicated in the definition of class `Programmer`. The class `Person` is an *indirect base class*. The class `Programmer` is *directly derived* from class `Employee` and *indirectly derived* from class `Person`. An object of class `Programmer` inherits attributes from all of its base classes, each of which is a subobject. This means that a programmer has three data members: `name`, `salary` and `favourite`.

Member functions can also be inherited. For instance, we can write:

```
Programmer pr;
pr.change_name("Hanna");
pr.change_salary(25000);
pr.change_favourite("C++");
pr.write_info();
```

In the last line, `write_info` in class `Employee` will be called.

Derived classes

> **class** D : *access* B {
>   . . .
> };

(*access* = **public**, **protected** or **private**)

- Class D is *directly derived* from class B.
- Class B is a *direct base class* of D.
- D *inherits* all the members from B.
  - Exceptions: constructors, destructors, friend functions and the assignment operator =.
- Members with the same name are *hidden*.

> **class** D2 : *access* D {
>   . . .
> };

- Class D2 is *indirectly derived* from class B.
- Class B is an *indirect base class* of D2.
- D2 *inherits* all the members from B and D.

There may be several independent subclasses to a particular class. For instance, we can define a class that defines temporary employees:

```
class Temp_emp : public Employee {
public:
  Date from, to;
};
```

Here we use a class `Date`:

```
class Date {
public:
  int year, mon, day;
};
```

We now declare two variables, a programmer and and a temporary employee:

```
Programmer pr;
Temp_emp te;
```

The variable `pr` is composed of three parts: a `Person` part, an `Employee` part and a `Programmer` part. The variable `te` is composed of a `Person` part, an `Employee` part and a `Temp_emp` part. This is illustrated in Figure 9.2.

The relations between the classes are illustrated in Figure 9.3.

Since a derived class `D` always contains the data members of a base class `B` as a subobject, we can easily carry out a type conversion from type `D` to type `B`. The data members of the derived type are then 'peeled away' to leave the base class subobject. In this way, conversion from a derived type `D` to a base type `B` therefore occurs safely and is also one of the type conversions that can occur automatically (see Section 5.7.1). This also applies to pointers. A pointer of type `D*` can be automatically converted to a pointer of type `B*`. As an example, we can look at the

Figure 9.2

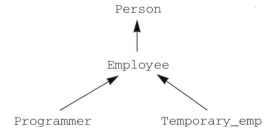

Figure 9.3

following function which compares the salaries of two employees and gives the higher one as result.

```
long int higher_salary(Employee a, Employee b)
{
  if (a.earns() > b.earns())
    return a.earns();
  else
    return b.earns();
}
```

If, as before, we have the variable pr of type Programmer and the variable te of type Temp_emp, we can make the call

```
cout << higher_salary(pr, te);
```

Here the first argument is automatically converted from type Programmer to type Employee, and the second from type Temp_emp to type Employee.

Conversion in the other direction, that is, from a base type to a derived type, cannot occur automatically. It can be done explicitly but this can be dangerous:

```
Employee *pa;
Programmer pr, *pp = &pr;
Temp_emp te;
pa = pp;                      // always safe
pp = (Programmer *)pa;        // unsafe but works
pa = &te;
pp = (Programmer *)pa;        // unsafe, may miscarry
pp->change_favourite("C++"); // and does!!
```

The first assignment pa=pp is safe because we convert from a derived type to a base type. The second assignment is unsafe because we cannot determine if the object pa points to is a Programmer or some other kind of employee. (But in this example it works.) The assignment in the penultimate line causes a catastrophe. The pointer pp should point to a `Programmer` but will, in fact, point to a `Temp_emp`. Now when we call the member function `change_favourite`, this will make a change in the object pointed to that we do not want. In Section 9.6 on page 310, we will be discussing the operator **dynamic_cast**, which carries out type conversion more safely.

9.2   **Constructors, destructors and inheritance**

Objects that belong to a derived class can be initialized, like other objects, with the aid of constructors. When a constructor is called for this purpose, the data members that have been inherited from the base class must also be initialized. This is done by calling a constructor for the base class. Then the part of the object (the subobject) that has been inherited from the base class will be initialized. The remainder of the object will be initialized by the constructor specially defined for the derived class. In this section we will look at how this happens, and see which rules apply. In our example we use the classes `Person`, `Employee` and `Programmer`. The class `Person` only had one constructor, a default constructor. Now we add another constructor:

```
class Person {
public:
  Person();
  Person(const char *n);
  ...
  char name[30];
};
```

The two constructors have the definitions

```
Person::Person()
{ name[0] = '\0'; }
Person::Person(const char *n)
{ strcpy(name, n); }
```

(The two constructors could have been combined into one if we had given the parameter a default value but in the interests of clarity we have not done this.) The new constructor is called when we make the declaration:

```
Person p("David");
```

We also complete class `Employee` with another constructor:

```
class Employee : public Person {
public:
  Employee() : salary(0) {};
  Employee(const char *n, long int l)
          : Person(n), salary(l) {}
  ...
  long int salary;
};
```

Look at the second constructor. We have used an initialization list to initialize the different parts of the object. The expression `Person(n)` is a call of the constructor for the base class `Person`. Let us now see what happens if we initialize an object of class `Employee`. We make the declaration:

```
Employee e1("Lisa", 20000);
```

Because the parameter `n` in our example has the value `"Lisa"`, we get the expression `Person("Lisa")` in the initialization list. As a result, the second constructor for class `Person` is called and the data member `name` initialized. Then the data member `salary` is initialized to `20000`. Note that the constructor for the base class is always called *before* the data members in the derived class are initialized and *before* the statements to be executed inside the braces are executed. In the constructor above we have written `Person(n)` in front of `salary(l)` in the initialization list but the order does not matter. The base class constructor is *always* called first.

We now initialize an object using the first constructor (the default constructor) for class `Employee`:

```
Employee e2;
```

An initialization list is also used in the first constructor but there is no expression for the base class `Person`. Since a constructor for a base class must always be called, a call of the base class default constructor (the constructor that can be called without parameters) is generated *automatically*. Here, too, the call takes place *before* the data members in the derived class are initialized and *before* the statements inside the braces are executed. In our example, the data member `name` will be initialized to a string of length zero. Only then is the data member `salary` initialized to zero.

Of course, for a default constructor of the base class to be called, one must exist. (The class `Person` has one.) If a base class does not have a default constructor, one of the constructors of the base class in the initialization list of the constructor of the derived class *must* be called. Otherwise the program will be faulty. If, for argument's sake, we suppose that a default constructor for class

`Person` did not exist, we would have to rewrite the first constructor for class `Employee`:

```
Employee() : Person(""), salary(0) {};
```

If we fail to define constructors for a class, default constructors are defined automatically (as we saw on page 210). We can say categorically, that base classes without their own constructors will be given a default constructor.

   If we do not define our own constructors for a derived class then this, too, will have an automatically defined default constructor assigned to it. Let us take an example in which we declare a new subclass of class `Person`:

```
class Athlete : public Person {
  ...
private:
  bool elite;
};
```

Note that we have not defined any constructors. We then get an automatically generated default constructor. We might imagine that it looks something like this:

```
Athlete() : Person() {}   // automatically generated
```

The default constructor of the base class is also called, in the automatically generated default constructor, for if this did not happen, we would get a compilation error.

   We can now declare a variable of class `Athlete`:

```
Athlete at;
```

The default constructor for class `Person` will be called and the data member `name` will be initialized, while the data member `elite` will be uninitialized.

   This is a suitable moment to recall that when we define a class, we usually get an automatically generated *copy constructor* (see page 216) and an automatically generated *assignment operator* (see page 254). This also applies to derived classes. Both operators make an automatic assignment to the part of an object consisting of the base class, or the base class subobject. This is done when the automatically generated copy constructor calls the copy constructor of the base class and the automatically generated assignment operator calls the assignment operator of the base class.

   If there are deeper inheritance relations, the call of constructors can extend to several sections. Here we give class `Programmer` from page 273 another constructor:

```
class Programmer : public Employee {
public:
  Programmer();
  Programmer(const char *n, long int l, const char *f);
  ...
  char fav[10];
};
```

The definition of the second constructor is:

```
Programmer::Programmer(const char *n, long int l, const char *f)
: Employee(n,l)
{ strcpy(fav, f); }
```

A constructor – the one with two parameters – for the base class Employee is called here in the initialization list, and this constructor, as we explained earlier, will in turn call a constructor for its base class Person. This results in the initializations in class Person being performed first, followed by the initializations in class Employee and, lastly, the initializations in class Programmer. In C++, initializations must be performed in a strict order. The members of the highest base class are initialized first, and we proceed down the hierarchy until the members of the classes derived last are initialized.

Fortunately, destructors are much easier to deal with than constructors. Destructors are not inherited. A destructor is normally only used when a corresponding constructor has allocated memory space that must be released. Destructors are handled like constructors except that everything is done in the

---

Inheritance and constructors

For a derived class D with a direct base class B, the following applies:

- In the initialization list of a constructor for D, a constructor for the base class can be called explicitly:

  D::D(*parameters*) : B(*parameters*), ... {*statements*}

  If this has not been done, a default constructor for B is called *automatically*.

- If class D has an automatically generated default constructor, the default constructor of the base class will be called in it.

- Initialization order in a constructor:
  - a constructor for the base class is called;
  - the data members of the class in question are initialized (in the order in which they occur in the initialization list);
  - the statements inside the braces { } are executed.

Inheritance and destructors

- Destructors are not inherited.
- The execution order for destructors:
  - the statements inside the braces { } are executed;
  - a destructor for the base class is called.

---

reverse order. This means that the destructor for the last derived class is executed first. Here is a simple example to demonstrate this:

```
class C1 {
public:
  C1(int n);
  ~C1();
private:
  int *pi, l;
};
C1::C1(int n): l(n)
{ cout << l << " integers are allocated" << endl;
  pi = new int[l];
}
C1::~C1()
{ cout << l << " integers are released" << endl;
  delete[] pi;
}
class C2 : public C1{
public:
  C2(int n);
  ~C2();
private:
  char *pc;
  int l;
};
C2::C2(int n): C1(n), l(n)
{ cout << l << " characters are allocated" << endl;
  pc = new char[l];
}
C2::~C2()
{ cout << l << " characters are released" << endl;
  delete[] pc;
}
main()
{
  C2 a(50), b(100);
}
```

When the program is run, we get the printout:

```
50 integers are allocated
50 characters are allocated
100 integers are allocated
100 characters are allocated
100 characters are released
100 integers are released
50 characters are released
50 integers are released
```

9.3 Access control

We have seen how, in a class definition, we can use the reserved words **public** and **private** to indicate whether the members of a class will be accessible outside the class. There is a third possibility, a sort of compromise between **public** and **private**, the reserved word **protected**. A class definition can have the form:

```
class C {
public:
  declarations of visible members
protected:
  declarations of protected members
private:
  declarations of private members
};
```

These three parts may come in any order. If nothing is written, all the members will be private. The following rules apply:

- If a member is declared in a class C and is *private* (declared in the **private** section), it can only be used by the member functions in C and by the friends of class C.

- If a member is declared in a class C and the member is *protected* (declared in the **protected** section), it can only be used by the member functions in C, friends of C and member functions and friends of classes derived from C.

- If a member is *public* (declared in the **public** section) it can be used everywhere, without restrictions.

A protected member is accessible *within* the inheritance hierarchy but not outside it. We will use class Clock to give an example:

```
class Clock {
public:
```

```
    Clock ();
    Clock (int hour, int min, int sec);
    void set (int hour, int min, int sec);
    int read_hour() const {return h;}
    int read_min() const {return m;}
    int read_sec() const {return s;}
    void write(bool write_sec = true) const;
    void tick();
protected:
    int h, m, s;
};
```

The only difference here is that we have written **protected** instead of **private** in the third line from the bottom. We will now define a subclass of Clock, the class Alarm_Clock. An alarm clock has the same properties as an ordinary clock but we have added the possibility of having an alarm at a specific time. There is a member function set_alarm with which we indicate when the alarm is to ring. We have also made a new variant of the function tick which will hide the one declared in class Clock.

```
class Alarm_Clock : public Clock {
public:
    void set_alarm(int hour, int min, int sec)
                    { ah=hour; am=min; as=sec; };
    void tick();
protected:
    int ah, am, as;
};
```

The definition of the new variant of the function tick is most interesting here:

```
void Alarm_Clock::tick()
{
    Clock::tick();
    if (h==ah and m==am and s==as)
        cout << "\a\a\a";
}
```

First we call the function tick, which was declared in the base class Clock. This moves the clock forward one second followed by a check to see whether it is time for the alarm to ring. But for this to happen, we must have access to the members of base class Clock. (We could use the functions read_hour and so on but do not do so in this example.) If h, m and s had been private members, this would not have been possible, but by declaring them as protected, we will have access to them in the subclass `Alarm_Clock`.

As a rule, it can be said that if a class is constructed with the intention of making it the base class for various derived classes, then its data members should be declared as protected rather than as private. We then have the option of formulating the member functions in the subclasses more efficiently.

When a class D is derived from a base class B then, as we have seen, it will inherit the members of B. We then accept the inherited members as members of D and, just as for other members, the accessibility of the inherited members must be specified. We do this by writing one of the words **private**, **protected** or **public**, in front of the name of the base class concerned. We can then write one of the following:

```
class D : private B {    // private inheritance
  ...
};
```

```
class D : protected B {    // protected inheritance
  ...
};
```

```
class D : public B {    // public inheritance
  ...
};
```

We call these *private, protected* and *public* inheritance, respectively. It is more common to use *public* inheritance. We can give the following rules, where B is the base class and D the derived class.

- *Private members* of B are never visible anywhere but in B, neither in D nor anywhere outside B. Their visibility is not affected by the type of inheritance involved.

- If *private inheritance* is involved (the word **private** is used), then all the members of B which are *protected* or *public* will be *private* in D.

- If *protected inheritance* is involved (the word **protected** is used), then all the members of B which are *protected* or *public* will be *protected* in D.

- If *public inheritance* is involved (the word **public** is used), then all the members of B which are *protected* will also be *protected* in D and all the members of B which are *public* will also be *public* in D.

We note that it is the most restrictive of any two types of access that applies. The exception is the private members of a base class which are never accessible in the derived class. Let us take some examples that illustrate the foregoing rules. We first declare a base class B with three derived classes D1, D2 and D3.

```
class Base {
public:
  int i1;
protected:
  int i2;
private:
  int i3;
};
class D1 : private Base {
  void f();
};
class D2 : protected Base {
  void g();
};
class D3 : public Base {
  void h();
};
```

None of the subclasses has access to member i3 in the base class B. But all three of the base classes can access members i1 and i2 *internally*. In the definition of the member function f (the same thing applies to g and h) we will get, for example:

```
void D1::f() {
  i1 = 0;   // OK
  i2 = 0;   // OK
  i3 = 0;   // ERROR!
};
```

Access for i1, i2 and i3 *outside* the three classes is shown in the following program.

```
main()
{
  Base b;
  b.i1 = 0;    // OK
  b.i2 = 0;    // ERROR!
  b.i3 = 0;    // ERROR!
  D1 d1;
  d1.i1 = 0;   // ERROR!
  d1.i2 = 0;   // ERROR!
  d1.i3 = 0;   // ERROR!
```

```
D2  d2;
d2.i1 = 0;    // ERROR!
d2.i2 = 0;    // ERROR!
d2.i3 = 0;    // ERROR!
D3  d3;
d3.i1 = 0;    // OK
d3.i2 = 0;    // ERROR!
d3.i3 = 0;    // ERROR!
};
```

By using private or protected inheritance, we can prevent a user accessing the members inherited from the base class from outside. An alternative method would be to use public inheritance, redeclaring all the public base class members in the derived class. Then the members of the base class would be hidden. This necessitates that *all* the public members are redeclared, otherwise they will not be hidden.

If we use private or protected inheritance, there is a way of selectively making individual members of the base class more accessible in a derived class – by making what is called an *access declaration*. This is done by simply *naming* one of the members of the base class at an appropriate place in the derived class. Here are a couple of examples:

```
class D4 : protected Base {
public:
  Base::i1;   // access declaration
};
```

By naming the member variable i1 in the **public** section of D4, we also make i1 *public* in D4. We are now allowed, for instance, to write the following in the function main:

```
D4  d4;
d4.i1 = 0;   // OK
```

In a similar way, we can make i2 *protected* in D5 by naming i2 in the **protected** section of D5. This will result in i2 being accessible in subclasses of D5.

```
class D5 : private Base {
protected:
  Base::i2;   // access declaration
};
```

We are not allowed to make a member more accessible than it is in the base class. For instance, if we had tried to name i2 in the **public** section of D5, we would have received an error message.

In the draft standard, *using* declarations are recommended instead of access declarations (see Section 14.1). We then write:

```
using Base::i1;
using Base::i2;
```

9.4   Reusable code, an example

We now give an example to demonstrate several of the points discussed so far. One of the fundamental ideas behind object-oriented programming is that we should be able to reuse program code by building on classes that are already available. We will be using this technique in our example.

Sometimes it is necessary to work with really large integers, numbers that consist of so many digits that they do not have enough space in a variable of type **int** or **long int**. In this example, we will construct a class SuperInt which enables us to work with such large integers. Large numbers will be represented with the help of an integer array, where a digit is placed in each element of the array. We make use of the class Vector (from Chapter 8) and make class SuperInt into a subclass of this:

```
class Vector {
public:
  Vector(int first_index=1, int number=0);
  Vector(const Vector& v);
  ~Vector();
  int first() const {return i1;}
  int last() const {return i1+num-1;}
  int length() const {return num;}
  const Vector& operator=   (const Vector& v);
  bool          operator==  (const Vector& v) const;
  bool          operator!=  (const Vector& v) const;
  const Vector& operator+=  (const Vector& v);
  Vector        operator+   (const Vector& v) const;
  const Vector& operator+=  (int d);
  Vector        operator+   (int d) const;  .
  const Vector& operator-=  (const Vector& v);
  Vector        operator-   (const Vector& v) const;
  const Vector& operator-=  (int d);
  Vector        operator-   (int d) const;
  const Vector& operator&=  (const Vector& v);
  Vector        operator&   (const Vector& v) const;
  Vector        operator-   () const;
  const Vector& operator++  ();      // prefix ++v
```

```
Vector          operator++  (int);    // postfix v++
const Vector&   operator--  ();       // prefix --v
Vector          operator--  (int);    // postfix v--
int&            operator[]  (int i);
int             operator[]  (int i) const;
const Vector    operator()  (int from, int to) const;
friend Vector   operator+   (int d, const Vector& v);
friend ostream& operator<<  (ostream& o, const Vector& v);
friend istream& operator>>  (istream& in, Vector& v);
private:
  int *p;
  const int i1;
  int num;
};
```

We define the new class `SuperInt` as a subclass of class `Vector`:

```
class SuperInt : protected Vector {
public:
  SuperInt(long int n = 0);
  Vector::length;
  int operator() (int k) const; // gives digit no. k
  SuperInt operator+ (const SuperInt& b) const;
  SuperInt operator- (const SuperInt& b) const;
  SuperInt operator- () const;
  SuperInt operator* (const SuperInt& b) const;
  SuperInt operator* (int i) const;
  SuperInt operator/ (const SuperInt& b) const;
  SuperInt operator/ (int i) const;
  bool operator== (const SuperInt& b) const;
  bool operator!= (const SuperInt& b) const;
  bool operator<  (const SuperInt& b) const;
  bool operator>  (const SuperInt& b) const;
  bool operator<= (const SuperInt& b) const;
  bool operator>= (const SuperInt& b) const;
  friend istream& operator>> (istream& is, SuperInt& b);
  friend ostream& operator<< (ostream& os, const SuperInt& b);
private:
  SuperInt(bool neg, int len)
      : Vector(0, len), negative(neg) {};
  bool negative;
};
```

The class `SuperInt` contains the most important operations that allow us to work with large numbers. There is a constructor for creating new objects. There is an automatically generated copy constructor for creating copies of other objects of class `SuperInt`. There are operators for the four arithmetic operations and the – operator has a further unary variant. There is a variant of the multiplication and division operators with an ordinary **int** as the right-hand operand. (Small integers, for instance 1, are very easy to multiply and divide by, so use is made of this.) There are a number of logical operations to compare SuperInt objects with each other. Finally, there are two friend functions, one to write and one to read objects of class SuperInt.

Protected inheritance is used in the definition of SuperInt (**protected** is on the first line). If we had used public inheritance, all the member functions inherited by class SuperInt from class Vector would have been visible for the user. There are many operators for class Vector which are not applicable to objects of type SuperInt. Even worse, there are operations which would give incorrect results if they were applied to objects of class SuperInt. For instance, the operator ++ for class Vector increases every element in a vector by 1. If this operator were performed for class SuperInt, each *digit* in a number would be increased by 1, which is not the correct way to add 1 to a number. Protected inheritance is implemented to prevent the user from making a mistake by using the wrong operator.

The only one of the inherited member functions to be made directly visible is that of length. This occurs in the fourth line of the definition of class SuperInt, where there is an access declaration. The function length returns the length of a vector. In the case of the derived class SuperInt, the number of digits in a large number is returned, so this operation has some significance.

Another inherited member function that could have been made visible, is the indexing operator []. It would have enabled a user to directly access individual digits in a SuperInt. The problem here is that the user would have been able to *change* individual digits in a number – perhaps not such a good idea! (It is not possible to allow only the constant version of the [] operator to be visible in an access declaration.) So we have done things differently. On the fifth line we declare a function call operator () with one parameter. We let this operator return a single digit in a number. We can then read but not change a particular digit. Our function call operator has another advantage: if, as parameter, we give the index of a digit not in the number concerned, we will get a value of 0. If, for instance, we have a variable x of SuperInt and x has the value 123456, the call x(2) will give a value of 4 (indexing takes place from the right, beginning with zero), while a call of x(6) will return a value of 0.

Another constructor is defined in the private section of class SuperInt. This constructor will only be used internally when the member functions of the class are implemented. It should not be visible outside the class. We also note that, in the private section, the class only has a single data member. This is the member negative, which indicates whether or not a number is less than zero. All the other necessary data members are inherited from the base class Vector. The class Vector allows us to work with vectors of varying lengths. We shall make use of this fact, therefore, and let every object of class SuperInt consist of an array that is just as long as necessary. Every digit in a SuperInt is stored in an element in the array and no preliminary zeros are stored. The only exception is the number zero which is stored in an array with a single element that contains a zero. When we work with integers, we usually number the digits from the right and begin numbering with zero. Units are represented by the digit number 0, tens by digit number 1, and so on. We will use this numbering sequence here. (This means that the digits in a SuperInt will þe backwards in an array.) Objects of type SuperInt will be of different lengths, and the memory space for them will have to be allocated and released dynamically. We will not have to do this explicitly in class SuperInt, since the constructors and the destructor in class Vector will take care of this automatically.

Before we discuss how the different member functions will be implemented, we show a program that simulates a simple calculator. The user will enter expressions of the form *x op y*, where *op* is one of the operators + - * and /. The numbers which are input as data can be of arbitrary length (but the input operator can only read numbers with a maximum of 500 digits). The program replies by writing out the result and terminates when the user writes the character combination for *end of file*.

```cpp
#include "superint.h"
#include <iostream.h>
main()
{
  SuperInt x, y;
  char op;
  cout << "? ";
  while (cin >> x and cin >> op and cin >> y)
  {
    if (op == '+')
      cout << (x+y) << endl;
    else if (op == '-')
      cout << (x-y) << endl;
    else if (op == '*')
      cout << (x*y) << endl;
    else if (op == '/')
      cout << (x/y) << endl;
    else
      cout << "Incorrect operator" << endl;
    cout << endl << "? ";
  }
}
```

We now show the program when it is run. (The data entered by the user has been underlined.)

```
? 1234567890123456789 * 987654321098765
1219326311370217418780678478765585

? 1219326311370217418780678478765585 /
1234567890123456789
987654321098765
```

```
? 66666644444433333377777888889999111111 +
6765765765765765
66666644444433333377778565465576487687 6
```

Now let us look at how the different operations in class `SuperInt` are implemented. We will begin with the constructors. The first one, which lies in the public section, allows us to initialize a `SuperInt` with a value of type **long int**. This constructor also functions as a default constructor and type conversion constructor from type **long int** to `SuperInt`. The constructor is called automatically in the following kinds of expressions:

```
SuperInt s1(6798), s2=2324, s3;
s3 = 518;
s1 = s1 + 9576;
```

In the last line the right-hand operand is converted to the type `SuperInt`. When the constructor is called it should ensure that a vector is allocated exactly big enough to hold the number given as parameter. For a positive number n to be stored, $1 + \log n$ digits is needed. On the basis of this, we can write the following help function to calculate the number of digits in a number n.

```
int num_dig(long int n)
{
   if (n==0)
     return 1;
   else
     return log10(labs(n)) + 1;
}
```

The number 0 is treated as a special case. We called the standard functions `log10` and `labs` which are declared in the header files `math.h` and `stdlib.h` respectively (see page 42). Now we can write the definition of the constructor:

```
SuperInt::SuperInt(long int n)
: Vector(0, num_dig(l))
{
   negative = (n<0);
   n = labs(n);
   for (int k=0; k<length(); k++)
   {
     (*this)[k] = n % 10;
     n /= 10;
   }
}
```

The Vector part of the object is initialized when the constructor for the base class is called in the initialization list. The first argument indicates that indexing will begin with 0, and the second argument indicates how many elements will be allocated for the vector. To compute this, the help function num_dig is used. The data member negative is initialized with the initialization of the Vector part. The allocated vector is then filled with all the digits, which are calculated one at a time by dividing the number n by 10 and seeing what remainder results. The expression (*this) [k] means that the inherited indexing operator for the actual object is called. This operator gives as result a reference to element number k in the array. The array cannot be accessed directly since the pointer to it lies in the private section of the base class. We must therefore use the indexing operator. (This is not a disadvantage as the operator will check that the index lies within the allowed limits.)

The second constructor is defined directly in the private section of the class definition:

```
SuperInt(bool neg, int len)
: Vector(0, len), negative(neg) {};
```

The constructor will get as parameters both a logical value stating whether or not the number is negative, and an integer indicating how many digits are to be allocated. We do not want this constructor to be accessible to outside users since it enables objects of type SuperInt to be created, where an array will not be correctly filled with digits. We will use the constructor internally in class SuperInt.

There is a third constructor, the copy constructor. As we know, this is declared automatically and is visible from outside. It is called in expressions of the form

```
SuperInt s4(s1), s5 = s2;
```

This constructor in turn calls the copy constructor of the base class. We wrote the copy constructor for class Vector ourselves in Chapter 7 (see page 219). It makes a deep copy. We also get an automatically generated assignment operator which is called when we write, for example

```
s4 = s5;
```

This assignment operator calls the assignment operator of the base class, which we also wrote ourselves (see page 255). This also makes a deep copy; when we initialize a SuperInt with another SuperInt or assign a SuperInt to another, we will automatically get a deep copy. All this happens because class SuperInt is derived from class Vector. It can be seen that we do not need to think of allocations of memory space and releasing memory space when we write the member functions in class SuperInt.

The next member function we will look at is the function call operator () which is used to read a particular digit in a SuperInt. The parameter k indicates which digit is involved.

```
int SuperInt::operator()(int k) const
{
  if(k < length())
    return (*this)[k];
  else
    return 0;
}
```

If a number has n digits, the most significant digit of the number will lie in element number $n-1$, since numbering always takes place from 0. We can find out the number of digits in a number by calling the inherited member function `length`. If the function **operator**() were called with a parameter value k greater than the number for the most significant digit, we would realize that a zero was in this position; in fact, the function would return a value of 0. If k, on the other hand, contains the number of a 'regular' digit, this will be read with the help of the indexing operator.

The next operator we shall define is simple. It is the unary minus operator which returns an object of reversed sign:

```
SuperInt SuperInt::operator- () const
{
  if (*this == 0)
    return 0;
  else
  {
    SuperInt s(*this);             // Create a copy
    s.negative = not s.negative;   // Change sign
    return s;
  }
}
```

If the number is not equal to 0, a copy of the actual object is created. (The copy constructor will be called.) We then change the sign in the copy and give it as result from the function. Note that we cannot make this change in the actual object since the function **operator-** is a constant function.

In class SuperInt we declared a whole collection of operators which compared two objects. The operators == and !=, which compare equality and inequality are simple:

```
bool SuperInt::operator== (const SuperInt& b) const
{
  return negative==b.negative and Vector(*this)==Vector(b);
}
```

```
bool SuperInt::operator!= (const SuperInt& b) const
{ return not (*this == b); }
```

The operator == first checks whether the numbers have the same sign. If so, the comparison operator for the base class is called to check whether the digits are equal. Note that the expressions Vector(*this) and Vector(b) are explicit type conversions to the base class Vector. The operator != is trivial. All it does is to invert the result from the operator ==.

Of the other comparison operators it is only the operator < that is slightly difficult, so we will take it first:

```
bool SuperInt::operator< (const SuperInt& b) const
{
  if (negative and b.negative)
    return -b < -*this;
  if (negative and not b.negative)
    return true;
  if (not negative and b.negative)
    return false;
  int n;
  if (length() > b.length())
    n = length();
  else
    n = b.length();
  for (int k=n-1; k >= 0; k--)          // Compare the digits
    if ((*this)(k) != b(k))
      return (*this)(k) < b(k);
  return false;
}
```

First, the operands are checked in case one is negative. If both are negative, their signs can be changed along with the inequality sign. (The unary minus operator which was defined above is called.) If only one operand is negative, we can dispense with the decision whether the first is less than the second.

If both operands are positive, the digits in them are compared, one by one. We begin with the most significant digit and terminate the comparisons as soon as we have found two digits that are different. The expression (*this)(k) != b(k) tests whether digit number k in both operands is different. Note that the operator () is used here, so it will make no difference if the two operands have different lengths.

When both operators < and == have been dealt with, defining the remaining comparison operators becomes self-evident.

```
bool SuperInt::operator<= (const SuperInt& b) const
{ return *this < b or *this == b; }
```

```
bool SuperInt::operator> (const SuperInt& b) const
{ return not (*this < b) and not (*this == b); }
bool SuperInt::operator>= (const SuperInt& b) const
{ return not (*this < b); }
```

Now let us tackle the operator + which adds two SuperInts.

```
SuperInt SuperInt::operator+ (const SuperInt& b) const
{
  if (b.negative)
    return *this - (-b);
  if (negative)
    return b - (- *this);
  // Calculate the number of digits in the sum
  int dig, i, m;    // m is the memory digit
  for (i=m=0; i<length() or i<b.length(); i++)
  {
    dig = (*this)(i)+b(i)+m;
    m = dig / 10;
  }
  SuperInt s(false,i+m);  // The sum gets the length i+m
  // Calculate the digits in the sum
  for (i=m=0; i<s.length(); i++)
  {
    dig = (*this)(i)+b(i)+m;
    s[i]= dig % 10;
    m   = dig / 10;
  }
  return s;
}
```

We first test whether an operand is negative. If so, we change the sign of this operand and call the operator – to perform a subtraction instead of an addition. If both operands are positive, an addition should be performed. The sum will be calculated in a new temporary SuperInt which we will call s. Before we declare the variable s, we must know how many digits it is to contain. The number of digits will be equal to the length of the longest of the two operands, with 1 added if there should be a memory digit when the two most significant digits are added. To calculate how long s should be, we perform the additions of the two operands but we do not keep the result. The only thing we keep track of is the variable i, which computes how many digits are added, as well as the variable m, which contains the memory digits that arise. After the last round m will contain either a value of 0 or 1. The variable s should therefore consist of i+m digits. When s has been declared, we perform the addition once more, but this time we save all the digits that arise in the variable s.

We will now turn our attention to the definition of the subtraction operator -:

```
SuperInt SuperInt::operator- (const SuperInt& b) const
{
  if (b.negative)
    return *this + (-b);
  if (negative)
    return - (-*this + b);
  if (*this < b)
    return -(b - *this);

  // Both numbers are positive and *this >= b
  SuperInt d(*this);        // Will contain the result
  int i, j;
  for (i=0; i<length(); i++)
  {
    d[i] = d[i]-b(i);       // Calculate digit no. i
    if (d[i] < 0)           // Borrow
    {
      for (j=i+1; d[j] == 0; j++)
        d[j] = 9;
      d[j]--;               // The first digit that is not zero
      d[i] += 10;
    }
  }

  // Compute the number of initial zeros in the result
  for (i=length()-1, j=0; i>0 and d[i]==0; i--, j++)
    ;
  if ( j == 0)
    return d;               // No initial zeros
  else
  { // j zeros. Create a new shorter result
    SuperInt d2(false, length()-j);
    for (i=0; i<d2.length(); i++)
      d2[i] = d[i];
    return d2;
  }
}
```

A test is carried out to see if one of the operands is negative. If so, this operand is negated and an addition is performed instead. If both operands are positive, another test checks if the first operand is not less than the second. If this is so, we let the operands change place and return the negated value of the subtraction.

If both operands are positive and the first is greater than or equal to the second, subtraction is performed digit by digit. The result is placed in a local variable d. In subtraction, we may need to 'borrow' exactly as if we were counting by hand. When subtraction is finished, we test whether there are zeros at the beginning of the result. There should not be any in a SuperInt. If there are, we declare a new temporary variable d2 which is shorter than d. We then copy the digits in d to d2, leaving out the zeros at the beginning.

The multiplication operator exists in two variants. We shall first look at the simpler of the two, the one that multiplies a SuperInt by an ordinary **int**. Our main reason for constructing this variant is that we will need it later when we will be multiplying a SuperInt by individual digits in another SuperInt. We give the definition below. If the right-hand operand lies in the interval from 0 to 10, the calculation is carried out directly; otherwise, the right-hand operand is also converted to a SuperInt, and the second variant of the multiplication operator is called to perform the multiplication.

```
SuperInt SuperInt::operator* (int i) const
{
  if (i == 0 or *this == 0)
    return 0;
  else if (i==1)
    return *this;
  else if (i>=2 and i<=9)
  {   // Perform repeated addition
    SuperInt r;
    for (int j=1; j<=i; j++)
      r = r + (*this);
    return r;
  }
  else if (i==10)
  {   // Move the digits one step to the left
    SuperInt r(negative, length()+1);
    r[0]=0;
    for (int j=1; j<r.length(); j++)
      r[j] = (*this)(j-1);
    return r;
  }
  else
    return (*this) * SuperInt(i);
}
```

If one of the operands is equal to 0, or if the right-hand operator is equal to 1, then calculating the result is a trivial operation. If the right-hand operand has a value between 2 and 9, multiplication is performed as repeated addition. (The value of the left-hand operand is added as many times as the right-hand operand indicates.) If the right-hand operand is equal to 10, we get the result by creating a SuperInt where all the digits are moved a step to the left.

With the aid of this operator we can write the variant of the multiplication operator that multiplies two operands of type SuperInt.

```
SuperInt SuperInt::operator* (const SuperInt& b) const
{
  if (*this == 0 or b == 0)
    return 0;
  else          '
  {
    SuperInt a(*this), r;
    a.negative = false;
    for (int i=0; i<b.length(); i++)
    {
      r = r + a * b(i);
      a = a * 10;
    }
    r.negative = (negative and not b.negative) or
                 (not negative and b.negative);
    return r;
  }
}
```

A special case arises when one of the operands is equal to zero. (This is done to ensure the sign will be right in the result, irrespective of the sign of the other operand.) Generally, multiplication is performed exactly as we do it by hand with pen and paper. The left-hand operand (the actual object) is copied to a temporary variable a. The result of the multiplication will be calculated in another temporary variable r, which has a value of 0 from the outset. We then multiply the variable a with the digits in b a digit at a time, first the units, then the tens and so on. The result is added to the variable r. Between every addition, a is multiplied by 10. To perform the multiplications, we call the second variant of the operator *, the variant that has an **int** as its right-hand operand.

The last operator is the division operator /. This also exists in two variants, one that has an ordinary **int** as right-hand operand and one that has a SuperInt. We begin with the one with **int** as right-hand operand. This takes care of the special cases when the right-hand operand is equal to 1 or 10. In all other cases, the right-hand operand is converted to a SuperInt, and the second variant of the division operator calculates the result. If the right-hand operand is equal to 1, calculating the result is a trivial operation. If it is equal to 10, we get the result by creating a copy of the actual object, one in which all the digits are moved one step to the right.

```
SuperInt SuperInt::operator/ (int i) const
{
  if (i==1)
    return *this;
  else if (i==10)
  {  // Move the digits one step to the right
    SuperInt r(negative, length()-1);
    for (int j=0; j<r.length(); j++)
      r[j] = (*this)(j+1);
```

```
      return r;
   }
   else
      return *this / SuperInt(i);
}
```

The second variant of the division operator can now be defined:

```
SuperInt SuperInt::operator/ (const SuperInt& b) const
{
   assert(b != 0);
   SuperInt num(*this), den(b), r;
   int num_steps = 0;
   num.negative = den.negative = false;
   // Move den to the left as far as possible
   while (num >= den)
   {
      den = den * 10;
      num_steps++;
   }
   for (int i=1; i<=num_steps; i++)
   {
      den = den / 10;   // Move den a step to the right
      r = r * 10;
      // Subtract den from num as many times as posssible
      while (num >= den)
      {
         r = r + 1;   // Note how many times it is possible
         num = num - den;
      }
   }
   r.negative = (negative and not b.negative) or
                (not negative and b.negative);
   return r;
}
```

Three local variables are used here. The numerator in the division is placed in the variable num, the denominator in the variable den and the result in the variable r. The calculation proceeds in the same way as in manual calculation. First the denominator is moved as far to the left as it will go, and then we try how many times the denominator will 'go into' the numerator. This is noted, then the numerator is moved back one step to the right. We see how many times the denominator 'goes into' what is left of the numerator and continue in this way until the numerator has been moved back to its original value.

To complete class SuperInt we only have to define the friend functions >> and <<, which perform the reading of input and writing of output, respectively, of objects of type SuperInt. The input operator >> is defined as follows:

```
istream& operator>> (istream& is, SuperInt& b)
{
  cin >> ws;     // Skip blank characters
  char s[500], *q=s, sign = '+';
  if (cin.peek() == '+' or cin.peek() == '-')
    cin >> sign;
  while (cin.peek() >= '0' and cin.peek() <= '9')
    cin >> *q++;
  *q = '\0';
  q = s;
  if (strlen(q) == 0)      // No digits
  {
    cout << "Incorrect integer" << endl;
    abort();
  };
  while (*q == '0')        // Skip leading zeros
    q++;
  if (strlen(q) == 0)      // The number 0 is a special case
    b == 0;
  else
  {
    SuperInt temp(sign == '-', strlen(q));
    for (int i=temp.length()-1; i>=0; i--)
      temp[i] = *q++ - '0';
    b = temp;
  }
  return is;
}
```

The manipulator ws is first used to skip leading blank characters (spacings, tab stops and end-of-line characters). Then we check whether the next character waiting to be read is a plus or a minus sign. If it is, the character is read in; if not, we assume it is ᶠ+'. Here we use the standard function peek, which tests the next character in the input stream without using it up.

A number of characters from the input stream are then read and placed in the character array s. The pointer q is used to point to the next free place in s. The input data is read as long as the character waiting to be read is a digit. When the last digit has been read, a zero character is placed last in the text string. If no digits could be read in, the user has written an incorrect integer. Then an error message is returned and the program terminated, in which case the standard function abort, declared in the header file stdlib.h, is used. If the number input is a correct integer, the function will continue by skipping all leading zeros. This is done by moving the pointer q forward until it points to the first character that does not contain the value '0'. If there are no more digits, the number 0 has been entered and this can be treated separately. If the number 0 has not been entered, a temporary variable temp of type SuperInt is declared, and the digits are placed in this variable, one by one. Note that the digits are placed backwards in temp compared to those in the text string. Finally, temp is assigned to the out parameter b.

The last function is the output operator >>. This is rather more straight-forward, and no commentary is necessary.

```
ostream& operator<< (ostream& os, const SuperInt& b)
{
  if (b.negative)
    os << '-';
  for (int i=b.length()-1; i>=0; i--)
    os << b[i];
  return os;
}
```

This section has been crammed with detail and perhaps difficult to digest. We have tried to demonstrate the benefit of using an already completed class and building onto it, instead of doing everything from the beginning. Note especially that in class SuperInt we never had to worry about memory allocation and deallocation. The base class Vector took care of all that.

9.5 Polymorphism and dynamic binding

In the so-called *typed programming languages*, such as C++ and Ada, types are used to monitor which operations can be carried out on the different data. If, for example, the variable x has type **double** and the function f(x) is called, the compiler will check if there is a function f that has a parameter of type **double**, or if there is a function f that has a parameter of type t and there is an automatic type conversion which can be made from type **double** to type t. If such is found to be the case, the compiler generates machine code which will cause the function f to be called when the program is run. Thus, which function is called is determined when the program is compiled. The call is said to be *bound* to the function f. In Section 4.3 we saw that in C++ there can be *overloaded* functions, which means that several functions can have the same name but take different types of parameters. For example, if the call g(x) is made, the compiler can decide which function should be called by comparing the type of x with the different types of parameter which different g functions take.

In Chapter 13 we shall see that it is possible to construct what are known as *generic* program units for different types. We can construct a class Vector, for example, where the elements do not need to be of type **int** but can be of arbitrary type.

Overloading and generic program units are two forms of what is called *polymorphism* (having many forms) in the context of programming. This means that a program construct which has a certain appearance can mean different things (for example, calls to different functions) depending on the types of the operands involved. Binding means deciding exactly which form is appropriate. For both overloading and generic units, binding occurs during compilation, and this is known as *static*, or *early* binding. Alternatively, *dynamic* or *late* binding can occur, and this takes place during program execution. In languages without typing, such as Smalltalk, only dynamic binding is used, while in other object-oriented languages, such as Ada and C++, both static and dynamic bindings are allowed. The polymorphism associated with static binding is usually called *ad hoc polymorphism*; if the term polymorphism is used alone it usually means polymorphism related to dynamic binding.

In the typed object-oriented languages, dynamic binding occurs in connection with inheritance. In C++ we use what are called *virtual functions* when we want to have dynamic binding. A member function is declared as virtual by writing the word **virtual** first in the declaration. A class which contains at least one virtual function, or which inherits a virtual function, is called a *polymorphic class*. To demonstrate polymorphism, dynamic binding and virtual functions, we will define a group of classes that describe different kinds of vehicle.

```cpp
class Vehicle {
public:
  virtual void give_info();
};

class Motor_vehicle : public Vehicle {
public:
  Motor_vehicle(char *no) { strcpy(reg_num, no); }
  char *number() { return reg_num; }
  void give_info();
protected:
  char reg_num[8];
};

class Private_car : public Motor_vehicle {
public:
  Private_car(char *no, int n)
    : Motor_vehicle(no), num_seats(n) {}
  void give_info();
protected:
  int num_seats;
};

class Bus : public Motor_vehicle {
public:
  Bus(char *no, int n, bool a)
    : Motor_vehicle(no), num_pass(n), aircond(a) {}
  void give_info();
protected:
  int num_pass;
  bool aircond;
};
```

```
class Minibus : public Bus {
public:
  Minibus(char *no, int n, bool a)
   : Bus(no, n, a) {}
};
class Truck : public Motor_vehicle {
public:
  Truck(char *no, int l)
   : Motor_vehicle(no), max_load(l) {}
   void give_info();
protected:
  int max_load;
};
```

The root class is Vehicle since all the other classes are either directly or indirectly derived from this class. The function give_info is declared in the class Vehicle. Note that the word **virtual** stands in the declaration. This means that give_info is a *virtual function*. All the classes, except the class Minibus, each have their own variant of the member function give_info, and all these variants will be virtual functions. The word **virtual** does not have to be repeated in all the subclasses. The class Minibus will inherit the variant of give_info from class Bus. It is extremely important to note that the function give_info must have *exactly* the same number of parameters and types in the parameters. The return type must also be the same in all the variants. If the parameters are different in a variant, this variant will not be virtual. Instead, the virtual function declared in the base class will be hidden. If the parameters are the same but the return type different, the program will be faulty (except in a special case which will be discussed later). For our example to work in a more realistic situation, there must be more member functions than simply give_info. It should be possible, for example, to read the data members. These functions have been left out here, for the sake of simplicity.

New ideas
• *Polymorphism*   – a particular construct can be executed in different ways.
• *Static binding*   – which function is to be called is decided during compilation.
• *Dynamic binding*   – which function is to be called is decided during execution.
• *Virtual function*   – a function that can be called with dynamic binding.
• *Polymorphic class*   – a class that declares or inherits at least one virtual function.

The definitions of the different variants of give_info have the following appearance:

```
void Vehicle::give_info()
{
  cout << "A vehicle" << endl;
}
void Motor_vehicle::give_info()
{
  cout << "A motor vehicle" << endl;
  cout << "Reg no: " << reg_num << endl;
}
void Private_car::give_info()
{
  Motor_vehicle::give_info();
  cout << "A private car" << endl;
  cout << num_seats << " seats" << endl;
}
void Bus::give_info()
{
  Motor_vehicle::give_info();
  cout << "A bus" << endl;
  cout << num_pass << " passengers" << endl;
  if (aircond)
    cout << "Has air-conditioning" << endl;
}
void Truck::give_info()
{
  Motor_vehicle::give_info();
  cout << "A truck" << endl;
  cout << max_load << " kg maximum load" << endl;
}
```

Suppose that we now declare three variables:

```
Private_car  pc("XYZ 555", 5);
Truck        tr("ZZZ 222", 10000);
Minibus      mb("CPP 999", 10, true);
```

If we make the call

```
pc.give_info();  // static binding
```

we get written out

```
A motor vehicle
Reg no: XYZ 555
A private car
5 seats
```

Here there is a call to the variant of `give_info` that was declared in class `Private_car`. Note that this function in turn calls the variant of `give_info` belonging to `Motor_vehicle`. These are examples of *static binding*. Since the type of the variable `pc` is known at compilation, the compiler can decide which variant of `give_info` is to be called.

To demonstrate dynamic binding, we declare a pointer `fp`:

```
Vehicle *fp;
```

The pointer's type is 'pointer to `Vehicle`', which means that `fp` can point to objects of this type. Earlier in this chapter (see page 275) we saw that type conversion from a derived class to a base class was always possible and could also occur automatically. This also applies to pointers. A pointer to a derived class can be automatically converted to a pointer to the base class. Pointer `fp` can, therefore, be made to point to objects that belong to any of the classes derived from class `Vehicle`. For example, we can let the pointer `fp` point to a truck by making the assignment:

```
fp = &tr;
```

If a call is made (the arrow operator should be used since `fp` is a pointer):

```
fp->give_info();   // dynamic binding
```

then it will not be possible to decide at compilation what kind of object `fp` points to. We only know that it must be of class `Vehicle` or of one of the classes that have been derived (directly or indirectly) from this class. Thus, at compilation it is not possible to decide which variant of the function should be called. We will therefore get *dynamic binding*. When the program is executed, there is a check to see what kind of object `fp` points to at that moment, followed by a call to the function for it. If, for instance, this statement has been executed before the call:

```
fp = &tr;
```

then the call, above, would be output as:

```
A motor vehicle
Reg no: ZZZ 222
A truck
10000 kg maximum load
```

If, instead, we had executed the statements

```
fp = new Private_car("AAA 333", 4);
fp->give_info();   // dynamic binding
cout << endl;
```

```
fp = &mb;
fp->give_info();   // dynamic binding
```

we would have had this output:

```
A motor vehicle
Reg no: AAA 333
A private car
4 seats

A motor vehicle
Reg no: CPP 999
A bus
10 passengers
Has air-conditioning
```

Note that the function give_info for class Bus is called in the last line in spite of the fact that fp points to a minibus. This is because class Minibus does not have its own variant of the function give_info but instead inherits the variant of class Bus.

In this example it is also possible to get dynamic binding with the aid of a pointer whose type is 'pointer to Motor_vehicle'. For instance, we can write:

```
Motor_vehicle *mp;
mp = &tr;
mp->give_info();   // dynamic binding
```

In C++ we differentiate between the *static* and *dynamic type* of an expression. The static type will depend entirely on how the type of the expression has been declared in the program. The static type is determined at compilation and is not changed while the program is executed. For instance, the static type for the expression *fp is Vehicle, since it was stated in the declaration of fp that it should have this type. The dynamic type for an expression is decided by the actual value of the expression and can be changed during execution. The expression can contain a pointer or a reference. If, for instance, the pointer fp happens to point to a Bus, the dynamic type for the expression *fp will be Bus.

When a virtual function is called, the dynamic type of the actual object will determine which function is to be called and when an ordinary, non-virtual function is called, the static type of the actual object determines which function will be called. Generally, this means that if we are to have dynamic binding, we must have *expressly* declared the function involved as virtual. If we had left out the word **virtual** in the declaration of give_info in class Vehicle, there would not have been dynamic binding in any of the above calls. In the call fp->give_info(), the static type of fp would have been decisive, and this would have meant that the variant of give_info declared for class Vehicle would have been called irrespective of what kind of object fp had happened to point to. Then

```
A vehicle
```

would have been written out in every case. One occasion when it is fruitful to use pointers to objects is when we want to monitor many objects belonging to the same group of classes, that is, classes that have a common base class. An array of pointers can be used, for instance, to define that a car hire firm owns certain vehicles:

```
Vehicle *ftab[50];
```

Now it is possible to add to the company's stock of vehicles:

```
ftab[i] = new Private_car("QWE 123", 4);
ftab[j] = new Minibus("ASD 003", 8, false);
```

Then we can write out information for all the cars of the company:

```
for (int i=0; i < 50; i++)
    ftab[i]->give_info();   // dynamic binding
```

Using dynamic binding in this type of problem can often lead to elegant solutions because we do not have to explicitly test what kind of object we are dealing with and because we do not have to make different calls for different objects. All this is built into the mechanism of dynamic binding. And there is another advantage: it is easy to add new objects afterwards. Suppose, for example, that the car hire firm also hires out bicycles. A new class `Bike` can then be constructed:

```
class Bike : public Vehicle {
public:
  Bike(int n) : num_gears(n) {}
  void give_info();
protected:
  int num_gears;
};
```

No changes are necessary to the parts of the program already completed. If we had not used dynamic binding, on the other hand, we would have had to add a new check in all the places of the program where we checked the kind of objects involved.

We saw that we could produce dynamic binding by having pointers to objects. References can also be used. This is demonstrated in the following function that outputs information about a `Vehicle`. This function is not a member function. Instead, it has a parameter which is a *reference* to a `Vehicle`.

```
void put(Vehicle& f)
{
  cout << "Information for a vehicle:" << endl;
```

```
    f.give_info();      // dynamic binding
}
```

For instance, we can make the call:

```
put(tr);
put(*fp);
```

The static type for the parameter f is always 'reference to `Vehicle`', while the dynamic type in the first call is 'reference to `Truck`'. The dynamic type of what fp happens to point to is determined in the second of these calls.

We saw earlier that when a virtual function is inherited, exactly the same parameters and return type should be declared in the derived class as in the base class. There is an exception to this rule in the case of the return type. Suppose that a virtual function f is declared in a base class B1 and that we create a subclass to B1 which we call D1. We will create in class D1 our own variant of the virtual function f. If f in class B1 returns a value that is a pointer or reference to a class B2, we may in class D1 indicate that f should return a pointer or reference to another class D2 provided that D2 is a subclass of B2. This is especially interesting if class B1 is equal to B2 and class D1 is equal to D2.

We will give an example of this, beginning once more with various kinds of vehicle. We will make it possible to make copies of different kinds of vehicle. Suppose, for instance, that we have two pointers of type 'pointer to `Vehicle`':

```
Vehicle *fp, *fp2;
```

Dynamic binding

- The actual function *must* be declared as virtual in the base class:
  virtual *return_type* f(*parameters*);
- It is redeclared in the subclasses with *exactly* the same parameters and return type (there is a special exception for a return type).
- The word **virtual** does not have to be repeated.
- *Static type* – The type an expression has according to the declarations.
- *Dynamic type* – The type an expression has at execution.
- Call of a virtual function:
  ```
  p-> f(...);      // p is a pointer to the base type
  r.f(...);        // r is a reference to the base type
  ```
- Which function is to be called, is determined by the dynamic type of p and r.

and that we let `fp` point to some kind of vehicle, a `Truck`, for instance:

```
fp = new Truck("BBB 777", 15000);
```

We will now create a copy of the vehicle `fp` points to. If `fp` points to a `Motor_vehicle`, we want to create a new `Motor_vehicle`; if `fp` points to a `Truck`, we should create a new `Truck`; if `fp` points to a `Private_car`, we should create a new `Private_car`; if `fp` points to a `Bus`, we should create a new `Bus` and if `fp` points to a `Minibus`, we should create a new `Minibus`. We therefore construct a new virtual function that we can call in the following way:

```
fp2 = fp->create_copy();
```

Clearly, the call here must occur with dynamic binding. We put the following declaration into the definition of class `Vehicle`:

```
class Vehicle {
public:
  virtual Vehicle *create_copy()
  { return new Vehicle (*this); }
  as earlier
};
```

We must now define our own variants of `create_copy` in the subclasses of `Vehicle`. In classes `Motor_vehicle` and `Truck` we write the following, for example (and similarly in the other classes derived from class `Vehicle`).

```
class Motor_vehicle : public Vehicle {
public:
  Motor_vehicle *create_copy()
  { return new Motor_vehicle(*this); }
  as earlier
};
class Truck : public Motor_vehicle {
public:
  Truck *create_copy()
  { return new Truck(*this); }
  as earlier
};
```

Here the return types for the function `create_copy` are not identical to the return type in the declaration in class `Vehicle`, but because of the special rule just described, it is allowed in any case.

9.6 The operators `typeid` and `dynamic_cast`

In using virtual functions we seldom have cause to check an object's dynamic type but there are occasions when this may be necessary. There are two operators we can make use of in C++: **typeid** and **dynamic_cast**. To be able to use these, we should include the file `typeinfo.h` (or simply `typeinfo` if the draft standard is followed) in our program.

With the operator **typeid**, we can directly compare an object's dynamic type with a particular type. If the variable has type `Vehicle *` as before, we can write, for instance:

```
if (typeid(*fp) == typeid(Private_car))
  cout << "This is a private car" << endl;
else if (typeid(*fp) == typeid(Bus))
  cout << "This is a bus" << endl;
else if (typeid(*fp) == typeid(Minibus))
  cout << "This is a minibus" << endl;
else if (typeid(*fp) == typeid(Truck))
  cout << "This is a truck" << endl;
```

If we had executed this statement earlier:

```
fp = new Minibus ("ASD 003", 8, false);
```

fp would point to a `Minibus` and we would get the output:

```
This is a minibus
```

The operator **typeid** returns a value of the predefined standard class `type_info`. Apart from the comparison operators == and !=, there is for this class a member function `name` which can be used to find out the name of the type for an expression. The function `name` returns a text string. We can write, for instance:

```
cout << typeid(*fp).name() << endl;
cout << typeid(123+94).name() << endl;
```

We then get the message:

```
Minibus
int
```

The second line shows that the operator **typeid** can also be used for types that are not classes.

Note that `*fp` must be the argument for **typeid** if the correct result is to be obtained. If we had tried to write:

```
if (typeid(fp) == typeid(Minibus *))  // ERROR!!
  cout << "This is a Minibus" << endl;
```

which logically seems to be the same thing, the expression after **if** would have been false. The reason is that the expression **typeid**(fp) gives the static type 'pointer to Vehicle' of fp. This can be seen if the following statement is executed:

```
cout << typeid(fp).name() << endl;
```

We then get the output:

```
Vehicle *
```

The operator **typeid** can also be used when we have references. For example, we can construct the following function which checks whether a Vehicle is a kind of bus:

```
bool a_bus(Vehicle& f)
{
  return (typeid(f) == typeid(Bus) or
          typeid(f) == typeid(Minibus));
}
```

The other useful operator is **dynamic_cast**. It can be used for two purposes: first, to check whether an object is of a particular type and second, to make type conversion safe from a base type to a derived type. Let us take an example. Suppose that the pointer fp, as before, points to any kind of Vehicle. Now we want to know whether fp might possibly point to a Motor_vehicle and if so, we want to write out the registration number for this Motor_vehicle. We can then write:

```
Motor_vehicle *mp;
if (mp = dynamic_cast<Motor_vehicle *>(fp))
  cout << mp->number() << endl;
```

First we declare a pointer mp which can point to Motor_vehicle but not to other kinds of Vehicle, bicycles, for example. The expression:

```
dynamic_cast<Motor_vehicle *>(fp)
```

checks whether the parameter fp points to a Motor_vehicle or to an object belonging to a subclass of Motor_vehicle. If this is so, the value of fp is converted to the type 'pointer to Motor_vehicle', and the pointer we then get will be the result of the operator **dynamic_cast**. If fp does not point to a Motor_vehicle, the operator **dynamic_cast** will give a null pointer (value 0) as result. In the **if** statement above, the result from the operator **dynamic_cast** is assigned to the variable mp. Since a value of 0 is understood as false and

---

The operators `typeid` and `dynamic_cast`

The file `typeinfo` must be included.

`typeid(*p) == typeid(C)`

or

`typeid(r) == typeid(C)`

where p is a pointer, r a reference and C the name of a class, checks whether the object pointed to (referred to) belongs to class C.

`typeid(*p).name()`

or

`typeid(r).name()`

gives a text string with the name of the type to which the object pointed to (referred to) belongs.

`dynamic_cast<C *>(p)`

if p is a pointer to an object of class C or a subclass of C, then p converted to the type 'pointer to C' is given as result, otherwise 0.

`dynamic_cast<C&>(r)`

if r is a reference to an object of class C or a subclass of C, then r converted to the type 'reference to C' is given as result, otherwise the exception `bad_cast` is generated.

---

all other values as true, the printout statement will only be performed if fp points to a `Motor_vehicle`, in which case mp will point to this `Motor_vehicle`.

The operator **dynamic_cast** can also be used when there is a reference to an object. Then this reference can be safely converted into a reference to a subclass. Since references can never have the value 0, another technique is used to mark an incorrect type conversion. The operator then generates what is known as an *exception*. We have not discussed this term yet but in order to complete our discussion we will give an example here of how a reference to a `Vehicle` can be converted into a reference to a `Motor_vehicle`.

```
void put_no(Vehicle& f)
{
  try {
    Motor_vehicle& m = dynamic_cast<Motor_vehicle&>(f);
    cout << m.number() << endl;
  }
  catch(bad_cast) {
    cout << "Not a motor vehicle" << endl;
  }
}
```

The function is called with a reference to Vehicle. If the reference refers to a Motor_vehicle, the registration number is written out, otherwise an error message is given. (Exceptions are described in detail in Chapter 10.)

Note that the operator **typeid** can be used to check whether an object is of a given class C, while the operator **dynamic_cast** can be used to check whether an object is of a particular class C or some other class derived from C.

9.7   Virtual destructors

Constructors and destructors are not inherited. But they do call, as we saw earlier, a constructor and a destructor, respectively, for a base class; thus they can be said to inherit behaviour from the base class. A constructor cannot be virtual. When we create a new object, we have to indicate exactly what kind of object we want. Destructors, however, can be virtual, and this can be very useful.

To demonstrate a situation where we need to use virtual destructors, we return to the classes Person and Athlete from page 270 and page 279, respectively. Earlier, class Athlete had a single data member, elite, but now we extend the class with another data member:

```
class Athlete : public Person {
public:
  Athlete(char *n, char *k);
  ~Athlete();
private:
  bool elite;
  char *club;
};
```

We let the data member club be a pointer to a text string which contains the name of the athlete's club. This means that space for the text string must be allocated dynamically each time a new Athlete is created. This is done in the constructor which has two parameters, the name of the athlete and the club. In the following definition of the constructor, we have included the last line merely for demonstration purposes.

```
Athlete::Athlete(char *n, char *k): Person(n)
{
  club = new char[strlen(k)+1];
  strcpy(club, k);
  cout << (strlen(k)+1)<<" bytes allocated"<<endl;
}
```

The class `Athlete` is a subclass of class `Person`. Therefore, the constructor for class `Person` is first called in the initialization list to initialize the `Person` part of the object. Memory space exactly large enough to hold the club's name is then allocated dynamically. Finally, the club's name is copied into the new memory space.

Since dynamic memory space is allocated in the constructor, we must also have a destructor that deallocates this memory space when it is no longer needed.

```
Athlete::~Athlete()
{
  cout << (strlen(club)+1)
       << " bytes deallocated" << endl;
  delete[] club;
}
```

A test program that uses the classes `Person` and `Athlete` is given below for demonstration purposes:

```
main ()
{
  Athlete i1("Maria", "City Judo Club");
  Person *p1, *p2;
  p1 = new Person("Lisa");
  p2 = new Athlete("John", "Westtown AC");
  delete p1;
  delete p2;
}
```

When we run the program, we obtain the following output:

```
15 bytes allocated
12 bytes allocated
15 bytes deallocated
```

The 15 bytes allocated for the variable `i1` are deallocated, exactly as they should be when execution reaches the last right-hand brace. The variable `p1` points to an object of class `Person`. No memory space is allocated for this object, so none will be deallocated, either. The problem is the object pointed to by the variable `p2`. This object is of the class `Athlete`, and memory space (15 bytes) is allocated when the object is created. When the statement **delete** `p2` is executed, however, memory space is not deallocated as it should be. This is because the pointer p2 has the type 'pointer to `Person`' and not the type 'pointer to `Athlete`'. The static type is thus 'pointer to `Person`'. When a non-virtual member function is called, it is, as we have seen, the actual object's static type that determines which variant of the member function is to be called. It is the destructor for the base class `Person` that is called in this case. We did not declare a destructor in our example for the class `Person`, although there is one that is generated automatically but does nothing.

The solution to our problem is to make the destructor of the base class *virtual*, for then the dynamic type of the actual object will determine which destructor is to be called. Thus we declare a virtual destructor in class `Person`:

```
class Person {
public:
  virtual ~Person() {};
  as earlier
}
```

The new constructor does nothing: there are no statements inside the braces. Since no dynamic memory space was allocated for class `Person`, there will be nothing to be deallocated. (If class `Person` had allocated memory space dynamically, the destructor would naturally have de-allocated this memory space here.) When we now test our program, we will get dynamic binding with execution of the statement **delete** p2. Then the destructor for class `Athlete` will be called. The text written out will now be correct

```
15 bytes allocated
12 bytes allocated
12 bytes deallocated
15 bytes deallocated
```

From this example we learn that we should *always* declare a virtual destructor in a class if this class is intended to be the base class for other classes. If this is not done, programs can be created that consume memory without releasing it, and this can lead to serious execution errors. The question arises whether C++ is poorly constructed where destructors are concerned. Surely all destructors should be automatically virtual? Then this problem would not arise.

9.8   Abstract classes

The member function `give_info` for class `Vehicle` (see page 304) is really quite meaningless because the only thing that happens when it is used, is that it writes out the text 'A vehicle'. But we defined it because we wanted to be sure that there would be a function `give_info` for every object of a class derived from class `Vehicle`. Suppose, for instance, that we declare a new subclass `Tram` of class `Vehicle`. Further suppose that we forget to define a new member function `give_info` for class `Tram`. Objects belonging to class `Tram` will then inherit the member function `give_info` from class `Vehicle`. The operation `give_info` should exist for all objects of a class derived from class `Vehicle` if we are to make use of the technique of dynamic binding. If, as previously, we have a pointer `fp`:

```
Vehicle fp;
```

and make the call

```
fp->give_info();
```

then the member function `give_info` must exist for all objects which `fp` could point to.

But we do not have to invent a 'meaningless' member function for a base class in order to be assured that all the objects will have this function. What can be done instead is to declare what is known as a *pure virtual function*. This member function will not be implemented (defined), thus we will not be able to call it. A pure virtual function is only a kind of marker for a true function. We will show how it looks by remaking the member function `give_info` in class `Vehicle` into a pure virtual function. The definition of class `Vehicle` will then look like this:

```
class Vehicle {
public:
  virtual void give_info() = 0;   // pure virtual function
};
```

It is the initialization to 0 that indicates that `give_info` is a pure virtual function. Since `give_info` should not be implemented, we cannot write a definition for it.

A class that contains at least one virtual function is called an *abstract class* (not to be confused with *abstract data type*, which was discussed in the introduction to Chapter 7). Since a pure virtual function cannot be called, it is not allowed to create objects of an abstract class. Thus we cannot declare variables of type `Vehicle` now. Objects can only be created for those classes where all the pure virtual functions have been replaced by 'true' functions. For example, it is permissible to declare an object of class `Bike` if this class, as previously, has its own version of the member function `give_info`:

```
class Bike : public Vehicle {
public:
```

```
   void give_info();
   etc.
};
```

If we define a new class that is derived from an abstract class, we are not forced to declare our own versions of the base type's pure virtual functions. If these functions are not redeclared, the new class will also be abstract, and we are not allowed to create objects of the new class. If, for instance, we take away the declaration of the function `give_info` in class `Motor_vehicle`, this class will be abstract, and it will not be permissible to create objects of this class. On the other hand, we are allowed to create objects of the classes derived from class `Motor_ vehicle` since these will have declared their own versions of `give_info`.

By making use of pure virtual functions, therefore, we can obtain an abstract base class. It is not our aim to create objects from an abstract class like this. It will merely serve as a pattern for the various subclasses. An abstract base class indicates which primitive operations must be present for all objects belonging to one of the classes derived from the base class. Good examples of this are applications which allow us to work with different graphic figures drawn on the screen. An abstract base class `Figure` can then be obtained. Starting from this, we can derive various subclasses for different figures such as circles, rectangles and lines. The class `Figure` can contain the pure virtual functions `draw`, `change_colour` and `move`.

To give a more concrete example of the use of abstract base classes, we will return to the program in Section 7.5, page 230. Here a player played the card game Twenty-one against the computer. A class `Player`, which defined the actions of a player, was implemented in the program. The problem with this class was that it had to define the actions of both the user and the computer. We were therefore obliged to have a member variable that indicated whether the player was a human or a computer. Let us redefine class `Player` so that it becomes an abstract base class instead:

```
class Player {
public:
   Player(Cardstack& cardpack) : pack(cardpack) {};
   virtual int play() = 0;
protected:
   Cardstack& pack;
   Cardstack hand;
   int points();
};
```

We have made two changes to the earlier version. The function `play` has been declared as a pure virtual function, and the member variable `computer`, which indicated whether or not the current player was a computer, has been removed. We now define two new subclasses of `Player`, `Human` and `Computer`:

```
class Human : public Player {
public:
  Human(Cardstack& cardpack) : Player(cardpack) {}
  int play();
};
class Computer : public Player {
public:
  Computer(Cardstack& cardpack) : Player(cardpack) {}
  int play();
};
```

These new classes each have their own variant of the virtual function `play`. If we compare these with the function `play` we had previously, we can see that they have been simplified, because each variant can be specially formulated for every subclass.

```
int Human::play()
{
  int p = 0;
  while (p < 21)
  {
    Card k = pack.deal_top();
    hand.lay_top(k);
    p = points();
    cout << "You got "; k.write_out();
    cout << " and has " << p << " points" << endl;
    if (p < 21)
    {
      char answer[10];
      cout << "One more card? " ;
      cin >> answer;
      if (answer[0] != 'y')
        break;
    }
  }
  hand.throw_cards();
  return p;
}
```

```
int Computer::play()
{
  int p = 0;
  while (p<16)
  {
```

Abstract classes

- A member function can be declared as a *pure virtual function*
  virtual *result type* f(*parameters*) = 0;
- Pure virtual functions have no implementation (definition).
- A class with at least one pure virtual function is an *abstract* class.
- No objects can be created from an abstract class.
- Subclasses that do not have their own versions of all the pure virtual functions are also abstract.

```
    Card k = pack.deal_top();
    hand.lay_top(k);
    p = points();
    cout << "The computer got "; k.write_out();
    cout << endl;
  }
  cout << "The computer has " << p << " points" << endl;
  hand.throw_cards();
  return p;
}
```

Now we only need to change the declarations of the two players you and I in the main program. Both of these variables previously had type Player. Instead we write:

```
Human     you (pack);
Computer  I   (pack);
```

(The parameter pack is a reference to the cardpack the two players have in common.) When later in the program the calls you.play() and I.play() are made, different versions of the function play will be called.

9.9   Virtual operators

As we saw, the concept of dynamic binding meant that it was the actual object's dynamic type that determined which function was to be called. If, for instance, we make the call p->f(x), where p is a pointer, x a parameter and f a virtual function, it is the type of the object that p points to that determines which variant of function f is to be called. Operators are also member functions. If we write an expression:

a *XX* b

where *XX* is an operator symbol, this would be the same thing as if we had written

```
a.operatorXX(b)
```

If the function **operator***XX* is declared as virtual and we make a call in the following form (p and q are pointers):

```
(*p) XX (*q)
```

it is then the type of the object the pointer p points to that determines which variant of operator *XX* is to be called. It does not matter what the pointer q happens to be pointing to. *C++ allows dynamic binding in the first operator only.* This could cause confusion if we want to write symmetrical operators with two parameters of the same type. Suppose, for example, that we want to construct an operator > that compares two motor vehicles of the same kind. (We use the same classes as we did earlier in this chapter.) If we have two pointers mp1 and mp2:

```
Motor_vehicle *mp1, *mp2;
```

we would like to be able to write, for instance:

```
if (*mp1 > *mp2)
```

That is, we would like to have dynamic binding so that different > operators would be called depending on what mp1 and mp2 happened to point to. If they point to trucks, for instance, then the maximum loads of the trucks should be compared; if they point to private cars or buses, the number of passengers should be compared. But what would happen if the pointers pointed to different kinds of vehicle, one for instance pointing to a bus and the other to a truck? The old saying that it does not do to compare apples and oranges is a good principle, and we would like it to apply here, too. Therefore, we regard it as an error when the two pointers point to different kinds of vehicle, and we allow the program to abort.

We begin now by declaring the operator > for class Motor_vehicle. We let the operator be a pure virtual function which means that class Motor_vehicle will be abstract. We do not want a situation where objects that are 'only' Motor_vehicle can be declared.

```
class Motor_vehicle : public Vehicle {
public:
  virtual bool operator> (Motor_vehicle& m) = 0;
  as previously
};
```

The next step is to declare our own variants of the operator > for the classes that are derived from class Motor_vehicle. The parameter for the operator has type 'reference to `Motor_vehicle`'. We begin with class `Private_car`. Our first attempt looks like this:

```
class Private_car : public Vehicle {
public:
  bool operator> (Private_car& m);   // ERROR!!
  as previously
};
```

Since this operator should be able to compare two private cars, we have indicated that the type of the parameters should be 'reference to `Private_car`'. Unfortunately, this is a mistake. The class definition can be compiled. Even the definition of the operator > can be compiled. But if we write a program and try to declare a variable of type `Private_car`, we will get a compilation error because the compiler understands `Private_car` to be an abstract class. There cannot be objects of an abstract class. `Private_car` is an abstract class because the parameter type in the declaration of the > operator, of course, in class `Private_car` does not tally with the parameter type in the corresponding declaration in the base class `Motor_vehicle`. Therefore, the new declaration is understood as a declaration of a *new* > operator which *hides* the one declared in the base class. The hidden operator is inherited and will still be a pure virtual function since it has not been redefined in class `Private_car`. The parameter type must therefore be the same as in the base class. Let us make another attempt:

```
class Private_car : public Motor_vehicle {
public:
  bool operator> (Motor_vehicle& m);   // Correct!
  as previously
};
```

Now the definition of class `Private_car` will be correct. Next, the definition for the > operator has to be written. Our first attempt is:

```
bool Private_car::operator> (Motor_vehicle& m)
{
  return num_seats > m.num_seats;   // ERROR!!
}
```

We will get a compilation error here! The compiler will complain about the expression `m.num_seats` and state that there is no member of class `Motor_vehicle` of that name. The parameter m does not have the correct type to enable us to access the data member `num_seats`. This parameter should have had type 'reference to `Private_car`' but it did not work, as we saw above. The solution to this problem is to make a type conversion. We now write the following correct definition of the > operator.

```
bool Private_car::operator> (Motor_vehicle& m)
{
  Private_car& r = dynamic_cast<Private_car&>(m);
  return num_seats > r.num_seats;
}
```

The operator **dynamic_cast** has been used to make a conversion from type 'reference to Motor_vehicle' to type 'reference to Private_car'. This conversion will work if parameter m happens to refer to a Private_car. If it does not, we will understand the program to be faulty and get an execution error because the operator **dynamic_cast** will generate an exception. (If we want to take care of this and write an error message, the same technique can be used as on page 312).

The > operator is defined for the other classes in a similar way. In class Truck we write, for example:

```
bool Truck::operator> (Motor_vehicle& m)
{
  Truck& r = dynamic_cast<Truck&>(m);
  return max_load > r.max_load;
}
```

9.10 Multiple inheritance

In all our examples of inheritance up to now, we have seen how derived classes have had a single direct base class. However, a class may have several direct base classes. This is called *multiple inheritance*. We can, for example, declare a class D that has three different, direct base classes, B1, B2 and B3:

```
class D : public B1, protected B2, private B3 {
  declarations of members
};
```

A class can have as many direct base classes as we like. They are simply listed after the colon, the only restriction being that a particular base class can only occur once in the list. We indicate for each one whether the inheritance should be *public*, *protected* or *private*, by writing one of the words **public**, **protected** or **private**. If none of these is indicated it will be assumed that inheritance is private. It is not important in which order the base classes come in the list.

With multiple inheritance the same rules apply regarding visibility, initializations, and so on, as for simple inheritance. When, for example, an object with several direct base classes is created, all the base class subobjects must be initialized, either by the derived class calling the constructors of the base classes, or by their default constructors being called automatically.

 We use multiple inheritance when we want to combine different properties from two or more base classes. We shall demonstrate this by adding to classes with different kinds of vehicle. Our goal is to construct a class that defines amphibious cars, a combination of cars and boats. We begin by defining the fundamental base class `Vehicle`:

```cpp
class Vehicle {
public:
  Vehicle() { weight = length = width = 0;}
  virtual void give_info() = 0;
protected:
  int weight, length, width;
};
```

The only difference compared with the previous version is that we have added, for demonstration purposes, the three data members `weight`, `length` and `width`, and we have defined our own default constructor that sets them to zero.

 We then declare two new classes, `Boat`, which defines boats in general and `Motor_boat`, which defines motor boats. Since boats are a kind of vehicle, they have been defined as a subclass of `Vehicle`. The class `Motor_boat` is, of course, a subclass of class `Boat`.

```cpp
class Boat : public Vehicle {
public:
  Boat(char *material) {strcpy(m, material);}
  const char *made_of() { return m;}
  void give_info()
  {cout << "This is a boat of " << m << endl; }
protected:
  char m[10];
};
class Motor_boat : public Boat {
public:
  Motor_boat(char *material, int prop)
  : Boat(material),num_prop(prop){}
protected:
  int num_prop;
};
```

 Now we can define the class `Amphibious_car`, which is derived from the classes `Private_car` and `Motor_boat`.

```
class Amphibious_car : public Private_car, public Motor_boat {
public:
  Amphibious_car(char *no, int seats, char *m, int prop)
  : Private_car(no, seats), Motor_boat(m, prop) {}
};
```

An Amphibious_car has a subobject that is a Private_car and a subobject that is a Motor_boat. Both subobjects must be initialized, and this occurs when their constructors are called in the initialization list in the constructor for Amphibious_car. The relations of the different classes are illustrated in Figure 9.4.

We can now declare an Amphibious_car:

```
Amphibious_car a("AMF 012", 4, "steel", 2);
```

An Amphibious_car inherits all the properties from both of its base classes. For example, we can make the calls:

```
cout << a.made_of() << endl;
cout << a.number()  << endl;
```

In the first line, the function made_of is called. This was inherited by Amphibious_car from class Boat. In the second line the function number, inherited from class Motor_vehicle, is called. We will now try to call the function give_info:

```
a.give_info();
```

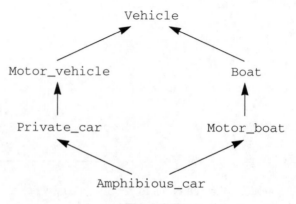

Figure 9.4

This does not work very well. When we attempt a compilation, we get an error message giving something like:

```
member is ambiguous
```

The class `Amphibious_car` has inherited the function `give_info` from two sources. The compiler does not know if it is the function `give_info` in class `Private_car` or the `give_info` in class `Boat` that is to be called. Therefore, we must explicitly indicate in the call which one is intended. For instance, we can write:

```
a.Private_car::give_info();
```

A better variant would be to redeclare `give_info` in class `Amphibious_car`:

```
class Amphibious_car : public Private_car, public Motor_boat {
public:
  void give_info();
  as before
};
```

Both of the inherited versions of `give_info` can be called in the definition:

```
void Amphibious_car::give_info()
{
  Private_car::give_info();
  Motor_boat::give_info();
}
```

Now we can call `a.give_info()`, and we obtain:

```
A motor vehicle
Reg no: AMF 012
A private car
4 seats
This is a boat of steel
```

Suppose that we now want to know how much an amphibious car weighs. We try to add the following line to the function `Amphibious_car::give_info`

```
cout << "Weight: " << weight << endl;
```

This does not work. Again we get the error message:

Member is ambiguous

This is because `Amphibious_car` has *two* data members with the name `weight`. The two base classes `Private_car` and `Motor_boat` are both indirectly derived from class `Vehicle`, which means that both subobjects each contain a data member with the name `weight`.

Of course, an `Amphibious_car` cannot reasonably have two collections of data members in the base class `Vehicle`. A particular `Amphibious_car` has only one `weight`, one `length` and one `width`. We must therefore make sure that only one set of data members is inherited. The solution is to use a *virtual base class*. We must then adjust our definitions of the classes directly derived from class `Vehicle`, that is, classes `Motor_vehicle` and `Boat`. We shall indicate that both of these classes are to inherit class `Vehicle` *virtually*. We do this by adding the word **virtual** when the base class is given. The new definitions of `Motor_vehicle` and `Boat` will then look like this:

```
class Motor_vehicle : public virtual Vehicle {
  as before
};

class Boat : public virtual Vehicle {
  as before
};
```

If in a class C it is indicated that a base class V should be virtual, then objects of all classes derived from C will contain exactly one subobject of class V.

Multiple inheritance

- A class can have several direct base classes
  class D : *access* B1, *access* B2, ... {
     declarations of own members
     };
- Each base class is included in its entirety as a subobject.
- All members from all base classes are inherited.
- Confusion with names may arise. Solved by the operator : :
- A *virtual base class* V is included as a subobject exactly *once* in an object.
  class C : *access* **virtual** V {
     declarations of own members
     };

Note that we must indicate that the base class is to be virtual as early as with the definitions of `Motor_vehicle` and `Boat`. It would be too late when we define class `Amphibious_car`. If we intend to use multiple inheritance, we must plan at an early stage, as early as with the construction of the basic base classes.

The question might arise with a virtual base class of how to initialize this single base class subobject. In this example it is quite simple because the constructor for the virtual base class `Vehicle` is not called explicitly in either of its subclasses, `Motor_vehicle` or `Boat`. The default constructor that sets the members `weight`, `length` and `width` to zero will be called here. But we could think of cases where the virtual base class is initialized differently at the different 'steps' up to the base class. What happens then? For virtual base classes, there is in C++ a complicated, special rule which states that the base class subobject corresponding to the virtual base class can only be initialized once. If we were to draw a figure, this would be done at the step furthest to the left. (The concepts of 'left' or 'right' are determined by the order in which the base classes are listed in the class definitions.) The best advice we can give is to avoid writing programs where the step at which a virtual base class is initialized takes on undue importance.

EXERCISES

9.1   Beginning with class `Person`, construct a new derived class `Student` with suitable members. In addition construct a new class `Course`, relating it appropriately to class `Student`.

9.2   Complete Exercise 9.1 with class `Teacher` according to Figure 6.9, page 192.

9.3   Beginning with classes `Person` and `Motor_vehicle`, define a class `Car_owner` to define a person who can be the owner of one `Motor_vehicle` or more.

9.4   In the previous exercise it was assumed that the owner of a vehicle is always a natural person 'of flesh and bone'. Write new class definitions which allow an owner to be a person in the legal sense, that is, a corporation of some sort. A corporation has, in turn, one or more owners. Beginning with two new base classes, `Owner` and `Thing` and making use of multiple inheritance, show whether it is possible to define the situation that certain classes, for example, persons, can be the owners of one or several things and that certain other classes, for example persons in the legal sense of corporations, can be both owned and owner at the same time.

9.5   Different kinds of animal can be defined using classes and inheritance. Define some animals by beginning with a class `Animal` and deriving the different animals from this. Feel free to use such intermediate classes as `Mammal`, `Insect`, `Bird`, and so on. Declare a virtual function `Sound` to define the sound made by the animal.

9.6 Descriptions of geometric figures are often used as examples in the context of object-oriented programming. First define a class Point that defines a point (*x*, *y*) in a two-dimensional coordinate system. Then declare a class Figure that contains a starting point. Let class Figure have a pure virtual function, Area.

In addition, define a number of subclasses of the class Figure, for example, Circle, Triangle and Rectangle. Give them suitable members. Let each subclass have its own version of the function Area.

Finally, declare an array with pointers to arbitrary figures and write the statements necessary to calculate and output the area for all the figures in the array.

9.7 Complete class SuperInt with friend functions enabling you to perform the operations + – * and / when the left-hand operand has type **long int** and the right-hand operand has type SuperInt. The result of such an operation should be a SuperInt.

9.8 Write a virtual function max which as result gives the larger of two Vehicles of the same make. If fp1, fp2 and fp3 have type 'pointer to Vehicle', it should be possible to perform a statement like fp3=fp1-max(*fp2). After this statement, fp3 should point to the larger of the two vehicles that fp1 and fp2 point to.

9.9 Start from class Vector and construct a new derived class Matrix, where the elements of the matrix are integers. A matrix consists of a certain number of rows and columns. Individual elements are indicated by the row and column number. For simplicity, the numbering of rows and columns should always start from 1. The indexing operator does not allow more than one operand, so the function call operator can be used instead. Let the new class Matrix get an appropriate collection of member functions and ensure that all operations visible for class Matrix are significant and correct for matrices.

9.10 Complete class Matrix in the previous exercise with the two member functions row and col with the help of which a particular row or column can be read. As result the functions should give a value of type Vector.

Exceptions

When a program is executed, unexpected situations may occur. Such a situation is called an *exception*. This may be the result of an error of some kind, for example, indexing outside the limits in an array, or giving faulty input data to a function. An exception is not necessarily the result of a logic error in the program. It can also arise from faulty input data.

When a function is being written, the algorithm should be as clear and easy to understand as possible. But if checks were inserted at each stage of the algorithm to handle every imaginable error and abnormal event, the algorithm would become very clumsy and hard to follow. In the latest versions of C++, a mechanism has been added to handle exceptions. This mechanism is technically similar to the one in the programming language Ada. The part of the program where the error arises generates an exception which, according to predetermined rules, is passed on to other parts of the program where the exception can be 'trapped' and appropriate action taken.

One thing that C++ has inherited from its predecessor C is its way of handling execution errors, although it might be more correct to say, its way of *not* handling execution errors. As we have seen, there is no way of controlling, for example, an index, so that it lies inside the allowed limits, and there are normally no controls to see that overflow does not arise in connection with numerical calculations. If controls are wanted in a program, they normally have to be put there by the programmer. This is where C++ differs from other high level languages in which a number of execution controls are normally carried out automatically. (If, in the interests of efficiency, these are not wanted, they can usually be turned off by giving a special instruction to the compiler.) If we want to use the technique of dealing with exceptions in C++, we *ourselves* usually have to make sure that exceptions are generated when errors arise, because the compiler will not normally do so. For instance, it will not generate an exception if indexing is not correct.

Earlier, we used the standard function `assert` in programs to insert execution controls. The problem with `assert` is that if the given condition is not true, the program will be terminated. The error cannot be taken care of, and so the program cannot be allowed to continue. But `assert` is not constructed for this purpose. It is meant to be used during program testing and discarded when the program has been tested. In this chapter we will learn how to use the new technique for handling exceptions. We will be using it from now on instead of the function `assert`.

10.1   Generating exceptions

Two separate stages can be distinguished when working with exceptions. In the first, an exception is generated and in the second stage, the exception is trapped. We will begin by describing what happens in the easier of these two stages, how exceptions are generated. How they are trapped, we will deal with later.

An exception is generated by the execution of a **throw** statement. When this statement is executed, the block being executed will be terminated immediately. Program control will then be transferred to the part of the program trapping the exception. If no part of the program does this, the program will be terminated prematurely. (This will occur when the standard function `terminate` is automatically called. This function in turn calls the function `abort`.)

A **throw** statement has the general form

```
throw expression;
```

where *expression* can be of any type. We could write, for example:

```
throw 28;
```

Even though the expression can be of arbitrary type, we ought to use the special classes given in the standard to signal exceptions. These classes are defined in the header file `stdexcept`. (See Appendix A.) In order to make use of them, this line should appear first in the program:

```
#include <stdexcept>
```

All the standard classes for exceptions have in common the fundamental base class `exception`. This has two subclasses, `logic_error` and `runtime_error`. The class `logic_error` is a base class for whatever classes are there to signal errors resulting from logic errors in the program, such errors as could have been avoided (at least in theory) if the program had been constructed differently. The other subclass, `runtime_error`, is a base class for classes used to signal execution errors that cannot be avoided by constructing a program differently. Figure 10.1 illustrates the different predefined classes.

One of the most derived classes, on the right in the figure, should be used. To generate an exception, we write:

```
throw exception_name("extra information");
```

To generate an exception of class `invalid_argument`, we write, for example

```
throw invalid_argument ("to my_funct");
```

When we write in this way, we create an object and 'throw away' this object so that it can be trapped later in another part of the program. All the classes in Figure 10.1, except the base class `exception`, have definitions of the form:

```
class class_name : public base_class {
public:
  class_name(const string& what_arg);
};
```

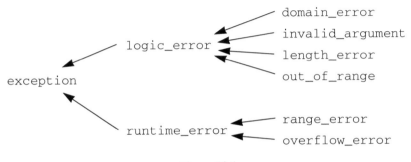

Figure 10.1

We see that there is only one constructor and that it will have an argument of the standard type string. Since ordinary text strings can be automatically converted to the class string, we can create objects of these classes by writing expressions of the form *class_name*("*text*"). The text given as argument can be read later when the exception is trapped. We can therefore use it to add extra information that could be useful, such as information about exactly where the error arose.

We worked with the class Vector in Chapter 8. There we used the function assert to check that the parameters of member functions had values that were allowed. A better way is to generate exceptions. Then a program will not have to be terminated merely because a function has been called with incorrect parameters. As an example we give a new version of one of the indexing operators. (Compare with page 256.) If the index does not lie in the allowed interval, an event of the class out_of_range is generated:

```
int& Vector::operator[] (int i)
{
  if (i < i1 or i > last())
    throw out_of_range("Vector::operator[]");
  return p[i-i1];
}
```

We have added the function's name here as additional information in the **throw** statement.

Another example is the operator += on page 248, that adds elements in a Vector to elements in another Vector. We recall that a requirement in this function is that both the vectors involved be of equal length. The new version will be this:

```
const Vector& Vector::operator+= (const Vector& v)
{
  if (num != v.num)
    throw length_error("Vector::operator+=");
  for (int i=0; i<num; i++)
    p[i] += v.p[i];
  return *this;
}
```

The other member functions in class Vector should also be similarly changed so that they generate exceptions.

We can also declare our own subclasses of the classes in Figure 10.1. For example, we can make the definition

```
class communication_error : public runtime_error {
public:
  communication_error(const char *what_arg = "")
  : runtime_error(what_arg) {}
};
```

We have given the parameter of the constructor a default value here. This means that
we can write the expression both with and without an argument:

```
throw communication_error("Timeout in reader");
throw communication_error();
```

In certain cases the system itself will generate exceptions. If we use the
operator **new** and try to allocate more memory space than is available, an exception
of class bad_alloc is generated. (Note that in earlier versions of C++, the
operator **new** returned a value of 0 in this case.) If we try to use incorrect type
conversions with the operator **dynamic_cast** (see page 310), an exception of
class bad_cast is generated and if we give the operator **typeid** a null pointer as
argument, an exception of class bad_typeid will be generated. These three
classes are all subclasses of class exception. The class bad_alloc is defined
in the header file **new,** and the classes bad_cast and bad_typeid are defined
in the header file typeinfo.

Classes derived from class exception are also used in several of the
suggested standard libraries to signal errors. This applies, for instance, to the library
where the standard class string is defined, and to the library which contains
classes for handling streams and files. In the latter library, there is a class failure
which is used to signal certain types of error with the reading and writing of data.

---

throw statement

> **throw** *expression*;

where *expression* can be of arbitrary type.

- Normal execution is terminated when a **throw** statement is executed.
- It is best to use a standard class *S* derived from the standard class
  exception
  > **throw** *S*("*text*");

  or a personally created class *E* derived from class exception
  > **throw** *E*();
- The following line must be found in the program
  > #include <stdexcept>

10.2   Handling exceptions

So far we have only discussed how exceptions are generated. If an exception is not trapped, the program will stop. If we have a program that controls an industrial process of some sort, it is not acceptable for the program to cease abruptly if an exception occurs. The program must deal with what has happened by writing a warning message to the operator or closing down a critical process, for example. It is also unacceptable for a program to cease because an operator happens to have written input data in the wrong format.

There are three levels of ambition in dealing with exceptions:

(1)   Take control of the exception and try to take suitable action to enable the program to continue.

(2)   Identify the exception and pass it on to another part of the program.

(3)   Identify the exception but ignore it: the program will stop when the exception occurs.

The basic principle should be that the exception is controlled in the part of the program where its effect can be handled most sensibly. The third level is the one we have seen so far. We have used the function `assert` and allowed the program to stop. This is fine when dealing with logic errors that have occurred while the program was being tested before it was properly run.

We shall begin with an example from the following function:

```
int f(int x)
{
  int a = fa(x);
  int b = fb(x);
  return a / b;
}
```

Both of the functions that are called, `fa` and `fb`, can be two arbitrary functions. If function `fb` should return a value of 0, we will have a problem. If we do nothing, division by 0 will be performed and this will give an undefined result. (Most C++ implementations ignore so-called arithmetic overflow.) If the variable `b` gets a value of 0, this will be apparent but what should we do? If we are operating on ambition level 1 (to take control of the exception), we have to find a suitable value to return from the function `f`. We try this:

```
int f(int x)
{
  int a = fa(x);
  int b = fb(x);
  if (b == 0)
    return INT_MAX;
  return a / b;
}
```

The constant INT_MAX is defined in the standard file `limits.h` and indicates the largest number that can be stored in a variable of type **int**. If, for example, type **int** is represented with 16 bits, INT_MAX will be equal to 32767. This is the nearest that we can get to the infinitely great number that should have been returned in the case when b equals 0. Naturally, this is mathematically absurd, and we must accept that ambition level 1 is too high for this example. It is simply not possible to return a reasonable value from the function f when b gets a value of 0. If we go to ambition level 3, the problem becomes easy. We simply add the following line after the value of b has been calculated:

```
assert(b != 0);
```

or we can write

```
if (b == 0)
{
   cout << "Overflow in the function f";
   abort();
}
```

But then the program will stop, and this may not be necessary. The result from function f may not be so important, after all. If the function that called f had found that an error had arisen, it might have been able to proceed anyway, even if it had not got a result from f. This is possible if we try to apply ambition level 2. Begin by writing a new version of function f to generate an exception when b becomes 0.

```
int f(int x)
{
   int a = fa(x);
   int b = fb(x);
   if (b == 0)
      throw overflow_error("Error in f");
   return a / b;
}
```

Let us look at the function that calls function f. When we call a function that can generate exceptions, we have to indicate specially that we are prepared to trap exceptions. This we do by making use of what is called a **try** block, which has the general form:

```
try {
   statements
}
catch (parameter) {
   statements
}
```

```
catch (parameter) {
  statements
}
etc.
```

After the word **try** we write a block that contains the statements to be performed, one that can possibly generate an exception. After this block there should be one or more *handlers*. Each handler is introduced with the reserved word **catch** and has a single parameter. The following things happen when the statements in the block after **try** are executed. If no exception occurs, the statements are performed as usual, and none of the handlers will be involved. If an exception of type $type_e$ is generated by one of the statements after **try**, execution of this statement will be interrupted, and the program will instead jump to the *first* of the handlers that has a parameter of a type that matches $type_e$. We will give the rules later for what is meant by 'match' but we now show an example instead.

```
void g()
{
  int i;
  while (1)
    try {
      cout << "? ";
      if (not (cin >> i))
        break;
      int r = f(i);
      cout << "The result was " << r << endl;
    }
    catch(overflow_error) {
      cout << "No result can be given" << endl;
    }
}
```

The function g keeps reading in integers from the keyboard. Input is terminated when the character combination for end-of-file is given (Ctrl-Z or Ctrl-D). For every number read, the function f is called, and the result from f written at the terminal. If a number happens to be read in such that b in the function f becomes equal to zero, the following statement is executed:

```
throw overflow_error("Error in f");
```

Since the exception that now arises does not lie in a **try** block, it will not be dealt with in the function f. Instead f will be interrupted and the exception sent further to the function g, which called f. In g there is then an exception at the point where f was called, that is, in the declaration:

```
int r = f(i);
```

This line is then aborted, and since it lies in a **try** block, the program will jump to the first of the **try** block's handlers that matches the type overflow_error. In the **try** block in g, there is only one handler, and since it has a parameter precisely of type overflow_error, the program will jump there. Then we obtain:

```
No result can be given
```

As soon as a handler is reached that traps the exception, the exception is eliminated. Execution then proceeds normally with the statement that comes *after* the **try** block, that is, with a statement that comes after the last of the handlers. It is important to note that there is no jump back to the statement that was aborted in the **try** block. (If in our example there had been several other statements after f(i) was called, these would not have been performed.) If we wanted to perform the statements in the **try** block again, we would have to put the whole **try** block into a repetition statement, as we did in our example, and execute the statements in it from the beginning.

The rules state that when an exception of $type_e$ arises, control will be transformed to the nearest 'suitable' handler. By 'suitable' we mean that it will have a parameter whose type matches $type_e$. And when we say 'nearest', we mean that the handler will be in the **try** block that was begun last of all the unfinished **try** blocks. This means that an exception is 'passed on' from the point where it arises – the interruption point – until there is a handler that can deal with the exception. The path the exception takes here is the reverse of the stages leading up to the interruption. If no suitable handler can be found on the way back, the program will be terminated.

We must also give the rules (in simplified form) for what is meant by types 'matching'. Suppose that there has been an exception of $type_e$. If a handler has a parameter of type T or type 'reference to T', then this parameter matches $type_e$ if:

- T and $type_e$ are the same type;
- T is a base class of $type_e$;
- T has type 'pointer to B' and $type_e$ type 'pointer to D', where B is a base class of D.

The most important point is, of course, the first one which states that if the types are the same, then they match. This is the rule that was applied in our function g above.

We shall now extend our example to demonstrate how we can have several handlers. We did not worry before about the two functions fa and fb which were called in function f. Suppose that fa looks as follows:

```
int fa(int x)
{
  int tab[100];
```

```
    ...  // initialization of tab
  if (x < 0 or x >= 100)
    throw out_of_range("in fa");
  return tab[x];
}
```

The function fa generates an exception of the standard class out_of_range if incorrect indexing is performed.

We now extend the function g with yet another handler:

```
void g()
{
  int i;
  while (1)
    try {
      cout << "? ";
      if (not (cin >> i))
        break;
      int r = f(i);
      cout << "The result was " << r << endl;
    }
    catch(overflow_error) {
      cout << "No result can be given" << endl;
    }
    catch(exception& e) {
      cout << typeid(e).name() << ": "
           << e.what() << endl;
    }
}
```

We let the parameter in the new handler have type 'reference to exception'. This means that according to the rules above, this parameter will match all classes directly or indirectly derived from class exception. This in turn means that the new handler will be a suitable handler for all the kinds of exceptions where the standard classes in Figure 10.1 are used. We have given the parameter in the new handler a name, e. It functions in roughly the same way as a parameter in a function call. When control is transferred to the handler, the handler gets the actual exception as argument. This means that we can use the parameter e to examine the exception in more detail. We first use the standard operator **typeid** to write out the name of the class the exception belongs to. Note that it is extremely important to let the parameter e be of type 'reference to exception' and not simply of type exception, because when we call **typeid**, we find out which subclass of exception e refers to. If e is merely of type exception, the argument is copied to e, and all the parts except for the exception part are peeled away. The expression **typeid**(e).name() would then always return the text 'exception'.

The standard class `exception` contains a very useful virtual member function with the name `what`

```
virtual const char* what() const;
```

This function is inherited by all the subclasses of `exception`. When we call it, we get as result the text that was given as extra information when the exception was generated.

Let us suppose that we have a main program that makes the call `g()`. Here is an example from the program when it is run:

```
? 0
No result can be given
? -1
out_of_range: in fa
```

When we give a value of 0 as input data, function `f` generates an exception of type `overflow_error`, and we land in function `g`. When we give a value of −1, an exception of type `out_of_range` is generated in function `fa`. Since there is no **try** block with a suitable handler either in function `fa` or function `f`, the exception is sent on to the **try** block in function `g`. Here we land in the second of the handlers since class `out_of_range` is derived from class `exception`. Note that we get the message 'out_of_range' and not 'exception'. This is because we use a reference parameter in the handler. We get the text 'in   fa' from the call of function `what`. The same text was given in the **throw** statement.

Only one exception handler can be executed in a **try** block. The first handler with a matching parameter is chosen. In our example this means that when we get an exception of type `overflow_error`, we land in the first handler in spite of the fact that the second handler also has a matching parameter. As a general rule, it can be said that if there are several handlers, the handlers for the most derived classes should be placed first. Otherwise they will be hidden by the handlers of the base classes.

As soon as function `g` has a handler with a parameter of type 'reference to `exception`' it can trap all the exceptions that are generated in `f`, `fa`, `fb` or any other function that belongs to a class derived from the standard class `exception`. But what would happen if some other kind of `exception` arose? Suppose that function `fb` should have the following appearance:

```
int fb(int x)
{
  if (x == 1)
    throw "Now there is an error";
  if (x == 2)
    throw x;
  return x;
}
```

The function fb can generate two different kinds of exceptions. None of the standard classes for exceptions are used here (if they had been, it would have been better). An exception of type **char** * is generated in the statement

```
throw "Now there is an error";
```

And in the statement

```
throw x;
```

an exception of type **int** is generated (since x has this type). Exceptions of this kind are not trapped by the **try** block in function g. They will, therefore, slip through the net to go on to the function that called g. Let us suppose that g is called directly from main. If the call does not lie in a **try** block with a handler that can handle this kind of exception, the program will be terminated. But we might also expect to find a **try** block in main:

```
main()
{
  try {
    statements
    g();
    statements
  }
  catch(char *s) {
    cout << s << endl;
  }
  catch(...) {
    cout << "Unknown error occurred" << endl;
  }
}
```

A call of g occurs inside the **try** block. There are two handlers. The first one deals with exceptions of type **char** *. What happens is simply that the text is written out. The second handler has a parameter list consisting of three dots. This is a special way of indicating that the handler will trap any kind of exception. If we are dealing with this kind of handler, it must come last as it hides all handlers coming after it. Here is an example of how the program looks when it is run:

```
? 0
No result can be given
? -1
out_of_range: in fa
? 1
Now there is an error
```
The program stops here

```
              try blocks

      try {
        statements
      }
      catch (parameter) {
        statements
      }
      catch (parameter) {
        statements
      }
      etc.
```

- When an exception occurs in statements after **try** there is a jump to the first handler (the **catch** part) whose parameter matches the exception type.

- When the statements in the handler have been executed, the **try** block is finished, and execution proceeds with the next statement. There is never a jump back to the place where the interruption occurred.

- If there are no handlers to deal with an exception, the **try** block is aborted and the exception is sent on.

When we give a value of 0 as input data, the function f generates an exception of type overflow_error, and when we give a value of −1, an exception of type out_of_range is generated in function fa. Both of these exceptions are trapped, as before, by the handlers in the **try** block in function g. When the exceptions have been trapped, they are eliminated. Since the **try** block in function g lies inside a **while** statement, the whole of it is repeated again and again, and this ensures that the program continues normally when the errors have been dealt with. But after we have given an input value of 1, the program will stop. This is because an exception of type **char** * is generated in fb. This exception is not trapped by any of the handlers in function g, so it is sent on to function main, and an exception arises at the point where g is called. There is then a jump to the first of the handlers that has a matching parameter. When the text string s has been written out, the handler is terminated and with it, the **try** block. There is no jump back to the point where g was called. The **try** block will not be repeated as it does not lie in a repetition statement. The function main has now come to its last statement and is completed in the normal way. The same thing happens when the program is run with a value of 2 given as input data:

```
? 2
Unknown error occurred
The program stops here
```

Parameters of exception handlers

Different forms:

```
catch (T)
catch (T e)
```
traps exceptions of type T

```
catch (T&)
catch (T& e)
```
traps exceptions of type T or (if T is a class type) of classes derived from T.

```
catch ( ... )
```
Traps exceptions of all kinds. Must come last.

Here, an exception of type **int** is generated, so we will end up in the last of the handlers in main, the one that can trap exceptions of all kinds.

Thus, by putting all the statements in main into a **try** block and letting this **try** block have a handler with the parameter . . . we can trap all the exceptions that arise in the program. Of course, there can also be handlers with the parameter . . . in other functions. To demonstrate this we write a new version of the function f:

```
int f(int x)
{
  try {
    int a = fa(x);
    int b = fb(x);
    if (b == 0)
      throw overflow_error("Error in f");
    return a / b;
  }
  catch (overflow_error) {
    throw;
  }
  catch (...) {
    cout << "Error in f" << endl;
    throw;
  }
}
```

All the statements in the function have been enclosed in a **try** block with two handlers. The first handler traps exceptions of type overflow_error, which we generate ourselves, and the second handler traps all other kinds of exceptions. We have an extra handler for type overflow_error because we do not want

'Error in f' written out for exceptions of this kind. This information can be obtained, of course, by using the member function what. When an exception is trapped in a handler, it is normally eliminated, and execution of the program proceeds normally with the next statement after the **try** block. Meanwhile, it is possible from inside a handler to indicate that the exception trapped is not to be eliminated but should be passed on, exactly as if it had not been trapped in the first place. This is done by writing a **throw** statement without expression. The statement:

```
throw;
```

in the handlers in function f passes on an exception to the function that called f. The program can be given the following test run:

```
? 0
No result can be given
? 2
Error in f
Unknown error occurred
The program stops here
```

Through the extra output text in f, it is now easier to discover where the error arose.

Something should be said about constructors and destructors in connection with exceptions. An exception involves a more complicated mechanism than a simple jump to an exception handler. When an exception occurs, the program 'cleans up' after itself exactly as if the functions and blocks remaining had been concluded in the normal way. This means that if variables of a class type have been declared and then cease to exist, the destructors for these variables are called automatically. But there is an important exception. Destructors are only called for objects whose constructors have been completed. Basically, this means that if an exception occurs in a constructor, the destructor is not called for this object. We should, therefore, take care that exceptions do not occur in constructors where memory is allocated dynamically. Care should also be taken that exceptions do not occur in destructors since these can be called automatically while another exception is being dealt with.

10.3 Defining our own exception **classes, an example**

The standard library for reading and writing from streams is comprehensive and contains many useful resources. The input and output operators >> and <<, for example, are often elegant and easy to use. There are shortcomings, however, and one of these is illustrated in the following lines from a program:

```
int i;
cout << "Indicate a number: "
cin >> i;
cout << "The number " << i << " was read" << endl;
```

We make a test run. In a typical C++ system, we can get the message:

```
Indicate a number: 50000
The number -15536 was read
```

Another test run can give the following output:

```
Indicate a number: 80000
The number 14464 was read
```

In this example, we have used a system where type **int** is represented with 16 bits. The input operator >> makes no check whatsoever that overflow does not arise when the digits are read in and for this reason the result is absurd. To make the reading of integers safer, we shall construct our own function get for the reading of input data. The function will generate exceptions if something goes wrong.

We will use the standard class overflow_error in function get to signal that we are attempting to read in large numbers. Two types of error can arise now. One is that an attempt can be made to read a number although end-of-file has occurred, and the other is that the user can write incorrect data, for instance, letters instead of digits. We shall define our own classes to point out these errors. We begin with the declaration of our own class io_error:

```
class io_error : public runtime_error {
public:
  io_error(const char *what_arg)
  : runtime_error(what_arg) {}
};
```

Clearly, we have let our new class io_error be a subclass of the standard class runtime_error. This means, among other things, that class io_error will inherit the virtual function what. We now declare two subclasses of the class io_error. These classes will each signal a particular kind of input error.

```
class end_error : public io_error {
public:
  end_error(const char *what_arg =
            "Reading when end of file")
  : io_error(what_arg) {}
};
```

```
class data_error : public io_error {
public:
  data_error(const char *what_arg =
             "Incorrect input data")
  : io_error(what_arg) {}
};
```

We will be using the class end_error to signal that we are attempting to read although end-of-file has occurred and class data_error to signal that the user has entered incorrect input data. For both these classes we have given a default value for the parameter of the constructor.

The input function get will now look like this:

```
void get(int& i)
{
  char c;
  char sign = '+';
  bool ok = false;
  i = 0;
  cin >> ws;  // Skip white characters
  if (cin.peek() == EOF)
    throw end_error("In the function get(int&)");
  if (cin.peek() == '+' or cin.peek() == '-')
    cin >> sign;
  while (cin.peek() >= '0' and cin.peek() <= '9')
  {
    ok = true;
    cin >> c;
    c -= '0';
    if (i <= INT_MAX/10 and i*10 <= INT_MAX-c)
      i = i*10 + c;
    else
      throw overflow_error("Input error");
  }
  if (not ok)
  {
    skip_line();  // See page 106
    throw data_error();
  }
  if (sign == '-')
    i = -i;
}
```

The function first skips all the blank characters. Then the standard function cin.peek is used to see whether end-of-file has occurred. If so, it is an error to try to read more, and we generate an exception of type end_error. If the user has written a plus or minus sign, this will be read and stored in the variable sign.

We use `cin.peek` in the **while** statement to see whether the next character waiting to be read is a digit. If it is, the digit is read in to the variable `c` and converted from ASCII code to an integer in the interval from 0 to 9 by subtracting the character code for the digit '0'. Before the new digit is added to the result, a check is made to ensure that it can be added to the end without overflow resulting. Overflow will not occur if the old value in variable `i` can be multiplied by 10 without the result being greater than INT_MAX, the largest number that can be stored in a variable of type **int**. The condition is thus `i*10<=INT_MAX` but we cannot write this since overflow would occur when `i*10` is calculated. We, therefore, rewrite this condition and check instead whether `i<=INT_MAX/10`. When the old value in `i` has been multiplied by 10, we should be able to add it to the new number in variable `c`, in which case the condition `i*10+c<=INT_MAX` should be true. But we also have to rewrite this in order to avoid the occurrence of overflow in the test itself. Thus we check that `i*10<=INT_MAX-c`. If our checks show that the latest digit can be added to the result, we can perform the expression `i=i*10+c` without the risk of overflow, otherwise we generate an exception of type `overflow_error`.

After the end of the **while** statement, we check to see that at least one digit has been read. To do this, we use the variable `ok`. This is initialized to the value **false** but is set to **true** as soon as a digit has been read in the **while** statement. If no digit has been read, the user will have written faulty input data, and an exception of type `data_error` is generated. But before this is done, the actual input line is 'cleaned' with the help of function `skip_line`; see Section 4.2.

Here is the main program that calls the function `get` and traps the various kinds of exception:

```
main()
{
  int k = 0;
  while (cin.peek() != EOF)
    try {
      get(k);
      cout << k << endl;
    }
    catch(data_error) {
      cout << "Faulty number. Try again!" << endl;
    }
    catch(exception& e) {
      cout << typeid(e).name() << ": "
          << e.what() << endl;
    }
}
```

A test run of the program can have the following appearance. The underlined parts have been written by the user.

```
30000
30000
50000
overflow_error: Input error
-qw
Faulty number. Try again!
-12
-12
Here the user writes ctrl-z or ctrl-d
end_error: In the function get(int&)
```

What is perhaps astonishing is that we have got the error `end_error` in spite of the fact that we made the test `cin.peek()!=EOF` in function `main` before trying to read the next number. The reason is this: when the last number, −12, was read, the last character to be consumed was '2'. The end-of-line character after this was not read, therefore, and this means that the end of the file was *not* reached and the test `cin.peek()!=EOF` gave the value **true**. When function `get` is called, it begins by skipping all the blank characters and so skips the end-of-line character. End-of-file occurs *now*, and `get` generates the exception `end_error`. A way of getting around this problem is by letting the main program itself make sure that the end-of-line character is read after every input data. The simplest thing to do is to insert a call of function `skip_line` after every call of `get`:

```
try {
  get(k);
  skip_line();
  cout << k << endl;
}
```

The only disadvantage with this is that we cannot input more than one number per line but this may not matter in an interactive program.

10.4   Specification of exceptions

The technique of handling exceptions is based, as we have seen, on trapping the exceptions that have occurred in the functions that have been called. Various means can be applied to deal with different kinds of exceptions. Meanwhile, the question might be asked: how do we know what type of exception a called function can generate? One way of knowing this is, of course, to read the program code for the actual function but this is not possible in practice when applied to functions that are a part of large programs and which themselves call other functions. Another way is to read the documentation available about the actual function and hope that it contains information about the different kinds of exception that can be generated. Unfortunately, such information cannot always be found.

C++ offers a third possibility. A function declaration can contain a *specification* of which exceptions the function can generate. Suppose, for example, that we construct a function f, and we know that only exceptions of type T1 and T2 can occur in this function. We can then define the function in the following way:

```
void f(parameters) throw(T1, T2)
{ ... }
```

Last in the function head we write the reserved word **throw** followed by an enumeration of types for the exceptions that can be generated. The suffix '**throw**(T1,T2,T3...)' on the first line is called an *exception specification*. When a function f is now used, we can be aware of the kinds of exceptions that will need to be trapped. If there are functions declared in one place and defined in another, the exception specification must be in both the declaration and the definition. Earlier in this chapter we gave a new version of the indexing operator for class Vector. We can now add an exception specification. The declaration will then be:

```
int& operator[] (int i) throw(out_of_range);
```

and a separate definition can be written:

```
int& Vector::operator[] (int i) throw(out_of_range)
{
  if(i < il or i > last())
    throw out_of_range("Vector::operator[]");
  return p[i-il];
}
```

An empty exception specification, as for example

```
void g(parameters) throw()
{ ... }
```

means that the function cannot generate any exceptions at all. If there is no exception specification such as, for example,

```
void h(parameters)
{ ... }
```

this will mean, as before, that the function can generate exceptions of any type.

If the compiler discovers that a function can generate an exception of a kind not given in the specification, this will not mean that the program is faulty. (Suppose, for example, that the function g should call the function f, above.) This will not be regarded as a compilation error because it is, in general, impossible for the compiler to know all the kinds of exception a function can generate. For it to be able to do this, it would have to analyse the program text in all the functions that the actual function could possibly call as well as all the functions that these functions could possibly call, and so on.

If exceptions of incorrect type are generated, these are dealt with instead when the program is executed. If in a function f, an exception arises of a type not given in the exception specification, a standard function called unexpected will be called. If nothing else has been indicated, function unexpected will in its turn call another standard function terminate, and this terminates the program.

For the examples that follow we will use once again function f from page 334. We write a new version where we use an exception specification to indicate the different kinds of exception that can be generated in the function:

```
int f(int x) throw(overflow_error, out_of_range)
{
  int a = fa(x);
  int b = fb(x);
  if (b == 0)
    throw overflow_error("Error in f");
  return a / b;
}
```

In the exception specification for f we indicated the type overflow_error since function f can itself generate exceptions of this type. To determine what other types should be listed in the exception specification for f, we have to know what exceptions can be generated in functions fa and fb. Let us suppose that these are functions written by someone else and that we do not have access to the program codes. What we can know, however, are the declarations of the functions which will exist in an appropriate header file. Suppose that they have the following appearance:

```
int fa(int x) throw(out_of_range);
int fb(int x);
```

From these declarations we can see that fa can generate exceptions of type out_of_range, so we can include this type in the exception specification for f. On the other hand, the exceptions that can be generated by fb are unknown since we do not have an exception specification for this function.

We can now write a **try** block where we call the function f:

```
try {
  cout << "? ";
  int r = f(i);
  cout << "The result was " << r << endl;
}
```

```
catch(exception& e) {
  cout << typeid(e).name() << ": "
       << e.what() << endl;
}
```

Since the classes `overflow_error` and `out_of_range` are both derived from class `exception`, we have to content ourselves with having a single handler that can trap both these kinds of exception. If as input data we give a value of 0, we could get the output text

```
? 0
overflow_error: Error in f
```

From the definition of function `fb` on page 339 we see that if we feed in a value of 2, `fb` will generate an exception of type **int**. We then get the output:

```
? 2
Program aborted
```

When the exception is passed on from function `fb` to `f`, the system discovers that `f` has an exception specification and that type **int** is not included in it. Function `unexpected` is therefore called. This in turn calls `terminate`, and the program is terminated.

We shall now illustrate how to avoid having a program terminated by redefining the function `unexpected`. We will show the whole program:

```
#include <stdexcept>
#include <exception>
#include <typeinfo>
#include <iostream.h>

void my_unexpected()
{
  throw bad_exception();
}

int fa(int x) throw(out_of_range);   // see page 337
int fb(int x);                       // see page 339

int f(int x)
throw(overflow_error, out_of_range, bad_exception)
{
  int a = fa(x);
  int b = fb(x);
  if (b == 0)
    throw overflow_error("Error in f");
  return a / b;
}
```

```
main()
{
  set_unexpected(my_unexpected);
  int i;
  while (1)
    try {
      cout << "? ";
      if (not (cin >> i))
        break;
      int r = f(i);
      cout << "The result was " << r << endl;
    }
    catch(exception& e) {
      cout << typeid(e).name() << ": "
           << e.what() << endl;
    }
}
```

To replace the standard function `unexpected` with our own function, we first call in `main` the standard function `set_unexpected`. As parameter we give the name of (that is, a pointer to) our own function. We have termed this function `my_unexpected`, and the definition is given first in the program. Now if there should be an exception in function `f` of a type not given in the exception

---

Specification of exceptions

- An exception specification can be added last in a function declaration:
    return_type f (*parameters*) **throw**(T1, T2, T3 ...);
  Then the function should only generate exceptions of the types given in the specification.

- An empty exception specification means that no exceptions should be generated by the function:
    return_type f (*parameters*) **throw**();

- If there is no exception specification, all types of exception can be generated:
    return_type f (*parameters*);

- If an exception of a type not given in the exception specification is generated, function `unexpected` is called, and this terminates the program. Function `unexpected` can be replaced by the non-standard function:
    set_unexpected(*name_of_nonstandard_function*);
  This can generate an exception of type `bad_exception`.

specification for f, function `my_unexpected` will be called automatically. This function merely generates an exception of the standard class `bad_exception`, a subclass of the standard class `exception`. Since `bad_exception` is in the exception specification for f, the program will not be terminated. Instead, the exception will be trapped in the handler in `main`.

Function `set_unexpected` is declared in the header file `exception`. The definition of class `bad_exception` is also in this file. As mentioned earlier, classes `out_of_range`, `overflow_error` and `exception` have been defined in the header file `stdexcept`. (See Appendix A.)

A test run may now look as follows. Note that the program will not stop if a value of 2 is given as input data.

```
? 0
overflow_error: Error in f
? 2
bad_exception:
? -1
out_of_range: in fa
```

EXERCISES

10.1   Change all the member functions in class `Vector` so that they generate exceptions, instead of using `assert`. Also use exception specifications to specify which exceptions the different functions can generate.

10.2   Write a version of the function `nfac` on page 126. The new function should give a floating point number as its result and, if the result is so great that it cannot be represented by the system in use, an exception should be generated.

10.3   The function `roots` on page 121 computes the roots of a quadratic equation. Rewrite this function so that it no longer has the output parameter `ok`. Instead, the function should generate an exception of class `numeric_error`. Define this class as a subclass of the standard class `runtime_error`.

10.4   Solve Exercise 5.7 on page 182 using an exception to indicate that copying has miscarried.

10.5   Write a function `try_to_get` that can be called to read an integer from the keyboard safely. The function should have two output parameters, the first of which should be a reference to the variable to which input data will be read. The second parameter should be of type **bool**, and it should be used to signal whether or not the reading of input data has gone according to plan. *Tip*: call the function `get` on page 345.

10.6 The function `get_enum` on page 175 reads input data from enumeration types. Make changes in this function so that it generates an exception of class `data_error` when the user writes incorrect input data, and an exception of class `end_error` when an attempt is made to read although end-of-file has occurred. Then make the necessary changes to the program on page 176 so that the new version of `get_enum` can be used.

11 Streams and Files

In this book we have used the C++ standard library to read and write data from the terminal. This library is text-oriented. It relies on data being read and written in textual form. In other words, it uses the keyboard and terminal like a kind of typewriter. The mouse is not used at all. But isn't this rather old-fashioned? Surely modern programs are windows-oriented, that is, they make use of a graphic screen and use windows, menus, icons and so on, to communicate with the user? Shouldn't we be describing these things in a book like this? There is justification for this argument but there are two reasons why, in spite of everything, we have used the C++ standard library. The first is that it is rather complicated to write windows-oriented programs. There are a great many help functions to be mastered, and these are, unfortunately, in no way standardized. There are many kinds of windows systems, and they are all different. Before writing windows-oriented programs, therefore, we have to decide on one particular system and learn it. The description of windows-oriented programs lies entirely outside the scope of this book but the reader is advised to learn the basics of C++ before studying the windows system which will be important to him or her.

The other reason why we use the C++ standard library is because it is actually useful, even in windows-oriented programs. A program does not only communicate with the user. It also has to be able to read and write data stored permanently in the form of files in secondary storage, for instance, on disks or CD-ROM. Sometimes we need to convert and edit data that has been read, or that will be written, using the help functions of a windows system. In both of these cases, we can use the C++ standard library. It is heartening to know that we program in exactly the same way as we do when reading from and writing to the terminal. The same help functions are used, the output and input operators << and >>, for example. What we have learnt so far is extremely useful, even for windows-oriented programs.

In this chapter we will be looking at the general notion of a stream and will use this opportunity to give a summary of all the different functions for reading and writing that we have used up to now (plus a few more). The book will then be easier to use as a reference work.

We then look at how files are read and written. In this connection we will illustrate how parameters can be given to the main program when a program is started. In particular, we will demonstrate how objects of different classes can be stored in files with information about which class an object belongs to. This will later facilitate reading files and recreating objects.

Data is most often stored in files in the form of text, usually called text files. We may sometimes want to store data in exactly the same form as it is stored in the primary memory, in what are called binary files, and this will be demonstrated.

Finally, there is a section on how to use the C++ standard library to convert and edit data internally in the primary memory.

11.1   The class ios

The idea of using *streams* for reading and writing data is a fundamental concept in the C++ library. A stream is simply a sequence of bytes. There are a number of operations in the library for reading from streams and writing to streams. A program can communicate with external media – for instance, disk memory – via streams. A stream can be connected to a particular file. Streams can even be connected to memory space in the primary memory or to the terminal. The interesting thing here, is that streams can always be handled in the same way, regardless of what they happen to be connected to.

In the standard library, streams have been implemented with the help of a number of classes. The most fundamental of these is the class ios[†], which contains data and operations for all kinds of streams. This is the base class for the two classes istream and ostream[‡]. These classes contain resources for handling streams that can be read and written. To read and write from files, we use the classes ifstream and ofstream[§], which are subclasses of istream and ostream, respectively. Streams can also be connected to the primary memory, when they can be used to edit and convert data internally in the program. In the draft standard there are two sets of classes that can be used. Classes istrstream and ostrstream are used when we want to handle character arrays as streams, while the other set, classes istringstream and ostringstream, is used when we connect streams with objects of the standard class string.,Figure 11.1 shows how the different classes are related to each other.

In the standard there are a number of predefined stream objects: cin, cout, cerr and clog. These are always automatically declared, so we should never try to declare them ourselves. The object cin is of class istream. It is automatically connected to 'standard input', which is normally the keyboard, but in some operating systems it can be redirected (see page 79). The other three standard objects are all of class ostream. The object cout is automatically connected to 'standard output', normally a text window at the terminal. 'Standard output' can also be redirected. The objects cerr and clog are used for output of error texts and program logs. These streams are normally connected so that output text reaches the terminal. It is a good idea to write all error messages in stream cerr instead of in cout. Then error messages will be visible at the terminal even if cout has been redirected.

If we want to work with a stream that has not been predeclared, we have to declare our own stream objects. Then objects of one of the classes furthest to the right in Figure 11.1 are normally declared.

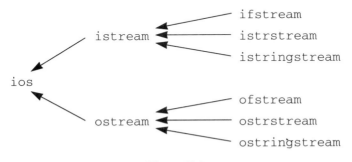

Figure 11.1

[†] Class ios is defined in the draft standard using the generic class ios_base.
[‡] These are defined in the draft standard using the generic classes basic_istream and basic_ostream, respectively.
[§] These are defined in the draft standard with the generic classes basic_ifstream and basic_ofstream.

The classes `ios`, `istream`, `ostream` and the predeclared stream objects are defined in the file `iostream.h` which must therefore be included in the program. Classes `ifstream` and `ofstream` are defined in the header file `fstream.h`. The header file `strstream.h` contains the definitions of classes `istrstream` and `ostrstream`. We will not look at classes `istringstream` and `ostringstream` but they are declared in the header file `sstream`.

In class `ios` there are three so-called *flags* which indicate the condition of a stream (see Table 11.1). If none of the flags is set, the stream is all right.

There is also a set of member functions in class `ios` that can be used to read and change the conditions in these flags. We can write, for instance:

```
if (clog.good())
  cerr << "The stream clog is all right";
if (cin.fail())
{
  cerr << "Reading miscarried";
  cin.clear();
}
```

The member function in the penultimate line in Table 11.2 is the operator `!` (**not**). This can be used as an alternative to calling the function `fail`. For instance, the condition in the last of the **if** statements above can be written:

```
if (!cin)
```

Table 11.1   State flags in class `ios`.

Flag	Indication
`failbit`	That the latest input or output operation miscarried for some reason.
`eofbit`	That end-of-file occurred at an earlier attempt at reading.
`badbit`	A serious error that usually concerns the stream's internal buffer.

Table 11.2   Member functions for handling state flags.

Function	Effect
void `clear();`	Clears all the flags.
bool `good();`	Gives **true** if none of the flags is set.
bool `fail();`	Gives **true** if `failbit` or `badbit` is set.
bool `eof();`	Gives **true** if `eofbit` is set.
bool `bad();`	Gives **true** if `badbit` is set.
bool operator! `();`	Gives the result `fail()`.
operator bool `();`	Gives the result **not** `fail()`.

The function `eof` needs some explanation. When the end of a stream has been reached there is no more input to be read. If we try to read when this has happened we say that end-of-file occurs. The flag `eofbit` is then set. For this flag to be set, we must actually have tried to read when there is no more input to be read. It is not sufficient merely to have reached the end of a file. (A programmer experienced in Pascal or Ada should especially note this, since the corresponding function in these languages gives the value 'true' when the end-of-file has been reached, regardless of whether or not an attempt to read has been made.) Suppose, for instance, that we wish to compute the number of characters written in by the user. We try the following program lines:

```
char c;
int n = 0;
while (not cin.eof())   // NB! ERROR!
{
  cin.get(c);
  n++;
}
cout << "You wrote in " << n << " characters" << endl;
```

Suppose now that the user writes in the text 'abc' and then presses the enter key. Then the end of the file is marked by writing Ctrl-Z (or Ctrl-D):

```
abc
The user marks the end of the file here
```

Something rather astonishing will be returned:

```
You wrote 5 characters
```

The **while** statement is therefore executed for five rounds. In the first three rounds the characters 'a', 'b' and 'c' are read. In the fourth round, the end-of-line character generated by the enter key is read. After the fourth round, there is no more input data to get, but the flag `eofbit` is not set yet. It is not set before an attempt is made to read when there is no more input. This means that the **while** statement is executed for a fifth round. When `get` is called the fifth time end-of-file occurs and the flag `eofbit` is set. (The variable c will then get the value EOF.)

To correctly compute the number of characters that have been read, we must adjust the **while** statement. We can then write, for instance:

```
while(true)   // Correct
{
  cin.get(c);
  if (cin.eof())
    break;
  n++;
}
```

After every attempt at reading, we check whether the flag `eofbit` has been set. If so, the **while** statements are terminated. With the same input data as above, we now get the correct printout:

```
You wrote 4 characters
```

But a correct **while** statement can be written more simply:

```
while(cin.get(c))   // Correct and simplest
   n++;
```

This may seem rather strange. The function `get` gives as result a reference to the stream that is read. The result is, therefore, of type 'reference to `istream`'. The condition in parentheses after **while** should be of type **bool** (or **int**, if it is one of the older compilers). The compiler then tests whether there is a type conversion that can be done automatically from type `istream` to type **bool**. In the last line of Table 11.2, we note that for class `ios` there is a type conversion operator precisely for type `istream` to type **bool**. This operator will be called automatically. It gives as result the value **true** if the latest reading has been successful, and a value of **false** otherwise. In our example, this means that the **while** statement is executed for four rounds. When the condition inside the parentheses is computed for the fifth time, reading will miscarry and the result will be **false**. Earlier in the book, we have used the input operator >> in several places and written expressions of the form:

```
while(cin >> i)
```

The result of the input operator is also of type 'reference to `istream`'. This means that the type conversion operator in Table 11.2 will also be automatically called in these cases.

The standard library for reading and writing in C++ was constructed before the language for handling exceptions was introduced and this is why the procedure with flags, which has to be monitored by the programmer, is now in use. If the library were constructed today, exceptions would most probably be used instead of flags to signal errors. However, in the draft standard there is a mechanism that enables the programmer to indicate whether he or she wants exceptions to be generated when the flags are set.

The member function `exceptions` is used to indicate when we want exceptions to be generated. The call should have the form:

```
str.exceptions(ios::flag|ios::flag|ios::flag);
```

where `str` is the name of the stream object in question and `flag` the name of one of the flags in Table 11.1. (The vertical line is the symbol for the bit operator 'or' – see Section 14.2.) One, two, or three flags can be indicated. If, for instance, we want an exception to be generated when the flag `eofbit` is set for stream `cin`, the following call should be inserted first in the program:

```
cin.exceptions(ios::eofbit);
```

and if we want exceptions to be generated if one of the flags `badbit` or `failbit` is set for stream `clog`, we make the call:

```
clog.exceptions(ios::badbit|ios::failbit);
```

If we make use of exceptions, the exceptions generated will be of class `ios::failure`, a subclass of the standard class `exception`. Thus we can use the standard function `what`, demonstrated in Chapter 10, to get information on the cause of the error.

Finally, it should be said that in class `ios` there are also flags that indicate how data should be read and edited. These flags can be used in different ways, both with the help of special member functions in class `ios` and by using manipulators. It can all be rather complicated. In this book we use manipulators throughout since they are easiest to read and understand. We will be looking at read and edit flags in our discussion on the reading and writing of streams.

11.2   Reading streams

Streams that we can read from all belong to class `istream`, or a class derived from it. This was illustrated by Figure 11.1. Class `istream` contains a great number of resources for reading streams. Many of the functions in class `ios` can also be used when reading. We have already demonstrated most of these in connection with stream `cin` but we will give a brief summary here so they are all found in one place in the book.

When we read input data, we differentiate between *formatted* and *unformatted* reading. With unformatted reading, data is read from the instream just as it is stored, byte by byte. With formatted input, on the other hand, input data can be interpreted and converted. Formatted reading is carried out making use of the operator >>, while unformatted reading is done with the help of special member functions. We will begin by describing formatted input.

11.2.1   Formatted input

The input operator >> can be used to read data of all the standard types. If we suppose that `is` is an object of class `istream` or of a class derived from it, we could write, for instance:

```
unsigned short int usi;
long double ld;
is >> usi >> ld;
```

The result of a reading expression is a reference to the actual stream, so several readings can be done in a chain, as demonstrated above. Normally, a reading begins with all the white characters being skipped. Note that this also applies when data is read to variables of type **char** and to character arrays. The user is thus free to write several items of input data on the same line, or to insert a line break between various input data items. When white characters have been skipped the characters are consumed one by one from the instream as long as the characters read can be included in a value of the actual type. If, for example, input data is read to an integer variable, the characters in the instream will be consumed as long as there are digits. Reading will stop at the first character not included in the read value.

If reading occurs to a variable of numeric type, conversion will occur from a stream of **char** containing character codes, to a value of the actual type. Suppose, for example, that the statements above are executed and the user enters the following input data:

```
76    -12.677
```

then the character sequence "76" is converted to a value of type **unsigned short int** and the character sequence "-12.677" to a value of type **long double**.

If, for some reason, reading miscarries (perhaps the user writes incorrect input data), the flag ios::failbit is set, and if end-of-file occurs when an attempt is made to read, the flag ios::eofbit will be set. This can generate exceptions if we have indicated that we want this to occur. As we saw earlier, we cannot be sure that an error will be indicated if there is overflow when data is converted.

Reading always stops at the next white character. This also applies when we read to a text string. For instance, if we have the lines from a program:

```
char a[11];
is >> a;
```

and give the following input data:

```
C++ From the Beginning
```

the array a will only contain the text string "C++". The rest of the line will remain in the instream. The next character to be read is the space character in front of F. Note that the input operator always adds a null character at the end in the variable that is read to. Thus in array a, a null character will be placed in position number 3. (Numbering occurs as usual from 0.)

There are a number of manipulators that can be used when input data is read. They are summarized in Table 11.3. (Some of them have been declared in file iomanip.h.)

Table 11.3   Manipulators for input.

Manipulator	Effect
setw(n)	Indicates the maximum number of characters that can be held in the array that will be read to.
ws	Jumps to the next non-white character in the stream.
skipws	Always skip leading white characters when the operator >> is used (standard setting).
noskipws	Do not skip leading white characters when the operator >> is used.
dec	Input data of integer type will be interpreted as decimal numbers.
oct	Input data of integer type will be interpreted as octal numbers.
hex	Input data of integer type will be interpreted as hexadecimal numbers.
boolalpha	Input data of type **bool** should be indicated as **false** or **true**.
noboolalpha	Input data of type **bool** should be indicated as 0 or 1.

When we read to a character array, there is no check to see that the array can hold the characters that have been read. If, in the example above, we were to feed in a connected text longer than ten characters, the characters read would end up outside array a and ruin the other data. To stop this happening, we can use the manipulator setw and indicate the maximum number of characters that can fit into the array:

```
is >> setw(11) >> a;
```

If setw(n) has been written, the input operator >> will read at most n-1 characters from the stream. (A null character is always added at the end.) The manipulator setw is good for *one* reading only.

The manipulator ws is used to indicate that white characters should be skipped. We write, for instance:

```
is >> ws;
```

As we have seen, all white characters will be automatically skipped when the input operator >> is used. If we do not want this to happen we can use the manipulator noskipws:

```
is >> noskipws;
```

Then no white characters will be skipped from then on. Note that if input data contains a numeric value with a white character in front, there will be an input error when an attempt is made to read to a variable of numeric type. If we want to return to the standard setting, the manipulator skipws can be used.

The manipulators dec, hex and oct specify whether numeric integers that are read should be interpreted as decimal, hexadecimal, or octal numbers, respectively. Look at the following lines:

```
int i, j, k;
is >> oct >> i >> hex >> j >> dec >> k;
cout << i << " "<< j << " "<< k;
```

It is specified here that i should be interpreted as being written in octal form, j in hexadecimal form and k in decimal form. If the stream is contains the following input data, for example:

```
45 a7 29
```

then the output will be (written in decimal form):

```
37 167 29
```

When values are read to variables of type **bool**, input data can be written either in the form of words as **false** or **true**, or as the integers 0 and 1. We choose the desired form with the help of the manipulators boolalpha and noboolalpha.

11.2.2 Unformatted input

Unformatted input is carried out with special member functions in the class istream. A summary of the functions available are given in Table 11.4.

A common element of all of these functions is that they *never* skip white characters. All the characters are read strictly in turn. The functions can set the flag ios::failbit if input miscarries. The flag ios::eofbit can also be set if end-of-file occurs when the functions try to read. Exceptions can be generated if an indication has been made that this should occur. If nothing else is stated, the functions in the table will give as return value a reference to the actual stream.

We have seen examples of how most of the functions can be used, and we will encounter a few more when we look at files. The functions read and readsome are used primarily when we work with *binary files*, files which do not contain text. We will come back to this later.

We will simply give an example containing a few statements, that counts the number of lines in the instream is. We assume that no line has more than 500 characters.

```
const int max_length = 500;
char row[max_length+1];
int i = 0;
while (is.getline(row, max_length))
   i++;
cout << "The stream contains " << i << " rows";
```

When end-of-file occurs, both the flags eofbit and failbit are turned on. Since the member function getline returns a reference to the stream is, the type

Table 11.4 Member functions for unformatted input.

Function	Description
gcount()	Returns the number of characters read by the latest function for unformatted input.
get()	Reads and returns the next character in the stream, gives EOF if end-of-file occurs.
get(c)	Reads the next character in the stream to the variable c.
getline(s, n, t)	Parameter t has default value '\n'. Reads in a number of characters to text string s until the next character to be read is the same as the stop character t. This character is read but is *not* put into text string s. Input is terminated early if end-of-file occurs or if n-1 characters have been read. A null character is always placed last in s.
get(s, n, t)	As getline but the stop character t is not read, instead remains as the next character in the stream.
read(s, n)	Reads n characters to the character array s points to. If end-of-file occurs before n characters have been read, flags eofbit and failbit are set.
readsome(s, n)	As read but the number of read characters are given as return. If this number is less than n, failbit is *not* set.
ignore(n, t)	The parameter n has default value 1, and t the default value EOF. Skips n characters in the stream. Stops earlier if the character waiting to be read is the same as t or if end-of-file occurs.
peek()	Returns the character waiting to be read but the character remains as the next character in the stream.
putback(c)	Puts back the character c into the stream.
unget()	Puts back the character last read into the stream.

conversion operator in Table 11.2 will be automatically called, and this will return the value **false** when flag failbit is on.

11.3   Output to streams

We can write to streams that are members of the class ostream or a class derived from it. (See Figure 11.1.) Class ostream contains resources for writing to streams. With output data, we distinguish between *formatted* and *unformatted* output. With formatted output, output data is converted to a sequence of **char**, and it can also be edited in many different ways. With unformatted output, data is written to the outstream just as it is, without being converted.

11.3.1 Formatted output

Formatted output is carried out with the help of the operator $<<$. We have already seen many examples of formatted output to the stream `cout` but we will give a summary of its uses here for the sake of completeness. The operator $<<$ is declared in class `ostream` for all the standard types.

With formatted output, output data can be edited in a great many ways. Editing is controlled by a collection of format flags that are defined in the base class `ios`. The format flags which have an effect on output are shown in Table 11.5. The standard setting for all the flags, apart from `right` and `dec`, is off.

Class `ios` also monitors the three values shown in Table 11.6.

In class `ios` there are member functions (`setf` and `unsetf`) with whose help we can read and set the flags in Table 11.5 and the values in Table 11.6. We

Table 11.5 Flags for formatted output in `ios`.

Format flag	Effect
left	Indicates that the written value should be left-adjusted, that is, any filler characters should be added after writing.
right	Indicates that the written value should be right-adjusted, that is, any filler characters should be added before writing.
internal	Indicates that any filler characters should be added between the number's sign and the first digit.
dec	Indicates that writing of integers should occur in decimal form.
oct	Indicates that writing of integers should occur in octal form.
hex	Indicates that writing of integers should occur in hexadecimal form.
fixed	Indicates that writing of floating point numbers should occur in a fixed format with a decimal point. The number of decimal places is given by `precision`.
scientific	Indicates that writing of real numbers should occur in the floating point format 999.999e99. The number of decimal places is given by `precision`.
uppercase	Indicates that upper case letters should be used with floating point writing of real numbers and with hexadecimal writing of integers.
boolalpha	Indicates that values of type **bool** should be written out in the form **false**, **true**, instead of 0, 1.
showbase	Indicates that octal numbers should be written with an initial zero and hexadecimal numbers with the characters 0x first.
showpoint	Indicates that the decimal point and terminating decimals with the value 0 should always be written for floating point numbers.
showpos	Indicates that positive numbers should be written with the sign + first.
unitbuf	Indicates that all characters should be written directly and not buffered.

Table 11.6 Values for formatted output in `ios`.

Value	Meaning
`width`	Indicates the least number of output positions in the next output. Standard value = 0.
`fill`	The character used as a filler if writing requires fewer than `width` positions. Standard value = the blank character.
`precision`	Used for writing floating point numbers. If the format is `fixed` or `scientific`, `precision` gives the number of decimal places, otherwise indicates the total number of significant figures. Standard value = 6.

will not describe these functions here, however. Instead, we will use manipulators, which are both simpler and safer to use. Manipulators are used together with the output operator <<. They are either defined in the header file `iostream.h` or the file `iomanip.h`. Table 11.7 shows the manipulators we can use to manipulate the formatting flags.

Certain formatting flags must be handled together since they cannot all be set at the same time. This applies for instance to the flags `dec`, `oct` and `hex`. The manipulators in Table 11.7 do this automatically.

If we suppose that `os` is a stream of class `ostream` or a class derived from it, we can write, for example:

```
os << uppercase << scientific;
```

Output of real numbers then occurs in the format:

```
1.234567E+12
```

If neither `fixed` nor `scientific` has been indicated, output, as we saw earlier, will be written in the format that is easiest to read but this will depend on the actual value.

The manipulators `setiosflags` and `resetiosflags` can be used to turn on and shut off, respectively, an arbitrary flag. If, for example, the compiler being used has not implemented the manipulator `uppercase`, we can instead write:

```
os << setiosflags(ios::uppercase);
```

Manipulators can also be used to change the values in Table 11.6. These manipulators are shown in Table 11.8, where a number of output manipulators of a more general kind have also been included.

Note that after every output of the form os<<x, the value `ios::width` is automatically set to zero. (The only exception occurs when x has type **char**. Then

Table 11.7 Manipulators for handling formatting flags.

Manipulator	Effect
uppercase nouppercase	Turns on and shuts off, respectively, flag ios::uppercase.
boolalpha noboolalpha	Turns on and shuts off, respectively, flag ios::boolalpha.
showbase noshowbase	Turns on and shuts off, respectively, flag ios::showbase.
showpoint noshowpoint	Turns on and shuts off, respectively, flag ios::showpoint.
showpos noshowpos	Turns on and shuts off, respectively, flag ios::showpos.
left	Sets flag ios::left, shuts off flags ios::right and ios::internal.
right	Sets flag ios::right, shuts off flags ios::left and ios::internal.
internal	Sets flag ios::internal, shuts off flags ios::left and ios::right.
dec	Sets flag ios::dec, shuts off flags ios::oct and ios::hex.
oct	Sets flag ios::oct, shuts off flags ios::dec and ios::hex.
hex	Sets flag ios::hex, shuts off flags ios::dec and ios::oct.
fixed	Sets flag ios::fixed, shuts off flag ios::scientific.
scientific	Sets flag ios::scientific, shuts off flag ios::fixed.

ios::width is not set to zero.) This means that if we want to have a certain number of output positions, the manipulator width(n) must be repeated for every set of output data.

The manipulator flush may need some commentary. When we feed out characters to a stream, they land in a buffer. If the stream is for instance connected to a file or standard output, we cannot be certain that the actual output will take place at the same time as the program feeds out characters into the stream. In the interests of efficiency, the output characters are collected into a buffer then written out later, all together. Normally we would not pay much attention to this but sometimes it can be difficult to find the error when a program is prematurely terminated, for we cannot be sure that the buffer is empty. There may be unwritten characters still in it. If test output has been inserted in different parts of the program and one of these is not seen at the terminal, it need not necessarily mean that the program has not executed the statement that generates the output.

Earlier, we saw several examples of the use of manipulators for editing output, so we will not go further into detail here. Instead, it will be left to the reader as an exercise to experiment with the various manipulators.

Table 11.8   Manipulators for formatted output.

Manipulator	Effect
setw(n)	Sets value `ios::width` to n.
setfill(c)	Sets value `ios::fill` to the character c.
setprecision(n)	Sets value `ios::precision` to n.
setbase(n)	setbase(10) same as manipulator dec. setbase(8) same as manipulator oct. setbase(16) same as manipulator hex.
flush	Empties the output buffer, that is, unwritten characters in the output buffer are written out.
endl	Inserts an end-of-line character in the stream. Then calls flush.
ends	Inserts a zero character in the stream.

11.3.2   Unformatted output

We carry out unformatted output with special member functions in class ostream. These functions are shown in Table 11.9. All the functions in the table give as return value a reference to the actual stream.

The call os.put(c) has the same effect as if we write os<<c. We discussed the effect of function flush above in connection with the manipulator flush. We will be showing examples of how function write works later when we look at binary files.

Table 11.9   Member functions for unformatted output.

Function	Description
put(c)	Writes the character c to the stream.
write(s, n)	Writes n characters to the stream from the character array s points to.
flush()	Empties the output buffer, that is, unwritten characters in the output buffer are written out.

11.4   Connecting files to streams

The variables used in a program are to be found in the primary memory of the computer and only exist as long as the program is being executed. We have to be able to store data permanently for many programs, however. To do this, we must use a secondary memory (most often a disk). Data in a secondary memory is stored in the form of *files*. A file is an arbitrarily long sequence of bytes which normally contain characters coded according to the ASCII code, or some other code. A file that contains such characters is called a *text file*. But files can exist that do not contain ASCII characters, for instance those that contain executable programs. Such files are usually called *binary files*.

A text file has a *line structure*. We can suppose that it consists of a number of lines, where each line can have an arbitrary number of characters and is terminated with a *line terminator*. The physical make-up of a line terminator can be one or more ASCII characters but different operating systems differ here. For instance, Unix normally uses a single character, LF (or 'line feed', ASCII code 10), while MS-DOS uses two characters, CR ('carriage return', ASCII code 13) and LF. When a C++ program reads a text file, the line terminator is automatically converted to a single end-of-line character which is normally indicated by '\n' in the program. The converse also applies. When an end-of-line character is written out to a text file, it is automatically converted to the character, or set of characters, which constitutes the line terminator in the text file. In MS-DOS, for instance, the end-of-line character is converted to the two characters CR and LF when output to a text file occurs.

There is no line structure in a binary file. The file consists only of a sequence of bytes that can contain any data. When binary files are read and written, therefore, there is no data conversion at all. Every byte is read or written exactly as it is.

How does the program know whether a file is a text file or a binary file? The answer is that the program must be told when the file is opened. We shall see examples of this later. If nothing in particular is indicated, it is assumed that the file is a text file.

All the programs we have studied up to now have been read from the stream `cin` and written in the stream `cout`. This means that in most cases input has come from the keyboard and output has been to a text window at the terminal. Now we will look at how streams can be connected to files. This is essentially a very simple matter. We use the two classes `ifstream` and `ofstream`. If we want to read from a file, we declare an object of class `ifstream` and if we want to write to a file, we declare an object of class `ofstream`. We begin by showing a program that reads a text file with the name `my_file.txt` and writes out the contents of the file at the terminal. Finally, the program writes out the number of lines in the file.

```
#include <iostream.h>
#include <fstream.h>
main()
{
  int n=0;
  char c;
  ifstream f1("my_file.txt");
  while (f1.get(c))
  {
    cout.put(c);
    if (c == '\n')
      n++;
```

```
    }
    cout << endl << "The file consists of " << n
        << " lines" << endl;
}
```

In the line

```
ifstream f1("my_file.txt");
```

the variable f1 is declared as a stream of class ifstream. We can indicate a text string as parameter of the constructor, as we have done here. The constructor will understand this as being the name of a file and so when the object f1 is initialized, the constructor will automatically link the corresponding file to stream f1. When a file is connected to a stream, we say that the file has been *opened*. We can also declare a stream without connecting it to a file, in which case a default constructor is used for the stream. The member function open can later be used to open a file and link it to the stream. We also could have written, therefore:

```
ifstream f1;
...
f1.open("my_file.txt");
```

When the name of a file is indicated, either a short file name can be given, as here, or the file's complete name can be given to the file system. For example, the name c:\own\diverse\my_file.txt, or something similar, could be given. If a short name is given, the file must exist in the actual file folder where the program is run.

When a stream has been declared and connected to a file, we can handle it exactly as we have handled streams before. Since class ifstream is a subclass of class istream, it inherits all the members from class istream, and these can be used directly for its own objects. In our program, for instance, we use the member function get (see Table 11.4).

When the connection between a file and a stream is cancelled, the file is said to be *closed*. To close a file, the member function close can be used. We could have inserted the following call at the end of the program, above:

```
f1.close();
```

But we do not generally need to close our files explicitly, since classes ifstream and ofstream have destructors that automatically call function close. This means that as soon as a stream of one of these classes ceases to exist in the program, the file connected to the stream is closed. In our program, for instance, the destructor for f1 is called when the program is coming to an end and the file my_file.txt will be closed then.

In the next example, we demonstrate that it is just as easy to write to files as it is to read from them. We will look at a program that copies file my_file.txt to a new file with the name `new_file.txt`. In the program, the new file is connected to an object `f2` of class `ofstream`. When the copying is finished, the program writes a text at the terminal giving the number of lines that have been copied.

```
#include <iostream.h>
#include <fstream.h>
main()
{
  int n=0;
  char c;
  ifstream f1("my_file.txt");
  ofstream f2("new_file.txt");
  while (f1.get(c))
  {
    f2.put(c);
    if (c == '\n')
      n++;
  }
  cout << endl << n << " lines copied" << endl;
}
```

This program is not really very useful since it can only copy `my_file.txt` and create the copy `new_file.txt`. For the program to be more useful, it must be able to copy any one file to any other file. This is not difficult to do. We simply let the program read the file's name at execution. Let us then make a new version (the output containing the number of lines that have been copied, has been removed).

```
#include <iostream.h>
#include <fstream.h>
#include <iomanip.h>
#include <stdlib.h>
main()
{
  char c;
  char name[100];
  cout << "Which file should be copied? ";
  cin >> setw(100) >> name;
  ifstream f1(name);
  if (!f1)
  {
    cout << "The file cannot be opened";
    exit(EXIT_FAILURE);
  }
  cout << "Name of the copy? ";
  cin >> setw(100) >> name;
  ofstream f2(name);
  if (!f2)
```

```
    {
      cout << "The file cannot be created";
      exit(EXIT_FAILURE);
    }
  while (f1.get(c))
    f2.put(c);
}
```

The problem is that when the user is allowed to indicate the file name, an incorrect file name can be given. If it is a file that must be read, it should exist first, among other things. Therefore, when we have tried to open a file, we should always check to see whether this has been successful or not. If the procedure has miscarried, either in the constructor or in the function `open`, the flag `failbit` will be set for the stream. We can check to see whether it has not been set. A simple way to do this is to use the operator ! in the actual stream (see Table 11.2.). In our program the expression ! f1, for example, will give the value **true** if opening the file to be copied has miscarried. If any of the files in the program cannot be opened an appropriate error message is given and, as a result, the program is terminated. To terminate a program ourselves, we can use the standard function `exit`. The function `exit` should have an integer as parameter. The value 0 means that the program has been successful, and it is then terminated in the usual way. Other values will mean that the program has miscarried. We can use one of the two predefined constants `EXIT_SUCCESS` and `EXIT_FAILURE` as parameter for `exit` to indicate whether or not the program has been successful. These constants and the function `exit`, are declared in the header file `stdlib.h`.

An alternative to using the operator ! to check whether a file was opened, is to call the member function `is_open`. This returns a value of type **bool**. For example, the expression `f1.is_open()` returns the value **true** if f1 is open.

Every stream has an internal *buffer* where the data belonging to the stream is placed. There should be a *file buffer* for every object, and this applies especially to classes `ifstream` and `ofstream`. Characters that are read from a file or to a file will land in the file buffer. In the standard classes for input and output there are several functions that make it possible to handle data directly in a buffer but, as luck would have it, we normally do not need to use these. We can manage very well with the functions for formatted and unformatted in- and output that we demonstrated earlier. We will only mention here a very useful and efficient operation that involves using a file buffer. This is when we want to copy a whole stream (file) to another one. In order to have access to a file buffer, we use the member function `rdbuf` which returns a pointer to the buffer. The call `f1.rdbuf()` gives as result, for example, a pointer to the file buffer belonging to stream f1. The output operator `<<` is defined, as we saw, for all the standard types. But there is also a version where the right operand is a pointer to a file buffer. When we call this version, the whole buffer will be written out. This means, for instance, that we can make the statement

```
cout << f1.rdbuf();
```

We then get the output of the whole file `f1` written at the terminal. If instead we want to copy to another file, we can write, for example:

```
f2 << f1.rdbuf();
```

The *entire* file `f1` is connected to, is copied to the file `f2` is connected to. This has exactly the same effect as writing:

```
while (f1.get(c))
  f2.put(c);
```

but it is simpler and more efficient; besides, there is less risk of faulty programming.

When we open a file, we can indicate what properties the file should have. There are a number of flags defined in the base class `ios`, and these are shown in Table 11.10.

File flags can be indicated as an extra parameter when a constructor or the member function `open` is called. For instance, we could have written in the program above:

```
ostream f2(name, ios::app);
```

If the file had then existed before, it would not have been overwritten. Instead, new output data would have been added at the end.

If an extra parameter for a constructor or the function `open` is not indicated, the default value `ios::in` will apply for streams of class `istream`, and the default value `ios::out` for streams of class `ostream`. Several of the flags listed in Table 11.10 can be combined. A vertical line is then typed between the flags. If, for instance, we want to open a binary file that can be both read and written, we can write:

Table 11.10   File flags in class `ios`.

Flag	Property
in	It should be possible to read from the file. The file should exist.
out	It should be possible to write in the file. If the file does not exist, a new file should be created. If the file exists earlier, it should be overwritten.[†]
app	It should be possible to write in the file. If the file does not exist, a new file should be created. If the file exists earlier, output data should be added at the end.
trunc	If the file exists earlier, it should be overwritten.
ate	Move to the end of the file directly when the file has been opened.
binary	The file will be handled as a binary file.

[†] This is not quite clear in the draft standard but in practice it works like this.

```
f.open(name, ios::in|ios::out|ios::binary);
```

In Table 11.11 we show some combinations together with the properties that are involved. The flag `binary` can be added here, if a procedure involves a binary file. Clearly, files can be both read and written but for this to be useful, we generally have to work with files that allow direct access.

We shall now demonstrate how text files can be used to build data registers of different kinds. As an example, we will be working with a file that contains names and telephone numbers according to the model shown on the following page:

Table 11.11   Combination of file flags.

Combination	Property
`in|out`	It should be possible to update the file (both reading and writing). The file should exist.
`in|out|trunc`	It should be possible to both read and write the file. If the file does not exist, a new file should be created. If the file exists earlier, it should be overwritten.
`in|out|app`	It should be possible to both read and write the file. If the file does not exist, a new file should be created. If the file exists, all updating should be done at the end of it.
`out|trunc`	It should be possible to write in the file. If the file does not exist, a new file should be created. If the file exists earlier, it should be overwritten.

Opening and closing files

Declare a stream object for each file. Use class `ifstream` for files that will be read and class `ofstream` for files that will be written.

```
ifstream f(file_name, mode);
```

where *file_name* is a text string and *mode* an expression of the form

```
ios::file flag|ios::file flag|etc.
```

Alternatively, use a default constructor and call `open` later:

```
ifstream f;
...
f.open(file_name, mode);
```

A file is closed automatically when the destructor of the stream object is called. Can also be closed by an explicit call of `close`

```
f.close();
```

```
Anderson Lisa 0181-712-3456
Browning Neil 01362-123456
Conway Ben 0116-889-9889
```

For each person there are three pieces of information: last name, first name and telephone number. It is an easy matter to construct a file of this sort with an ordinary text editor but for practice we will look at a program that generates such a file. The program should let the user write information for an arbitrary number of persons, and this information should be kept in the file. We will assume that the file with the telephone number is called `telephone.txt`. If the file already exists, the new information will be written at the end of it. So as not to destroy an existing file, we indicate the file flag `ios::app` when the file is opened. The program will finish by writing out the file `telephone.txt` at the terminal. Here we make use of the technique of writing out the file buffer directly. Before the file `telephone.txt` can be read and written out at the terminal, it must be closed:

```cpp
#include <iostream.h>
#include <fstream.h>
#include <iomanip.h>
main()
{
  ofstream fout("telephone.txt", ios::app);
  char ln[30], fn[30], tel[20];
  cout << "Give last name, first name and tel. no. "
       << "Terminate with Ctrl-Z" << endl;
  while (cin>>setw(30)>>ln and
         cin>>setw(30)>>fn and
         cin>>setw(20)>>tel)
    fout << ln << ' ' << fn << ' ' << tel << endl;
  fout.close();
  // Write out contents of the file
  ifstream fin("telephone.txt", ios::in);
  cout << "Telephone list:" << endl;
  cout << fin.rdbuf();
}
```

Our next step is now to look at how we change data inside a file, and as an example, we use one containing telephone numbers. We shall write a program that makes it possible to change a telephone number for one of the persons in the file. If we want to change the contents of a file, there are two ways of doing it. One is to use direct access, which enables us to change certain characters. (We will be looking at how this is done later.) The problem with this method is that it is complicated to insert new characters or remove them, and we are usually able to simply *exchange* characters. This will not work in our example. When a telephone number is changed, there is, of course, no guarantee that the new number will have as many digits as the old one. We will therefore use the second method which involves copying to a temporary file. The program has two stages. In the first, file telephone.txt is read and a copy is written to file tempfile. If during the copying process the given person is found, the new telephone number is placed in file tempfile. In the second stage of the program, file tempfile is copied back to file telephone.txt. The program has the following appearance:

```
#include <iostream.h>
#include <fstream.h>
#include <iomanip.h>
#include <string.h>
#include <stdio.h>
main()
{
  char ln1[30], fn1[30], tel1[20];
  char ln2[30], fn2[30], tel2[20];
  bool found = false;
  cout << "Give last name, first name and new tel. no. "
       << "for the person who will be changed" << endl;
  cin >> ln1 >> fn1 >> tel1;
  {
    ifstream fin("telephone.txt");
    ofstream fout("tempfile");
    while ( fin>>setw(30)>>ln2 and
            fin>>setw(30)>>fn2 and
            fin>>setw(20)>>tel2)
    {
      fout << ln2 << ' ' << fn2 << ' ';
      if (strcmp(ln1, ln2)==0 and
          strcmp(fn1, fn2)==0)
      {
        found = true;
        fout << tel1 << endl;  // Write new tel. no.
      }
      else
        fout << tel2 << endl;
    }
  }  // fin and fout are closed automatically
  if (found)
  {  // Copy tempfile to telephone.txt
    ifstream f1("tempfile");
    ofstream f2("telephone.txt");
    f2 << f1.rdbuf();
  }
  else
    cout << "The person is not there" << endl;
  remove("tempfile");
}
```

Note that after the first stage files telephone.txt and tempfile will be closed, since the declarations of fin and fout lie in an internal block in main.

The file `string.h` must be included because the program uses the standard function `strcmp` to compare the first and last names input, with the names in the file. The file `tempfile` created in the program will be a temporary file. This means that the program should 'clean up' after itself, removing this file from the file system. To do this, we use the standard function `remove` that is declared in the header file `stdio.h`. File `stdio.h` contains declarations of the functions that are included in the C standard library for reading and writing. These functions should not normally be used at the same time as the C++ standard library functions but it is all right to use function `remove`. Another useful function in `stdio.h` is the function `rename` which changes the name of a file. This function has the declaration:

```
rename(const char *oldname, const char *newname);
```

In our program we have given the temporary file the name `tempfile` but there is a certain risk involved. Suppose that we run the program in a file folder where there is already a file with the name `tempfile` and that this file, in spite of its name, contains important information. Our program will destroy this file. To avoid the risk of destroying an existing file, we can use the function `tmpnam`. This is declared in `stdio.h` and returns a pointer to a text string containing a file name guaranteed to be unique. Thus we could insert the following declaration into the program:

```
char *tname = tmpnam(0);
```

We must then change the program so that `tname` will replace `tempfile` everywhere in it:

```
ofstream fout(tname);
...
ifstream f1(tname);
...
remove(tname);
```

11.5   File names as arguments to `main`

In traditional command-oriented operating systems such as Unix and MS-DOS, a program is started by writing a command line. (This can also be done in a windows-oriented system such as Windows 95. You simply open an MS-DOS window which simulates a simple terminal.) In a command line, we first give the name of the program and then what usually follows are the names of the arguments for the program. The arguments are normally names of files but we can also have other kinds of arguments such as flags of different kinds. The program and the different arguments are usually separated by blank characters. For instance, if we write the following command line:

```
> demo -x /r fill
```

it means that the program called `demo` will be run and that it will have the three arguments `-x`, `/r` and `fill`.

How do these arguments get into function `main` then? Up to now we have said that function `main` does not have parameters but this is not really true. In fact, `main` has two parameters, usually called `argc` and `argv`. (Certain C++ compilers, the Borland compiler for instance, can have additional parameters but these are not standardized.) The first line in function `main` can therefore be written:

```
main(int argc, char *argv[])
...
```

The first parameter, `argc`, is an integer that gives the number of arguments written in the command line. The program name is also counted as an argument. When the program `demo` is started by the command line above, for example, the parameter `argc` will have a value of 4. The other parameter, `argv`, is an array where each element in the array is a pointer to a text string. The array `argv` contains `argc+1` elements. When `main` starts, `argv[0]` contains a pointer to a text string with the program name, `argv[1]` contains a pointer to a text string with the first parameter in the command line, `argv[2]` contains a pointer to a text string with the second parameter and so on. The last element, `argv[argc]`, contains a value of 0, that is, a null pointer. An illustration of the program `demo` when it has been called by the command line is given in Figure 11.2.

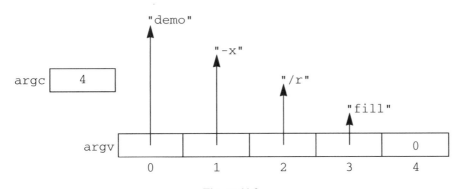

Figure 11.2

We assume now that the following program has been compiled and that the executable program has been stored in the file `demo`.

```
// The program demo
#include <iostream.h>
main(int argc, char *argv[])
{
```

```
    cout << "program name: " << argv[0] << endl;
  for (int i=1; i<argc; i++)
    cout << "Argument " << i << ": "
          << argv[i] << endl;
}
```

First the program writes its own name and then all the parameters given in the command line when the program was started. If the program is called with the command line above it will write out:

```
Program name: demo
Argument 1: -x
Argument 2: /r
Argument 3: fill
```

(Note that some compilers give the complete file name, for example, `c:\own\demo.exe`.) It is common to indicate the file name as argument in the command line. Most of the standard commands in MS-DOS and Unix have file names as arguments, for example. We will demonstrate such a program below.

We often prefer to write a tabulator character instead of several blank characters when using a text editor but this often causes problems when we want to edit the file in another program. The program we are going to write will read a text file that contains tab characters. The text file will be copied to a new file, and all the tab characters will be replaced by a number of blank characters. The name of the file to be read and the name of the new file will be given as arguments in the command line. If we want to, we can also include in the command line, by way of a final argument, the number of blank characters that will replace each tab character in the new file. If this final argument is not given, the program will assume that every tab stop is to be replaced by three blank characters. Let us suppose that the executable program has been stored in the file `tab`. The program can then be started with one of the command lines, for instance:

```
> tab my_file.txt new_file.txt
> tab report report2 4
```

When a program that gets its arguments from the command line is written, care must be taken to see that the correct number of arguments has been given and that all the arguments contain values that are allowed. A program like this is, therefore, often introduced with a number of controls. Our program, below, is an example of this:

```
// The program tab
#include <iostream.h>
#include <fstream.h>
#include <stdlib.h>
#include <string.h>
```

```
main(int argc, char *argv[])
{
  if (argc<3 or argc>4)
  {
    cerr <<"Incorrect number of arguments" << endl;
    exit(EXIT_FAILURE);
  }
  ifstream fin(argv[1]);   // Try to open the in file
  if (!fin)
  {
    cerr << "Cannot open the file " << argv[1] << endl;
    exit(EXIT_FAILURE);
  }
  ofstream fout(argv[2]);   // Try to open the out file
  if (!fout)
  {
    cerr << "Cannot create file " << argv[2] << endl;
    exit(EXIT_FAILURE);
  }
  int n = 3;
  if (argc == 4)
    if (strlen(argv[3])==1 and
        argv[3][0]>='0' and argv[3][0]<='9')
      n = argv[3][0]-'0';
    else
    {
      cerr << "Incorrect last argument" << endl;
      exit(EXIT_FAILURE);
    }
  char blank[] = "        ";
  blank[n] = '\0';

  char c;
  while(fin.get(c))
    if (c == '\t')
      fout << blank;
    else
      fout << c;
}
```

First the program checks that the correct number of arguments has been given. Since the program name is also counted, the counter `argc` must have a value of 3 or 4. The program then tries to declare, each one in turn, the streams that are connected to the in file and the out file. The file names are taken from `argv[1]` and `argv[2]`.

The variable n indicates how many blank characters are to replace each tab character, and it is initialized to 3. The program then checks to see whether a final argument, `argv[3]` has been indicated. If so, the argument must be a text consisting of a single character (element number 0 in the text string `argv[3]`), and this character must be a digit. (Only values in the interval 0–9 are allowed.) If the last argument has been indicated and is correct, the variable n is changed. The character array `blank` is initialized with a text string consisting of nine blank characters, and the program inserts a null character in element number n. From now on, therefore, `blank` will be taken to be a text string consisting of n blank characters.

The final part of the program is simple. Here the in file is read character by character and every time a tab character is encountered, the text string `blank` is written to the out file instead.

11.6 Direct access

Up to now we have read and written all our files in a sequence, from beginning to end. Classes `istream` and `ostream`, however, contain resources which make it possible to move back and forth in a file, almost in the same way as can be done when indexing in an array is carried out. We usually say that we have *direct access* to a file. When we read or write a file, the system automatically monitors an *actual position* in the file. (This really applies to all streams, not only to those connected to files. But it is most useful for files.) The actual position marks the place in the file from which the next character will be read, or to which the next character will be written. The actual position is an integer of type `streampos`. (This type is automatically declared when we include the file `iostream.h`. Type `streampos` is the same as one of the standard types, **long int**, for instance.) Numbering always takes place from 0, so that position number 0 means the file's first byte. When a file is opened, the actual position is automatically set to 0. When we read or write from a file, the actual position is automatically moved forward so that it points to the next position waiting to be read or written.

There are two operations that can be performed when we work with direct access: *tell* and *seek*. We use *tell* to read the actual position and *seek* to change the actual position. There are six different functions that can be used. These are summarized in Table 11.12. There are, as we can see, two sets of functions, one for instreams and one for outstreams (g stands for 'get' and p for 'put'). When we want to move the actual position in a file, we can either do it absolutely by calling the operation *seek* with an integer of type `streampos` as parameter, or we can perform a relative shift (forwards or backwards) with respect to the file's beginning, its end, or the actual position.

We now show a program that demonstrates how the functions in Table 11.12 can be used.

```
#include <iostream.h>
#include <fstream.h>
main()
{
  ofstream fout("testfile.txt");
  fout << "First line" << endl;
```

```
    fout << "Line 2" << endl;
    fout.seekp(0, ios::beg);
    fout << "XY";
    fout.seekp(4, ios::cur);
    fout << 'Z';
    streampos pos = fout.tellp();
    fout.seekp(0, ios::end);
    fout << "The last line" << endl;
    fout.seekp(pos);
    fout << 'W';
    fout.close();
    // Print out the file
    ifstream fin("testfile.txt");
    char c;
    while (fin.get(c))
        cout << c;
    // Print out the end of the file again
    fin.clear();    // NB! Is necessary
    fin.seekg(-8, ios::end);
    while (fin.get(c))
        cout << c;
}
```

First the program writes out the two lines

```
First line
Line 2
```

to a new file with the name `testfile.txt`, then it goes back to the beginning of the file and writes out the two characters XY, which will overwrite the characters Fi. The current position after this is the third character in the first line. The program then moves four characters forward. The new current position is the one containing

Table 11.12 Member functions for direct access in files.

Function	Effect
is.tellg() os.tellp()	Gives actual position in instream is and outstream os. Result is of type streampos.
is.seekg(pos) os.seekp(pos)	Sets actual position in instream is and outstream os to pos (pos should be a non-negative integer of type streampos).
is.seekg(off, dir) os.seekp(off, dir)	Moves actual position in instream is and outstream os to the point dir indicates, plus off positions. off should be an integer (possibly negative). dir should be one of: – ios::beg (beginning of file), – ios::end (end of file), – ios::cur (actual position in file).

the character L, and the program overwrites this with the character Z. The current position is then read (this points at the character i) and saved in the variable pos. The program then moves to the end of the file and finally prints out a third line, after which it returns to the position saved in the variable pos and writes the character W there. (Thus the character i will be overwritten.)

The file testfile.txt is closed and then reopened for reading. First the whole file is printed on the screen. After that the program goes back eight characters from the end and prints these characters once more. The output is:

```
XYrst ZWne
Line 2
The last line
t line
```

Note that it is important to call the function clear after reading the whole file for the first time. When we come to the end of the file, the flag eofbit is set. We will not be able to read from the file again until this flag has been cleared. In the last line of the printout, above, we can only see six characters although the program went back eight positions. This is because this program has been test run on a PC where the line terminator consists of two characters CR plus LF. These two characters come last in the file.

Up to now we have shown files which we either read from or write to. (To be able to read a file which we wrote earlier, we had to close it first then open it again.) When we use direct access, it is often necessary to have files which can be both read from and written to and for this to be possible, two conditions must be satisfied. First, the file must be opened with file flags that allow us to both read and write (see Table 11.11) and, second, there must be member functions for both reading and writing, for the stream connected to the file. The stream in question cannot be of class ifstream, because this only has resources for reading, nor can it be of class ofstream, as this only has member functions for writing. In many implementations of C++ there is a class called fstream, which is a combination of the two streams. Class fstream thus contains member functions for both reading and writing, but it is not to be found in the draft standard. We, therefore, begin by demonstrating how class fstream can be defined if it is not already in the compiler being used.

We use multiple inheritance and let class fstream be a subclass to both class ifstream and class ostream. The definition of class fstream looks like this:

```
class fstream : public ifstream, public ostream {
public:
    fstream()
    : ifstream(), ostream(ifstream::rdbuf()) {}
```

```
fstream(const char * name, int mode)
  : ifstream(name, mode),
    ostream(ifstream::rdbuf()) {}
};
```

Note that `fstream` is a subclass of `ostream`, not of `ofstream`, which might have seemed more natural. This has to do with the buffer used internally by stream objects. When we create an object of class `ifstream` or `ofstream`, a file buffer is always formed, but since we are dealing with one file, we want a buffer that can be used for both reading and writing. We have not created objects of class `istream` or `ostream` before. (We have only used the predefined objects `cin` and `cout`.) Meanwhile, there are constructors available for these classes. Such constructors do not create buffers. Instead, they require as parameter a pointer to a buffer which must be created by the programmer before the constructor is called.

The only members we define for the new class `fstream` are two constructors, a default constructor and a constructor with two parameters, one of these being a file name, the other an integer that is used to indicate file flags. (This means that class `fstream` has exactly the same constructors as classes `ifstream` and `ofstream`.) Both constructors use initialization lists to initialize subobjects of the two base classes. Initialization of the base class `ifstream` is the easiest. We simply call the default constructor for class `ifstream` in the default constructor for `fstream`. In the second constructor, we call the constructor for class `ifstream` that opens a file and connects it to the stream. When a subobject of class `ifstream` is initialized, a file buffer is created. The member function `rdbuf` can be called to get a pointer to this buffer. When we initialized the subobject of class `ostream`, we used `ifstream::rdbuf` to give the constructor a pointer to the buffer to be used. Thus, the same buffer will be used by both subobjects.

Here is a simple example that demonstrates how the new class `fstream` can be used:

```
#include <iostream.h>
#include <fstream.h>
#include <string.h>
main()
{
  fstream f("testfile.txt",
     ios::in|ios::out|ios::trunc);
  // Write two lines to the file
  f << "This is line no 1" << endl;
  streampos pos2=f.tellp();  // Line 2 begins here
  f << "Line number 2" << endl;
  // Write out the file at the terminal
  f.seekp(0);
  char s[100];
  while(f.getline(s, 100))
    cout << s << endl;
  f.clear();  // NB! Necessary after end-of-file
```

```
// Change the first word to stars
f.seekp(0);
f >> s;
f.seekp(0);
for (int i=1; i<=strlen(s); i++)
  f.put('*');
// Write an X in the middle of the second line
f.seekp(pos2);
f.getline(s, 100);
f.seekp(pos2+strlen(s)/2);
f << 'X';
// Write out the file at the terminal
f.seekp(0);
cout << f.rdbuf();
}
```

The program creates a new file with the name `testfile.txt`. In the first stage, two lines are written to the file, and the file's contents are written out at the terminal. In connection with this, we use the variable `pos2` to mark the position where line 2 begins. In the second stage, two changes are made in the file. The file's first word is replaced by stars, and the character in the middle of the second line is changed to an X. After this the file's contents are written out at the terminal again. The program's output will be:

```
This is line no 1
Line number 2
**** is line no 1
Line nXmber 2
```

In the program two different ways of writing the file at the terminal are shown: by reading and writing a line at a time and by writing out the file buffer directly. Note that when a line is read at a time, the flag `eofbit` is set when end-of-file occurs. We have to call `clear` before we can carry on working with the file.

When we work with streams of class `fstream`, where reading may alternate with writing, we cannot always assume that shifts relative to the actual position will work. It is, therefore, best to do as in this example, by indicating absolute file positions.

We will now look at an example that is perhaps a little more useful. It is very common to use binary files to store databases of various kinds. An example of such a program is a booking program which monitors the number of reserved places at hotels and concerts, for instance. Another example is a stores management program which monitors how many articles of a particular sort there are in stock. This type of program is characterized by the storage of *entries* in a binary file. The file will contain a number of entries of the same kind. An entry is a collection of data that belongs together. An entry can, for instance, relate to a particular room in a hotel, or a certain article in a stock program. The entries are stored in binary form in the file, which means that *no* conversion to ASCII characters will occur. The entries in the file will have exactly the same appearance as entries in the primary memory. This means in particular that numeric data is stored in the same way as integer types or floating point number types. When entries are read and written from and to a file, a *whole entry* is transferred at a time. Thus, the individual components of an entry are not read and written one at a time.

Naturally, we define entries in C++ with the help of classes. Classes that define entries must, however, be very simple. They can only contain pure data. They cannot contain pointers or references since it is pointless to store primary memory addresses in a file. (If the file is read at a later stage by the program that wrote it, or some other program, the program would no doubt be loaded into a different place in the primary memory.) In addition, classes that define entries cannot contain extra, hidden information. This means that they cannot have virtual functions or base classes. The following class is a simple one that is used to define a bank account:

```
class Account_Entry {
public:
  long int account_no;
  double balance;
  Person account_holder;
};
```

An `Account_Entry` has three data members, all of them public. An entry contains an account number, a balance and an account holder. An account holder is of class `Person`, which can be defined in the following way, for example:

```
class Person {
public:
  char name[20];
  char address[30];
};
```

Class `Account_Entry` only contains pure data. There are no pointers or references or hidden information. Note that it would have been an error to use type `char` `*` in class `Person`. If we had written, for instance:

```
char *name;   // ERROR!
```

The component `name` would have been a pointer to a text string found somewhere else. By declaring the components `name` and `address` as character arrays with given lengths, the text strings themselves will be in the entry.

We will now look at a program that monitors bank accounts. We suppose that there is a binary file with the name `account` that contains entries of class `Account_Entry`. The file is sorted so that the entries are in account number order. We can imagine the program being run by an employee at a bank. Every time there is a new customer, the program will ask for an account number. It then searches for the entry in the file that contains the given account number. After this, the program will ask for an amount. A positive amount means a deposit and a negative one means a withdrawal. The program then performs the given transaction and updates the account entry in the file.

The entries in the file are numbered from 0 upwards. Since all the entries have the same length, we can calculate the starting position in the file for a given entry by multiplying the entry number by the size of the entry. A binary search is used to search for a particular entry in the file (see the discussion on page 102). We can calculate the number of entries in the file by moving to the end of the file, reading the position, then dividing this by the size of the file.

A variable with the name `entry` of type `Account_Entry` is declared in the program and this is used when we want to read and write entries to the file. A whole entry is read or written at a time, using the member functions `read` and `write`. These will have, as a first argument, a pointer to a character array that will be read to, or written from. A pointer to the variable `entry` will be this argument in the program. This pointer must be converted to type **char** `*` to get the right type. We give the program below. The file `banktype.h` in the program contains the definition of classes `Account_Entry` and `Person`.

```
#include <iostream.h>
#include <fstream.h>
#include <iomanip.h>
#include "banktype.h"
main()
{
  fstream f("account",
            ios::in|ios::out|ios::binary);
  while(true)
  {
    cout << "Account_num? ";
    long int searched;
    if (not (cin>>searched))
      break;
    Account_Entry entry;
    const int entry_size = sizeof (Account_Entry);
    // Binary search
    bool found = false;
    f.seekp(0, ios::end);
    long int entry_no, first=0,
             last=f.tellp()/entry_size-1;
    while (not found and first <= last)
    {
      entry_no = (first+last)/2;;
      f.seekp(entry_no*entry_size);
      f.read((char *) &entry, entry_size);
      if (searched < entry.account_no)
        last = entry_no-1;
      else if(searched > entry.account_no)
        first = entry_no+1;
```

```
     else  // equal
       found = true;
   }
   if (not found)
     cout << "Incorrect account_num" << endl;
   else
   {
     cout << entry.account_holder.name << endl
          << entry.account_holder.address << endl
          << "balance: " << setiosflags(ios::fixed)
          << setprecision(2) << entry.balance << endl
          << "Amount? ";
     double amount;
     if (not (cin>>amount))
       break;
     if (amount<0 and entry.balance+amount<0)
       cout << "Withdrawal cannot be done" << endl;
     else
     {
       entry.balance += amount;
       f.seekp(entry_no*entry_size);
       f.write((char *)&entry, entry_size);
       cout << "New balance: " << setprecision(2)
            << entry.balance << endl;
     }
   }
 }
}
```

11.7   Storing heterogeneous objects in files

We have now seen how binary files and direct access can be used to store entries in files efficiently. For it to be possible to use this technique, we pointed out that the classes defining the entries had to be very simple. When we discussed inheritance we saw that there could be collections of objects from different classes but that the classes had to have a common, fundamental base class. We saw, for instance, how different kinds of vehicle could be defined by the creation of different subclasses of class Vehicle. Such a collection of objects is usually called a *heterogeneous* object collection as opposed to a *homogeneous* object collection where all the objects have the same type. This technique for storing objects in binary files, demonstrated in the previous section, presupposes that we are dealing with homogeneous object collections.

In this chapter, we will demonstrate a technique for the storage of heterogeneous object collections in files. It will be possible to write out objects of different types in a file and to read in the objects on a later occasion. A particular problem is that for every object in the file, information about the class the object belongs to must be stored in the file so that it will be possible to recreate a similar object when the file comes to be read.

Suppose we would like to define a class with the name Storable. There will be two member functions in the class, read and write, which read and write objects in files. We can then define subclasses of class Storable which will inherit functions read and write. Before discussing the mechanism involved, we will demonstrate the procedure seen from the user program's point of view. Suppose that we have defined a class Animal with three subclasses: Dog, Horse and Cow. We have defined class Animal as a subclass of class Storable. Let us look at the following program:

```
main()
{
  Storable *tab[100];
  tab[0] = new Dog("dachshund", "Nick");
  tab[1] = new Horse(5, "black");
  tab[2] = new Cow(5000);
  tab[3] = new Horse(7, "brown");
  tab[4] = new Cow(4000);
  tab[5] = new Dog("labrador", "Napoleon");
  ofstream f("animal_file");
  for (int i=0; i<6; i++)
    tab[i]->write(f);
};
```

The program creates six different kinds of animal object and keeps pointers to the objects in the array tab. Since all the objects are derived from class Storable, array tab has elements that are of type 'pointer to Storable'. When all the objects have been created, the program opens a new file with the name animal_file and writes out all six objects to this file. Function write, inherited from class Storable, is called to write the output.

When the program has been executed, the file animal_file will remain. Suppose now that on a later occasion we want to run another program that reads in the file and recreates the six objects. This program will look like this:

```
main()
{
  Storable *tab[100];
  Dog a_dog;
  Horse a_horse;
  Cow a_cow;
  a_dog.example();
  a_horse.example();
  a_cow.example();
  ifstream f("animal_file");
  int n = 0;
```

```
  while (tab[n]=read(f))
    n++;
  for (int k=0; k<n; k++)
    ((Animal *) tab[k])->info();
}
```

First, a similar table to the one in the previous program is declared. For the program to recreate the objects to be found in file animal_file, it must know what kind of object the file can contain. Therefore, the program begins by giving examples of the three different objects that can occur in the file. With these examples serving as models, the program can then construct similar objects. Examples are given by calling the member function example that has been inherited from Storable.

In the next step, the file animal_file is opened for reading. The objects are read one at a time with the aid of the inherited function read. This gives as result a pointer to a newly created object of the right class. When end-of-file occurs, function read returns a null pointer. The pointers we get as a result from function read are stored in array tab.

In the last step, we run through array tab from the beginning, performing as many rounds as the number of objects read. At every round, the virtual function info is called, and this writes out information about the objects. Every animal class has its own version of function info. Function info is declared as virtual in class Animal. We must therefore do a type conversion from class 'pointer to Storable' to class 'pointer to Animal' for the compiler to find the function and produce dynamic binding. The program will write out:

```
A dachshund called Nick
A black horse that is 5 years old
A cow that gives 5000 litres/year
A brown horse that is 7 years old
A cow that gives 4000 litres/year
A labrador called Napoleon
```

Thus we can store heterogeneous object collections in files in a relatively simple way by using class Storable. We will now look at the mechanism behind all of this and begin by looking at the base class Storable:

```
class Storable {
public:
  void example() const;
  void write(ostream& fout) const;
  friend Storable *read(istream& fin);
  enum {max=100};
private:
  virtual Storable *create_similar() const = 0;
  virtual void write_mem(ostream& fout) const = 0;
  virtual void read_mem(istream& fin) = 0;
```

```
    static Storable *ex[max];
    static int number_ex;
    static Storable *search(const char *class_name);
};
```

The three functions that were called in the two programs above, are declared in the public section. We use the member function `example` to say that the actual object will be an example of a class that can be found stored in a file. The member function `write` is called when we want to write out the actual object in a file. Function `read` reads data from a file, checks which class the read object is to have and then creates, with the help of the given examples, an object of the right class. Function `read` cannot be a member function, since there is no actual object the function can be called for. It is of course a function's job to create such an object.

In the private section of the function there are declarations of everything necessary to administrate reading and writing. First, the three pure virtual functions `create_similar`, `write_mem` and `read_mem` are declared. Because these are pure virtual functions, class `Storable` will be an abstract class. It is not our intention to create objects that are 'only' of class `Storable` but we do want the objects we create to belong to some subclass of `Storable`. All such subclasses that will not be abstract must have their own versions of the virtual functions. The function `create_similar` will create a new object of the same kind as the actual object. For instance, if we call this function for an object of type `Dog`, the function should give as result a pointer to a new object, also of class `Dog`. We will not describe the other two virtual functions just yet.

Two static data members, `ex` and `number_ex` are declared in the private section of the class. These are used to monitor the example objects that have been given, using the member function `example`. That the two data members are static, means, as we know, that they only exist in a single edition common for all objects belonging to class `Storable` or a subclass of it. The member `number_ex` is an integer that contains the number of given example objects, and the member `ex` is an array whose individual members are pointers to objects of class `Storable`. This array is used to point out the different example objects. The size of the array has been indicated with the aid of the enumeration value `max`, which has been given a value of 100 (see page 174). We usually use anonymous enumeration types in this way to indicate constants in classes. If we had declared a constant data member:

```
const int max;
```

every object of class `Storable` or one of its subclasses would have contained a copy of this constant. In addition, it would have had to have been initialized in a constructor for class `Storable`.

We place the definition of class `Storable` in a file with the name `store.h`, so the static data members should be defined in file `store.cpp`:

```
Storable *Storable::ex[Storable::max];
int Storable::number_ex = 0;
```

The third static member in class `Storable` is a function `search` that is used for finding a suitable example object among the examples in array `ex`. As parameter, this function gets a text string that contains the name of a class. The function checks the array `ex` and tries to find an object that belongs to a class with the given name. If it finds such an object, it gives as result a pointer to it; otherwise a null pointer is returned. An ordinary linear search is used, and the definition is quite simple:

```
Storable *Storable::search
        (const char *class_name)
{
  for (int i=0; i<number_ex; i++)
    if (strcmp(typeid(*ex[i]).name(),class_name)==0)
      return ex[i];
  return 0;
}
```

The function runs through the array `ex`. For every example object in the array, the operator **typeid** in combination with the function `name` is used to find out the name of the class the example object belongs to (see Section 9.6, page 310). This name is compared to the name that was given as parameter.

We can now give the definition of the member function `example`. The job of this function is to insert new example objects into array `ex`. There need not be more than one example for each class. Before the new example object is inserted into the array, it is checked to make sure that no example object of this class already exists in the array. Function `example` has the following appearance:

```
void Storable::example() const
{
  if (not search(typeid(*this).name()))
  {
    if (number_ex < max)
      ex[number_ex++] = create_similar();
    else
      cerr << "Too many examples" << endl;
  }
}
```

We could have kept a pointer to the actual object in array `ex` in which case we would have written

```
ex[number_ex++] = this;   // Dangerous
```

This is rather dangerous as we cannot be sure that the actual object exists throughout the time of execution. To avoid this problem with lingering pointers, we create another object, of the same class as the actual object and insert a pointer to this object instead. This is done by using the virtual member function create_similar.

For class Storable, it now remains to show the definitions of the member function write and the friend function read. We begin with function write:

```
void Storable::write(ostream& fout) const
{
  fout << typeid(*this).name() << ' ';
  write_mem(fout);
  fout << endl;
}
```

As parameter the function gets a reference to the stream the data will be written in. Binary files are not used. Instead, the information is written in the file in text form. For every object written, we begin by writing the name of the class the object belongs to. We also use the operator **typeid** and function name here.

We now write out all the data members there are for the actual object. But there is a problem here. Class Storable will naturally have no knowledge of how all of its subclasses look and which data members they contain. Therefore the individual data members cannot be written in function write. This problem is solved, however, by requiring every class that will be storable to have its own implementation of the virtual member function write_mem. This member function will simply write out the individual members for the actual class. Function write can, therefore, call write_mem to produce output from all the data members. Finally, an end-of-line character is written. Thus every object will begin on a new line in the file. So that the file can be read later, there must be at least one white character, for example, a blank character, between the output of each data member. The member functions write_mem must take care of this.

As an example, let us suppose that we shall write out an object of class Horse. A horse has (as we shall soon see) two data members, an integer that gives its age and a text string that gives the horse's colour. When function write is called for an object of class Horse, the following line can for instance, be written to the file:

```
Horse 5 black
```

Class Cow only has one data member (an integer that indicates how many litres of milk the cow gives per year). If, instead, we want to write out an object of class Cow, the following line can therefore be written to the file:

```
Cow 5000
```

The job of function `read`, a friend function of class `Storable`, is to read a file that has been produced with function `write`. As result the function gives a pointer to a newly created object, or a null pointer if reading has miscarried. Function `read` has the following appearance:

```
Storable *read(istream& fin)
{
  char class_name[100];
  if (not (fin >> setw(100) >> class_name))
    return 0;
  Storable *lp = Storable::search(class_name);
  if (lp)
  { lp = lp->create_similar();
    lp->read_mem(fin);
  }
  return lp;
}
```

The function begins by trying to read in the class name to a text string. If this reading miscarries (end-of-file might have occurred), a null pointer is returned. Otherwise the function continues by calling the static member function `search`, to see if there is an example object of the actual class. If such an object is found, `search` returns a pointer to it. We then call the virtual function `create_similar` and get as result a pointer to a new object of the same kind as the example object, that is, of the class given by the class name that was read from the file. The user must him or herself implement the virtual function `read_mem` for every non-abstract subclass of class `Storable`. This function reads in data to the individual members in an object of the actual class. Thus, it functions like `write_mem` but the other way round. If, for example, the next line in the file has the appearance:

```
Horse 5 black
```

and function `read` is called, it will create a new object of type `Horse` and fill in this object so that the horse becomes 5 years old and black.

The definition of class `Storable` is now finished. To complete our example, we now give the definitions of classes `Animal`, `Dog`, `Horse` and `Cow`. Class `Animal` is an abstract class and is intended to serve as base class for the other three classes. Since this class will be abstract, we do not need to implement the virtual functions inherited from class `Storable`.

```
class Animal : public Storable {
public:
  virtual void info() = 0;
};
```

```
class Dog : public Animal {
public:
  Dog(const char *b = "", const char *n = "")
  {strcpy(breed, b); strcpy(name, n);}
  void info()
  {cout << "A " << breed << " called "
       << name << endl;}

private:
  char breed[30], name[20];
  virtual Storable *create_similar() const
  { return new Dog; }
  virtual void write_mem(ostream& fout) const
  { fout << breed << ' ' << name; }
  virtual void read_mem(istream& fin)
  { fin >> breed >> name; }
};
```

```
class Horse : public Animal {
public:
  Horse(int a=0, const char *c = "") : age(a)
  {strcpy(colour, c);}
  void info()
  {cout << "A " << colour << " horse that is "
       << age << " years old" << endl;}

private:
  int age;
  char colour[20];
  virtual Storable *create_similar() const
  { return new Horse; }
  virtual void write_mem(ostream& fout) const
  { fout << age << ' ' << colour; }
  virtual void read_mem(istream& fin)
  { fin >> age >> colour; }
};
```

```
class Cow : public Animal {
public:
  Cow(int l=0) : milk(l) {}
  void info()
  {cout << "A cow that gives " << milk
       << " litres/year" << endl;}

private:
  int milk;
  virtual Storable *create_similar() const
  { return new Cow; }
  virtual void write_mem(ostream& fout) const
  { fout << milk; }
  virtual void read_mem(istream& fin)
  { fin >> milk; }
};
```

11.8   Connecting text strings to streams

Up to now, we have used streams to communicate with units outside the program (files, terminal keyboard). But, it is in fact possible to use streams internally in a program. An ordinary text string can be connected to a stream. If we connect a text string to an input stream, we can read data from the text string, exactly as if we had used `cin` and input data had been written at the keyboard. Similarly, if we connect a text string to an output stream, we can write data in the text string just as if we were writing output data to the terminal. Making use of streams in this way is very practical if in a program we want to make type conversions to and from text strings; for instance, if we have a real number given in the form of a text string and want to convert it to type **double**, or if we have an integer in the form of an **int** and would like to convert it to a text string and edit it in some way.

We will begin by describing how input from text strings takes place. To do this, we will use a stream of class `istrstream`. For this there are three different constructors:

```
explicit istrstream(const char* s);
explicit istrstream(char* s);
istrstream(const char* s, streamsize n);
```

This presupposes that we have a character array which the parameter s points to. This character array will contain the data to be read to the stream. The first two constructors require that the text string s points to, should end with a null character. The third constructor can be used if there is a character array that does not terminate with a null character. So we will indicate, instead, the length of the character array as second parameter of the constructor. (Type `streamsize` is an integer type, for example, **long int**.) Here is a short program that demonstrates the use of class `istrstream`. Three different streams, `st1`, `st2` and `st3` are created with the help of the three different constructors.

```
#include <strstream.h>
#include <string.h>
main()
{
  int i;
  double x;
  char txt1[10], txt2[10];
  istrstream st1("12 34.5");
  st1 >> i >> x;
  cout << i << '_' << x << endl;

  char s2[100];
  strcpy(s2, "25 degrees Celsius");
  istrstream st2(s2);
  st2 >> i >> txt1 >> txt2;
  cout << i << '_' << txt1 << '_' << txt2 << endl;
```

```
    char s3[3];
    s3[0] = '9'; s3[1] = '7'; s3[2]='5';
    istrstream st3(s3, sizeof s3);
    st3 >> i;
    cout << i << endl;
}
```

The printout from the program will be:

```
12_34.5
25_degrees_Celsius
975
```

Output to text strings takes place analogously. Output to the stream will land in a character array instead of being written at the terminal or in a file. We make use of class `ostrstream`. To create a stream `ost` and connect it to a character array `s`, we write:

```
ostrstream ost(s, n);
```

Here `s` will be a pointer to a character array, and `n` will be an integer that gives the length of the array. When we write to a character array, we ourselves have to place a null character at the end of the output so that the array will contain a text string. The simplest way of doing this is to use the manipulator `ends`, which functions analogously to the manipulator `endl`. The following program uses two streams `os1` and `os2`, which write to the two character arrays `s1` and `s2`, respectively.

```
#include <strstream.h>
#include <iomanip.h>
#include <math.h>
main()
{
    char s1[100];
    ostrstream os1(s1, sizeof s1);
    os1 << "C++ from the Beginning" << ends;
    s1[4] = 'F';
    cout << s1 << endl;
    char s2[100];
    ostrstream os2(s2, sizeof s2);
    double x = 5, y = sin(x);
    os2 << "The result:" << endl
        << "sin(" << x << ")="
        << setiosflags(ios::fixed) << setprecision(3)
        << y << endl << ends;
    cout<< s2;
    cout<< os1.pcount() << ' ' << os2.pcount() << endl;
}
```

Output from the program will then be:

```
C++ From the Beginning
The result:
sin(5)=-0.959
23 27
```

Note that output both to `s1` and `s2` terminates with `ends`. The text string `s1` does not contain an end-of-line character, and this is why `endl` has been added when `s1` is written out in `cout`. The text string `s2`, on the other hand, contains end-of-line characters after every line. Therefore, there is no extra `endl` when `s2` is written to `cout`. On the last line, the member function `pcount` is called. This gives as result the number of characters that have been written in an outstream. Thus we can see how many characters have been written to `s1` and `s2`.

It should be said that for class `ostrstream` there is also a constructor without parameters. For instance, we could write:

```
ostrstream os;
```

We do not have to indicate to which text string output data will be written. The stream itself will allocate sufficient memory space to hold the text that will be written. When the output data has been written, we can use the member function `str` to get a pointer to the text string that has been allocated.

```
os << 15*32 << ends;
cout << os.str() << endl;
```

This seems simple enough but, of course, there is a snag. From the moment function `str` has been called, the outstream becomes *frozen*, which means that nothing further can (or should) be written in it. In addition, we ourselves have to deallocate the memory space that was allocated for the output data. When we no longer need the text string, therefore, we have to give the statement:

```
delete[] os.str();
```

We said that streams could be used to carry out type conversions simply to and from text strings. As an example, we will show the function `add_date`, which can add a number of years to a given date. The function has three parameters. The first is a pointer to a text string that contains a date in the format 'yyyy-mm-dd', the second is a pointer to an uninitialized character array sufficiently long to contain a date and the third is an integer that indicates how many years are to be added. If, for instance, we make the call `add_date("1997-03-26", s, 15)`, the function will fill in the character array `s` points to so that it contains the text `"2012-03-26"`.

```
void add_date(char *d1, char *d2, int n)
{
  istrstream is(d1);
  ostrstream os(d2, 11);
  int year;
  is >> year;
  os << (year+n) << (d1+4) << ends;
}
```

When windows-oriented programs are written, the streams `cin` and `cout` are not used to read and write. Instead, there are special help functions for the windows system that is used. If we want to write output data, we can call, for example, a help function that produces a display window containing a text. There is usually a little button with 'OK' or some other qualifying text in it which we can click when we have read the message. This help function must know which text is to be written out, and it is usually indicated as a text string given as parameter to the help function. Reading input data works in a similar way. A help function is called, and this produces a window in which the user is expected to write input data. When the user has finished, the help function gives as result a text string that contains what has been written.

In this type of program, streams can be used to convert data that is to be written out or that has been read. We will illustrate this with an example. Suppose that there are two help functions `win_input` and `win_output`. (These functions have been invented for this example. In a real windows system they will have other names and parameters.) Both generate a window at the terminal. Function `win_output` gets a string as parameter and writes it out in the window. The function `win_input` has two parameters, both pointers to text strings. The first text string contains the question to be written out in the window, and the other text string is an outparameter that is filled in with the answer the user has given. In Chapter 2 we wrote a simple program that calculated how much it cost to rent a car. We can now write some program lines which do the same thing:

```
const int length = 100;
char text[length];
int day_number, daily_rate;
{
  win_input("Number of days? ", text);
  istrstream is(text, length);
  if (not (is>>day_number))
    throw data_error();
}
{
  win_input("Rate per day? ", text);
  istrstream is(text, length);
  if (not (is>>daily_rate))
    throw data_error();
}
{
```

```
    ostrstream os(text, length);
    os << "Total cost: "
        << day_number * daily_rate << ends;
    win_output(text);
}
```

Note that we check whether reading has been successful. If it has not, an exception is generated. (We have used the class `data_error`, which was defined on page 345.) In this type of program we cannot write error messages in the streams `cout` or `cerr` since we are dealing with text windows.

EXERCISES

11.1   Write a program that reads in text from the terminal and stores the text in a new text file with the name `myfile.txt`. The new file should have the same line structure as the text file written from the terminal. In addition, all the lower case letters should be translated into upper case letters.

11.2   A secret message is kept in the text file `secret.txt`. This has not been stored as straightforward text but in the form of a coded message so that it cannot be easily read without authorization. Each letter in the original message has been coded to another using this table

```
        code letters:  guwyrmqpsaeicbnozlfhdkjxtv
        original text: abcdefghijklmnopqrstuvwxyz
```

If, for example, the file contains the text 'lnybrt jgshsbq jrybrfygt rsqph oc', the uncoded message is 'rodney waiting wednesday eight pm'. Write a program to read the file with the secret message and write it out in plain language. The program should begin by reading in the code (the first line in the table above) from the terminal.

11.3   Write a program to read an existing text file and write out its contents at the terminal. No empty lines (containing only a line terminator) or lines containing only blanks should be written out. Otherwise the output should have the same structure as the text file. The program should be applicable to any text file; the text file's name should be read from the terminal.

11.4   A command that is often used in the Unix operating system, is one called `cat`. The task here is to write your own version of this program. The program `cat` can be used to combine files but it can also serve to write out the contents of one or more files at the terminal. The command has the form:

```
        cat f1 f2 f3 ...
```

Thus the program name is written followed by an arbitrary number of file names. The program writes out the files one at a time in standard output. If you wish to use the program to combine files, the standard output could be redirected. The following call, for instance, provides that `fc` will contain a copy of `fa` combined with `fb`.

```
cat fa fb > fc
```

Note that a redirection is not an argument which is sent to `main`. In this line, therefore, the program will only get `fa` and `fb` as arguments.

11.5   Suppose that the file `telephone.txt` with names and telephone numbers on page 376 is sorted in alphabetical order. Write a program that adds a new person. The program should read in a name and telephone number for the new person from the terminal and then insert this information in the correct place in the file so that it will remain sorted. Use a temporary file.

11.6   Information about a number of people has been collected in a binary file for statistical purposes. The information stored is the name, height, weight, shoe size, age and civil status for each person. In order to process the data the sex of every person has to be known, although this information is not included in the file.

Write a program that reads the file and creates two new files, one containing only women and one with only men. For every person in the file, the program should ask the operator whether a person is a man or a woman.

11.7   A company has a register of its customers in the form of a binary file. There is an entry in the file for each customer, containing the customer's name and two lines of address including the postal code. Each of these three items is at most 20 characters in length. To send out information to customers, a program is required that can print self-adhesive address labels with the customers' names and addresses. A printing terminal is used loaded with special paper on which the labels are stuck contiguously, three in a row. The total width of the paper is 72 characters, so each label will be 24 characters wide. The height of each label is five lines.

Write a program that reads the file of customers and produces a text file which can later be sent to the customers. Use only the three centre lines of each label. The program should work even if the number of customers is not an exact multiple of three.

11.8   When we handle files, they are usually sorted. Some particular component among the entries, for instance, a car registration number, is normally chosen to institute the sort procedure. This component is called the *sorting key*. A problem that often occurs is one where there are two sorted files with the same kind of entries and a new, sorted file has to be made containing the entries of both files. We say that the two original files have been *merged*. Write a program that merges two binary files containing entries which define cars. The sorting key is the car registration number. You may decide yourself what the other entries are to be.

11.9 A company has prepared a list of its employees' room and telephone numbers in a binary file. There is an entry for every employee and each entry contains a name, a room number and a telephone number. The file is sorted in alphabetical order. Write a program that can insert entries for new employees, change already existing entries, or remove entries from the file. The program should repeatedly ask for the name, the room number and the telephone number of an employee. If a name not in the file is given, a new entry should be inserted in the correct place. If a name already existing in the file is given, the corresponding entry should either be changed or removed. The operator indicates that an entry is to be removed by writing a room number of 0 in the entry. The entries existing in the file but otherwise not indicated by the operator, should not be changed. The program may require names to be read in alphabetical order.

11.10 Information about the status of football teams taking part in a league has been stored in a binary file so that for each team there is an entry in the file. An entry contains the team's name, the points it has and the number of goals scored for and against. Entries in the file are in arbitrary order.

Write a program that sorts the file so that the team with most points comes first and the one with least points comes last. If several teams have the same number of points, the team with the best goal aggregate comes first. Teams with the same number of points and goal aggregate should be placed in alphabetical order. *Tip*: Read all the teams into an array, sort it, then write it out in the file.

11.11 A company has a sorted binary file `stockfile` with which all the articles in its stock are monitored. There is an entry for every kind of article, each entry containing the article designation (a code consisting of ten characters), a definition of the article (a text of 30 characters), the number in stock and the price. Write a program that can deal with the following commands from the terminal:

`info` *artno*	The program writes out information stored for articles of *artno* type at the terminal.
`buy` *artno* *n*	The program should update the stock file with the information that *n* articles of *artno* type have been purchased and added to the stock.
`sell` *artno* *n*	The program should update the stock file with the information that *n* articles of *artno* type have been sold from the stock.

11.12 A sports club has stored a register with all its members in a file. The club handles several sports, for instance, football, athletics and wrestling. So it has different kinds of information to be stored for its members, depending on which sport they take an interest in. Certain information is common to all its members (name, address, etc.). The different kinds of members can therefore be defined with the help of classes and inheritance. The register file is produced by a program that has used `Storable` in

Section 11.7 to be able to store heterogeneous objects. Define a class hierarchy that describes some different categories of member in the sports club. Then write a program that can be used for finding information about individual members. The program should first read the register file to an array. Then it should repeatedly ask for a member's name. If the member is in the register, appropriate information should be written out at the terminal. (Use dynamic binding.)

11.13 Develop the program in the previous exercise so that it will add new members or allow information to be changed for a given member of the club. The new data must, of course, be kept in the register file before the program is terminated.

11.14 Assume that the time of day is defined by a text string in the format 'hh.mm.ss'. Write a function which updates a time of day by adding a certain number of seconds (which can be greater than 60). The function should have two parameters: a pointer to the text string to be updated and an integer that indicates how many seconds should be added. *Tip*: Use the technique of connecting text strings to streams.

11.15 Write a program that reads a text from a text file and writes it out in edited form in standard output. The name of the file should be given as argument to `main`. As a second argument to `main`, the desired line size should be indicated in the output. (Use a connection to a stream to convert this argument to an integer.) Assume that the input file contains a number of words (sequences of non-white characters) with an arbitrary number of white characters between every word. In the output there should be one blank character between words. The line structure in the output should not be the same as that of the input file. Each line of the output should contain as many words as possible in the given line length, so that the lines are roughly the same length.

12 Dynamic Data Structures

When we have wanted to define similar objects in a program, we have used arrays. Arrays are, as we have seen, very useful things but there are situations where their value is limited. In some applications, for example, we may have collections of data without a definite idea of how many objects we need. In such cases we have to construct so-called dynamic data structures, which can grow and shrink during program execution. In this chapter, we will be looking at how we can create, with the aid of classes and pointers, dynamic data structures in C++. We will be paying particular attention to the following common data structures: *lists*, *queues*, *stacks*, *sets* and *trees*.

12.1   Linked lists – the basics

We shall begin by discussing *linked lists*. In this section we will be describing the fundamental technical aspects – how linked lists are constructed and how they are handled. There are singly linked lists and doubly linked lists. In Section 12.2, we will be using linked lists as building blocks when we construct abstract data types – stacks, queues and sets – on a higher level.

12.1.1   Singly linked lists

A linked list, with three integers, is illustrated in Figure 12.1. A linked list consists of a number of elements, and each element has two components, a pointer to the next element in the list and a value, which can be of any type. In this chapter we will assume, for the sake of simplicity, that this value is an integer. We will see later, in Chapter 13, how this can be generalized to give components of arbitrary value. The first element of a list is usually called its *head*, and that element is pointed to by a special pointer. We have called this pointer `first`. The last element in the list contains a value of 0, that is, a null pointer. This marks the end of the list.

Building up a list

A list element can be defined with the aid of the following class:

```
class Element {
public:
  Element *next;
  int data;
  Element(Element *n, int d) : next(n), data(d) {}
};
```

In class `Element` there are two data members, `next`, which is a pointer to the next element, and `data`, which contains the value of the list element. The type for the data member `next` is `Element *`, that is, 'pointer to `Element`'. A constructor that is called when new list elements are created has been added to class `Element`.

Figure 12.1

Figure 12.2

For simplicity, we have placed all the members in the **public** section, where they are visible.

Now a linked list will be built up using class Element. We begin by declaring the pointer variable first, which will point to the first list element:

```
Element *first=0;
```

The pointer first has been initialized to a value of 0, which says that the list is empty (has no elements). We can now create a list element and place it in the list:

```
first = new Element(first, 5);
```

The pointer first will point to the new element, which is initialized by the constructor in class Element. Since the pointer first earlier had a value of zero, the data member next in the new element will have a value of 0. It will then look as in Figure 12.2.

Assume now that we wish to create a new list element with a value of 3 and place it first in the list. This we do simply by writing:

```
first = new Element(first, 3);
```

This is exactly the same statement that was used earlier to insert the first element! The only difference is that the value 3 has been indicated instead of 5. Since the pointer first points to the element with value 5 before the statement is performed, data member next in the new element will point to the element with value 5. The situation is shown in Figure 12.3.

To get the list in Figure 12.1, we can use the statement again:

```
first = new Element(first, 4);
```

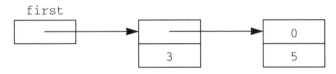

Figure 12.3

Running through a list

If we want to run through all the elements in a list, we can simply start at the first element and continue until the last element is reached. The following statement can be used to write out all the elements in a list:

```
for (Element *p=first; p; p=p->next)
   cout << p->data << ' ';
```

Another pointer p is used here, of type 'pointer to Element' and this is initialized so that it points to the first element in the list. The condition for continuing is p, which may seem rather strange. The condition is 'true' if variable p contains a value not equal to 0, that is, if p does not contain a null pointer. A null pointer is interpreted as the value 'false'. We could also have written p!=0. At every round, p->data is written out. Note that the arrow operator has to be used here, as p is a *pointer* to an object. At the end of every round, the statement p=p->next is performed, thus pointer p will point to the next element in the list. In the last round, p will have a value of 0.

The same technique can be used if we want to search in a list, for instance. The function below searches for a particular value in the list. As parameter, the function gets a pointer to the first element in the list and the value searched for. If this value is in the list, the function gives as result a pointer to the list element where the value is to be found. If it is not in the list, the function gives a null pointer as result.

```
Element *search(Element *first, int searched)
{
  Element *p;
  for (p=first; p and p->data!=searched; p=p->next)
    ;
  return p;
}
```

In the function, p is simply allowed to run through the list until the end (p gets the value 0) or until the value searched for has been found, in which case p will contain a pointer to this list element.

Note that the tests must be performed in the correct order in the **for** statement. We have to test whether p is different from 0 *before* the expression p->data is computed. If this is not done, there will be an execution error when p happens to be the same as 0.

Putting elements into a list and removing them

We have seen from the above that we can easily put a new element first in a list with a single statement. A function can be constructed that does this:

```
void put_first(Element *& first, int d)
{
   first = new Element(first, d);
}
```

If we want to create a list with two elements that contain the values 10 and 20, for example, we can call the function twice:

```
Element *h=0;
put_first(h, 20);
put_first(h, 10);
```

Here we use a pointer with the name h to point to the first element in the list.

The function put_first has two parameters. The last one is the value that will be put in the new list element. The type of the first parameter may look rather strange. Parameter first has the type '*reference* to a pointer to Element'. We know that we have to use a reference parameter if we want to change a parameter's value in a function, and we have to do this here, since the pointer indicated in the call must be changeable. In our example, we have to be able to change the *pointer* h *itself*. It is not sufficient to be able to change what h points to.

Thus it is not difficult to put an element first in a list. To put a new element last in a list is a little more difficult because the whole list has to be run through until the end is reached. The following function creates a new list element and puts it last in the list. We must also have a reference parameter here, since we have to be able to change the pointer itself in case the list has been empty from the beginning.

```
void put_last(Element *& first, int d)
{
   if (not first)
     // Empty list, put in new element first
     first = new Element(0, d);
   else
   {
     Element *p;
     for (p=first; p->next; p=p->next)
       ;
     // p points to the last element now
     // Put in a new element after p
     p->next = new Element(0, d);
   }
}
```

The case of the empty list must be treated separately because in that case the parameter first has to be changed. If the list is not empty, the pointer p is made to run through the whole list until the end has been reached. Note especially that the test condition in the **for** statement is p->next, not p. This means that the **for** statement is terminated when p points to the last element in the list. If the test condition had been p, we would have gone one round too many and p would have got the value 0. When the new list element has been created, the data member next in the previous last element will contain a pointer to the new element. This is why p->next is changed in the last statement.

It is sometimes necessary to place a new element in a particular position in a linked list. Suppose, for example, we have an element in a list and a pointer p is pointing to it. Now suppose we want to put a new element with value 4 *after* this. The new element can then be created and placed in the list with a single statement:

```
p->next = new Element(p->next, 9);
```

Figure 12.4 illustrates this. The dashed line shows the situation before the statement above is executed. If we had wanted to insert a new element in front of a particular element that is pointed to, it would have been much more problematic. Then we would have had to run through the list from the beginning in order to get a pointer to the element in front of the one pointed to.

In certain cases it is simple to remove elements from a list. The first element can be removed with the statement:

```
first = first->next;
```

This is demonstrated in Figure 12.5 where the dashed lines show the situation before the statement is executed. It is also easy to remove the element coming after one to which there is a pointer. For example, we can remove the element that lies after the one that p points to:

```
p->next = p->next->next;
```

It is a little more difficult to remove the last element in a list or a particular element in the list.

Figure 12.4

Figure 12.5

Linked lists and recursion

A list can be seen as a *recursive data type* and it can be said that a list is either empty, or consists of two components, a *head* and a *tail*. The head is the value in the first element of the list (an integer, for instance), and the tail is a list consisting of all the elements except the first. The tail is, therefore, a list that is one element shorter than the original. This perspective can be extremely useful in solving certain problems involving list handling.

We saw above that it is possible to write out the contents of a list by going through the elements of the list from start to finish, using a **for** statement. This was easily done. It would have been much harder if we had wanted them written out in reverse order, with the last element written first, but this problem can be solved elegantly using recursion. The following function will write out a list in reverse order:

```
void write_reverse(Element *first)
{
  if (first)
  {
    write_reverse(first->next);
    cout << first->data << ' ';
  }
}
```

This says that a list can be written out in reverse order if we first write out its tail in reverse order and then write out its head. The list head is first->data and first->next is a pointer to the list tail. An empty list has no elements, and there is nothing to write for such a list.

We have already studied the problem of placing a new element at the end of a list but it can be solved much more simply by using recursion. The following algorithm is used: If the list is empty, then the new element is the list's only element and so is placed at the start of the list, otherwise the new element should be placed at the end of the tail.

```
void put_last_rec(Element *& first, int d)
{
```

```
  if (not first)
    first = new Element(0, d);
  else
    put_last_rec(first->next, d);
}
```

Note that there must be a reference parameter here, since we must be able to change the parameter `first`.

12.1.2   Doubly linked lists

One problem with the lists studied so far is that the whole list has to be run through – using either iteration or recursion – if an element has to be inserted or removed at the end of the list or in front of an element pointed to. If we have to work with a list and these operations are used frequently, it can be appropriate to construct a *doubly linked* list. In such a list, each element contains two pointers, apart from the element's value. One pointer points to the next element in the list, and the other points to the previous element. This is illustrated in Figure 12.6. Such a list is often made circular, as in the figure, by making the forward pointer of the last element point to the first element and the first element's backward pointer point to the last element.

To describe an element in a doubly linked list with values of type **int**, we can use the following class. Apart from the two pointers and the value of the list element, the class contains a constructor with which new list elements can be constructed. This constructor will also function as a default constructor.

```
class Element {
public:
  Element *forward, *backward;
  int data;
  Element(Element *f=0, Element *b=0, int d=0)
    : forward(f), backward(b), data(d) {}
};
```

first

Figure 12.6

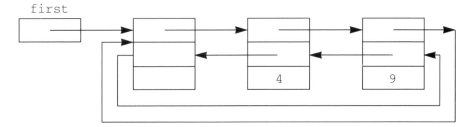

Figure 12.7

When working with linked lists, an empty list must be handled in a special way. This makes functions handling the lists a little longer and more complicated. To avoid this problem, it is useful to let every list have a special element at the start of the list but which does not belong to the list itself. This is particularly useful when handling doubly linked lists. If, for example, we want to represent a list of integers that contains two elements, 4 and 9, we can do this with the list in Figure 12.7. Note that the first element, whose value is of no importance, does not belong to the logical list. If this technique of a special first element is used, the empty list can be described as in Figure 12.8. To build up the structure in this figure, the following statements can be executed:

```
first = new Element;
first->forward = first->backward = first;
```

If we use a special element at the start of the list, the pointer `first` can never be equal to 0 because it will always point to this element. If we want to test whether a list is empty, therefore, there is no point in testing whether `first` is equal to 0. But we can write instead:

```
if (first->forward == first)
```

The advantage of a doubly linked list is that it is never necessary to run through one in order to make changes. The following function, for example, removes an element from a list.

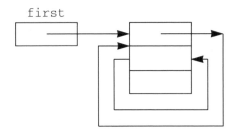

Figure 12.8

```
void remove(Element *e)
{
  e->backward->forward = e->forward;
  e->forward->backward = e->backward;
  delete e;
}
```

The parameter e points to the element to be removed. The first statement in the function means that the forward pointer in the element in front of the element pointed to, will point to the element after the one pointed to. Correspondingly, the second statement means that the backward pointer in the element after the one pointed to, will point to the element in front of the one pointed to. The result is that the element pointed to has been 'linked out' of the list. (We do not need to change the pointers in the target element, since this will be removed in the last statement.) Because there is a special element at the start of the list, it will not matter if the target element is the first, last, or some other element in the list. The code remains the same.

We shall take another example. The following function will insert a new element in front of a given element. The parameter e points to the element in front of which the new element will be put and d is the value the new element will have.

```
void put_previous(Element *e, int d)
{
  Element *pnew = new Element(e, e->backward, d);
  e->backward->forward = pnew;
  e->backward = pnew;
}
```

Memory space is first allocated for the new element, and pointer pnew is set to point to it. The new element is initialized so that the forward pointer gets the value e (thus it will point to the element e points to), and the backward pointer gets the value e->backward (which means that it points to the element in front of the one e points to.) The value in the new element is initialized to d. The new list element is now initialized. It only remains to see that it is linked in the list in the right place. This is done with two statements. The statement e->backward->forward= pnew means that the forward pointer in the element in front of the one e points to, will point to the new element instead; and the statement e->backward=pnew changes the backward pointer in the element e points to, so that it points to the new element.

Note here too, that it is of no importance where in the list the new element is placed.

The function put_previous can now be used to implement the function that puts a new element first in the list:

```
void put_first(Element *first, int d)
{
    put_previous(first->forward, d);
}
```

Note that we must have `first->forward` and not `first`. The new starting point should of course be placed in front of list element number two. The special start element should always remain first in the list. However, inserting a new element after a given element pointed to is a trivial case. We can write the function:

```
void put_after(Element *e, int d)
{
    put_previous(e->forward, d);
}
```

Since the backward pointer in the special first list element points to the last element of the list, it will be a simple matter to insert a new element last in the list. We can also write a function here:

```
void put_last(Element *first, int d)
{
    put_after(first->backward, d);
}
```

If we want to run through a doubly linked list, we do so in the same way as with a singly linked list. When dealing with a circular list, however, the trap of a never-ending round is certainly to be avoided. The following function writes out a doubly linked list that has a special start element:

```
void write(Element *first)
{
    Element *p;
    for (p=first->forward; p!=first; p=p->forward)
        cout << p->data << ' ';
}
```

Note that p is initialized so that it points to the second list element in the first round. Thus we jump over the special start element. Note also the end condition `p!=first`. When p has reached the last node in the list, the forward pointer points to the start element, since the list is circular. If we had tested whether p was equal to 0, the program would have got itself into a never-ending round.

When working with doubly linked lists, there is scarcely any need for recursion because it is as simple to scan a list forwards as in reverse order. If we want to write out a list in reverse order, we can use the following function:

```cpp
void write_reverse(Element *first)
{
  Element *p;
  for (p=first->backward; p!=first; p=p->backward)
    cout << p->data << ' ';
}
```

12.2   Linked lists – applications

In this section we will be constructing classes that define some common abstract data types – stacks, queues and sets. Classes will be implemented making use of linked lists. In Chapter 13, we will demonstrate a general list class that is implemented with a doubly linked list.

12.2.1   Stacks

A *stack* is a data structure that uses the principle 'last in, first out'. A stack can be likened to a pile of plates in a self-service cafeteria. When a new plate is placed in the pile, it is put on top of the plates already there; when we want to take one, we have to take the one at the top of the pile. It is said that the top data element in a stack constitutes the stack's *top*. There are two operations for a stack, *push* and *pop*. The operation *push* places a data element on top of the stack and *pop* removes the top element from the stack. A stack is illustrated in Figure 12.9.

A stack can easily be constructed with a singly linked list. We let the first list element contain the stack's top. A push operation means that a new element is put

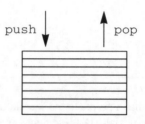

Figure 12.9

first in the list, and a pop operation removes the first element from the list. We can define a class `Stack` and place the definition in a file with the name `stack.h`. We will assume that the data elements to be placed in the stack have type **int**.

```
// File stack.h
#include <stdexcept>
class Element;

class Stack {
public:
  Stack()  : first(0) {};
  ~Stack();
  void push(int d);
  int pop() throw(length_error);
  bool empty();
private:
  Element *first;
  Stack(const Stack&) {};
  Stack& operator= (const Stack&) {};
};
```

There are three operations: `push` and `pop`, as described above, and `empty` which indicates whether or not a stack is empty. If we try to perform the operation `pop` on a stack that is empty, it will generate an exception of the standard class `length_error`. In the declaration of function `pop`, an exception specification is used to state this.

A stack has a single data member, the pointer `first` that points to the first element in a linked list. The default constructor initializes this pointer to 0, which means that every new stack created will be automatically empty from the beginning. There is also a destructor which releases all the allocated list elements.

The last two lines in the private section of class `Stack` are particularly noteworthy. There we define our own versions (which do nothing) of a copy constructor and assignment operator. As we know, there is an automatically defined copy constructor and assignment operator for every class, and these copy the data members one by one. If we do not define our own copy constructor and assignment operator for class `Stack`, the pointer `first` will be copied when one stack is copied to another during an initialization or assignment. This would mean that two different stack objects would point to the *same* linked list, which would, naturally, be quite wrong. By defining our own versions of the assignment operator and copy constructor and placing them in the **private** section, a user will not be allowed to carry out assignments and initializations of stacks. The risk of two stacks pointing to the same list is thus avoided.

Note that the file only contains a *declaration* of class `Element` and not a complete definition. Just as the user of class `Stack` does not need to know how the internal implementation of a stack looks (and should not, either), neither does the definition of class `Element` need to be in the header file. But there must be a definition that says that `Element` is a class, otherwise it would not be possible to declare the data member `first`. We put the definition of class `Element` into the file `stack.cpp`, together with the definitions of the member functions in class `Stack`:

```
// File stack.cpp
class Element {
  friend class Stack;
  Element *next;
  int data;
  Element(Element *n, int d):next(n), data(d) {}
};
void Stack::push(int d)
{
  first = new Element(first, d);
}
int Stack::pop() throw(length_error)
{
  if (empty())
    throw length_error("Stack::pop");
  Element *p=first;
  int d=p->data;
  first = first->next;
  delete p;
  return d;
}
bool Stack::empty()
{
  return not first;
}
Stack::~Stack()
{
  while(not empty())
  {
    Element *p=first;
    first = first->next;
    delete p;
  }
}
```

Class `Element` is defined in the same way as on page 406. The only difference is that all the members have been placed in the **private** section (**private** is understood when nothing to the contrary is stated). Class `Stack` has been indicated as a friend class and, therefore, has access to everything in class `Element`.

The member function `push` in class `Stack` is constructed in the same way as the function `put_first` on page 409, although the reference parameter `first` is not needed here. Instead, function `push` uses the data member `first`, which is, of course, directly visible since `push` is a member function.

The function pop is easy. If the stack is empty, an exception is generated. Otherwise, the first element is linked out of the list, and the value that was found in this element is returned. The memory space occupied by this element is deallocated.

In the destructor there is a **while** statement that is executed until the list is empty. In every round the first element is linked out of the list and the memory space it occupied is released.

The following program demonstrates how class Stack can be used. The program reads a text from the terminal and writes it out in reverse order. (The individual characters that are read have type **char** but they are automatically converted to type **int** when they are put into the stack.)

```
#include "stack.h"
#include <iostream.h>
main()
{
  Stack s;
  char c;
  cout << "Write a text. Finish with Ctrl-Z" << endl;
  while (cin.get(c))
    s.push(c);
  while (not s.empty())
  {
    c = s.pop();
    cout << c;
  }
}
```

12.2.2 Queues

A queue is a data structure that works on the well-known principle 'first in, first out'. We shall let a queue have the operations put_in and take_out. If a linked list is used to implement a queue, all the new elements should be put in last in the list and all the elements taken out of the list should be taken out from the beginning. As we know, it is easy to take out the first element in a singly linked list. It is more difficult to put in a new element last. Iteration or recursion must be used to run through the whole list from the beginning. Since the operation put_in has to be performed often for a queue, this would not be very efficient. An alternative is to use a doubly linked list when, as we know, it becomes an easy matter to put new elements last. The problem with using a doubly linked list is that it is unnecessarily complicated and uses a great deal of memory space since every list element contains two pointers instead of one.

But there is yet another alternative. We shall implement a queue with a singly linked list but besides the usual pointer pointing to the beginning of the list, there will also be a pointer that points to the last element of the list. An illustration of this is shown in Figure 12.10.

first

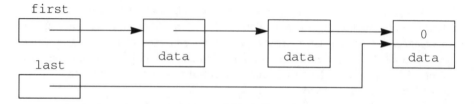

last

Figure 12.10

We will now define a new class `Queue`, in which elements of type **int** can be put in and taken out of queues. We let the pointers `first` and `last` be data members. There are three member functions: `put_in`, `take_out` and `empty`. The last one can be called to test whether or not a queue is empty. The member function `take_out` generates an exception of standard class `length_error` if an attempt is made to take out an element from an empty queue. We put the definition of class `Queue` into a file `queue.h` that looks like this:

```
// File queue.h
#include <stdexcept>

class Element;

class Queue {
public:
  Queue() : first(0), last(0) {};
  ~Queue();
  void put_in(int d);
  int take_out() throw(length_error);
  bool empty();
private:
  Element *first, *last;
  Queue(const Queue&) {};
  Queue& operator= (const Queue&) {};
};
```

In the constructor both the pointers `first` and `last` are set to null pointers, so that all new queues automatically become empty right from the beginning. The destructor goes through the entire linked list and releases all the list elements.

We have put our own versions of the copy constructor and assignment operator in the **private** section. This prevents a user from copying entire queues when initialization and assignment are carried out. (See the description of stacks on page 416.)

In the same way as when we constructed class `Stack`, we only give a *declaration* of the help class `Element` in the header file. The complete definition of class `Element` is given in the file `queue.cpp`. We will put the definitions of the member functions `put_in`, `take_out` and `empty` there as well:

```
// File queue.cpp
#include "queue.h"
class Element {
  friend class Queue;
  Element *next;
  int data;
  Element(Element *n, int d):next(n), data(d) {}
};
void Queue::put_in(int d)
{
  Element *pnew = new Element(0, d);
  if (empty())
    first = pnew;   // The queue was empty, put in first
  else
    last->next = pnew;   // Put in after last
  last = pnew;
}
int Queue::take_out() throw(length_error)
{
  if (empty())
    throw length_error("Queue::take_out");
  Element *p=first;
  int d=p->data;
  first = first->next;
  if (empty())   // The queue was empty
    last = 0;
  delete p;
  return d;
}
bool Queue::empty()
{
  return not first;
}
Queue::~Queue()
{
  while(not empty())
  {
    Element *p=first;
    first = first->next;
    delete p;
  }
}
```

A new element is created in function put_in, and this will be 'linked in' last in the list, that is, normally after the element the pointer last points to. We must also deal with the separate case when the queue was empty before insertion of the new element. In this case, the new element is put first in the list. In both cases, the pointer last will point to the new element after it has been inserted.

We must deal separately, in function `take_out`, with the case that the queue is empty once the first element has been removed. The pointer `last` then gets the value 0.

12.2.3 Sets

The concept of a *set* is often used in theoretical mathematics. We shall demonstrate how sets can be constructed with the aid of linked lists. We can define a class `Set`:

```cpp
// File set.h
class Element;
class Set {
public:
  Set() : first(0) {};
  Set(const Set& s);
  ~Set();
  const Set& operator+= (int d);
  const Set& operator-= (int d);
  const Set& operator= (const Set& s);
  Set operator+ (const Set& s) const;   // union
  Set operator^ (const Set& s) const;   // intersection
  bool empty() const;
  bool member(int d) const;
  bool operator== (const Set& s) const;
  bool operator<= (const Set& s) const;
private:
  Element *first;
  Set(Element *p) : first(p) {};
};
```

We implement a set with the aid of a singly linked list. The class `Set` contains as its only data member a pointer to the first element in the list, and the default constructor initializes this pointer to 0. (There is also a copy constructor and a constructor in the private section but we will be dealing with them later.)

We hide the complete definition of class `Element` in the file `set.cpp` since the user of class `Set` does not need to know what the individual list elements look like. The definition of class `Element` looks like this:

```cpp
class Element {
public:
  Element *next;
  int data;
  Element(Element *n, int d) : next(n), data(d) {}
  ~Element() { delete next; }
};
```

One difference from our previous definition is that we have let all the members be visible. Therefore, it has not been necessary to indicate class Set as a friend class. We have done this because we will be using help functions that are not member functions of class Set, and they will need to know how the list is built up. In spite of everything in class Element being outwardly visible, there is no risk of a user of class Set accessing individual list elements in a Set object. None of the member functions in class Set returns a pointer to a list element.

Another difference in the present class Element is that a destructor has been added. This looks quite simple but, in fact, it releases the memory space for all the elements in the linked list. Let us see how the destructor in class Set is defined:

```
Set::~Set()
{
   delete first;
}
```

When this destructor is called, the first element in the list is released. Then the destructor for class Element will be called for this element. The statement **delete** next is performed, which means that the memory space for element number two is released and the destructor for this element called. This, in turn, releases element number three whose destructor is called, and so on. The destructor in class Element will thus be called recursively until we reach the end of the list. (If the pointer next is equal to 0, nothing is performed in the **delete** statement.)

In this example we will be using recursion for demonstration purposes when we implement the different member functions in class Set. As we saw earlier, recursive functions used in connection with linked lists have pointers to the list elements as parameters. The member functions of class Set do not have any such parameters. Instead, the pointer first to the linked list is a data member. Thus, the member functions cannot be called recursively. Instead, we use a common technique where we make the member functions call recursive help functions internally, letting them do the work. We begin by seeing how the member function for the operator += is constructed. This function adds a new element to the actual set:

```
void add(Element *& p, int d)
{
   if (not p or d < p->data)
      p = new Element(p, d);
   else if (p->data != d)
      add(p->next, d);
}
const Set& Set::operator+= (int d)
{
   add(first, d);
```

```
    return *this;
}
```

A recursive help function called add is used here. Note that this is not a member function but it can still know what class Element looks like because all the data members here have been declared in the **public** section.

We are working with sets that contain integers. A set is implemented with a linked list where there is one list element for each integer in the set. The different integers are placed in the list so that this is *sorted* in order of size, the smaller integers coming first. When a new integer is to be added to a set, the following recursive algorithm can, therefore, be used in the function add: if the list is empty, or if the list is not empty but the new number is less than the list's first number then the new number is placed first in the list. Otherwise, ignore the first number, and put the new number at a suitable place in the list's tail. (If the new number happens to be equal to the first number in the list, nothing at all should be done since the number will then belong to the set already.) Note that the parameter p is a reference parameter since we must be able to change the pointer itself when a new element is put into the list.

The operator - =, which removes an element from a set, can be implemented in the following way:

```
void sub(Element *& p, int d)
{
  if (p and p->data==d)
  {
    Element *q=p;
    p=p->next;
    q->next = 0;   // NB!
    delete q;
  }
  else if (p and p->data < d)
    sub(p->next, d);
}
const Set& Set::operator-= (int d)
{
  sub(first, d);
  return *this;
}
```

If the list is not empty and the integer to be taken out from the set comes first in the list, the first list element will be linked out and its memory space released. Before this is done, we have to make sure that the pointer next has been set to 0. Otherwise, as we know, the destructor for class Element will be called recursively, and all the elements in the rest of the list will be released as well. If the integer to be removed from the set is not first in the list, we check whether the list's first number is less than the number to be removed. If it is, the number (assuming it exists) must be further along the list, in its tail, and we call the function `sub` recursively to remove it.

The next member function we will look at is the assignment operator =. When data structures are implemented using pointers, we almost always have to carry out deep copying if we want to assign one object to another. If we do not define our own assignment operator for class `Set`, the pointer `first` will be copied when we make an assignment. This would mean that different set objects would be able to point to the same linked list. When one set is copied to another, all the list elements have to be copied one by one so that a new list is built up. The old list then has to be wiped out.

```
Element *copy(Element *p)
{
   if (not p)
      return 0;
   else
      return new Element(copy(p->next), p->data);
}
const Set& Set::operator= (const Set& s)
{
   if (first != s.first)   // to itself?
   {
      delete first;
      first = copy(s.first);
   }
   return *this;
}
```

A recursive help function `copy` is used here to do the copying. It can also be used when we implement the copy constructor. Deep copying must also be done here:

```
Set::Set(const Set& s)
{
   first = copy(s.first);
}
```

The member function `member` checks whether a particular integer belongs to the set. We use a help function with the name `exists`. The number searched for is in the list if it is in the first list element or the tail of the list:

```
bool exists(Element *p, int d)
{
```

```
      return (p and p->data==d) or
             (p and exists(p->next, d));
  }
bool Set::member(int d) const
{
    return exists(first, d);
}
```

To be able to define the operator == which checks whether two sets are equal, we write a help function with the name equal that uses the following recursive idea: two lists are equal if they are both empty; if they are not both empty, then they are equal if their first elements are equal and their tails are equal.

```
bool equal(Element *p1, Element *p2)
{
    return (not p1 and not p2) or
           (p1 and p2 and p1->data == p2->data and
            equal(p1->next, p2->next));
}
bool Set::operator== (const Set& s) const
{
    return equal(first, s.first);
}
```

Two operations commonly performed on sets are *union* and *intersection*. The union of two sets s1 and s2 is a new set that contains all the elements that are *either* in s1 or s2. An intersection is a new set that contains all the elements that are *both* in s1 and s2. In class Set we have declared the two operations + and ^ which compute a union and an intersection, respectively. We begin by defining the operator +. To implement this operator, we use a recursive help function, uni. This gets a pointer to two linked lists and gives as result a new list that contains the union of elements in the lists:

```
Element *uni(Element *p1, Element *p2)
{
  if (not p1 and not p2)
    return 0;
  else
    if (not p2 or (p1 and p1->data < p2->data))
      return new Element(uni(p1->next,p2), p1->data);
    else if (not p1 or (p2 and p2->data < p1->data))
      return new Element(uni(p1,p2->next), p2->data);
    else  // Same first element
      return new Element(uni(p1->next, p2->next),
                         p1->data);
}
```

```
Set Set::operator+ (const Set& s) const
{
   return Set(uni(first, s.first));
}
```

The function uni uses the following algorithm: if both lists are empty, their union is empty; otherwise, we check the first element in each list and choose the list whose first data element is smallest. This element will be in the union, so a new list element is created that will contain this data element. The tail in the new list will be the same as the union of the rest of the lists. If the two lists should have the same first element, this element will only be included once in the new list. If one list is empty and not the other, we choose the first element in the list that is not empty and let this be included in the union.

In the definition of the operator +, the function uni is called, and this gives as result a linked list that contains the elements to be included in the union set. The constructor that is declared in the **private** section of class Set is used to initialize the new set object to be given as result.

The next operator we will look at is the operator ^ that computes the intersection of two sets. The operator ^ is implemented according to the same model as the operator +. A recursive help function, inter, is used. Function inter gets pointers to the two linked lists as parameters. As result it gives a new list containing the elements included in both lists. A set that contains this list is given as result in the operator ^. We give the definitions here:

```
Element *inter(Element *p1, Element *p2)
{
   if (not p1 or not p2)
      return 0;
   else if (p1->data == p2->data)
      return new Element(inter(p1->next, p2->next),
                         p1->data);
   else if (p1->data < p2->data)
      return inter(p1->next, p2);
   else
      return inter(p1, p2->next);
}
Set Set::operator^ (const Set& s) const
{
   return Set(inter(first, s.first));
}
```

Function inter first checks if one of the two lists is empty. If so, a value of 0 is returned, since no common element can be found in the lists. If neither of the lists is empty, a test is made to see whether the two first elements are equal. If they are, a list element with the value of these list elements will be included in the result. If not, we jump over the smallest of these two elements and compute the intersection of the remaining elements.

The only member function that remains to be defined is the operator <= which checks whether the left operand is a subset of the right. This can be done using the member functions we have already constructed. We can check whether a set s1 is a subset of another set s2 by forming the intersection of s1 and s2. If the intersection is the same as s1, then s1 only contains such elements as can be found in s2, that is, s1 is a subset of s2. We can now define the operator <=.

```
bool Set::operator<= (const Set& s) const
{
  return (*this ^ s) == *this;
}
```

12.3 Iterators

In the three classes Stack, Queue and Set we constructed in the last section, there are operations that we can use to add or remove individual data elements in a collection. What is lacking in all three classes, however, are operations that run through all the elements in a collection. For instance, we might want to write out all the values that belong to a particular set, or that are in a particular stack. We might also like to have operations that allow the user to change some data element in a collection. We cannot, for example, find a certain value in a queue and replace this with another one. Naturally, it is possible to extend the classes that we have with member functions that make it possible to do these things. There is, however, an important method of doing these operations and this is the one that uses iterators.

An *iterator* is a separate object similar to a pointer, that can be connected to a collection of data, a stack for instance, or a set. An iterator can refer to a particular element in a collection. It might be helpful to compare its operation with how an ordinary pointer points to a particular element in an array. When we run through a collection of data with an iterator, it is as though this collection were a simple array and the iterator were a pointer to it. An iterator has the two operations ++ and -- which send it forwards or backwards in a collection and the * operator which gives the data element the iterator refers to. An iterator can thus be used as a cursor that points out a certain position in the collection where an element is to be read, updated, inserted or removed. Collections of data, regardless of how they are implemented, can be handled uniformly when we use iterators. For example, if a queue is scanned using an iterator it makes no difference to a user whether the queue is implemented as a linked list, an array, or in some other way. Another advantage when using iterators is that several independent scans of the same data collection can be made at the same time. There are iterators that can run through a data collection in different ways. For instance, you can run through a queue from the beginning to the end at the same time as you run through it backwards from the end to the beginning.

In the draft standard for C++ there are a number of ready-made classes, lists and sets, for instance, and these classes make consistent use of iterators. To be able to use these standard classes, we have to understand how iterators function. We will be showing examples of iterators which function in the same way as the ones in the standard classes given in the draft standard. In this section we will construct iterators that make it possible to run through a set, then in Chapter 13 we shall construct a generic class that defines lists. This class uses iterators and is built up in exactly the same way as class `List` in the draft standard.

We begin by completing class `Set` with an iterator class. We will call the new class `Iterator`. Since the new class will go together intimately with class `Set`, its definition is placed *inside* the definition of class `Set`. The complete name of the new class is thus `Set::Iterator`. Before we go into detail, we will show an example of how class `Iterator` can be used. We write an output operator `<<` for class `Set` which can be used in the same way as the output operator for other types. Now suppose that we have defined a variable s of type `Set` and that s contains the numbers 5, 12 and 19. We can then have the statement:

```
cout << s << endl;
```

and we get written out:

```
[5, 12, 19]
```

The function **operator**`<<` has the following appearance. Note that it is not a member function:

```
ostream& operator<< (ostream& os, const Set& s)
{
  bool first=true;
  Set::Iterator it;
  os << '[';
  for(it=s.begin(); it!=s.end(); ++it)
  {
    if (not first)
      os << ", ";
    os << *it;
    first = false;
  }
  os << ']';
  return os;
};
```

The function gets as parameter the set s that should be written out. An iterator with the name it is declared in the third line, and in the **for** statement two new member functions – begin and end – are called. Function begin gives as result an iterator that refers to the first element in the set. Function end also gives an iterator as result. This does not refer to the set's last element, as we might think, but to an imagined first element that lies just *outside* the set. (This can be compared to an array. Suppose that we have declared an array m[10]. Then the expression m is a pointer to the array's first element and the expression m+10 is a pointer to the first element that lies outside the array.) In the **for** statement, the variable it is initialized to s.begin(). The condition to continue for another round is that the iterator it is not the same as s.end(). To make the iterator it go forward so that it refers to the next element in the set, the operator ++ is used. The operator * is employed inside the **for** statement to access the data element the iterator it refers to. Thus, with the aid of an iterator we can handle a set in the same way as if it were an ordinary array. We do not need to know how the set is implemented.

Now it is time to look at the definition of class Iterator. As we explained, it lies inside the definition of class Set. We also add the two new member functions begin and end for class Set:

```
class Set {
public:
  class Iterator {
  public:
    Iterator() : point(0) {};
    bool operator== (const Iterator& i) const
                      {return point == i.point;}
    bool operator!= (const Iterator& i) const
                      {return point != i.point;}
    const int& operator* () const
                                  throw(out_of_range);
    Iterator& operator++ ()    throw(out_of_range);
    Iterator operator++ (int) throw(out_of_range);
  private:
    friend class Set;
    Element *point;
    Iterator(Element *e) : point(e) {};
  };

  Iterator begin() const {return Iterator(first);}
  Iterator end()   const {return Iterator(0);}
  as before
};
```

No further changes need to be made to class Set. Class Iterator has only one data member, the pointer point, which points to an individual list element in the linked list a set is built up from. The default constructor for class Iterator sets point to 0. If we have an iterator it and a set s and write the statement:

```
it = s.begin();
```

then the data member `point` in `it` will point to the first list element in the set `s`. This follows since function `begin` returns an iterator object where `point` is initialized to the value `first`. Function `end` correspondingly returns an iterator object where `point` has the value 0.

There is both a prefix and a postfix version of the operator `++`. Both versions move the pointer `point` forward so that it comes to point to the next list element for the actual set. If we reach the end of the list, that is, if `point` is equal to 0 and we try to perform one of the operators `++`, an exception will be generated. Note that the complete class name, `Set::Iterator`, must be given when the member functions are defined.

```
// prefix ++i
Set::Iterator& Set::Iterator::operator++ ()
     throw(out_of_range)
{
  if (not point)
    throw out_of_range("Iterator::operator++");
  point = point->next;
  return *this;
}
```

```
// postfix i++
Set::Iterator Set::Iterator::operator++ (int)
             throw(out_of_range)
{
  Iterator temp = *this;   // Keep the old value
  ++ (*this);              // Move forward
  return temp;             // Return the old value
}
```

The operator `*` is used to access the data element an iterator refers to. This operator is constructed as a member function, **operator***. As result it gives a reference to the integer that is in the list element the iterator refers to. Note that the result is a reference to a *constant* integer. This means that the operator `*` cannot be used to change an individual element in a set. Only its value can be read. (If we want to change something in a set, we should use the operators `+=` and `-=` as before, to add or remove elements from the set.) If the actual iterator does not refer to a list element, an exception is generated. The definition of the operator `*` is then

```
const int& Set::Iterator::operator* () const
             throw(out_of_range)
{
```

```
  if (not point)
    throw out_of_range("Iterator::operator*");
  return point->data;
}
```

If we construct an iterator for another collection of data where we want individual elements to be changeable, a queue for example, we can let the operator * return a reference to a value that can be changed. The word **const** will then not be in the return type.

Apart from the member functions mentioned previously, class Iterator has a copy constructor and the two operators == and != which test whether two iterators are equal or unequal.

It may seem as though this is an unnecessarily complicated mechanism for writing out the contents of a set. Might it not have been easier to let the output operator << be a friend function to class Set? Then individual elements in a set could have been accessed directly without the use of an iterator. This is true of course but the whole point of using iterators is that they offer a general method that can be used in different contexts. Where sets are concerned, it is not necessarily the case, for instance, that we will always want to write one out in the format [5, 12, 19]. As an example, we will show a program that reads in two lines from the terminal. The program then writes out which characters occur in one of the lines and which characters occur in both of the lines. The program uses two sets, s1 and s2. All the characters in the first line are placed in s1, and all of those in the second line are placed in s2. After this the union set and the intersection of the two sets are computed.

```
#include <iostream.h>
#include "set.h"
main()
{
  Set s1, s2;
  char line1[200], line2[200], *p;
  cout << "Write two lines" << endl;
  cin.getline(line1, 200);
  cin.getline(line2, 200);
  for (p=line1; *p; p++)
    s1 += *p;
  for (p=line2; *p; p++)
    s2 += *p;
  cout << "Characters in one of the lines:" << endl;
  Set s3 = s1 + s2;
  Set::Iterator it(s3.begin());
  while(it != s3.end())
    cout << char(*it++);
  cout << endl;
  cout << "Characters in both lines:" << endl;
  s3 = s1 ^ s2;
```

```
    it = s3.begin();
    while(it != s3.end())
      cout << char(*it++);
    cout << endl;
}
```

Here is an example of how the output might look when the program is run.

```
Write two lines
C++ From the Beginning
The Road to C
   Characters in one of the lines:
   +BCFRTadeghimnort
   Characters in both lines:
   Cehot
```

12.4   Trees

In the section on doubly linked lists we saw that each element could have two pointers. There is, naturally, no limit on the number of pointers in each element, and these pointers do not need to point in such a way as to define a linked list. Using pointers, it is possible to build up data structures with elements that are connected arbitrarily. In this section we shall study *trees*. A tree is shown in Figure 12.11.

The elements of a tree are usually called *nodes*. The topmost node is called the tree's *root*. (It is usual to draw and think of a tree in an upside-down position compared with the real thing.) From the root there can be pointers to other nodes in the tree but there can never be pointers to the root from any of the tree's nodes. In general, there are only pointers 'downwards' from each node in the tree. To each node there is only one path from the root. (For example, in Figure 12.11 it is only

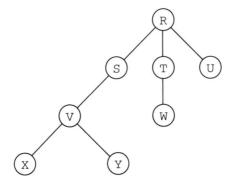

Figure 12.11

Trees

- A *root* is a node that no other node in the tree points to.
- To any one node there is a *unique* path from the root.
- The nodes that do not have pointers to other nodes are called *leaves*.

---

possible to take path R-S-V-Y to get to the node Y.) Thus, there may only be one pointer to any one node. If a node A points to a node B in a tree, the node B is said to be the *child* of A and A is said to be the *parent* of B. The root is the only node that is without a parent. The nodes that have no children, X, Y, W and U in the figure, are usually called *leaves*, and the pointers in the tree are sometimes called *arcs*.

12.4.1 Binary trees

In the tree in Figure 12.11 the nodes have up to three children. We shall limit ourselves, however, to trees in which a node can have at most two children. Such trees are common in the construction of data structures, and they are generally called *binary trees*. An example of a binary tree is shown in Figure 12.12.

In C++ a node in a binary tree can be defined by a class:

```
class Node {
public:
    int data;
    Node *left, *right;
    Node(int d=0, Node *l=0, Node *r=0)
        : data(d), left(l), right(r) {}
};
```

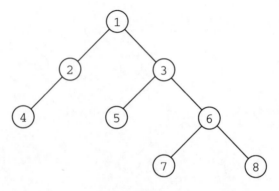

Figure 12.12

For simplicity's sake, we let all the declarations lie in the **public** section of the class. Each node has a data member that defines the contents of the node and two pointers that point to the node's left and right children, respectively. In addition, there is a constructor which initializes all the data members. In our example, the data part consists of an integer but this can easily be generalized so that it is any information at all. If a node is lacking a child, the corresponding pointer has a value of 0. In a leaf, both pointers are equal to 0. The tree in Figure 12.12 can be built up as indicated in Figure 12.13. A special pointer root points to the root of the tree so that the whole tree can be accessed. If we have an empty tree (a tree with no nodes), then root has the value 0.

Suppose that we have declared a variable root:

```
Node *root;
```

and want to build up a tree according to Figure 12.14. We can write the statements:

```
root = new Node;
root->data = 10;
root->left = new Node;
root->right = new Node;
root->left->data = 20;
root->right->data = 30;
```

Or, we can use a single statement

```
root = new Node(10, new Node(20), new Node(30));
```

Figure 12.13

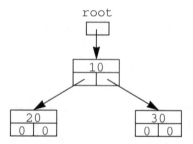

Figure 12.14

The nodes that lie to the left of the root can be considered as a new, smaller tree, with the left child of the root as its root. This tree is said to be the *subtree* of the original tree. In the same way, the nodes to the right of the root form a right subtree. This is illustrated in Figure 12.15. (For example, the left subtree in Figure 12.12 has node 2 as its root and comprises nodes 2 and 4. The right subtree has node 3 as its root and comprises nodes 3, 5, 6, 7 and 8.)

With the aid of subtrees, a tree can be regarded as a recursive data type, and the following definition can be given:

> A binary tree is either
> empty (has no nodes)
> or consists
> of a root, a left subtree and a right subtree.

This concept is useful in the design of programs for handling trees. We shall start by studying how to visit all the nodes of a given tree. We assume that we have a pointer `root` which points to the root of the tree. When we considered linked lists, it was natural to visit all the elements starting at the beginning and running through to the end but it is not that simple with a tree. It is possible to think of several alternative ways of traversing a tree. If we look at the tree in Figure 12.12, for example, we may think of visiting the nodes in the order, 1-2-3-4-5-6-7-8.

Figure 12.15

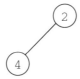

Figure 12.16

However, to write a program for this (level by level) is rather difficult. It is much simpler and more common to apply the three visiting orders – *preorder*, *inorder* and *postorder* – which are defined recursively. Let us start with the most common, *inorder*:

If the tree is not empty, then:

    (1)   Visit the tree's left subtree.
    (2)   Visit the tree's root.
    (3)   Visit the tree's right subtree.

      We shall now try to apply this visiting order to the tree in Figure 12.12. First we note that the tree is not empty and so the three stages of the algorithm should be carried out. The first stage, 'visit the tree's left subtree', means that the tree in Figure 12.16 should be visited. Since this is also a tree, the visiting algorithm (second instance) should be applied. The tree is not empty and so we carry out stage 1, that is, the subtree in Figure 12.17 is visited. We now apply a third instance of the algorithm. Since the tree is not empty, we carry out the first stage, 'visit the left subtree'; this means that we have to apply a fourth instance of the algorithm. This time the tree to be visited is empty because node 4 has an empty left subtree and the fourth instançe of the algorithm thus does nothing. We return to the third instance of the algorithm and carry out its second stage, 'visit the tree's root'. This means that node 4 is visited. The third stage, 'visit the tree's right subtree', starts a fifth instance of the algorithm, which does nothing because the right subtree is empty. Now all the stages of the third instance of the algorithm have been carried out, and we return to the second instance. We carry out the second stage, 'visit the tree's root', for the tree in Figure 12.16. Thus node 2 gets a visit.
      Since the tree in Figure 12.16 has an empty right subtree, nothing happens when a sixth instance of the algorithm is carried out, and we return eventually to the

            ④

Figure 12.17

first instance of the algorithm. We carry out the second stage, which means that the root of the original tree, node 1, is visited. Now we have visited nodes 4, 2 and 1, in that order, and continue by applying the algorithm in the same way to the right subtree. We eventually find that all the nodes in the tree are visited, in the order 4 - 2 - 1 - 5 - 3 - 7 - 6 - 8.

The following recursive function visits and writes out the contents of the nodes of a binary tree according to the *inorder* principle. The function gets a pointer to the root of the tree as parameter.

```
void inorder(Node *p)
{
  if (p)
  {
    inorder(p->left);
    cout << p->data << ' ';
    inorder(p->right);
  }
}
```

The functions for the other two visiting orders can be constructed in a similar way. The only difference is that the three stages in the algorithm already studied are rearranged. In the visiting order *preorder*, the value in the root is written out before the subtree is visited. We then get:

```
void preorder(Node *p)
{
  if (p)
  {
    cout << p->data << ' ';
    preorder(p->left);
    preorder(p->right);
  }
}
```

In the visiting order *postorder*, the value in the root is written out after the subtree has been visited. Function `postorder` can then be written:

```
void postorder(Node *p)
{
  if (p)
  {
    postorder(p->left);
```

```
    postorder(p->right);
    cout << p->data << ' ';
  }
}
```

As we see, the algorithms for trees are naturally expressed using recursion. We shall now study a function that evaluates the *depth* of a binary tree. The function takes a pointer to the root of the tree as parameter. The depth of a tree can be defined as the number of nodes on the longest path from the tree's root to a leaf. An empty tree has depth 0, and a tree that consists of only a root has depth 1. We write the function:

```
int depth(Node *p)
{
  if (not p)
    return 0;
  else
  {
    int ldepth = depth(p->left);
    int rdepth = depth(p->right);
    if (ldepth > rdepth)
      return ldepth + 1;
    else
      return rdepth + 1;
  }
}
```

The simplest case is if the tree is empty. The function then returns the value 0 as its result. If the tree is not empty, the depths of the left and right subtrees are evaluated separately and saved in the variables ldepth and rdepth. The function depth is called recursively to evaluate these depths, with pointers to the respective subtrees as parameter. The function returns the depth of the deepest subtree plus 1 (the root itself) as its result.

12.4.2 Binary search trees

We shall now study a special form of binary tree, a *binary search tree*. The value of each node in such a tree is greater than the values of all the nodes in its left subtree and less than or equal to the values of the nodes in its right subtree. The tree in Figure 12.18 is an example of a binary search tree.

A binary search tree has the property that, if the principle of *inorder* is used to traverse the tree, the nodes will be visited in order of size. The nodes in the tree in Figure 12.18 will be visited in the order $1-3-4-5-6-7-7-8-9$. A binary search tree can be used when information has to be found quickly. Let us study the example of a binary search tree in which each node contains information about a person. Each node stores a person's name and membership number. We define class Node

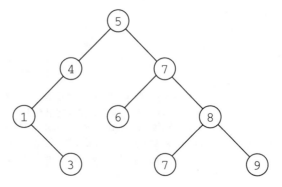

Figure 12.18

below. Apart from its data members, the class contains a constructor that makes it possible to initialize all the data members. This constructor can also serve as a default constructor:

```
class Node {
public:
  int memno;
  char name[20];
  Node *left, *right;
  Node(int mem=0, char *n=0, Node *l=0, Node *r=0)
    : memno(id), left(l), right(r)
    {strcpy(name, n);}
};
```

We can use the following function to find the node in the tree which contains the information about a particular person. The function has two parameters, a pointer to the tree and a membership number for the required person. As result, the function returns a pointer to the node in which the information about the person is stored. If the person sought is not found in the tree, the function returns as result the value 0.

```
Node *search(Node *p, int searched)
{
  if (not p)
    return 0;
  else if (searched == p->memno)
    return p;
  else if (searched < p->memno)
    return search(p->left, searched);
  else
    return search(p->right, searched);
}
```

The search works as follows. First it checks to see whether the tree is empty and, if so, a result of 0 is returned because there are no entries in the tree. If the root contains the person sought then the task is easy: the result is simply a pointer to the root. In other cases it must look further into one of the subtrees. The particular subtree depends on whether the membership number required is smaller or greater than the membership number in the root. This further searching is achieved by calling the function search recursively with a pointer to the left or right subtree as parameter.

To remove nodes in such a way that the tree remains a binary search tree is somewhat complicated (see Exercise 12.16). However, to insert new nodes is simple, and we will finish by showing a function for placing information about a new person into a binary search tree. As parameters, the function gets a pointer to the root of the tree and the new person's membership number and name. The procedure will create a new node for the new person and insert it in the correct place in the tree so that it remains a binary search tree:

```
void put_in(Node *& p, int new_mem, char *new_name)
{
  if (not p)
    p = new Node(new_mem, new_name);
  else if (new_mem < p->memno)
    put_in(p->left, new_mem, new_name);
  else
    put_in(p->right, new_mem, new_name);
}
```

If the tree is empty, it is easy to insert the entry in the right place. The new node is then the root of the tree, and the pointer p is set to point to this node. Notice that the parameter p must be a reference parameter because it must be both read and updated. If the tree is not empty, a choice must be made as to whether to insert the new node in the left or right subtree, depending on whether the new person's membership number is smaller or greater than the membership number in the root of the tree.

12.4.3 A tree class

All the functions we have used for handling trees so far have had a pointer to a node as parameter. For instance, we can make the call inorder(root) to write out the tree the pointer root points to. This way of doing things is not in the object-oriented spirit of C++. For a C++ programmer it would have been more natural if there had been a class Tree. A variable t of type Tree could then have been declared and a call made of a member function for class Tree. We should then be able to write:

```
Tree t;
...
t.inorder();
```

Is it not then possible to refashion class Node so that the different functions, inorder, for example, could be member functions instead of independent functions? Surely we could then rename class Node and call it Tree instead? Unfortunately this is not possible. The main reason is that certain operations on trees, for instance, writing out trees and inserting new nodes, we must also be able to perform on empty trees. So empty tree objects must be able to exist. So far, we have represented empty trees by a null pointer of type 'pointer to Node' but it is not possible to apply member functions to a null pointer. If we want to have a class that defines trees, we have to go about it in a different way. In this section we will show how this can be done.

We shall define a new class with the name Tree. The class will have a single data member, a pointer to the root of the tree. This pointer is of type 'pointer to Node'. An empty tree can then be represented by a tree object where this pointer has the value 0. We will also change the definition of class Node. The type for the two pointers left and right will be changed from 'pointer to Node' to 'pointer to Tree'. This is in line with our observation that a tree is a recursive data type. A tree is either empty or it has a root and two subtrees. To demonstrate the new structure, we have redrawn the tree in Figure 12.14, and Figure 12.19 shows how it now looks. We see that we need an extra pointer inserted between each node. At the bottom there are four leaves. These are empty trees and are represented by null pointers.

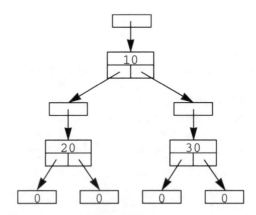

Figure 12.19

We begin by redefining class Node:

```
class Node {
  friend class Tree;
```

```
   int data;
   Tree *left, *right;
   Node(int d);
   ~Node();
};
```

Thus, the type for the pointers `left` and `right` has been changed. The constructor has changed and a destructor has been added. Since **private** is understood here, everything is invisible from outside except for class `Tree`, which is declared as a friend class. The definition of class `Tree` has the following appearance:

```
class Tree {
public:
   Tree() : root(0) {};
   Tree(int d) {root=new Node(d);};
   Tree(const Tree& t) {copy(t);};
   ~Tree() {delete root;};
   bool empty() const {return not root;};
   int& value() const throw(range_error)
                {check(); return root->data;}
   Tree& l_child() const throw(range_error)
                     {check(); return *root->left;};
   Tree& r_child() const throw(range_error)
                     {check(); return *root->right;};
   Tree& operator= (const Tree&);
   bool operator== (const Tree&) const;
   void inorder() const;
private:
   Node *root;
   void check() const
              {if (empty()) throw range_error("Tree");}
   void copy(const Tree& t);
};
```

There are three constructors. The first is a default constructor which constructs an empty tree, that is, the pointer root is set to 0. The second is a constructor that constructs a tree consisting only of a root. This constructor calls the constructor of class `Node` and has the definition:

```
Node::Node(int d)
: data(d), left(new Tree), right(new Tree) {}
```

Since the pointers `left` and `right` are initialized with the aid of the default constructor for class `Tree`, a new node will be initialized so that its two child trees are empty.

The third constructor for class `Tree` is a copy constructor that creates a tree which is a copy of another tree. The private member function `copy` is called to carry out the copying itself. We will return to this.

There is a destructor for class `Tree`. The only thing that this does is to perform the statement **delete** root. If the pointer `root` is equal to 0, nothing happens. Otherwise the node that `root` points to is deallocated. In addition, the destructor for class `Node` is called, and this has the simple definition:

```
Node::~Node()
{delete left; delete right;}
```

Here the destructor for class `Tree` will be called both for the left and the right subtree. This means that the destructor is called recursively for all the subtrees until the leaves are reached, and here the pointer root will be equal to 0. All subtrees and nodes will, therefore, be deallocated.

The member function `empty`, which checks whether a tree is empty, is easy to implement. We only have to see if the pointer `root` is equal to 0 or not.

The three member functions `value`, `l_child` and `r_child` give as result references to a tree's root value and the left and right subtree, respectively. For these functions to return a value, the actual tree must not be empty. If the tree is empty, the three functions will generate an exception. A check is made in the private member function with the name `check`.

Two operators have been defined for class `Tree`, an assignment operator that assigns a copy of a tree to another tree and a comparison operator, which tests whether two trees are equal. We begin by studying the implementation of the assignment operator:

```
void Tree::copy(const Tree& t)
{
  if (t.empty())
    root = 0;
  else
  {
    root = new Node(t.value());
    l_child().copy(t.l_child());
    r_child().copy(t.r_child());
  }
}

Tree& Tree::operator= (const Tree& t)
{
  if (root != t.root)   // to itself?
  {
    delete root;
    copy(t);
```

```
    }
    return *this;
}
```

The assignment operator first tests whether an assignment to itself is involved. If this is the case, nothing at all is done. In any other case the whole of the old tree is released. The private help function `copy` is then called to carry out copying. (This function is also called by the copy constructor.) Function `copy` is recursive. If the tree `t` to be copied is empty, then it is simple. The pointer `root` simply has to be equal to 0 in the actual tree as well. If tree `t` is not empty, the actual tree should have a root that is a copy of the root of tree `t`. A new node, initialized with the value in the root of `t`, is therefore allocated. The constructor for class `Node` sees to it that the two child trees are empty from the beginning. The two child trees in `t` must then be copied. We should not write:

```
root->left=t->root->left;      // ERROR!
root->right=t->root->right;    // ERROR!
```

Then the actual tree would point to the *same* two subtrees as `t`, which would mean that the actual tree would be changed if `t` were changed and vice versa. Instead, we also have to copy the subtrees, which is done by calling the function recursively for the two subtrees.

   The comparison operator is somewhat simpler. Two trees are equal if they are both empty or, if they are not, if they have the same root value, their left subtrees are equal and their right subtrees are equal. Making use of this, we can define the comparison operator. Recursion is also used here.

```
bool Tree::operator== (const Tree& t) const
{
   return (empty() and t.empty()) or
          (not empty() and not t.empty() and
           value() ==t.value() and
           l_child() ==t.l_child() and
           r_child() ==t.r_child());
}
```

   The last member function to be defined is the function `inorder`, which writes out the contents of a tree. This can be easily implemented with the help of the other member functions:

```
void Tree::inorder() const
{
   if (not empty())
   {
```

```
        l_child().inorder();
        cout << value() << ' ';
        r_child().inorder();
    }
}
```

We conclude by demonstrating how class `Tree` can be used to build up and write out the tree in Figure 12.9.

```
Tree t;
t=Tree(10);
t.l_child()=Tree(20);
t.r_child()=Tree(30);
t.inorder();
```

EXERCISES

12.1 A queue of cars is to be described using a linked list. Write the part of a program that creates a list describing a queue of three cars. For each car, the registration number, make and year should be stored.

12.2 Write a function to evaluate the length of a linked list.

12.3 Assume you have a linked list in which the data part of each element contains an integer. Write a function to determine whether the list is sorted.

12.4 A register of club members has been built up in the form of a linked list. Each member is represented by an element in the list, in which the name, address and telephone number are stored. The list is sorted alphabetically according to the member's name. Write a procedure to insert a new member into the list, so that the list remains sorted.

12.5 Write a function that gets a pointer to a singly linked list `l` as parameter. As its result, the function should return a pointer to the new list containing copies of all the elements of `l` but in reverse order.

12.6 In Exercise 8.9, a class `Polynomial` was constructed using an array. The exercise here is to implement class `Polynomial` with the aid of a linked list, where each element in the list corresponds to a term in the polynomial.

12.7 A sparse matrix is one in which most of the elements are zero. To save storage space, such a matrix can be represented as a linked list. In the list there is one element for each non-zero matrix element containing its line and column members and its value. Write a function that gets a sparse matrix in the normal format (a two-dimensional array) as a parameter. Assume that all the elements in the matrix are integers. The function should create a list to represent the sparse matrix. The result of the function should be a pointer to the list.

12.8 Write a procedure that swaps two neighbouring elements in a doubly linked list. The procedure should take as parameter a pointer to the first of the two elements to be swapped.

12.9 Complete class `Queue` in Section 12.2.2 with an iterator class which makes it possible to read and update individual elements in a queue.

12.10 Rewrite class `Queue` in Section 12.2.2 so that a doubly linked list is used to represent the queue. In addition, construct an iterator class that allows the queue to be scanned forwards and in reverse order.

12.11 Rewrite class `Set` in Section 12.2.3 so that a doubly linked list is used to represent the set.

12.12 Write a function to count the number of leaves in a binary tree.

12.13 A binary tree can be used to represent an arithmetic expression. The expression:

$$\frac{2 \times 3}{8 - 4} + 1$$

can, for example, be represented by the tree in Figure 12.20. The value of the binary tree can be defined as the value obtained when the corresponding expression is evaluated. The nodes can be defined by a class that contains the pointers to the two child trees, and we can let this have different subclasses for the different kinds of nodes involved. Make the class definitions necessary to describe an arithmetic expression in this way, and write a function that calculates the value of a given binary tree.

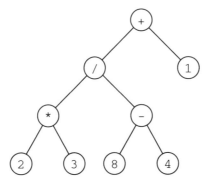

Figure 12.20

12.14 Two binary trees can be said to be reflections of one another if: (1) both are empty, or (2) both are non-empty, their roots contain the same information, and the right subtree of one is the reflection of the left subtree of the other and vice versa. Write a function that determines whether the two trees are reflections of one another.

12.15 Write a program that reads in a text from a text file and computes how many times different words appear in the text. Use a binary search tree to store the words read together with a counter. Each time a new word has been read from the text file, search to see whether it already appears in the search tree. If it does, increase the word's counter by one. Otherwise, create a new node for the word and insert this node in the correct place in the tree. The program should finish by writing out all the words that have appeared, in alphabetical order, together with the number of times they appeared.

12.16 It is not very difficult to insert a new node into a binary search tree. To remove a node is a little harder. The following algorithm can be applied:

> Call the node to be removed P.
>
> If P is a leaf, set the pointer in P's parent that points to P to 0.
>
> If P has a left child but no right child, let P's parent point to P's left child instead of pointing to P.
>
> If P has a right child but no left child, let P's parent point to P's right child instead of pointing to P.
>
> Otherwise, find the node Q in P's right subtree with the smallest value data part.
>
> Copy the data part of Q to the node P and remove node Q.

Note that the last step is recursive, since we can apply the algorithm to remove node Q.

Write a procedure to remove a given node from a binary search tree.

12.17 Complete the tree class in Section 12.4.3 with suitable member functions so that it can be used to handle binary search trees.

13 Templates

When handling programs, there is almost always a need to be able to have collections that consist of several objects. The different objects in such classes can either all have the same type – when we speak of *homogeneous object collections* – or they can be of different type, in which case they are called *heterogeneous object collections*. Arrays can be used to construct object collections but as we saw in the previous chapter, other constructions can also be used. Lists, stacks and trees can be used, for instance. A class that can be used to construct object collections is called a *container class*. The classes that we studied in Chapter 12 – classes `Stack`, `Queue` and `Set` – are all examples of container classes. The problem with these container classes, however, is that they can only be used to construct collections where the different objects have type `int`. If we should want to construct a queue, for instance, with an object of class `Person`, we could not use class `Queue`. Naturally, it is easy to use class `Queue` as a model for the construction of a new class `Person_Queue`; it is simply a matter of changing type `int` to type `Person` in a few places in the class. But this is an inefficient way of working and means that we would have to construct a new queue class for every element type.

C++ offers instead the possibility of using what are called *generic classes*. A *template* is written for the class, and the compiler automatically generates the different classes required from this template. The class does not have to be written more than once. If, for instance, a class template

449

called `List` has been constructed, the compiler can, with this information, generate the classes `List<int>` and `List<Person>`, which describe a list of integers and a person list, respectively.

We can also construct *generic functions*. If we want to construct a function that sorts an array, for instance, we can write a *function template*. The compiler can then use this to automatically generate functions which can sort different kinds of arrays.

Templates have not always been a part of C++. Inheritance used to be used to construct object collections. If we wanted to construct a list of persons, for instance, we let class `Person` be a subclass of the predefined class `Listable`. Class `Person` then inherited the property of being able to be a part of a list. But we had a problem if class `Person` needed several properties. Perhaps we also wanted to be able to write out the class, or include it in a tree. In order to solve problems such as these, the concept of multiple inheritance was introduced into the language. Various properties could then be inherited from different sources. A difficulty with using inheritance to construct object collections, however, is that we have to decide in advance how a particular class is going to be used. As early as the definition of the class `Person`, we have to know whether we want it to be listable, readable, stackable and so on. Another problem is that the programmer needs detailed knowledge of how the classes inherited from are built up in order to know what properties the new class should get. This puts a great deal of responsibility on the programmer.

It turned out that the use of generic classes was a much better method of constructing object collections than inheritance. Writing object-oriented programs does not mean that we have to use inheritance all the time. This is quite clear if, for a moment, we consider the relations discussed in Chapter 6. Inheritance defines the relation 'is'. An American is a person. But is it really correct to say that a person is listable? To be able to be included in a list, is hardly a natural property of any person. Persons have nothing to do with lists, so it is better to make lists independent of the things they contain. If we want to create a list containing people, we can do it with a separate class `List<Person>`.

Templates were introduced relatively late in C++. (Obviously, the programming language Ada has been used as a model but the syntax of the two languages is very different.) There are a number of container classes in the draft standard. They are all generic and use templates. Container classes do not make use of inheritance. There is also a collection of generic functions in the draft standard that can perform algorithms on object collections. There are, for example, generic sort and search functions.

In this chapter we will be looking at how templates are used to construct generic classes and functions. Unfortunately, the syntax for templates is not very elegant in C++, but we will not allow ourselves to be frightened off by that. Templates are very useful things indeed.

13.1   Class templates

13.1.1   Templates and instances

To begin our discussion of class templates, let us look at the following non-generic class that defines matrices:

```
class Matrix {
public:
  Matrix(int i=0, int j=0)
    : r(i), c(j), a(new double[r*c]) {}
  Matrix(const Matrix& m) : a(0) {*this = m;}
  ~Matrix() {delete[] a;}
  int num_row() {return r;}
  int num_col() {return c;}
  Matrix& operator= (const Matrix&);
  double& operator() (int i, int j);
private:
  double *a;
  int r, c;   // Number of rows and columns, respectively
};
```

As we know, a matrix is an arrangement of a number of rows and columns. The individual elements of a matrix in the above class have type **double**. To represent a matrix of r rows and c columns, we use an ordinary one-dimensional array of r*c elements internally in the class. The data member a is a pointer to this array. The elements of the matrix are placed in rows in the array so that row number 1 comes first, row number 2 second, and so on. The first constructor, which can also be the default constructor, is used when we want to create a new matrix with a certain number of rows and columns. The expression Matrix(3,5), for instance, indicates a matrix of 3 rows and 5 columns. The constructor initializes the data members r and c that contain the size of the matrix and allocate an array consisting of r*c elements. The other constructor is a copy constructor, and this uses the assignment operator to initialize a matrix to be a copy of another matrix.

The two member functions num_row and num_col are self-explanatory and are defined directly in the class definition. There are two operators, the assignment operator = and the function operator (). The assignment operator is, of course, used to assign one matrix to another. The function call operator is used to make indexing possible in a matrix. It has two parameters that indicate the row and column number, respectively. If the variable m has type Matrix, then the expression m(x,y) gives a reference to the element that is in row number x, column number y. The operator () checks that the coordinates occur within the bounds allowed. The definitions of the two operators = and () are given separately:

```
Matrix& Matrix::operator= (const Matrix &m)
{
  if (this != &m)   // to itself?
  {
    r=m.r;
    c=m.c;
    delete[] a;
    a = new double[r*c];
    for (int i=0; i<r*c; i++)
      a[i] = m.a[i];
  }
  return *this;
}
double& Matrix::operator()(int i, int j) {
  if (i<1 or i>r or j<1 or j>c)
    throw out_of_range("Matrix::operator()");
  return a[(i-1)*c + j-1];
}
```

Class Matrix makes working with matrices easy, but matrices can only be constructed where the elements have type **double**. We, therefore, rewrite class Matrix so that it becomes a template:

```
template<class T>
class Matrix {
public:
  Matrix(int i=0, int j=0)
   : r(i), c(j), a(new T[i*j]) {}
  Matrix(const Matrix& m) : a(0) {*this = m;}
  ~Matrix() {delete[] a;}
  int num_row() {return r;}
  int num_col() {return c;}
  Matrix& operator= (const Matrix&);
  T& operator() (int r, int c);
private:
  T *a;
  int r, c;   // Number of rows and columns, respectively
};
```

There are two changes to the earlier class Matrix. The first is that there is a new first line. The reserved word **template** indicates that class Matrix is a template and not an ordinary class. The *template parameters* (*generic parameters*) are indicated inside the characters <   >. In this case there is only one template parameter, and this has been given the name T. The word **class** indicates that T is a *type parameter*. This means that T designates a type, any kind of type. (Note that

T can also designate an 'ordinary' type such as **int** or **char** *, even though the word **class** is used.) As soon as T has been defined in this way it can be used *inside* class Set in the same way as a normal type name.

The second change that we have made in class Matrix is that we have changed type **double** to T everywhere. For instance, the member variable a has type T * instead of **double** *, and the function call operator () returns a value of type T& instead of **double**&.

We can now make use of the class template Matrix to create different kinds of matrices. We can write, for instance:

```
Matrix<int>    mi(5,8);
Matrix<Person> mp(3,4);   // See page 270.
```

Two variables are declared here. The variable mi is a matrix whose elements are of type **int** and mp is a matrix where the elements are of class Person. What happens here is that the compiler uses the template Matrix to generate two ordinary classes. We say that two *instances* of class Matrix are formed. (The terms *generated classes* and *specializations* are also used in the draft standard.) In the first instance, it would seem that the type parameter T has been replaced by **int** everywhere, while in the second instance it would seem that T has been replaced by Person. The easiest way of explaining this is to say that the compiler automatically makes these changes in the text for class Matrix and then compiles text in the ordinary way. (In fact the mechanism works in a more complicated way than this but it is something that the compiler does by itself.) An expression of the form Matrix<X>, where X is the name of a type (an ordinary type or class type) is the name of the class generated. This name can be used in the same way as an ordinary class name, and function parameters or variables of such a class can be declared in the usual way.

In class Matrix, the two member functions **operator**= and **operator**() will be defined separately. Since class Matrix is a template, its member functions must also be templates. The definitions will have the form:

```
template<class T>
Matrix<T>& Matrix<T>::operator= (const Matrix &m)
{
  if (this != &m)   // to itself?
  {
    r=m.r;
    c=m.c;
    delete[] a;
    a = new T[r*c];
    for (int i=0; i<r*c; i++)
      a[i] = m.a[i];
  }
  return *this;
}
```

```
template<class T>
T& Matrix<T>::operator()(int i, int j) {
  if (i<1 or i>r or j<1 or j>c)
    throw out_of_range("Matrix::operator()");
  return a[(i-1)*c + j-1];
}
```

Both definitions must be introduced by:

```
template<class T>
```

that is, the same line that introduced the definition of class template `Matrix`. This says that a definition of a template follows and that there is a type parameter called `T`. Since every instance of a class template will have its own instances of its member functions, we have to write `Matrix<T>::` in front of the function name when we indicate the full name of the member function. (If, for example, an instance should be created where `T` is equal to **int**, the member functions would be defined with the prefix `Matrix<`**int**`>::`.) If we want to indicate the name of a class template *inside* the class itself, we do not have to write `<T>` after the class name, the class name will be sufficient. This applies, for instance, to the parameter type of the operator =. `Matrix` is written and not `Matrix<T>`.

Class templates

```
template<class T>   // class definition
class C {
  return_type  f (parameters);
  ...
};

template<class T>   // definition of member
function
return_type  C<T>::f (parameters)
{ ...}
```

- `T` is a type parameter and is used as an ordinary type inside the class.
- Both the class definition and definitions of the member functions should be placed in the header file.
- *Instances* of the class are created when we write
  `C<type_name>`
  Then `T` is replaced by *type_name* everywhere in this instance.
- The expression `C<type_name>` can be used as an ordinary class name.

We spoke earlier of the placement of classes (see Section 7.2) and learned that for every class, two files should be created, a header file (that normally has a name ending in .h) and a definition file. We further established that the class definition should be placed in the header file and the definitions of the member functions in the definition file. For class templates, we would make slightly different recommendations. Since it should be possible for the compiler to automatically generate a class from a class template, it must have access to the whole text that defines the class. The program text defining the member functions must also be accessible. This means that for a class template, the definitions of the member functions should also be placed in the header file. As a result, there is normally no need for a definition file. (Different compilers may have solved this problem in different ways but the recommendations given here should work for all compilers.)

On page 180 we demonstrated a function add that could add two matrices whose elements were integers. The problem with this function was that it only worked for matrices with four columns. We can now give a more general function that adds matrices using the class template Matrix. The new function gets two integer matrices a and b as parameters and as result gives a matrix that contains the sum of the two matrices. For the operation to be carried out, the two matrices given as parameters must have the same dimensions. If this is not the case, an exception will be generated. The result is calculated in a local variable c, initialized with the aid of the copy constructor so that from the beginning it is a copy of a.

```
Matrix<int> add(Matrix<int>& a, Matrix<int>& b)
{
  if (a.num_row()!=b.num_row() or
      a.num_col()!=b.num_col())
    throw range_error("add");
  Matrix<int> c(a);
  for (int i=1; i<=c.num_row(); i++)
    for (int j=1; j<=c.num_col(); j++)
      c(i,j) += b(i,j);
  return c;
}
```

Here is a program where a matrix is read then all its elements are updated so that their values are doubled:

```
int x, y;
cout << "Number of rows? "; cin >> x;
cout << "Number of columns? "; cin >> y;
Matrix<int> m(x,y);
for (int i=1; i<=m.num_row(); i++)
  for (int j=1; j<=m.num_col(); j++)
    cin >> m(i,j);
m = add(m,m);
```

13.1.2 Static members

Just like ordinary classes, a class template can have static data members and member functions. For example, we can complete the class template `Matrix` with a static data member `mn` that monitors the number of matrices of a certain kind and a static member function `num_matrices` that can be called to read `mn`. (Naturally, the constructors and the destructor are also changed so that they can count up and down the static data member `mn` but we will not show these changes here.)

```
template<class T>
class Matrix {
public:
  . . .
  static int num_matrices();
private:
  . . .
  static int mn;
};
```

For ordinary non-generic classes, we know that a static data member is common for all objects belonging to the class. It then exists in one edition only. Where class templates are concerned, each *instance* of the class has its own edition of a static member variable. For instance, if we have the three instances, `Matrix<int>`, `Matrix<Person>` and `Matrix<double>`, the variable `mn` will exist in three editions, one for each instance.

Static member functions are defined in the same way as non-static member functions. For example, the definition of the static member function `num_matrices` is:

```
template<class T>
int Matrix<T>::num_matrices()
{ return mn; }
```

Static data members must always be defined outside the class definition; this applies to class templates as well. Since there will be an instance of the static data member for every instance of the class template, the definition of a static data member in a class template must also be a template and be preceded by the word **template**. For example, the definition of the static data member `mn` is:

```
template<class T>
int Matrix<T>::mn=0;
```

Static members in class templates

- Exist in one edition for *every* instance of the class.
- Static member functions are defined in the same way as non-static member functions.
- Static data members are templates and must be defined separately. A static data member v in class C will have the definition:
  ```
  template<class T>
  ```
  type C<T>::v = *initialization value*;

      If there is a static member function f for an ordinary class C, then f, as we know, can be called in two different ways. Either we can take an object x from class C and make the call x.f(), or we can indicate the class name and make the call C::f(). The same situation applies in the case of class templates but instead of the class name, we will take the name of the actual instance. Let us assume, for example, that the variable mp has type Matrix<Person>. Then the following lines will write out how many person matrices and integer matrices, respectively, currently exist:

```
cout << mp.num_matrices() << endl;
cout << Matrix<int>::num_matrices() << endl;
```

13.1.3   Friends and help classes

If there is an ordinary non-generic class, it can be transformed into a class template in a relatively simple way. In Section 12.2 we constructed a class Stack where the individual stack elements were of type **int**, and this was implemented with the aid of a singly linked list. We will now remake this class into a class template. We begin with the definition (see page 417). We call the type parameter T and change all the **int** to T.

```
template<class U>
class Element;

template<class T>
class Stack {
public:
  Stack() : first(0) {};
  ~Stack();
  void push (T d);
  T pop () throw(length_error);
  bool empty();
private:
  Element<T> *first;
```

```
Stack(const Stack&) {};
Stack& operator= (const Stack&) {};
};
```

To implement a stack, we use the help class `Element`, which defines individual elements in a singly linked list. Class `Element` must also be generic as the list elements will contain data elements of different types for the various instances of class `Stack`. The first line, above, is a declaration (not a definition) which indicates that `Element` is a class template with type parameter U. The data member `first` in class template `Stack` is declared as a pointer to an object of type `Element<T>`, that is, to a list element where the data element will be of type T, the same type as in the actual instance of `Stack`.

The complete definition of class template `Element` has the following appearance:

```
template<class U>
class Element {
  friend class Stack<U>;
  Element *next;
  U data;
  Element(Element *n, int d):next(n), data(d) {}
};
```

Note that class `Stack` must be able to see inside class `Element`. It has therefore been defined as a friend class. (The type parameters T and U must designate the same type. Therefore `Stack<U>` is written and not simply `Stack`.)

The definitions of the different member functions are simple to change. As an example we show the function `push` and the destructor (see page 418).

```
template<class T>
void Stack<T>::push(T d)
{
  first = new Element<T>(first, d);
}
```

```
template<class T>
Stack<T>::~Stack()
{
  while(not empty())
  {
    Element<T> *p=first;
    first = first->next;
```

```
    delete p;
  }
}
```

13.1.4 Template parameters

The class templates we have seen so far have only had one template parameter, but a class template (or function template) can have an arbitrary number of template parameters. There are two categories of template parameter, *type parameters* and *value parameters*. Type parameters are preceded by the word **class** and designate arbitrary types. Value parameters look like ordinary function parameters but may not be of floating point type.

As an example we will look at the following class template. Here we implement a stack using an array instead of a linked list. There are two data members, the array s, where the individual stack elements are placed and a counter n which monitors how many elements are currently in the stack. The class template has two template parameters. The first, T, is a type parameter used to designate the type of the individual elements in the stack, and the other, size, is a value parameter that indicates the maximum size a stack can have. The ordinary member functions empty, push and pop are defined.

```
template<class T, int size>
class Stack {
public:
  Stack() : n(0) {};
  bool empty () {return n<=0;}
  void push (const T& e){s[n++]=e;}
  T pop () {return s[--n];}
private:
  T s[size];
  int n;
};
```

When we create instances of this class template, we must give the values for both template parameters. For example, we can declare an integer stack with a maximum of 200 elements by writing:

```
Stack<int,200> x;   // A stack with a maximum of 200 int
```

When the value is given to the value parameter, a constant expression must be indicated that has a value which can be evaluated at compilation.

Template parameters

- A template can have an arbitrary number of template parameters:

  template<*param1*, *param2*, *param3* ...>

  where *paramN* is either a type parameter of the form

  class T

  or a value parameter that looks like an ordinary variable declaration:

  type_name V
- A value parameter may not be of floating point number type.
- Default values can be indicated.

Just like ordinary function parameters, template parameters can have default values. For instance, we would be able to change the first line in the class definition to:

```
template<class T=double, int size=100>
```

If a template parameter has a default value then all subsequent template parameters must also have default values. When there are default values we can leave out one or more of the parameters when we create an instance of the class. We can write, for example:

```
Stack<Person> y;   // A stack with a maximum of 100 persons
Stack<> z;         // A stack with a maximum of 100 double
```

13.1.5   Property classes

When we create an instance of a class template that has a type parameter T, type T is replaced everywhere inside the class with the actual type. For example, if we create an instance of class template Matrix for type Person, T is replaced by Person everywhere. This may work perfectly well for all imaginable types in class template Matrix but is not the case with all class templates. To demonstrate this, we will construct a class template that describes binary search trees. We begin with class Tree from page 443 and rewrite the class to make it a template:

```
template<class D>
class Tree {
public:
  as before
void inorder() const;
void put_in(D d);
D* search(D d);
private:
```

```
  class Node {
    friend class Tree<D>;
    D data;
    Tree *left, *right;
    Node(D d): data(d), left(new Tree),
              right(new Tree) {}
    ~Node() {delete left; delete right;}
  };
  as before
};
```

The changes we have made to the previous definition include changing type **int** to
D everywhere inside the class. To simplify things, class Node has been moved into
the private section of class Tree. To enable binary search trees to be built up, we
have also included two new member functions, put_in and search. The
definitions of these have the following appearance (see the functions on pages 440
and 441):

```
template<class D>
void Tree<D>::put_in(D d)
{
  if (empty())
    root = new Node(d);
  else if (d < value())
    l_child().put_in(d);
  else
    r_child().put_in(d);
}
template<class D>
D* Tree<D>::search(D d)
{
  if (empty())
    return 0;
  else if (d == value())
    return &value();
  else if (d < value())
    return l_child().search(d);
  else
    return r_child().search(d);
}
```

Now we can create an instance of the class for type **int**, for example:

```
Tree<int> t;
```

This works very well, and we can use the member functions put_in, search and
inorder to handle the binary search tree:

```
cin >>i;
t.put_in(i);
...
cin >> i;
if (t.search(i))
  cout << "is in the tree" << endl;
t.inorder();
```

Now suppose that we have declared a class Person with the following appearance:

```
class Person {
public:
  char pno[10];
  char name[30];
};
```

We want to build up a binary search tree where each node contains information about a person. As search argument we will use a national insurance number. We will try to create an instance of class Tree where the type parameter D is set to Person:

```
Tree<Person> tp;   // ERROR!
```

When this line is compiled, we will get a number of strange error messages, something in the style of 'illegal structure operation'. There will also be an indication that the errors lie in class Tree and not in the program code we have written ourselves. (In the draft standard it is stipulated that the line where the instance is created should be indicated as incorrect but not all compilers work like this today.)

The reason for these errors is that in functions put_in and search, the operations == and < are carried out on objects of type D. In addition, function inorder uses the output operator << to write out information in the nodes. This does not cause any problems when the type parameter D has been replaced by **int**, since these three operations exist for type **int**. But when we try to create an instance for type Person, there is a compilation error because the operations ==, < and << are not defined for type Person.

There are several things we can do to get around this. The easiest is simply to say that class template Tree can only be used for types where the three operations are defined. Another way of solving the problem is to make use of a *property class*. (This method is used in the draft standard in the library definition for reading and writing. The term 'traits' is used to designate property classes.) We let class template Tree have one more type parameter E that contains the necessary operations. We begin by rewriting the class definition:

```
template<class D, class E>
class Tree {
```

as before
};

The next step is to reconstruct our definitions of `put_in`, `search` and `inorder` so that they do not use the operations <, == and <<. Instead, we leave it to them to assume that there are three static functions with the names `less`, `equal` and `write` in class E:

```
template<class D, class E>
void Tree<D,E>::put_in(D d)
{
  if (empty())
    root = new Node(d);
  else if (E::less(d, value()))
    l_child().put_in(d);
  else
    r_child().put_in(d);
}
template<class D, class E>
D* Tree<D,E>::search(D d)
{
  if (empty())
    return 0;
  else if (E::equal(d, value()))
    return &value();
  else if (E::less(d, value()))
    return l_child().search(d);
  else
    return r_child().search(d);
}
template<class D, class E>
void Tree<D,E>::inorder() const
{
  if (not empty())
  {
    l_child().inorder();
    E::write(value());
    r_child().inorder();
  }
}
```

Note that the complete name of the function starts with the prefix `Tree<D,E>::`.

When we now create an instance of the class, we must give two type parameters. The first one indicates as before what type the data elements in the nodes are to have. The other is a property class which must have the three static member functions, `less`, `equal` and `write`. Since the operators <, == and <<

are defined for most of the ordinary types, it is appropriate to implement the three static member functions making use of these operators. We will construct the following class template to be used with class Tree in order to avoid the need of defining a property class for every ordinary type.

```
template<class D>
class TreeE {
public:
  static bool equal(const D& d1, const D& d2)
                     {return d1 == d2;}
  static bool less (const D& d1, const D& d2)
                     {return d1 < d2;}
  static void write(const D& d)
                     {cout << d << ' ';}
};
```

If we create an instance of this class for class **int**, for example, we will get a property class that can be used when we want to create instances of class Tree for type **int**. As a result, we can write the following to get a binary search tree, ti, where the data elements have type **int**:

```
Tree<int, TreeE<int> > ti;
```

A corresponding procedure can be followed for all types where the operators <, == and << are defined. For instance, if we want to have a search tree, tu, with data elements of type SuperInt (see page 288), we can write:

```
Tree<SuperInt, TreeE<SuperInt> > tu;
```

According to the draft standard, it is allowed in class Tree to indicate a default value for type parameter E with the following as model:

```
template<class D, class E = TreeE<D> >
class Tree {
  ...
```

This is useful since we do not then need to indicate the property class when we create instances of class Tree. Instead, we can write:

```
Tree<char> tc;
Tree<SuperInt> tu;
```

If we have a type, for instance, type Person, where the operators <, == and << are missing, we can write a special version of the property class just for this type.

This class can be called anything we please although it could be useful to call it TreeE. This is because it is allowed to define a *special instance* (or 'explicitly specialized class', according to the draft standard) of a template for a particular class. We can then give the definition:

```
class TreeE<Person> {
public:
  static bool equal (const Person& d1, const Person& d2)
         {return strcmp(d1.pno, d2.pno)==0;}
  static bool less (const Person& d1, const Person& d2)
         {return strcmp(d1.pno, d2.pno)<=0;}
  static void write (const Person& d)
         {cout << d.pno << ' ' << d.name << endl;}
};
```

If we now declare an instance of class TreeE for type Person, this definition will be used instead of the class template above.

Finally, here is an example involving part of a program that reads a number of national insurance numbers. For each one, a check is made to see if the actual person exists in the binary search tree tp. If this is the case, the person's name is written out. The user is also allowed to change the person's name (but not the national insurance number). The program concludes by writing out all the persons in the tree in order of their national insurance numbers.

```
Tree<Person, TreeE<Person> > tp;
...  // Here the tree is built up
while (true)
{
  Person p;
  cout << "National insurance number? ";
  if (not (cin >> p.pno)) break;
  Person *pp = tp.search(p);
  if (pp)
  {
    char answer[5];
    cout << pp->name << endl
    << "Should the name be changed? "; cin >> answer;
    if (answer[0] == 'y')
    {
      cout << "New name? "; cin >> p.name;
      strcpy(pp->name, p.name);
    }
  }
  else
    cout << "Does not exist" << endl;
}
tp.inorder();
```

13.1.6 Generic standard classes

In the draft standard there are a number of standardized container classes, for instance, sets, queues and lists. They are all class templates and use iterators. We cannot go through all the standard classes here. (Definitions for them can be found in the draft standard or in the documentation for your compiler.) So that the reader can understand how these classes function and how they can be used, we will, instead, study our own, somewhat simplified version of the standard class List which can be used to build up and handle lists. This class is extremely useful. (This is a fairly technical section. The most important thing, however, is not to know how class List is implemented but to understand the principles involved.)

To implement a list, we use a doubly linked list with an extra start element that does not belong to the list itself. (See page 412). We begin by giving a class template for the list elements. The forward pointer is called suc (successor) and the backward pointer pre (predecessor).

```
template<class T>
class Element {
public:
  Element *suc, *pre;
  T data;
  Element() {}
  Element(Element *s, Element *p, T d)
        : suc(s), pre(p), data(d) {}
};
```

We will now show the whole definition of class template List. It is quite long since, in fact, it describes two classes. Class Iterator is declared as an internal class *inside* class template List.

```
template<class T>
class List {
public:
  //------------------------------------------------------------------
  class Iterator {
  public:
    Iterator() : the_list(0), cur(0){};
    bool operator== (const Iterator& i) const
                        {return cur == i.cur;}
    bool operator!= (const Iterator& i) const
                        {return cur != i.cur;}
    T& operator* ();   // Gives a ref to an actual element
    Iterator& operator++ ();     // Moves forward
    Iterator operator++ (int);   // Moves forward
    Iterator& operator-- ();     // Moves backwards
    Iterator operator-- (int);   // Moves backwards
```

```
private:
    friend class List<T>;
    List<T> *the_list;
    Element<T> *cur;
    Iterator(List<T> *l, Element<T> *c)
                : the_list(l), cur(c) {};
};
//-------------------------------------------------------------------
List() :  f(new Element<T>), sz(0)
            {f->suc=f->pre=f;}
List(List& l);
List& operator= (List&);
bool empty() const {return sz==0;}
long int size() const {return sz;}
T& front();   // Gives reference to first element
T& back();    // Gives reference to last element
Iterator begin() {return Iterator(this, f->suc);}
Iterator end() {return Iterator(this, f);}
Iterator insert(Iterator pos, const T& d);
void insert(Iterator pos, int n, const T& d);
void insert(Iterator pos,Iterator i, Iterator j);
void erase(Iterator pos);
void erase(Iterator pos1,Iterator pos2);
void push_front(const T& d) {insert(begin(),d);}
void push_back (const T& d) {insert(end(),d);}
void pop_front() {erase(begin());}
void pop_back() {erase(--end());}
~List() {erase(begin(), end()); delete f;}
private:
    Element<T> *f;
    long int sz;
};
```

Class `List` contains two data members: `f` is a pointer to the first list element (the extra one), and `sz` is an integer that contains the number of elements in the list. The iterator class is constructed along the same lines as the iterator class that was used together with class `Set` in Section 12.3. As we can see, an iterator has two data members. The first, `the_list`, is a pointer that will point to the list which the iterator is connected to. The other, `cur`, will point to the current list element in the list. When we make the iterator run forwards and backwards in a list, the pointer `cur` will be changed. But the pointer `the_list` will not be changed as long as the iterator is tied to a particular list. The default constructor for class `Iterator` initializes both pointers `the_list` and `cur` to 0. An iterator is not, therefore, connected to any special list from the beginning.

We will first look at the member functions for class `List`. The default constructor creates a new empty list, and it does this by allocating the first extra list element then letting it point forwards and backwards to itself (see Figure 12.8). There is also a copy constructor and an assignment operator, both of which carry out deep copies. How this is done will be discussed later.

The member functions `empty` of `size` are of no consequence. Only the value of the member variable `sz` is used. The member functions `front` and `back` give as results a reference to the list's first and last data element, respectively. If the list is empty, an exception is generated. Note that the first element in the list is the extra start element. The first data element is, therefore, in list element number two.

```
template<class T>
T& List<T>::front()
{
  if (empty())
    throw length_error("List::front");
  return f->suc->data;
}
```

```
template<class T>
T& List<T>::back()
{
  if (empty())
    throw length_error("List::back");
  return f->pre->data;
}
```

The member functions `begin` and `end` are important. Both are defined inline and give an iterator as result. (They call the constructor for class `Iterator`, defined in the **private** section.) Function `begin` gives as result an iterator referring to the list element that contains the first data element (that is, to list element number two). Function `end` does *not* give a reference to the list's last element. It gives a reference to the first element that could lie *just outside* the list. Since the list is circular, this element will be equal to the extra list element that is placed first.

We use the member functions `begin` and `end` when we want to connect an iterator to a particular list. Suppose, for instance, that we declare a list of real numbers and that we want to have two iterators which refer to the beginning of the list and the first element outside the list, respectively. We can then write:

```
List<double> dlist;
List<double>::Iterator it1(dlist.begin()),it2(dlist.end());
```

We also could have used an assignment.

Iterators can be used to run through the list. For instance, all the numbers can be written out:

```
List<double>::Iterator it;
for (it=dlist.begin(); it!=dlist.end(); ++it)
  cout << *it << endl;
```

There are three versions of the member function, `insert`, which inserts new elements in a list. The first has an iterator, `pos`, and a new value, `d`, as parameter. The new value will be inserted *in front of* the element iterator `pos` refers to. As result is given an iterator that refers to the newly inserted element. For the operation to be allowed, `pos` must be connected to the current list – the list the member function `insert` is applied to. If it is not, an exception will be generated. The definition can now be written in the following way. (Function `put_previous` from page 414 has been used as a model.) The new value d will be inserted in front of the list element `pos.cur` points to.

```
template<class T>
List<T>::Iterator List<T>::insert(Iterator pos, const T& d)
{
  if (pos.the_list != this)
    throw invalid_argument("List::insert");
  Element<T> *pnew = new Element<T> (pos.cur, pos.cur->pre, d);
  pos.cur->pre->suc = pnew;
  pos.cur->pre = pnew;
  sz++;
  return List::Iterator(this, pnew);
}
```

Note that all iterator values are allowed. If, for instance, `pos` were equal to `begin()` then the new value would be placed first in the list. If `pos` were equal to `end()`, the new value would be placed in front of the imagined element not belonging to the list. In other words, the new value is placed last in the list in this case.

The two other versions of `insert` can now be easily defined using the first version. Version number two inserts n new elements with the value d in front of the element iterator `pos` refers to. It is simply a matter of calling version number one of the function n times:

```
template<class T>
void List<T>::insert(Iterator pos, int n, const T& d)
{
  if (n<0)
    throw invalid_argument("List::insert");
  for (; n>0; n--)
    insert(pos, d);
}
```

The third version of `insert` has three iterators, `pos`, `i` and `j` as parameters. Iterator `pos` will be connected to the current list and `i` and `j` to another list. The function reads a number of elements from the list i and j are connected to, and inserts them in front of the element pos refers to. (The elements in the interval i to j are read.) The list i and j are connected to will not be influenced by this. If we have two lists 11 and 12, we can insert a copy of 12 first in 11 by making the call:

```
11.insert(11.begin(),12.begin(),12.end());
```

The definition of the third version of insert will have the following appearance:

```
template<class T>
void List<T>::insert(Iterator pos, Iterator i, Iterator j)
{
  if (i.the_list!=j.the_list or i.the_list==this)
    throw invalid_argument("List::insert");
  for (Iterator it(i); it!=j; ++it)
    insert(pos, *it);
}
```

The function checks that iterators i and j are connected to the same list and that they are not connected to the current list.

There are two versions of function erase that remove elements from a list. The first version gets an iterator pos as parameter and removes the element pos.cur this iterator refers to. For the operation to be performed the iterator must be connected to the current list, and it must refer to an element inside the list. (The value end() lies outside the list and is, therefore, not allowed.) We then give the following definition. (Function remove from page 414 has been used as a model.)

```
template<class T>
void List<T>::erase(Iterator pos)
{
  if (pos.the_list != this)
    throw invalid_argument("List::erase");
  if (pos == end())
    throw out_of_range("List::erase");
  pos.cur->pre->suc = pos.cur->suc;
  pos.cur->suc->pre = pos.cur->pre;
  delete pos.cur;
  sz--;
}
```

The other version of erase has two iterators pos1 and pos2 as parameters and looks like this:

```
template<class T>
void List<T>::erase(Iterator pos1, Iterator pos2)
{
  for (Iterator it(pos1); it!=pos2; )
    erase(it++);
}
```

The function removes a number of elements in the list from and including pos1 up to and including the element *in front of* pos2. For instance, the following call removes all the elements from list 11:

```
11.erase(11.begin(), 11.end());
```

The four member functions push_front, push_back, pop_front and pop_back insert and remove elements first and last in a list. They can be easily implemented with the aid of the member functions insert and erase. The definitions have been put inline directly into the class definition. Note that to remove the last element in a list, the call erase(--end()) should be made. If erase(end()) is written, this will mean that we are trying to remove an element outside the list.

The destructor for class template List has also been placed directly in the class definition, and it can easily be implemented using the second version of erase. All the elements are simply removed. Note that the destructor must then remove the special start element in the list.

It remains for us to define the copy constructor and the assignment operator for class List. The copy constructor will first allocate the special start element and ensure that it points forwards and backwards to itself. Then it can easily make the deep copy by calling the third version of insert:

```
template<class T>
List<T>::List(List& l)  : f(new Element<T>), sz(0)
{
  f->suc = f->pre = f;   // Create start element
  insert(end(), l.begin(), l.end());
}
```

The assignment operator functions in a similar way but it will not allocate a special start element. Instead, the old elements will be removed.

```
template<class T>
List<T>& List<T>::operator= (List& l)
{
```

```
  if (f != 1.f)
  {
    erase(begin(), end());
    insert(end(), 1.begin(), 1.end());
  }
  return *this;
}
```

In conclusion, we will give the definitions of the member functions in class
Iterator. They are all very simple. The * operator gives as result a reference to
the data part in the current list element. The operators ++ and -- are used to move
forwards and backwards in the list. They exist in both prefix and postfix versions.
It is permissible to move forward to the first element lying just outside the list – the
element that end() refers to; but it is not permissible to move backwards in front
of the first element. All the operators require the iterator to be connected to a list;
that is, the member variable the_list may not be a null pointer.

```
template<class T>
T& List<T>::Iterator::operator* ()
{
  if (not the_list or *this == the_list->end())
    throw out_of_range("Iterator::operator*");
  return cur->data;
}

template<class T>
List<T>::Iterator& List<T>::Iterator::operator++ ()
{
  if (not the_list or *this == the_list->end())
    throw out_of_range("Iterator::operator++");
  cur = cur->suc;
  return *this;
}

template<class T>
List<T>::Iterator List<T>::Iterator::operator++ (int)
{
  Iterator temp = *this;
  ++ (*this);
  return temp;
}

template<class T>
List<T>::Iterator& List<T>::Iterator::operator-- ()
{
  if (not the_list or *this == the_list->begin())
    throw out_of_range("Iterator::operator--");
  cur = cur->pre;
  return *this;
}
```

```
template<class T>
List<T>::Iterator List<T>::Iterator::operator-- (int)
{
  Iterator temp = *this;
  -- (*this);
  return temp;
}
```

This terminates our somewhat simplified version of the standard class List. The iterator class, as stipulated by the standard, has been defined as an internal class inside the class template List. This might cause problems for some older compilers which cannot handle nested class definitions in combination with templates. If so, Iterator can be defined as a class template outside List.

13.2 Function templates

13.2.1 Definitions and instances

Classes are not the only things that can be generic. Templates, so-called *function templates*, can also be constructed for ordinary functions. In order to demonstrate how this is done, we will begin by looking at a problem that is by no means uncommon. When we write programs, we often have to compare two variables with each other and see which one is the smaller. Instead of doing this in an **if** statement, we can write a function to return the least value. The following function compares two integers of type **int** and gives as result the smaller of the numbers.

```
int min(int a, int b)
{
  if (a < b)
    return a;
  else
    return b;
}
```

It is not difficult to call this function. For instance, we can write k=min(i,j). But if we wanted to calculate the smaller of two variables not of type **int**, this function would not work. We would have to write a new version of the function. It is very inconvenient to have to write a new version of the function for every type a parameter can have. It is better to use a function template. So we rewrite the function:

```
template<class T>
const T& min(const T& a, const T& b)
```

```
{
  if (a < b)
    return a;
  else
    return b;
}
```

The first line indicates as before that what is to come is a template and that T is the name of the type parameter. The following lines contain the definition of the function itself. Type **int** has been replaced everywhere by T. (To simplify matters, we have rewritten the parameters a and b into constant reference parameters, thereby avoiding having to copy whole objects, which is an advantage if type T happens to designate a 'large' type).

It is simple to create an instance of a function template. We simply make a call. We can write, for example:

```
double x, y;
long int m, n;
...
cout << min(x, y) << endl;
cout << min(m, n) << endl;
```

In the penultimate line, an instance of the function min is automatically created where the type parameter T is replaced by **double**. On the last line, an instance is created where the type parameter T is replaced by **long int**.

An instance of a function template does not have to be created explicitly. It will occur automatically when a call is made. Then the compiler will try to fit together the actual parameters with the function's formal parameters and determine which type the generic type parameters will have. If the parameters can be matched together, there is a check to see whether there already is an instance for the actual parameters. If there is not, a new instance is automatically generated.

For this to be possible, all the generic type parameters must occur in the type specification of at least one of the function's usual parameters. For example, in the function template min, T occurs both in the type specification for parameter a and the one for parameter b. When instances of function templates are created, there are not the great number of automatic type conversions as there are with calls of ordinary functions. The actual parameters must correspond to the formal parameters more exactly. For instance, it is wrong to try to mix the types in a call of function min:

```
cout << min(m, y) << endl;   // ERROR!
```

In fact, in a function call it is permissible to *explicitly* indicate what types the generic type parameters should have and we write this in the same way as we do when creating instances of class templates. We can write, for instance:

```
cout << min<double>(m, y) << endl;   // GOOD!
```

Normal type conversions occur here since min<**double**> is no longer a template but an ordinary function. The value of argument m will, therefore, be converted to type **double**.

We will demonstrate some more useful function templates. The following function changes the value of two variables. (We have called the function swap since there is a standard function with that name.) We have to use reference parameters here because we want to be able to change them inside the function.

```
template<class T>
void swap (T& a, T& b)
{
  T temp=a;
  a=b;
  b=temp;
}
```

To change the values of the two **int** variables i and j, we can simply write swap(i,j), and the call swap(x,y) changes the values in the two **double** variables x and y.

It is often useful to use function templates that have arrays as parameters. The following function, for instance, searches for the smallest element in an array:

```
template<class T>
T& min_element(T f[], int n)
{
  int m=0;
  for (int i=1; i<n; i++)
    if (f[i] < f[m])
      m = i;
  return f[m];
}
```

As parameters, the function gets an array (that is, a pointer to the array's first element) and an integer that indicates how many elements the array contains. As result is given a reference to the smallest element in the array. In the following call an instance is created where T designates the type **float**:

```
float a[100];
...
cout << min_element(a, 100) << endl;
```

Sorting an array is a common operation, so it is inconvenient to write a sort function for every kind of array that has to be sorted. This is an appropriate occasion to use a function template. We shall use the sort algorithm 'search for the least and swap' described on page 65. Since we already have the function `min_element`, which searches for the smallest number in an array, and function `swap` to change two values, it should be a simple matter. We write a sort function that has two parameters, an array that will be sorted and an integer that indicates the number of elements in the array.

```
template<class T>
void sort(T f[], int n)
{
  for (int k=0; k<n; k++)
  {
    swap(f[k], min_element(f+k, n-k));
  }
}
```

When an instance of function `sort` is created for a particular type `T`, instances of functions `swap` and `min_element` will automatically be created for the same type. The call `min_element(f+k,n-k)` gives as result a reference to the smallest number in the subarray that begins at position number k. There are n-k elements in this subarray. We can now create instances of the sort function. For example, to sort the array a, above, we write:

```
sort(a, 100);
```

Function templates

```
template<class T1, class T2, ...>
```
return_type f (*parameters*)
{ ... }

- T1, T2 etc. are parameters and are used as ordinary types inside the function. All the type parameters must occur in a type specification in the parameter list.

- *Instances* of the function are automatically created when it is called
    f (*arguments*)
  The compiler then matches the arguments with the formal parameters and determines which type will replace T.

- We can indicate explicitly which type T is to have:
    f<*type*> (*arguments*)

- A *special instance* for a particular type V can be created. The function body is then rewritten and T is replaced by V.
    return_type f (*parameters*)
    { *special version* }

Just as if class templates were involved, we can create a *special instance* of a function template for a special type. The function template min_element will not work, for instance, if we have an array with text strings. A text string is, of course, defined by a pointer to a character array, so if we have two such pointers, s1 and s2, and make the comparison s1<s2, it is not the texts that will be compared but the values of the pointers, which is of little interest to us. We must construct a *special instance* of the template min_element:

```
char *& min_element(char *f[], int n)
{
   int m=0;
   for (int i=1; i<n; i++)
     if (strcmp(f[i],f[m])<0)
       m = i;
   return f[m];
}
```

Everywhere type T has been replaced by **char** *. The comparison operator < has also been replaced by a call of the standard function strcmp, which returns the value −1 if the first text string is alphabetically smaller than the other.

If we now have an array tab where the individual elements are pointers to text strings, the array can be easily sorted:

```
char *tab[100];
...
sort(tab, 100);
```

When function sort is called, an instance is created where T will designate type **char** *. When function min_element is then called from within sort, an instance will also be needed of min_element for type **char** *. But then the compiler discovers that there is a special instance and uses this one instead of generating a new instance from the template.

Of course, we can have function templates with several template parameters. Both type parameters and value parameters are allowed.

13.2.2   Generic standard functions – the algorithm library

In the draft standard, in the so-called *algorithm library*, there is a large collection of function templates. These can perform several different operations on container classes and other data collections. We can carry out searches, sort data and make other changes to data. The function templates in the algorithm library are defined in the header file algorithm.

All function templates have in common the method of using iterators to handle collections of data. The function templates min_element and sort, from the previous section, exist for instance as standard functions but they use iterators. We will begin by looking at the function template min_element.

```
template<class IT>
IT min_element(IT first, IT last)
{
  IT m=first;
  for (IT i = ++first; i!=last; i++)
    if (*i < *m)
      m = i;
  return m;
}
```

The generic type parameter IT designates an iterator or a pointer type. Suppose, for instance, that we have an integer array a:

```
double a[10];
```

Then we can call the function min_element

```
cout << *min_element(a, a+10);
```

Since the type of a is 'pointer to **double**', an instance of function min_element is created where the type parameter IT gets type **double** *. This means that the variables first, last, i and m inside the function min_element are ordinary pointers. The operations ++ and * that are performed on these variables are the normal pointer operations. The function leaves a result of type IT, that is, a 'pointer to **double**' for this instance. This pointer points to the smallest number in the array, which means that the expression *min_element(a, a+10) is the value of the smallest number in the array, so this value will be returned.

The function templates in the algorithm library are not only useful for arrays. They can also be applied to all the container classes for which iterators exist. We can declare a list of integers, for instance

```
List<int> l;
```

We use the class template List from page 466 here. The smallest number in the list l can now be found and written out by writing:

```
cout << *min_element(l.begin(), l.end());
```

In the instance of min_element that is now created, the type parameter T will get the type List<**int**>::Iterator, since it is the type the functions begin and end give as result. The operators ++ and *, which we ourselves defined for type List<T>::Iterator, will now be called inside the function min_element.

Here is the definition of the function template `sort`:

```
template<class IT>
void sort(IT first, IT last)
{
  for (IT k=first; k!=last; k++)
  {
    swap(*k, *min_element(k, last));
  }
}
```

This also has a generic type parameter `IT` that can designate a pointer or iterator. The parameters `first` and `last` refer to the first and last element in the data collection to be sorted. If we want to sort an ordinary array, we can make the call:

```
sort(a, a+10);
```

Then an instance is created where `IT` gets the type **double** `*`. We also automatically get instances of the functions `swap` and `min_element` for this type. (Function `swap`, which we showed on page 475, is also a standard function.) The variables `first`, `last` and `k` are pointers. In the call `min_element`, the pointers `k` and `last` demarcate the subarray in which we will search for the least value.

If we want to sort the integer list `l` that we defined earlier, this can be done just as easily:

```
sort(l.begin(), l.end());
```

We now get an instance where `IT` is equal to `List<int>::Iterator` and where the variables `first`, `last` and `k` are therefore iterators.

The operator `<` is used in the function template `min_element`. This function template and, therefore, the function template `sort`, will only work if there is an operator `<` defined for the actual element type. This has not caused any problems in our examples. In one case, the element type was **double** and in the other it was **int**. So that function templates can also be used for data collections where the element type does not have an operator `<`, several of the function templates can be found in an alternative version where a property class can be given as an extra template parameter. The alternative version of `min_element` will look like this:

```
template<class IT, class Compare>
IT min_element(IT first, IT last, Compare comp)
{
  IT m=first;
  for (IT i=++first; i!=last; i++)
```

```
    if (comp(*i, *m))
       m = i;
  return m;
}
```

The type parameter `comp` designates a property class. The interesting thing, however, is on the sixth line where the call `comp(*i, *m)` is made. Class `comp` is called as though it were a function! For this to be possible, there must be a function call operator for class `comp`. This operator will have two parameters that are of the type `i` and `j` point to, that is, of the same type as the individual elements in the data collection. Let us then define a class that has such a function call operator. We want to be able to compare text strings, so we define the following property class:

```
class Str_Less_Than {
public:
  bool operator () (char *s1, char *s2)
  { return strcmp(s1, s2) < 0;}
};
```

Suppose now that we have declared a list where the individual elements are pointers to text strings, that is, they have type **char** *:

```
List<char *> tl;
```

To read texts and place them in the list, statements like this can be given:

```
char s[100], *p;
cin >> s;
p = new char[strlen(s+1)];
strcpy(p, s);
tl.push_back(p);
```

Suppose now that we want to search the text in the list that comes first alphabetically. To be able to call the alternative version of function `min_element`, we first have to declare an object of class `Str_Less_Than`.

```
Str_Less_Than lt;
```

This object is only a sort of dummy. It does not contain any data members, only the function call operator. We can now write out the smallest text in the list:

```
cout << *min_element(tl.begin(), tl.end(), lt);
```

Function `sort` can also be found in an alternative version:

```
template<class IT, class Compare>
void sort(IT first, IT last, Compare comp)
{
  for (IT k=first; k!=last; k++)
  {
    swap(*k, *min_element(k, last, comp));
  }
}
```

The only difference compared with the other version, is that an object of the extra property class is given as argument in the call of `min_element`. We can now sort the texts in list `tl` in alphabetical order by making the call:

```
sort(tl.begin(), tl.end(), lt);
```

Just as with the earlier sections on iterators and standard classes, this section has contained a good deal of syntax that may be difficult to understand at times. We've worked through it so that the reader has an opportunity to understand and use the standard classes and function templates which exist in the draft standard.

13.3 Heterogeneous object collections

The contents of this chapter may have given the impression that inheritance and the use of templates are two different techniques competing with each other: we must choose one or the other. However, this is not the case at all. The two methods can be used together – in fact, they can complement each other to good effect. This is especially true in the case of heterogeneous object collections – where the objects are of different types. We shall confine ourselves here to describing collections where the objects, though of different type, are related to each other. These different objects will all have a common fundamental base class.

We first describe how the 'classical' technique, without the use of templates, is used to construct heterogeneous object collections. Then we will demonstrate how the use of templates and inheritance can be combined. Finally, there will be a comprehensive program involving both templates and inheritance.

13.3.1 The classical method

We now show how heterogeneous data collections can be built up simply by making use of inheritance. This technique was used before the concept of templates was introduced into C++. It is also the technique used in various object-oriented languages, like Smalltalk for example, that do not have generic program units.

We begin with the following class which defines elements that can be included in singly linked lists:

```
class ListElement {
public:
  ListElement() : next(0) {};
  ListElement *next_elem() { return next; }
private:
  friend class List;
  ListElement *next;
};
```

We see that there is only one data member, next, and this is a pointer to the next element in the list. There is no data member that contains information. There is a default constructor that sets the pointer next to zero. The member function next_elem allows an outsider to read but not to change next. The only class that can change next is the friend class List. It has the following definition:

```
class List {
public:
  List() : first(0) {};
  void put_last(ListElement *e);
  void remove_first();
  ListElement *first_elem() {return first; }
private:
  ListElement *first;
};
```

Using class List, we can build up linked lists where the list elements have type ListElement. The only data member is a pointer first that points to the first element in the list. The default constructor sets this pointer to zero from the beginning. The pointer first can be read from outside – but not changed – using the member function first_elem. For the sake of simplicity, we have only declared two member functions in class List. These have the following definitions (compare with those on page 409):

```
void List::remove_first()
{
  if (first)
    first=first->next;
}

void List::put_last(ListElement *e)
{
```

```
  e->next=0;       // e should always be last
  if (not first)   // Empty list, insert e first
    first = e;
  else
  {
    ListElement *p;
    for (p=first; p->next; p=p->next)
      ;
    // p is now pointing to the last element
    // Insert e after p
    p->next = e;
  }
}
```

It is not particularly interesting building up linked lists with elements of class ListElement, because the list elements do not contain any information apart from the pointer to the next element. But now we can use class ListElement as a base class for objects that we may want to put in a list. On page 302 we defined a group of classes which described different kinds of vehicle. The fundamental base class in this group was the class Vehicle. We will now redefine class Vehicle so that it, in turn, becomes a subclass of class ListElement. (The other classes are not changed.)

```
class Vehicle : public ListElement {
  public:
    virtual void give_info();
};
```

With this definition, class Vehicle and all its subclasses have inherited the property of being able to be included in lists. Every object of one of these classes will have the inherited data member next.

We can now declare a list and put different vehicles into it:

```
List l;
l.put_last(new Private_car("xyz111", 5));
l.put_last(new Bus("bus999", 40, true));
l.put_last(new Truck("bly555", 10000));
```

Function put_last expects a pointer to a ListElement as parameter but pointers to private cars, buses and trucks can be automatically converted to this type since these classes are subclasses of class ListElement. Figure 13.1 illustrates this.

To run through the list and write out information about the different vehicles, we can do the following.

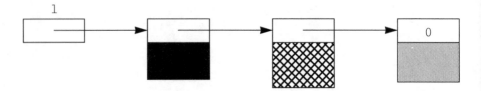

Figure 13.1

```
ListElement *p;
for (p=l.first_elem(); p; p=p->next_elem())
  ((Vehicle *)p)->give_info();
```

The expression in the last line may seem rather strange. The idea here is to call the virtual function give_info which is defined in class Vehicle. The pointer p has the type 'pointer to ListElement', it is also this type that the functions first_elem and last_elem give as result. So we cannot write p->give_info(), since there is no function with the name give_info in class ListElement. We need an explicit type conversion where the value of p is converted to type 'pointer to Vehicle'. The function give_info will be called with dynamic binding since it is virtual. We will, therefore, get different output data for different kinds of vehicle.

The type conversion carried out here is really quite dangerous since it is performed downwards in the class hierarchy. This is one of the disadvantages of the classical method of constructing heterogeneous object collections. Apart from being obliged to make risky type conversions, there is another disadvantage. As early as the class declaration – class Vehicle could be an example – the decision has to be made how the class will be used so that the inheritance of properties from the right base classes can be inherited. For instance, if we wanted to build up binary trees with vehicles, instead, we would have to make Vehicle the subclass of a base class other than ListElement.

13.3.2   The combination of inheritance and templates

Templates are good tools for constructing container classes, and inheritance is an excellent method for describing objects that can be classified in different groups and subgroups. The two things can be combined. If we again take the different kinds of vehicle as an example, we can use inheritance as we did before to describe the relation between different kinds of vehicle: 'a bus is a vehicle', 'a minibus is a bus', etc. But a vehicle is not a list element and the relation is not natural. To construct a list, we need a class template instead. We can use the class template List from Section 13.1.6 and declare the list l:

```
List<Vehicle *> l;
```

We give the type parameter T the value Vehicle *. As a result, the type of the elements that will be stored in the list is 'pointer to Vehicle'. The vehicles themselves will not be stored in the list, only the pointers to them. The definition of class Vehicle together with all its subclasses looks exactly as it does on page 302. No other pointers or anything else need to be added. We can now create some new vehicles and insert pointers to them in the list:

```
l.push_back(new Private_car("xyz111", 5));
l.push_back(new Bus("bus999", 40, true));
l.push_back(new Truck("bly555", 10000));
```

The situation is shown in Figure 13.2. The two top pointers in each node are the pointers pred and succ used by class List. The third pointer is the data component data, which in this instance of class List has the type 'pointer to Vehicle'.

To run through the list and write out information about the different vehicles, we, of course, use an iterator:

```
List<Vehicle *>::Iterator it;
for (it=l.begin(); it!=l.end(); it++)
  (*it)->give_info();
```

The expression *it gives as result a reference to a list element, that is, a reference to a pointer. This pointer has type 'pointer to Vehicle'. The pointer, therefore, has the right type for us to call the virtual function give_info. A type conversion is not necessary.

This has none of the disadvantages that we found in the classical solution of the previous section. No risky type conversions are necessary, and we do not have to make forced decisions as to whether objects of a certain class should be capable of inclusion in lists or other kinds of object collections. If, for example, we have a matrix of cars, we can use the class template Matrix. Any object can even be part

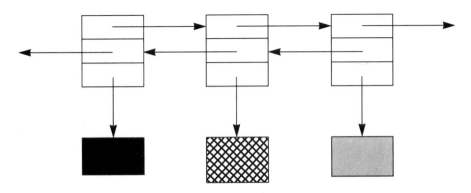

Figure 13.2

of several independent object collections at the same time, and there do not have to be extra data members in a particular object.

13.3.3   An example – spreadsheets

Certain calculation programs work with arrangements of figures, or 'spreadsheets', consisting of a number of rows and columns. Each 'square' in a spreadsheet contains what we call a cell, and we access a particular cell by indicating its row and column number. (Another way of expressing this is to say that a spreadsheet is a matrix whose elements are cells.) Each cell can contain a formula. (A cell can also be undefined.) A formula is an arithmetic expression that can contain the usual arithmetic operators but it need not contain any operator at all. In its simplest form, a formula can consist of a single term. The terms in a formula can be constant values. The interesting thing about calculation programs is that a term can also be a reference to another cell in the spreadsheet. Cell number (3,4) can, for instance, contain the formula (3,1)+(3,2), which means that cell number (3,4) will contain the sum of the values in cells (3,1) and (3,2).

This type of program can be very useful when we work with budgets and accounting procedures, for example. Certain rows and columns can be defined so that they connect to other cells in the spreadsheet. The calculation program can calculate the interconnected rows and columns automatically, and all we have to do is to give input data.

In this section, we shall demonstrate how such a calculation program can be built up. Naturally, we are not able to show a complete program – there is not enough space – but we will be showing the central constructions where the spreadsheet itself is built up.

We begin with the subject of *formulas*. A formula can have many forms but all formulas have a number of common properties. One of these is that we should be able to calculate a formula and get a value as result. So, we can look at formulas as a family of classes which all have an abstract base class in common, and this would have the following appearance:

```
class Formula {
public:
  virtual double calculate() = 0;
  virtual ~Formula() {};
};
```

This class has no data members. There are only two member functions, a virtual destructor and a pure virtual function, calculate. Because calculate is a pure virtual function, class Formula will be an abstract class. Objects of this class cannot be created. The class only exists to be a base class.

All the subclasses of Formula must have their own version of the member function calculate. Because the destructor has been declared as virtual, the

destructor of the subclass will be called when we deallocate an object with
Formula as its base class.

The simplest kind of formula is one that only contains a constant value. Such
a formula can be described with the following subclass:

```
class Constant : public Formula {
public:
  Constant(double value) : v(value) {}
  double calculate() {return v;}
private:
  double v;
};
```

The constant value is kept in the data member v, and function calculate gives
as result the value of v. There is a constructor which makes it possible to indicate
the value that v should have but there is no need to have a destructor since the class
does not itself allocate memory space dynamically.

We shall now study the kind of formula that has an operator with two
operands, that is, expressions of the form a *op* b, where *op* is an operator and a and
b are operands. As an example, let us look at a class that defines addition:

```
class Add : public Formula {
public:
  Add(Formula *left, Formula *right)
       : l(left) , r(right) {}
  double calculate(){return l->calculate()+r->calculate();}
  ~Add() {delete l; delete r;}
private:
  Formula *l, *r;
};
```

The two operands are defined with the two data members l and r which are
pointers to other formulas. So, a more complicated expression can be built up in the
form of a tree. The pointers l and r are given values in the constructor. The member
function calculate is simple. It calls the virtual function calculate for the
two operands l and r and gives as result the sum of their results. The call in the
expressions l->calculate() and r->calculate() occurs with dynamic
binding since l and r are pointers to the base class and calculate is a virtual
function. Hence, we do not know exactly which functions are called. It will depend
on what kinds of objects l and r point to.

The destructor releases memory space for the two operands so that the
destructors for these formulas will, in turn, be called. So, if we deallocate an
addition object, all the underlying formula objects will be deallocated.

The classes Sub, Mul and Div, which perform the three other modes of calculation, can easily be constructed in a similar way. The only difference, when compared with class Add, is that the operator + will be changed to - and * to / in the member function calculate. We do not have to show these classes.

To describe a formula which refers to another cell in a spreadsheet, we first have to define the class Cell. This class describes a particular 'square' in the spreadsheet:

```
class Cell {
public:
  Cell() : f(0), is_calculated_now(false) {}
  ~Cell() {delete f;}
  void define(Formula *form) {delete f; f=form;}
  bool defined() {return f!=0;}
  operator double();   // Calculates the cell's value
private:
  Formula *f;
  bool is_calculated_now;
};
```

There are two data members. The pointer f points to a formula. This pointer is initialized in the constructor to the value 0, which means that the cell is not defined. We can check whether a cell is defined by calling the member function defined. To insert a formula in a cell, to define the cell, we call the member function define, which has a pointer to a formula as parameter. This function releases memory space for the formula that was in the cell before and puts the new formula in its place.

The other data member, is_calculated_now, is rather special. It has been included so that no 'circular' calculations will begin. Suppose, for example, that cell number (3,4) contains the sum of the values in cells (3,1) and (3,2). To be able to calculate these values, we must first calculate the cells. Suppose further that cell number (3,1) contains the formula (3,3)*0.5 and that cell (3,3) contains the formula 100+(3,4). There will then be a circular calculation that has to be broken. The data member is_calculated_now is normally equal to **false** but as soon as we try to calculate the cell's value, it is set to **true**. It is restored to **false** when the calculation is finished. Each calculation begins with is_calculated_now being checked. If it has the value **true**, this means a circular calculation has occurred, and the calculation is aborted.

All of this is clarified by the definition of the member function **operator double**(). This is really a type conversion operator from type Cell to type **double** but we use it because it is convenient for calculating the value in a cell. If, for instance, we have a variable c of type Cell and want to calculate its value and assign it to a variable x of type **double**, we can simply write x=c. Then the type

conversion operator from type Cell to type **double** is called automatically. The
type conversion operator has the definition:

```
Cell::operator double()
{
  if (not f)
    throw calculation_error("Undefined cell");
  if (is_calculated_now)
    throw calculation_error("Circular calculation");
  is_calculated_now = true;
  double d = f->calculate();
  is_calculated_now = false;
  return d;
}
```

We can carry out the calculation itself by calling the member function calculate
for the formula in the cell. Two types of error can occur. The cell can be undefined,
that is, f can have the value 0, or a circular calculation can have occurred. If there
is an error, an exception of class calculation_error is generated. This class
is a non-standard subclass of the standard class logic_error:

```
class calculation_error : public logic_error {
public:
  calculation_error(const char *what_arg = "")
    : logic_error(what_arg) {}
};
```

Now class Cell has been completely defined, and we can define the last formula
class, class Other, which refers to another cell:

```
class Other : public Formula {
public:
  Other(Cell *other) : o(other) {}
  double calculate() {return *o;}
private:
  Cell *o;
};
```

This is really very simple. Class Other has a single data member, o, which is a
pointer to the other cell. Function calculate gives as result the value *o. This
expression has type Cell, since o is a pointer to a cell. But the result from function
calculate should be of type **double**, so the type conversion operator we

defined for type `Cell` is called automatically. As a result, the value in this cell is calculated.

Now we can use the class template `Matrix` from page 452 to construct a spreadsheet, w, with 10 rows and 7 columns:

```
Matrix<Cell> w(10,7);
```

Since each cell contains a pointer (the data member `f`) to the base class of a family of related classes (formal classes), we have created a heterogeneous object collection with the aid of the class template `Matrix`. We are now in exactly the same situation as described in Section 13.3.2. (We can ignore the fact that there is another data member in class `Cell`.)

We can now carry out indexing in matrix w and call the member function for individual cells. For instance, we can write:

```
w(2,5).define(new Constant(15));
w(3,5).define(new Constant(20));
w(4,5).define(new Add(new Other(&w(2,5)),
                      new Other(&w(3,5))));
cout << w(4,5) << endl;  // 35 is returned
```

We can redefine one of the cells:

```
w(2,5).define(new Constant(40));
cout << w(4,5) << endl;  // 60 is returned
```

Note that the value of cell (4,5) is changed, in spite of the fact that we do not make any changes in this cell. It is simply that cell (2,5) has been redefined.

This way of defining individual cells is not very elegant. In this type of program, the situation often arises where entire rows and columns have to be handled at the same time. We may want to stipulate that column number 7 should contain the sum of columns 3 and 6 and that the values in row number 8 should be 12% of the values in row number 7. One way of making things easier for the programmer is to enclose the matrix in a class `Spreadsheet` which describes a complete spreadsheet, and to provide class `Spreadsheet` with a set of useful member functions. We make the following definitions:

```
enum op {add, sub, mul, divi};

class Spreadsheet {
public:
  Spreadsheet(int nrow, int ncol)
           : m(new Matrix<Cell>(nrow, ncol)) {}
  ~Spreadsheet() {delete m;}
  int num_row() {return m->num_row();}
  int num_col() {return m->num_col();}
  Cell& operator()(int r, int c) {return (*m)(r,c);}
  void def_row(int row, int r, op o, double d);
```

```
    void def_col(int col, int c, op o, double d);
    void sum_row(int row, int r1, int r2, op o=add);
    void sum_col(int col, int c1, int c2, op o=add);
private:
    Matrix<Cell> *m;
};
```

Class `Spreadsheet` has as its only data member a pointer to a matrix with cells. This matrix is allocated dynamically in the constructor, which as parameters will get the number of rows and columns, respectively, that the matrix will have. To create a spreadsheet z with 20 rows and 10 columns, for example, we make the declaration:

```
Spreadsheet z(20,10);
```

The member functions `num_row` and `num_col`, which can be used to read the size of a spreadsheet, are easy to write. They simply call the corresponding member functions for class `Matrix`.

The function call operator `()` gives a reference to a particular cell in a spreadsheet. The expression z(5,7), for instance, gives the value in the cell in row number 5 and column number 7. The function call operator is implemented using the function call operator for class `Matrix`. The expression `(*m)` is the matrix m points to, and the expression `(*m)(r,c)` then means element number r,c in the matrix m points to.

The four remaining member functions allow the programmer the possibility of indicating properties for whole rows or columns in a spreadsheet. We begin by looking at the function `def_col`, with which we can indicate that a certain column is to be calculated from another column. To indicate, for example, that column number 8 should be equal to column number 3 but with all the cells multiplied by 2.5, we write:

```
def_col(8, 3, mul, 2.5);
```

Function `def_row` functions in a similar way. To indicate, for instance, that row number 10 should be equal to row number 8 but with a value of 100 added to each cell, we can write:

```
def_row(10, 8, add, 100);
```

We shall soon see how function `def_col` is implemented but first we will show a help function, `new_formula`, which is used by all of the last four member functions:

```
Formula *new_formula(Formula *f, op o, Formula *g)
{
    if (o==add)
        return new Add(f, g);
```

```
    else if (o==sub)
      return new Sub(f, g);
    else if (o==mul)
      return new Mul(f, g);
    else
      return new Div(f, g);
}
```

This function gets as parameters the pointers f and g which point to formulas and a value o, from the enumeration type op. The function creates a new formula, where the functions that f and g point to become operands. What kind of formula is created, depends on the value of the parameter o. As result, the function gives a pointer to the new formula that has been created.

Now we can study the definition of the function def_col. Its purpose is to define column number col from column number c. Any changes are determined by the operator o and the constant d. The function begins by checking that the parameters col and c do not indicate the same column. (A particular column cannot be calculated, of course, from itself.)

```
void Spreadsheet::def_col(int col, int c, op o, double d)
{
  if (col==c)
    throw invalid_argument("Spreadsheet::def_col");
  for (int i=1; i<=num_row(); i++)
  {
    Formula *f = new Other(&(*m)(i,c)),
            *g = new Constant(d);
    (*m)(i, col).define(new_formula(f, o, g));
  }
}
```

The function will put new formulas in all the cells in column number col. (It is, of course, this column that is to be defined.) To bring this about, it runs through all the rows of the matrix. For every row, i, two new formulas are created, and the pointers f and g point to them. Pointer g will point to a formula that contains the constant d. Pointer f points to a formula that refers to a cell in the corresponding row of column number c. The constructor for class Other will have a pointer to a cell as parameter. The expression (*m) means what m points to, that is, the matrix. The expression (*m)(i,c) is a reference to cell number (i,c) in this matrix, and the expression &(*m)(i,c) is thus the address to cell number (i,c) in the matrix. The help function new_formula, which constructs a formula with operands f and g, is then called. The new formula will be placed in the cell in column number col in row number i, which is done by calling the member function define for this cell.

The member function `def_row` is just the same, except that the columns are exchanged for rows. New formulas are put into all the cells in row number `row`, and so we run through all the columns. We do not need to show this function.

The two last member functions, `sum_row` and `sum_col`, are used to indicate that a certain row or column will constitute the sum of a certain number of other rows and columns, respectively. For instance, to indicate that row number 20 will contain the sum of rows 1 to 10, we make the call:

```
sum_row(20, 1, 10);
```

The last parameter has the default value `add`, but another operator can also be used. To indicate that row number 19 will contain the difference between row 3 and 4, for instance, we can write:

```
sum_row(19, 3, 4, sub);
```

In a similar way, function `sum_col` will make sums of columns. For example, to indicate that column number 7 is to contain column numbers 2, 3 and 4 multiplied by each other, we write:

```
sum_col(7, 2, 4, mul);
```

We will now show the definition of `sum_row`. (Function `sum_col` is written in a similar way but with the rows exchanged for columns.)

```
void Spreadsheet::sum_row(int row, int r1, int r2, op o)
{
  if (r1>r2 or (row>=r1 and row<=r2))
    throw range_error("Spreadsheet::sum_row");
  for (int j=1; j<=num_col(); j++)
  {                 '
    Formula *f=new Other(&(*m)(r1,j));
    for (int i=r1+1; i<=r2; i++)
      f = new_formula(f, o, new Other(&(*m)(i,j)));
    (*m)(row,j).define(f);
  }
}
```

The parameters `r1` and `r2` will indicate a row interval, so `r1` must be less than or equal to `r2`. The row to be defined, row number `row`, must not lie in the interval between `r1` and `r2`. It cannot be defined by starting from itself. After the preliminary checks have been made, the function runs through all the columns. For every column `j`, it builds up a sum formula that will be put into row number `row` in column `j`. To make the sum formula, it runs through all the rows in the interval between `r1` and `r2`. First a formula is created to refer to the cell in column `j` in row `r1`, then it is built up with references to rows `r1+1` to `r2`. The formulas are put together by the operator o. If o has the value add, a formula will be built to indicate that the cells in column number j in rows r1 to r2 should be added. At the end of each round the sum formula is inserted in row number row, and this is done by calling the member function define.

We finish now by showing a little main program that uses class Spreadsheet. The program reads a number of sales figures which are fed in exclusive of sales tax. As result it gives a printout of these initial figures, the amount of sales tax to be added to each and the amount of each including sales tax. To conclude, the program sums up all the sales figures, the sales tax and the sales figures including sales tax. When the program is run, it can look like this:

```
Indicate amount excluding sales tax
5000
2500
1000
12500
```

Amount	sales tax	incl. sales tax
5000	1250	6250
2500	625	3125
1000	250	1250
12500	3125	15625
=====	=====	=====
21000	5250	26250

The lines written by the user have been underlined. The program looks like this:

```
main()
{
  Spreadsheet s(1000, 3);
  s.def_col(2, 1, mul, 0.25);
  s.sum_col(3, 1, 2);
  cout << "Indicate the amount excluding sales tax" << endl;
  double b;
  int r=0;
  while (cin>>b)
    s(++r,1).define(new Constant(b));
  s.sum_row(s.num_row(), 1, r);
  cout<<"         Amount      sales tax    incl. sales tax"<<endl;
  for (int i=1; i<=r; i++)
  {
    for (int j=1; j<=s.num_col(); j++)
      cout<< setw(14) << s(i,j);
    cout << endl;
  }
  cout<<"         =====         =====        ====="<<endl;
  for (int j=1; j<=s.num_col(); j++)
    cout<< setw(14) << s(s.num_row(), j);
  cout << endl;
}
```

The program uses a spreadsheet, s, that contains 3 columns and a maximum of 1000 rows. Function def_col is used to indicate that column number 2 will be calculated as column number 1 multiplied by 0.25 (the current percentage sales tax). Then function sum_col is used to indicate that column number 3 will contain the sum of columns 1 and 2.

The figures fed in are then read and placed in column number 1. The variable r is used to calculate the number of amounts that have to be fed in. When reading has finished, function sum_row is called to indicate that the last row in the spreadsheet will contain the sum of rows 1 to r.

Now the spreadsheet is finished, and it will write out its contents. Rows 1 to r are written first and finally, row 1000.

We conclude with a little warning. Class Cell is not complete. An assignment operator and a copy constructor that makes deep copies are missing. As the class looks now, we would not be able to assign or initialize one cell with another. For instance, we could not assign one spreadsheet to another. If we were to complete class Cell with an assignment operator and a copy constructor, we could also add a constructor that had a parameter of type **double**. This would then function as a type conversion constructor and would make it easy to add new constant values to a cell. Instead of writing s(i,j).define(**new** constant(d)), we could write s(i,j)=d. This is left as an exercise for the reader.

EXERCISES

13.1 In Chapters 7, 8 and 9 we worked with a class Vector (the definition is on page 287). Rewrite this class so that it becomes a class template. (Not all the member functions need be rewritten; it will suffice to practise on a few.)

13.2 Rewrite class Queue from Section 12.2.2 so that it becomes a class template.

13.3 Rewrite class Set from Section 12.2.3 so that it becomes a class template.

13.4 Class Set in Exercise 13.3 requires that the operators ==, != and < should exist for the actual type. Write a version of class Set that uses a property class and which can be used for such element types where the operators are missing.

13.5 To run through a binary tree in the order *preorder*, *inorder* and *postorder* is, as we have seen, very easy. The exercise here is to write a function to visit a tree in order of level. This means that the root (at level 1) should be visited first, then the nodes at level 2, from left to right, followed by the nodes at level 3, from left to right and so on.

The following algorithm can be used. First examine how deep the tree is. Then create a separate queue for each level. Each queue should contain pointers to nodes. Then run through the tree in the order *inorder*, adding pointers to the nodes in the correct queues. Finally, run through the queues one at a time, in the correct order. Use class List from Section 13.1.6 to build the queues.

13.6 Write a function template that can be used to search for a particular element in an array of arbitrary type. The function should have as parameters an array and the element it is to search for. As result is given a pointer to the element searched for. If this element cannot be found, a null pointer should be returned.

13.7 A function template in the draft standard called reverse, changes a data collection so that the elements occur in reverse order. This function template has two iterators as parameters. Write the function template reverse.

13.8 Complete class Cell from Section 13.3.3 with an assignment operator and a copy constructor that makes deep copies. In addition, write a constructor that has a parameter of type **double**. This constructor should insert a formula of type Constant in the actual cell.

14 The Final Pieces of the Puzzle

This last chapter will describe some constructs which we need for a complete picture of C++. These constructs have no direct connection with each other but have been collected here for the simple reason that they did not fit in anywhere else in the book. The fact that they are being dealt with last does not mean that they are necessarily less important than earlier material. Name spaces, which we will deal with first are, for instance, an important new mechanism in C++.

14.1 Name spaces

Most substantive C++ programs are composed of a number of different, separately compiled program text files. Header files are used to access declarations of program units defined in other files. Header files can either be standard files as, for example, `iostream.h`, or non-standard files not in the draft standard. The total number of files included in any one compilation can be large since header files in turn include other header files. This means that there will normally be a great number of identifiers declared when a program is compiled, with the considerable risk that two different items will be given the same name in different header files. For instance, there might be two different constants declared with the name `size`. The program cannot then be compiled since the identifier `size` will be doubly defined. It is very irritating, when something in a program has been named, to find an error message warning that there has been a double declaration when the identifier in question has only been used once.[†] A *name space*, a new construct in C++, can be used to solve this problem. Then we can enclose a group of declarations, for instance, all the declarations in a header file, in a name space, and these declarations will not normally be visible outside this name space. The declarations will not then conflict with declarations made outside the actual name space or in other name spaces.

14.1.1 Definition of name spaces

In this section we will study how name spaces are defined. In the next section we shall see how we can access what has been declared inside a name space. A name space is a construct which has a form similar to that of a class. The construct is introduced with the reserved word **namespace** followed by the name of the name space. Then there will be a block that can contain a number of arbitrary declarations:

```
namespace name {
  declarations
}
```

Suppose now that we want to use two libraries with help functions in a program. There are two header files, one for each library. These files are called `alib.h` and `blib.h`. They have the following appearance:

```
// File alib.h
namespace Alib {
  void initialize();
  double result(double x);
```

[†] The keen reader may have wondered why the identifier `divi` and not `div` was used in the enumeration type `op` on page 490. This is because in the standard file `stdlib.h` there happens to be a function with the name `div`, and for some reason the file `stdlib.h` was included when the program was tested.

```
  const int max_num = 20;
  void write_out(double x);
}
```

```
// File blib.h
namespace Blib {
  void initialize();
  double result(double x);
  const int max_num = 100;
  const int least_num = 2;
}
```

We see that the declarations have been enclosed in two name spaces with different names. If we had not used name spaces and had included both the files in the same program, the compiler would have complained that the variable max_num was doubly defined. (The declarations of the functions initialize and result would have been compiled since it is not an error to repeat declarations of functions. But there would have been problems with linking because the linker would not have known which of the two versions was to be linked.)

The definitions, that is, the implementations, of the functions in the two help libraries are made as usual in separate definition files with names ending in .cpp. We can use the same syntax here as when we define member functions of classes. File alib.cpp can look like this:

```
// File alib.cpp
#include "alib.h"

void Alib::initialize()
{ statements }

double Alib::result(double x)
{ statements }

void Alib::write_out(double x)
{ statements }
```

The complete names of the functions can, thus, be explicitly indicated by beginning with the name of the name space followed by a double colon. There is a simpler way, however, because it is permissible to *extend* a name space with further declarations or definitions. For instance, file blib.cpp can have the appearance:

```
// File blib.cpp
#include "blib.h"
namespace Blib {
  void initialize();
    { statements }
```

```
double result(double x)
{ statements }
}
```

Here the name space `Blib`, originally defined in file `blib.h`, has been extended by the definitions of functions `initialize` and `result`. We do not then have to indicate the rather awkward `Blib::` in front of every function name. (It would be nice to be able to do this with the definitions of member functions for classes but unfortunately this is not possible.)

We can also define *unnamed name spaces*. Then the name of the name space is simply omitted.

```
namespace {   // unnamed name space
   declarations
}
```

The definitions inside an unnamed name space are automatically accessible in the part of the program where the unnamed name space is located. But they are not accessible from a separately compiled section of the program, and we can use this fact to hide internal help functions. Suppose, for example, that functions `initialize` and `result` make use of two help functions, `internal1` and `internal2`. We can then let file `blib.cpp` have the appearance:

```
// File blib.cpp
#include "blib.h"
namespace {
   void internal1()
   { statements }
   void internal2()
   { statements }
}
namespace Blib {
   void initialize()
   { ... internal1(); ... }
   double result(double x)
   { ... internal2(); ... }
}
```

Functions `internal1` and `internal2` are visible in file `blib.cpp` and can be called by `initialize` and `result` but it is not possible (by mistake) to call `internal1` and `internal2` from some other section of the program. (Alternatively, an old technique inherited from the programming language C can be used. Functions are declared with the keyword **static**, whereupon they become invisible to a linker. This has nothing to do with static member functions.)

Definition of name spaces

> **namespace** *name* {
>   *declarations*
> }

- If *name* has not been defined before, it is a definition of a *new* name space.
- If a definition of a name space with the name *name* has been given before, it is an *extension* of this name space.
- If *name* is omitted, it is a *unnamed* name space. The definitions in an unnamed name space are directly visible in the part of the program where the definitions have been made but they are not accessible from another, separately compiled part of the program.
- An alternative name (*name2*) can be defined instead of the original name (*name1*):
>   **namespace** *name2=name1;*

Name spaces can sometimes have cumbersome names. A manufacturer may be reluctant to see the company name omitted. Suppose, for instance, that a name space has the name `ChalmersSoftwareLibrary`. To avoid using this lengthy name, an alternative can be defined and used from then on:

```
namespace CSL = ChalmersSoftwareLibrary;
```

The syntax for name spaces and class definitions may look similar but there is an important difference between a name space and a class. A class is a type; therefore, instances of it can be declared. A name space, on the other hand, is not a type, so there cannot be instances of a name space. A name space is only a language construct that makes it possible to enclose a number of declarations belonging together, into a kind of package. (In fact, a similar construct in the programming language Ada is called a 'package'.)

14.1.2   Using name spaces

Whatever has been declared in a name space will be invisible from outside if no other measures have been taken. However, there are three ways of accessing the contents of a name space: with an 'explicit qualification', with a 'using declaration' and with a 'using directive'. To demonstrate these procedures, we will assume that we have a function f that includes the two files `alib.h` and `blib.h`:

```
#include "alib.h"
#include "blib.h"
void f()
```

```
{
    statements
}
```

Suppose now that we put the following line in the function statements:

```
write_out(2.6);   // Error, invisible
```

We get a compilation error, because whatever is inside a name space is not directly visible. One way of accessing something that has been declared inside a name space is to use the *explicit qualification*. We can write, for example:

```
Alib::write_out(2.6);   // OK, explicit qualification
```

Every time an identifier is used, its full name is written with the name space name coming first.

The second way of making a particular declaration visible is to give a *using declaration*. This begins with the reserved word **using**, and then comes the complete name of the identifier that is to be visible. Here we make the function least_num in Blib directly visible:

```
using Blib::least_num;   // using declaration
...
cout << least_num << endl;   // OK, visible
```

A using declaration means that the identifier indicated is declared in the actual place, just as if it had been an ordinary declaration. In this way, the identifier becomes directly visible.

The third way of making declarations in a name space visible, is by making a *using directive*. This makes *all* the declarations in a name space visible. The reserved word **using** is written, followed by the name of a name space. Here we make all the declarations in the name space Alib visible:

```
using namespace Alib;   // using directive
```

Employing a using directive means that everything that has been declared in Alib will be accessible, exactly as if the declarations had been made openly instead of in a name space. (There is a difference between a using declaration and a using directive. With a using declaration, the identifier is declared inside the function – in this case f. With a using directive, however, all the declarations will certainly be visible but will lie *outside* the function.)

Now everything that has been declared in Alib can be directly used in function f. We can make the statements

```
cout << max_num << endl;   // OK, all of Alib visible
initialize();
```

Using name spaces

- *Explicit qualification.* Give the complete name every time it is used:
  space_name : : *name*
- *Using declaration.* Declare *one* particular identifier at the indicated place:
  using *space_name* : : *name* ;
- *Using directive.* Makes the *whole* name space open:
  using namespace *space_name* ;

Using directives can be given for several name spaces:

```
using namespace Alib;
using namespace Blib;
```

Of course, there will now be ambiguities. If we write, for instance:

```
initialize();   // Error, ambiguous
```

the compiler will not know if the function `initialize` in `Alib` or `Blib` is to be called. So the name should be indicated explicitly:

```
Alib::initialize();
```

Using declarations or using directives can be placed anywhere in a program. To avoid unnecessarily making the contents of name spaces visible, we can ensure that our using declarations or using directives are only put in the functions or classes where the name space will be used. This is preferable to putting using directives at the outermost level in program files.

14.1.3   Name spaces and standard libraries

In the draft standard, a number of header files have been specified. These are both new files that are specific to C++ and new versions of all the header files that have been inherited from the programming language C. According to the draft standard, all header files should have file names which do *not* end in `.h`. The new versions of the C header files should have the same names as before but with a `c` in front. The new version of the C header file `math.h` is called `cmath`, for instance. But all the new header files will have the form:

```
namespace std {
   declarations
}
```

Hence, all the declarations occur in a common name space having the name `std`. Since all name spaces can be extended, the declarations in all the standard files that we include will be automatically found in the name space `std`. Declarations in header files do not automatically become visible in user programs. The three methods described in the previous section have to be used to gain access to them, so this makes it possible to include standard files without the danger of finding conflicting names when we declare something that happens to have the same name as a declaration in a standard file. If this problem does not arise and we want everything to be directly visible (as it always used to be in C and C++), then we only have to add this line at the outermost level of our program:

```
using namespace std;
```

So that C++ will be compatible with C, the C++ draft standard stipulates that all the old versions of header files (those where the names end in `.h`) should remain. When a file like this is included, the using declarations are given automatically for everything declared in the file. Everything will, therefore, be visible without the need for any action.

Let us take an example. The header file `cmat` contains declarations of mathematical standard functions. It has the form:

```
namespace std {
  double acos(double);
  double asin(double);
  etc.
}
```

The file `math.h` then has the appearance:

```
#include <cmath>
using std::acos;
using std::asin;
etc.
```

14.2   Bit operators

From the beginning the programming language C was constructed as an alternative to assembler languages when 'machine level' programs were to be written. These were programs which worked closely with the computer's operating system and hardware. In such programs we often need to be able to handle individual bits in memory cells. In C and C++, there are a number of operators that can be used to handle integer variables as though they contained bit patterns instead of integers.

Note that the operators described here are only defined for integer types. The operator ~ is the simplest one. It only has one operand and as result gives a bit pattern where all the zeros in the operand have been exchanged for ones, or vice versa. We will give an example. (In the following statements we assume that all of the variables have type **unsigned short int** and are 16 bits long.)

```
a = 7;    // a = 0000 0000 0000 0111
b = 20;   // b = 0000 0000 0001 0100
c = ~a;   // c = 1111 1111 1111 1000
```

The operators &, | and ^ carry out the operations *and*, *or* and *exclusive or* bit by bit. The operator *exclusive or* means that a particular bit in the result will be a 1 if exactly one of the operands contains a one in the corresponding position. If none or both of the operands contain a one, the result bit will be zero.

```
d = a & b;   // d = 0000 0000 0000 0100
e = a | b;   // e = 0000 0000 0001 0111
f = a ^ b;   // f = 0000 0000 0001 0011
```

According to the draft standard, it is permissible to use the reserved words **compl**, **bitand**, **bitor** and **xor** instead of the symbols ~, &, | and ^, respectively. The last two statements might then be written:

```
e = a bitor b;
f = a xor b;
```

The operators << and >> perform *left shift* and *right shift*, respectively, moving bits to the right or the left. The left operand contains the bit pattern to be moved, and the right operator indicates how many steps the bits should be moved. (If the right operand is negative or greater than the number of bits in the left operand, the result is undefined.) When a left shift is performed, zeros are always inserted from the right; when right shift is performed on a value that is positive or **unsigned**, zeros are inserted from the left. (If right shift is performed on a negative value that is **signed**, it remains undefined whether ones or zeros are inserted from the left.) Here are a couple of examples:

```
g = b << 5;   // g = 0000 0010 1000 0000
h = c >> 2;   // h = 0011 1111 1111 1110
```

The operator & is often used to perform *masking*, the selection of certain bits from a bit pattern. For instance, the following statement masks the eight bits in the middle of the bit pattern contained by the variable h:

```
i = h & 0xf00f;   // i = 0011 0000 0000 1110;
```

The operator | can be used to add ones to certain bits. The following statement will put ones in the eight bits furthest to the right:

```
j = i | 0x00ff;   // i = 0011 0000 1111 1111;
```

<table>
<tr><td colspan="3">Bit operators</td></tr>
</table>

•	Are only defined for integer types.	
•	Perform all operators bit by bit.	

~	`compl`	changes 0<–>1
&	`bitand`	and, bit by bit
|	`bitor`	or, bit by bit
^	`xor`	exclusive or
<<		left shift
>>		right shift

It should be noted that none of the operators we have shown here have any effect on *their* operators. If such operators are required, the corresponding assignment operators can be used. We can write, for instance:

```
a &= 0x000f;
```

which is the same thing as writing:

```
a = a & 0x000f;
```

14.3 struct

In the programming language C, there is a construct called **struct**. With **struct** we can construct types that are built up from several subcomponents, which can be of different type. (**struct** corresponds to the construct usually called 'record' in most other common programming languages.) When C++ was created, **struct** was used from the beginning to determine how classes were to function. The new construct **class** was similar to **struct** in C but new features were added, among them member functions and inheritance. Because C++ had to be compatible with C, it was decided that **struct** should also be present in C++, and it was allowed to have the same options as **class**. In other words, in C++, **struct** is the same thing as **class**. A **struct** can also have member functions and inherit from another **struct** or **class**. There is only one slight difference, and this has to do with access. All the members in a **struct** are automatically visible if neither of the words **private** or **public** is indicated. In a class, as we know, they would all end up in the **private** section. And the same thing applies to inheritance. When a **struct** is derived from another **struct** or from a class, public inheritance is automatically used if neither of the words **private** or **public** appears. Private inheritance is used in classes when nothing else is indicated. Here are some examples:

```
struct S1 {
  S1(int n=0) : i(n) {};
  void write() {cout << i << endl; }
  int i;
};
```

In S1 all the members are directly visible. We can write, for instance:

```
S1 a;
a.i=7;
a.write();
```

And another **struct** can be derived from S1:

```
struct S2 : S1 {
  S2(int n, double x) : S1(n), d(x) {}
  double square() {return d*d;}
private:
  double d;
};
```

In S2 the constructor and member function square are visible while the data member d is, of course, private. Public inheritance is used here in spite of the fact that the word **public** does not stand on the first line. The following statements might be given:

```
S2 b(5, 2.5);
cout << b.square() << endl;
b.write();
```

The construct **struct** really is easier to use than **class** when we want the visible members of a class to be indicated first. It is simpler to write:

```
struct D : B {
  ...
};
```

than writing everywhere:

```
class D : public B {
public:
  ...
};
```

```
                    struct

  The same thing as a class but data members and
  base classes are visible if nothing else is indicated.

     struct D : B {
         . . .
     };

  is exactly the same thing as

     class D : public B {
     public:
         . . .
     };
```

Paradoxically, the construct **class**, so central a concept in C++, is completely unnecessary. It would be just as efficient and, in fact, somewhat easier, to use **struct** in its stead. But a language that is object-oriented must, perhaps for different reasons, contain a construct that is simply called 'class'.

14.4 union

As we know, we can give a class a number of data members. We can write, for instance:

```
class C {
  int no;
  double v;
  char txt[6];
};
```

An object of class C, thus contains three components, an **int**, a **double** and a character array with six **char**. The number of bytes that are needed in the primary memory to store an object of class C is determined by the lengths of the three components. A **union** is a kind of class that can only contain *one* of its data members at a time. We can give the definition:

```
union Data {
  int no;
```

```
  double v;
  char txt[6];
};
```

If we now define an object, a, of type Data, a can *either* contain an **int**, a **double** or a character array. The three data members lie in the same place in the primary memory, thus competing for this space. An object of type Data will then take up as many bytes as the *longest* of its data members needs.

Unions can be used in cases where it is known that different objects can be of different kinds and that different data members will be used. In this way, memory space is saved by not reserving places for unnecessary components. Union objects can be declared and used as ordinary objects, but it must be remembered that such objects can only contain one kind of object at a time. We can write, for instance:

```
Data a;
a.no = 5;
cout << a.no << endl;
a.v=3.67;
cout << a.v << endl;
strcpy(a.txt, "Hello");
cout << a.txt << endl;
```

The same rules apply to a **union** as to a **struct**, which means that all members will be public if nothing else has been indicated. We can then access the different data members here directly.

A **union** may not be used in connection with inheritance. (It cannot have base classes, be a base class itself, or have virtual member functions.) On the other hand it is permissible to have ordinary member functions, constructors and destructors. We can complete the union Data with some constructors:

```
Data() {}   // default constructor
Data(int i) : no(i) {}
Data(double x) : v(x) {}
Data(char *s) {strcpy(txt,s);}
```

It is now possible to write:

```
Data a(5);
a = "Goodbye";
```

What happens if the variable a contains a value of a certain type and we try to interpret it as a value of another type? There will simply be an error. A **union** does not itself have knowledge about what type of data it currently contains. The programmer has to know this.

To avoid the risk of data being misinterpreted, we often enclose unions in a class that has an extra data member to indicate what type of data the union contains. For instance, we might want the union Data to describe different kinds of message.

> **union**
>
> - A class where the objects can only contain *one* of the data members at a time. An object is big enough to hold the largest of the data members.
> - May not be used in connection with inheritance.
>
> ```
> union U {
>     ...
> };
> ```

There are messages that contain a number (an integer), a value (a real number) or a text. We then construct a class `Mess` in which we enclose the union `Data`:

```
enum Kind {number, value, text, undef};
class Mess {
public:
  Kind k;  // discriminant
  Data d;  // union
};
```

The data member `d` is a union, so it can contain values of different type. Such a data member is usually called a *variant*. Data member `k` is of enumeration type and can contain one of the values `number`, `value`, `text` or `undef`. It indicates what kind of data is in `d`. The data member `k` is an example of what we call a *discriminant*. The discriminant can be tested before the value of `d` is interpreted:

```
if (m.k==text)  // m has type Mess
  cout << m.d.txt;
```

There is still room for error but if class `Mess` were extended with a few member functions, it could be made safer. We, therefore, place the data members `k` and `d` in the **private** section so that the user cannot access them directly. All access will occur via the member functions which will monitor that the type in `d` is correct. Here is the extended definition of class `Mess`:

```
enum Kind {number, value, text, undef};
class Mess {
public:
  Mess() : k(undef) {}
  Mess(int i) : k(number) {d.no=i;}
```

```
  Mess(double x) : k(value) {d.v=x;}
  Mess(char *k) : k(text) {strcpy(d.txt, k);}
  Kind what() {return k;}
  int the_number() {assert(k==number); return d.no;}
  double the_value() {assert(k==value); return d.v;}
  const char *the_text() {assert(k==text); return d.txt;}
private:
  Kind k;   // discriminant
  Data d;   // union
};
```

There are four constructors, a default constructor and a constructor for every possible type that d can contain. These constructors not only initialize d, they also place information on the type involved in the discriminant k. The member function what can be used to read but not change the discriminant. It can also be called to find out what is in d. Finally, for every one of the three types, there is a member function that makes it possible to read the value in d. With the aid of the discriminant, the member functions check that d contains the correct type. Since neither d nor the discriminant k can be changed without using one of the constructors, the data in d cannot be wrongly interpreted. If we were to try to use d incorrectly, we would get stuck in function assert:

```
Mess m(19);
cout << m.the_number() << endl;   // OK
m = "Hello";
cout << m.the_text() << endl;     // OK
cout << m.the_number() << endl;   // ERROR (in assert)
```

We will very briefly mention that there is something called *anonymous union*. A union can be declared without a name, in which case a variable is declared – and not a type. We could have declared class Mess in the following alternative way:

```
class Mess {
  ...
private:
  Kind k;
  union {
    int no;
    double v;
    char txt[6];
  };
};
```

The union then designates a member variable in class Mess. The names no, v and txt are directly accessible in class Mess. (In this way, we jump over the extra level with d which we used earlier.) The last three member functions will, for instance, have the appearance:

```
int the_number() {assert(k==number); return no;}
double the_value() {assert(k==value); return v;}
const char *text() {assert(k==text); return txt;}
```

14.5 Bit fields

When individual data members are declared in a class (or **struct**), we can indicate that they should be *bit fields* which consist of a certain number of bits packed together. When we declare a bit field, we write a colon after the data member's name then indicate the number of bits to be used for the actual data member. An example of the use of this procedure is when we have a number of objects of a certain type and want to save memory space. Suppose that we have a register of cars. For every car we wish to monitor the car's registration number (six characters), the model (a number between 0 and 99), whether the tax has been paid and the car has passed its inspection test and, lastly, whether the car is no longer running (has been taken off the road). We can then give the following class definition:

```
class Car {
public:
  char reg_no[6];
  unsigned int model : 7;
  unsigned int tax_paid : 1;
  unsigned int inspected : 1;
  unsigned int not_run : 1;
};
```

The data members model, tax_paid, inspected and not_run are bit fields here. Seven bits are reserved for model. The other three bit fields require only one bit each. A bit field must be of integer or enumeration type. It should be indicated, as it is here, whether a bit field is **unsigned** or **signed**, since it is not clear what it will be if only **int** is written.

Bit fields can be accessed just like ordinary data members. For example, we can write the following:

```
Car c;
strncpy(c.reg_no, "abc123", 6);
c.model = 97;
c.not_run = false;
```

```
cout << c.model << endl;
if (c.tax_paid and c.inspected)
  cout << "OK";
```

(To save space, no terminating zero has been stored at the end of the registration number, so `strncpy` and not `strcpy` must be used.)

When we write machine-level programs, for example *drive routines* which handle input and output from external units, bit fields can be very useful. We then have to access special, so-called *control registers*, which are found at given primary memory addresses. The individual bits in such a register have special functions. A register may look as it does in Figure 14.1. (We only give the general principles here. Registers may differ from system to system.)

The register consists of 16 bits numbered from right to left. (This will vary from computer to computer. Sometimes numbering occurs from left to right.) The bit on the right is set to a one if we want the external unit to be able to generate a hardware interrupt. The external unit itself puts a one in the sixth bit from the right when it is ready to accept (or has finished sending) data. The data to be sent to the external unit (or read from it) is placed in the eight bits furthest to the left. The program will fill in these bits for output while the external unit fills them in for input. The shaded bits in the register are unused in our example. We can now define a class that describes how a register will look, in keeping with Figure 14.1:

```
class Register {
public:
  unsigned int enable : 1;
                      : 4;
  unsigned int ready  : 1;
                      : 2;
  unsigned int data   : 8;
};
```

We have added *unnamed bit fields* to fill out the unused bits.

In any computer system there are several control registers, and these will be in fixed places in the primary memory. Different external units will have different

Figure 14.1

Bit fields

- We can indicate for individual data members the number of bits they should consist of.
- Bit fields must be of integer or enumeration type.
- Explicitly indicate **unsigned** or **signed**.
- Unnamed bit fields can act as fillers.

```
class C {
    type B1 : n1;
    type B2 : n2;
         : k1; ◦ // unnamed bit field
    type B3 : n3;
};
```

- The address operator & cannot be used in bit fields.

---

control registers. As an example, let us suppose that at the (hexadecimal) primary memory address `ffa0` there is a control register which is used to write one byte at a time to a particular external unit. We can declare a pointer, `r`, to point to this register:

```
volatile Register *r = (Register *)0xffa0;
```

We have not met the reserved word **volatile** before. It is used to indicate that what `r` points to can be changed in some way, without it being done by the program. (Of course, the external unit itself changes the bit `ready`.) This is written so that the çompiler will not try to make optimizations of the generated machine code for the variable `r`. This variable is initialized to the hexadecimal value `ffa0`. Since the type of this expression is **int**, an explicit type conversion must be made to 'pointer to `Register`'.

We can now access the special control register via the pointer `r`. Suppose that we want to write out a byte to the actual external unit. We have to wait until the unit is ready to accept data, then the data to be written out should be put in the register's data field:

```
while (not r->ready)    // Wait until the unit is ready
    ;
r->data = 'X';          // Write out data
```

If the word **volatile** had not been used in the declaration of `r`, the compiler might have tried to optimize the apparently meaningless **while** statement and get rid of it.

14.6   The do statement

We have used **while** and **for** statements in this book to produce repetition. But there is a third repetition statement, the **do** statement. It has the form:

```
do
    statement
while (expression);
```

This statement is similar to the **while** statement. The difference is that the test expression is calculated and tested *after* instead of before each round. This means that the statement inside a **do** statement is always performed at least once. Braces can be used if several statements have to be performed at each round. We usually write **do** statements in the following way:

```
do {
    statements
} while (expression);
```

It is useful to write the right brace first in the last line so that when we read the program we are not fooled into thinking that the word **while** begins a statement.

Here is an example of a type of program where it can be expedient to use a **do** statement. In the program, repeated calculations are carried out for different input data. After each calculation, the user is asked if further calculations should be performed.

```
main()
{
    double x;
    char answer[5];
    do {
        cout << "Give input data: " ; cin >> x;
        cout << "The result=" << res(x) << endl;
        cout << "Continue? (y, n) "; cin >> answer;
    } while (answer[0] == 'y');
}
```

14.7   The switch statement

A **switch** statement is one which can be used instead of an **if** statement where there is a multiple choice situation. (A **switch** statement is a primitive form of the *case* statement usually found in high level languages such as Ada and Pascal.) We will show, by way of an example, a part of a program that simulates a very simple calculator. The program reads and calculates expressions of the form x *op* y.

```
double x, y;
char op;
while (cin >> x >> op >> y)
  switch(op) {
    case '+':
      cout << (x+y) << endl;
      break;
    case '-':
      cout << (x-y) << endl;
      break;
    case '*':
      cout << (x*y) << endl;
      break;
    case '/':
      if (y != 0)
        cout << (x/y) << endl;
      else
        cout << "Division by zero" << endl;
      break;
    default:
      cout << "Incorrect operator" << endl;
}
```

A **switch** statement is introduced with the reserved word **switch**. Then there should be a *test expression*, which must be of integer or enumeration type, in parentheses. (This can also be a value of a class type if there is a type conversion operator for the class that converts to an integer type.) Every alternative in a **switch** statement is introduced with the word **case**. The expressions which come after **case**, the **case** expressions, must be constant. There cannot be two or more **case** expressions with the same value. There may also be a **default** alternative.

When a **switch** statement is executed, the test expression after the word **switch** is first calculated, and the value of this is compared with the values of the different **case** expressions. If the test expression has the same value as a **case** expression, there is a jump to the statement following this **case** expression. If none of the **case** expressions has the same value as the test expression, there is a jump to the statement after the word **default**. If the **default** alternative is absent and none of the **case** expressions is acceptable, nothing is carried out in the **switch** statement.

Note that a **break** statement must come last in every alternative (except in the last one). This results in the alternative being terminated. There is then a jump to the end of the **switch** statement. If there were no **break** statement in a given alternative, there would not be a jump. Instead, execution would continue with the statements in the next alternative!

---

switch statement

```
switch (integer_expression) {
    case constant_value1 :
        statements
        break;
    case constant_value2 :
        statements
        break;
    . . .
    default :
        statements
}
```

- Expressions after **case** must have different values.
- The **default** alternative can be omitted.
- There can be several **case** expressions in front of a given alternative.
- Upon execution there is a jump to the alternative for which the *integer_expression* is equal to a *constant_value*.
- If there is no suitable alternative, there is a jump to the **default** alternative. If there is a default alternative, nothing happens.

It is permissible to have several **case** expressions introducing a given alternative. For example, we can write:

```
switch(c) {
  case '0': case '1': case '2': case '3': case '4':
  case '5': case '6': case '7': case '8': case '9':
    number_digits++;
    break;
  case ' ': case '\t': case '\n':
    number_white++;
    break;
  default:
    number_others++;
}
```

Unfortunately this is not very elegant as the word **case** has to be repeated.

14.8   The conditional operator

There is an operator that programmers can possibly manage without, but we should be familiar with it, in any case. This is the *conditional operator*. With this operator, *conditional expressions* can be formed. Suppose, for instance, that we want to test which of the variables x and y is the larger and then assign the greater value to the variable z. Naturally, this is easily done with the aid of an **if** statement:

```
if (x>y)
   z = x;
else
   z = y;
```

However, a conditional expression can also be used:

```
z = (x>y) ? x : y;
```

The conditional operator has three operands. The first is a test expression. If this is true, the second operand, the one coming after the character ?, is calculated, and the result of the conditional expression will be equal to this operand. If the test expression is false, the third operand, the one after the character :, is calculated, and the result of the conditional expression will be equal to this operand.

A conditional expression is, therefore, a kind of **if** statement that leaves a value as result. The type of this result is determined by the last two operands. If they have the same type, the result will have this type; otherwise there will be the same kind of ordinary type conversions that occur with addition, for instance. The result type will, therefore, be equal to the longer of the two types.

As an example, we will show some program lines which write out a text string s in such a way that all the upper case letters (A–Z) are translated to lower case letters. Other characters are written out unchanged. (Assume that the variable c has type **char**.)

```
for (int i=0; c=s[i]; i++)
   cout<< char((c>='A' and c<='Z') ? c+'a'-'A' : c);
```

The result of the conditional expression has type **int**, so an explicit type conversion must be made to type **char**.

The conditional operator

expression1 ? expression2 : expression3

- If *expression1* is **true**, the result will be equal to *expression2*, otherwise the result will be equal to *expression3*.
- If *expression2* and *expression3* have the same type, the result type will be equal to this type, otherwise an ordinary arithmetic type conversion is made so that the result type will be the longer of the two types.

EXERCISES

14.1 In Chapter 4 we created our own library, `simpleio`, with a few functions for reading and writing (see page 115). Adjust this library so that all the declarations in it end up in its own name space with the name `Simpleio`.

14.2 In Section 12.2.3 we constructed a class `Set`. Place this class in its own name space. Several local help functions are used when the member functions are implemented. Place these in an anonymous name space so that they cannot be accessed from outside.

14.3 Assume that variable c of type **char** contains two small integers in the interval from 0 to 15. One of the integers is stored in the four bits on the left and the other in the four bits on the right. Write a program section that returns the sum of these two small numbers.

14.4 Suppose that we use an array, f, with element type **char** to store an array with logic values. Every logic value will be represented by only one bit, so there will be eight logic values in every **char**. Write a program section to show how indexing in the array can be carried out. In other words: given a variable k, the logic value number k should be taken out.

14.5 A process known as a *lexical analysis* occurs in the first stage in the workings of a compiler. The program text written by the programmer is interpreted, and divided into so-called *lexical tokens*. These lexical tokens are then sent to the second stage in the compiler. Examples of lexical tokens are identifiers, reserved words, integer constants, real constants and text strings. A lexical symbol must contain two pieces of information: there must be some indication of what kind of symbol it is, and the value of this symbol must be given. This value will depend on the kind of symbol in question. For instance, for an identifier, the value will be a text string with the identifier's name, and for an integer constant it will be an integer. Use a **union** to declare a type that describes lexical tokens.

14.6 Write a program that reads a date in the format yyyy-mm-dd. The program should write out the day number of the date during the year, that is, a number between 1 and 365, or 366 if it is a leap year. (Leap years are years that are divisible by 4 but years exactly divisible by 100 are not leap years unless they are also divisible by 400.) Use a **switch** statement with the different months as an alternative.

APPENDIX A

`<stdexcept>`

In this book we have frequently used the prescribed standard class `exception` and its subclasses to signal various kinds of error. These classes are defined in a standard file called `stdexcept` but if this file is not available in your compiler, the following files can be used instead. (To avoid the use of the standard class `String`, the type for the parameters of the different constructors has been changed from `String&` to **char** `*`.)

```cpp
// The file stdexcep.h
#ifndef STDEXCEP
#define STDEXCEP
#include <string.h>
class exception {
public:
  exception() throw();
  exception(const exception& e) throw();
  exception& operator=(const exception& e) throw();
  virtual ~exception() throw();
  virtual const char* what() const throw();
protected:
  char *m;
};
class logic_error : public exception {
public:
  logic_error(const char *what_arg)
  { m = new char[strlen(what_arg)+1];
    strcpy(m, what_arg);
  }
};
class domain_error : public logic_error {
public:
  domain_error(const char *what_arg)
  : logic_error(what_arg) {}
};
```

```
class invalid_argument : public logic_error {
public:
  invalid_argument(const char *what_arg)
  : logic_error(what_arg) {}
};
class length_error : public logic_error {
public:
  length_error(const char *what_arg)
  : logic_error(what_arg) {}
};
class out_of_range : public logic_error {
public:
  out_of_range(const char *what_arg)
  : logic_error(what_arg) {}
};
class runtime_error : public exception {
public:
  runtime_error(const char *what_arg)
  { m = new char[strlen(what_arg)+1];
    strcpy(m, what_arg);
  }
};
class range_error : public runtime_error {
public:
  range_error(const char *what_arg)
  : runtime_error(what_arg) {}
};
class overflow_error : public runtime_error {
public:
  overflow_error(const char *what_arg)
  : runtime_error(what_arg) {}
};
#endif
```

```
// The file stdexcep.cpp
#include "stdexcep.h"
exception::exception() throw() : m(0) {};
exception::exception(const exception& e) throw()
{
  if (e.m)
  {
    m = new char[strlen(e.m)+1];
    strcpy(m, e.m);
  }
  else
    m = 0;
}
exception& exception::operator=(const exception& e) throw()
{
  if (this != &e)
```

```
  {
    delete m;
    if (e.m)
    {
      m = new char[strlen(e.m)+1];
      strcpy(m, e.m);
    }
    else
      m = 0;
  }
  return *this;
}
exception::~exception() throw()
{ delete m;};
const char* exception::what() const throw()
{ return m;};
```

Index of Information Windows

Index

0800 957 9000